Sea

Bay
of
Biscay

0 25 50 100 150 200 Miles

FRANCE

KU-404-097

Bilbao San Sebastian

**Basque
Country**

Vitoria

Pamplona

Haro **Navarre**

Logroño

La Rioja

Tudela

ANDORRA

Soria

Huesca

Vic

Zaragoza

Calatayud **Catalonia**

Girona

Aragon *Ebro River* Lerida

Barcelona

Tarragona

Teruel

Cuenca

Balearic Sea

Castellón

Valencia

Majorca Minorca

Valencia

Albacete

Ibiza

Balearic Islands

Formentera

Murcia Alicante

Murcia

Cartagena

Canary Islands

Atlantic Ocean

Sea

N

THE FOOD
OF
Spain

the Food of Spain

A CELEBRATION

CLAUDIA RODEN

With photography by Jason Lowe

MICHAEL JOSEPH
an imprint of
Penguin Books

MICHAEL JOSEPH

Published by the Penguin Group

Penguin Books Ltd
80 Strand,
London WC2R 0RL, England

Penguin Group (USA) Inc.
375 Hudson Street,
New York, New York 10014, USA

Penguin Group (Canada)
90 Eglinton Avenue East, Suite 700,
Toronto, Ontario, Canada M4P 2Y3
(a division of Pearson Penguin Canada Inc.)

Penguin Ireland
25 St Stephen's Green,
Dublin 2, Ireland
(a division of Penguin Books Ltd)

Penguin Group (Australia)
250 Camberwell Road,
Camberwell, Victoria 3124, Australia
(a division of Pearson Australia Group Pty Ltd)

Penguin Books India Pvt Ltd
11 Community Centre,
Panchsheel Park, New Delhi – 110 017, India

Penguin Group (NZ)
67 Apollo Drive, Rosedale, Auckland 0632,
New Zealand
(a division of Pearson New Zealand Ltd)

Penguin Books (South Africa) (Pty) Ltd
24 Sturdee Avenue, Rosebank,
Johannesburg 2196, South Africa

Penguin Books Ltd, Registered Offices:
80 Strand, London WC2R 0RL, England

www.penguin.com

First published 2012
7

Copyright © Claudia Roden, 2012

Photography © Jason Lowe, 2012

Photography on pages: 22 (border), 37, 100, 105
(centre bottom), 106, 109, 119, 261, 311
© Alistair Richardson, 2012

Photography on pages: 5, 47, 54–5, 205 © istock

Photography on pages: 2, 15, 18, 64, 77, 83, 125
(centre), 227, 309, 504 © Alamy

Bespoke chapter opener designs copyright
© Tina Hannay of Hannay Design Ltd
www.tinahannaytiles.com

The moral right of the author has been asserted

Set in Caslon and Garamond

Printed in China

A CIP catalogue record for this book is available from
the British Library

ISBN: 978–0–718–15719–7

www.greenpenguin.co.uk

Penguin Random House is committed to a
sustainable future for our business, our readers
and our planet. This book is made from Forest
Stewardship Council® certified paper.

FOR MY CHILDREN, *Simon, Nadia and Anna,*
GRANDCHILDREN, *Cesar, Peter, Sarah,*
Ruby, Nell and Lily,
and also for Clive and Ros

CONTENTS

INTRODUCTION

THE FAINT AROMA OF LEMON ZEST AND CINNAMON

Recipes, I have come to understand, have a special place at the heart of the Spanish identity. And they give the measure of a man. It was always so. In the early seventeenth century, Miguel de Cervantes began the first paragraph in his masterpiece *Don Quixote* by describing the gentleman who rode a scraggy horse, carrying a wooden lance and an ancient shield, as a man who ate lentils on Fridays, eggs on Saturdays, sometimes a pigeon on Sundays, and an occasional stew with more beef than mutton.

Spain figured powerfully in my life long before I first went there for the BBC television series *Claudia Roden's Mediterranean Cookery* in 1987. My grandmother Eugénie Alphandary spoke an old Judeo-Spanish language called Judezmo or Ladino, which she said was old Castilian. She was from Constantinople (now Istanbul) and was descended from Jews who had been expelled from Spain in 1492 and went on to live in Ottoman lands. Her friends, who were mainly from Salonica, Smyrna and Constantinople, were labelled 'Spaniolis' within the Jewish community of Egypt that I grew up in. They were proud of their Spanish ancestry. They sang ballads about *hidalgos* (knights) and *moros* (Moors), as Muslims were called in medieval Spain, and about princesses who became slaves. Some of their names – Toledano, Cuenca, Carmona, Leon, Burgos, Soria, Saragossa – are a record of the cities their ancestors came from. The dishes they clung to – *albondigas* (meatballs), *almodrote* (vegetable flan), *maronchinos* (almond biscuits), *pan d'espanya* (sponge cake) – were their badge of identity.

As I travelled through Spain to research this book, names of cities and streets conjured up in my mind the familiar faces of my family and friends in Egypt. I recognized the names of vegetables and dishes. Traces of the old Muslim

presence – arabesque carvings, blue-and-white tiles, a fountain spouting cool water in a scented garden – evoked nostalgic memories of the Arab world I was born in. At the sight of an old minaret I imagined hearing the call to prayer of a muezzin. The streets lined with orange trees made me understand why my family makes orange cakes and crystallized orange peels, and why we put the distilled essence of orange blossom in so many of our desserts and pastries. The way people cook in Spain, the ingredients they put together, their little tricks, their turns of hand, are mysteriously familiar. A word, a taste, a smell trigger memories I never knew I had. It is surprising how dishes can appeal directly to the emotions. With food, as with music, you can touch people and make them cry.

I am intrigued by how interested Spanish people are when they learn that I am a *sefardita* (the name of Jews whose ancestors came from Spain). For centuries the country had wiped out its Muslim and Jewish past from national memory. The drama of the centuries-long *reconquista* – the reconquest of Iberian land from the Muslims that was finally completed in 1492 – was the official and cherished feature of Spanish history and self-image that was taught at school. But the legacies of the once huge population of Muslims and significant minority of Jews, and the consequences of their expulsion or conversion, are now matters of scholarly research and public interest and discussion.

It is an exceptional time to be travelling and eating in Spain today. The country has changed dramatically in less than thirty years. After the horrors of their civil war (1936–39), when thousands died and parts of the country knew famine, and after a long period of oppression and hardship when food was rationed during General Francisco Franco's dictatorship (1939–75), Spain is now a rich, modern, dynamic country, where everything, especially food, arouses great passion. And there has been a revolution in the restaurant kitchens.

In the past, Spanish food never received praise from foreigners. In the nineteenth century, although the French were fascinated with their neighbour and their accounts of travels in Spain were immensely popular, they described the food with disdain. French writers of that time, such as Théophile Gautier in his *Un Voyage en Espagne* ('Travels in Spain'), Alexandre Dumas in his *Adventures in Spain* and *From Paris to Cadiz*, and Prosper Mérimée in the novella *Carmen*, on which the opera of the same name was based, complained that the food was poor and that too much oil and too much pork fat, too much garlic and too much *pimentón* (Spanish paprika) made it unpalatable. Dumas sometimes insisted on cooking his own food in the hostels where he stayed. Richard Ford's English *A Handbook for Travellers in Spain* (1845) had nothing good to say about the food; neither did the Hispanophile Gerald Brenan in the twentieth century. At a dinner in Cordoba recently I was asked politely if the food in England was all that good in Richard Ford's time. His comments obviously still hurt. In the second half of the twentieth century, a bastardized tourist cuisine of the fixed-price menu and fake *paellas* developed during the massive expansion of cheap 'sand-sea-and-sun' tourism. It is still there in parts and tourists still complain, but otherwise Spain has transformed itself into one of the world's effervescent centres of gastronomic creativity.

San Sebastian in the Basque Country has become the culinary capital of Europe with the greatest concentration of Michelin three-star restaurants. Ferran Adrià at El Bulli in Roses in Catalonia, who is famous for using science and technology in the kitchen, is fêted abroad as the greatest living chef. Food and travel writers rave about the extraordinary and fantastic *nueva cocina*, the Spanish novelle cuisine, and its star chefs are rightly acclaimed throughout the world. These avant-garde chefs use machines, cook *sous vide* and with syringes, freeze-dry and caramelize, create hot jellies, instant mousses, bubbling froths and foams, vapours and explosions. They deconstruct traditional dishes, some use exotic foreign ingredients. Their food is what they call a *'cocina de autor'* – unique, creative signature dishes invented by the chef – and it is constantly changing. There have been several phases in the gastronomic revolution over the last three decades. Among the top influential chefs are Juan Mari Arzak, Pedro Subijana, Andoni Luis Aduriz, Martín Berasategui, Sergi Arola, Dani García and Carme Ruscalleda. Some developments have been crazy, but the kitchen revolution has led to an exquisite and refined professional *alta cocina* (haute cuisine) that Spain never had before, and to an updating of the traditional culinary know-how that had been passed down through the generations for centuries. The ways to do things better – to fry and roast better, to boil and stew better, to present food better and make it more delicious and appealing – have reached home cooks. And there has been a new appreciation of traditional Spanish food, which is what this book is about.

Many innovative chefs now say that they are inspired by their roots. They talk about their parents' and grandparents' cooking and about rescuing old rural traditions and local ingredients that are in danger of disappearing. The revered Catalan chef Santi Santamaría, whose restaurant El Racó de Can Fabes is in San Celoni near Barcelona, says that cooking has to be about sentiment as well as technique and that without 'ideology' it is simply a matter of manual skills and technology. His ideology, he says, is rooted in the life of his peasant family and the progressive politics of his youth. He quoted the painter Joan Miró: 'To be universal you have to be local.' The young Basque chef Andoni Luis Aduriz at his restaurant Mugaritz in San Sebastian spoke with touching intensity when he said that, apart from giving pleasure, his aim was to provoke 'memories and emotions – even bad ones'. This is the refrain today of most of the innovative chefs.

Despite the glamour of the innovators (in a catering school I visited in Galicia, the students all wanted to be like Ferran Adrià), a huge fraternity of chefs has stuck to traditional ways. In their old-style informal *mesones* (inns) and their grand establishments they offer what Spaniards have always known and loved. Because people cook very little nowadays – they do not come home for lunch, children eat at school, women work and there is just time to make a pasta or a grill in the evening during the week, or else if a family has a maid she is most likely to be Latin American or North African and so will cook dishes such as tagine or Peruvian potato stew – restaurants, taverns and bars have become places where Spaniards go to find the traditional and regional home cooking they hanker after.

Throughout the country there is a palpable feeling of nostalgia for the old rural life that was too quickly swept away by a booming tourist economy. It has translated into a newly found passion for regional cooking and food products. During the Franco regime, regional cultures were suppressed and artisan products were discouraged in favour of mass-produced industrial ones that could feed the population cheaply. When the autonomous communities (as the historic regions are now called) gained political recognition and the right to govern themselves in 1978, people felt free to celebrate their regional heritage and began valuing their cuisines and their local products, which had sometimes almost been lost. In a mood of regional nationalist hedonism, organizations were formed in the last ten years to preserve their culinary heritage by recording recipes. Such organizations have collected 900 recipes in Catalonia, 600 in the Balearic Islands of Majorca and Minorca, and 900 in Galicia! Producers rushed to defend their wines, their olive oils, their hams, their charcuterie and their cheeses, their beans and honeys, and their indigenous breeds of cows, pigs and capons. They obtained official *Denominaciones de Origen* (DOs) – designations of origin that guarantee quality and specify geographical origin and time-honoured traditional methods of production. As Spaniards became affluent and could afford to buy good wines and foods it was worth investing effort and money into greater quality. The European Union helped with subsidies, and the world has come to appreciate the result.

Like language and music, food in Spain is about local patriotism. The historic regions, now seventeen autonomous communities (nineteen with Ceuta and Melilla, Spanish enclaves on the Moroccan coast), each divided into provinces, were born out of the old medieval kingdoms. Each has its own history and culture, sometimes its own language, and a cuisine that springs from the land – the *comarca* or terroir – and also reflects the past. The first thing you discover about Spain is the extraordinary geographical diversity. The greatest difference is between the very long, narrow coastal plains, with their string of vibrant port cities, and the vast empty interior, a high plateau and huge mountain ranges. Travelling through the interior, you see plains and gentle hills, great rivers, mountain forests, marshlands and deserts. There are seas of wheat and of rice, and endless landscapes carpeted by grapevines and olive trees. Until roads began to be built in the 1960s, high mountains made internal transport difficult. Rural communities were isolated and culinary styles developed separately. That is one reason why every province, every town and every village has its own distinctive dishes or versions of a dish, and why every coastal region has at least three distinctive culinary styles – one of the sea, one of the rural coastal plain and one of the nearby mountains.

Regional cooking has survived because it is loaded with emotional associations and because Spaniards are attached to their roots. Until the mid twentieth century, the majority of the population lived and worked on the land. Most people now live in towns and cities, but they regularly go back to the village where their parents or grandparents came from, and where there is usually a family home. What their grandparents cooked has become something to be proud of.

During my travels through Spain, I asked everyone I met what their favourite foods were, how and where their parents and grandparents lived and how they cooked. People were happy to give me old family recipes and to take me to bars and restaurants where I could taste their favourite dishes; some invited me into their homes. I had a few mentors who helped me and gave me contacts in different regions. I talked with food writers and scholars, chefs and producers, with fishermen who remembered when fish and seafood were regarded as poor food, with people who had once worked on the land as virtual serfs, with landed aristocrats and with nuns who made pastries. I never learnt Spanish formally but I understood almost everything they said, and they understood my mix of Italian, French, Judaeo-Spanish and the Spanish I gradually picked up in Spain. I taught myself to read Spanish and went through old and new cookery books. My greatest mentor was Alicia Ríos (see page 219). Alicia is a food writer and historian and an olive oil expert. I stayed in her studio in Madrid and had access to her huge library and archive of cookery books.

The recipes in this book represent traditional home cooking from all the regions, as it is cooked today. My aim has been to feature the best dishes I could find, the most interesting and delicious – those I loved best and that I thought we would all enjoy cooking and eating. Sometimes a dish was good but the effort to make it was too great. I had a rule (because most of us are short of time) that there should be a balance between the effort of making a dish and the pleasure of eating it. This was the case for Catalan *canelones* (cannelloni), which I made when my granddaughters stayed the night and they watched me prepare it. The stuffing is complex and intriguing, with many ingredients, and the process of filling the pasta, then making the sauce and baking the dish is long and finicky. I had told the girls of my rule and that if a dish was fantastic it should go in the book no matter how difficult and how long it took to make. We all liked the *canelones* but we agreed that, considering the time it took to make them, we did not love them enough to give the dish an obligatory place in the book. There are dishes that you will not find here. For instance, I have included only a few recipes using salt cod, although there are dozens throughout Spain, because it is hard to find in Britain and I doubt many people would be encouraged to use salt cod as it is not part of our culture in the way that it is in Spain. I do not feature many recipes with pigs' ears, feet and other offal for the same reason.

Most Spanish dishes were born in the life of the peasantry, in a rural world where there were no proper ovens or modern kitchen gadgets, when people worked hard and needed warming, fatty foods that gave them energy for arduous work in the fields. Now things have changed – the manual labour is done by foreign immigrant workers and peasant life as it was has disappeared. People have every kitchen gadget. They are concerned with healthy eating and want to make cooking easier, quicker and lighter, with less fat and less frying. In many parts of the country where people once cooked exclusively with pork fat, they now mostly use olive oil (that is why I have allowed myself to use olive oil rather than pork fat throughout the book). Fish and seafood are cooked much more briefly. Where once long-cooked vegetables were preferred, they might now be served slightly al dente. And people do not always dredge everything with flour before frying, as they did in the past.

Although traditional Spanish cooking has evolved, it has not lost its character and identity. As with poetry and music, cuisines have rhymes and tunes and recurrent themes that characterize them. Spain's signature tune is the *sofrito* of fried onion and tomato to which garlic and green peppers are often added. The bits of chopped cured ham that find their way into most dishes; the *chorizo* and blood sausage that feature together in bean and chickpea stews; the wine or sherry and the brandy that go together in sauces – these are all among its themes. The *picada*, a ground paste of nuts crushed with garlic and fried bread, tells you that a dish is Catalan. The gentle flavour of saffron tells you that you are on the Mediterranean coast or perhaps in the south. *Pimentón* (Spanish paprika) or the faint aroma of grated lemon zest and cinnamon tells you that a dish is Spanish.

Part of the appeal of traditional dishes is that they hold memories of the past. The Catalan chef Santi Santamaría wrote, 'We are products of our history,' and that the reference points of his cooking were the memories of his grandparents' generation and medieval Catalan cookery books. The past in Spain is an intimate part of the present. I have found that history is a sensitive subject that arouses great passions. I like to imagine that past against the backdrop of Roman aqueducts, Moorish and Romanesque palaces and medieval villages. During festivals, a taste for the spectacular and the macabre, left over from the Middle Ages, is on show. During *Semana Santa* (Easter Week), when statues of the Virgin adorned with fine clothes are paraded through the streets, men lead the processions dressed up in the tall pointed hoods and robes worn by penitents during the public sentencing at the courts of the Spanish Inquisition (they were much later adopted by the Ku Klux Klan). The popular festival of *Moros y Cristianos* is a costumed re-enactment of the battles of the *reconquista* that is celebrated throughout the whole of Spain at different times of the year. Many old monasteries, castles and palaces have been restored into state-run luxury hotels called *paradores*. Their menus offer regional and 'historic' dishes. A little booklet produced in 1998 to celebrate the seventieth anniversary of the first paradores explains that Spanish gastronomy is as varied as its history, and gives recipes to illustrate the influences, dating back to Roman times. The stories behind what you eat in Spain are like the pieces of a puzzle. Working on this book was for me a delicious and exciting way of finding all the fragments and putting them together to discover the real Spain.

At home in London, as I roast red peppers and aubergines and sprinkle them with olive oil, as I caramelize onions, or fry almonds with garlic and bread, wonderful aromas fill my house, and I remember the Spanish mountains and the olive groves, the old churches and the convents. Most of all I miss the conviviality of the Spanish way of life. I recreate it with my friends, who come to try the dishes I discovered. They are used to me calling to invite them just a day before. I tell them what is on the menu. When I was cooking pigs' feet and ears, one or two said, 'I'll pass on that.' For five years now – that is how long I have been working on this book – I have invited many friends, some of them passing through from abroad, to these tasting and testing dinners. That too has been part of the pleasure of writing this book.

HISTORY AND CULTURE

CELTS, ROMANS, VISIGOTHS:
of pigs and olive trees

Cristóbal Lovera, an olive grower and olive oil mill owner from Baena whom I met in Cordoba, told me that recently there had been a long-running nationwide controversy about Spanish culture. Was it Roman or was it Arab? After a lot of argument it was decided that Spanish culture was Roman. At a dinner party in Madrid, when I said that I was researching the history and culture of Spanish food the hostess, Antonieta, said, 'You have to know that we are of Roman and Visigoth stock. Did you see the Roman aqueduct in Segovia?' She was angry, she said, at the way foreigners always noticed Moorish architecture and influences. 'By the thirteenth century almost all of the peninsula had been repossessed and Muslims remained only in the small enclave of Granada.' My rather earnest recitation of what I had just learnt about the actual Muslim presence in Spain as late as the seventeenth century must have made her feel that I was upset and perhaps that I saw her as prejudiced, because she put on a Moroccan belly-dancing costume and showed me a recipe for hummus stuck on her refrigerator. Spaniards like to see themselves as Romans and Visigoths or Celts, and even Phoenicians. Obviously, these early civilizations have a place in this book.

Early on in the Iberian peninsula, Phoenicians, Greeks and Carthaginians formed trading posts and settlements along the Mediterranean coast and in the Balearic Islands, while Celtic tribes coming over the Pyrenees established themselves in the north. The Phoenicians created salt pans and introduced the preservation of fish in salt, to make it appropriate for trade, and also brought their way of baking fish in a salt crust. The Carthaginians are said to have brought chickpeas. Greeks cultivated vines, olives and almond trees. The Celts were swineherds. They venerated the indigenous oak, which they believed had magical powers, and chestnut trees, and they fed their pigs acorns and chestnuts. One of their legacies is the cured pork products that came to have a hugely important place in Spanish gastronomy. They also reared cattle for dairy. When the entire Iberian peninsula came under Roman rule (the Romans called it Hispania), starting in 219 BC with the first invasion, vineyards and olive groves were expanded and wheat was established in the

plains, reaffirming the classical Mediterranean triad of bread, wine and olive oil on which Spanish gastronomy is based. The Romans also introduced peaches, apricots and lemons. The great lasting legacy the Romans left is the Latin language, from which the languages spoken in Spain – apart from the Basque language Euskara – are derived.

When the Roman Empire began to crumble, pillaging Germanic tribes passed through in waves until the Visigoths, whose ruling families of Germanic origin had been in the service of the Roman emperors, arrived as occupiers at the beginning of the fifth century. They established the capital of their kingdom in Toledo. Their king, Reccared, converted to Catholicism in AD 587 and the kings who followed continued to rule over a Roman Catholic Visigothic kingdom that gradually covered all of the peninsula. The Visigoths were stock-raising herders. They kept pigs and let them feed on acorns and berries in the woods and forests. They rejected olive oil and cooked with pork fat. They knew the art of salting and smoking their meats. They reared geese, kept goats and made cheese. They also made apple cider and beer from fermented barley. Their conquered subjects continued as in Roman times – cultivating grapes and olive trees; grains such as wheat, oats, barley, millet and rye; broad beans, peas, chickpeas and lentils; and vegetables such as cabbages and leeks. They had hazelnut and walnut trees, figs, pears, apples and plums. They picked wild berries, collected snails, reared pigs, sheep and goats and hunted deer, wild boar and small game such as rabbits and birds. Most of their fish came from rivers rather than the sea. There are no documents relating to the cooking of the time but foreign travellers noted that it was rough and primitive, that pork was the most popular food and that pork fat was preferred to olive oil.

AL-ANDALUS:
an exotic culinary invasion

Many years ago, when I visited El Molino, a restaurant and centre of gastronomic research outside Granada where they hold courses on the history of Spanish food, I asked about the origins of Spanish cooking. A man there told me the origins were 'Arab and Jewish' and gave roast pork, which is forbidden to Jews and Muslims, as an example, explaining, 'When they converted to Christianity they cooked pork in the same way they cooked lamb, which was to rub it with cumin seeds.' Now you know why you may find cumin seeds on Spanish roast belly of pork. The Muslim presence in particular had a huge impact on the gastronomy of Spain, even in parts of the country where it was brief.

In 711, an Arab army crossed the Straits of Gibraltar with their North African Berber foot soldiers and vanquished the Visigoths. Except for a pocket of resistance in the north, all of the Iberian peninsula fell under the rule of the Umayyad caliph based in Damascus and it became known as al-Andalus. After the massacre in 756 of the Umayyads by the Abbasids, who relocated the capital of the Islamic Empire to Baghdad, al-Andalus took on an autonomous existence under the rule of the emir Abd-al-Rahman I, an Umayyad prince who had managed to escape and find his way to Spain. In 929, Abd-al-Rahman III declared himself caliph of a state independent from Baghdad, the Caliphate of Cordoba. Under the caliphs of Cordoba, a glittering culture flourished in Spain in many fields, including philosophy, poetry, music, medicine, science and mathematics, architecture, agriculture and gastronomy.

The Arabs introduced irrigation techniques – a system of canals and the noria, a large wheel placed over a fast-flowing stream driven by a mule that lifts water in a series of earthenware pots – and horticultural practices such as grafting techniques. New crops arrived from all over the Islamic Empire, some indigenous to India and China. Among them were rice, a new species of wheat and sugar cane; vegetables such as artichokes, aubergines, spinach and carrots; fruits such as bitter oranges, melons and watermelons, dates, bananas, quinces; new types of almonds and also saffron. The grapes of Jerez province, which are used to make sherry, are said to have come from Shiraz in Persia. Lemons and pomegranates, which had disappeared since Roman times, were reintroduced. Market gardens and orchards sprang up around every city. Grand Moorish houses had private gardens and patios

with fruit trees. New varieties of sheep, including the Merino prized for its quality wool, were brought over from North Africa, as were new species of pigeons, and dovecotes were introduced. Libraries became full of works on botany and agriculture. In mosques and markets, agronomists taught when to plant, when to graft, when to harvest, what fertilizer to use, how to fight insect pests, which types of soil were best for which plants, how to grow crops in rotation and how to predict the weather. The greatest medieval treatise on botany and agriculture was written by a Muslim, Abu Zakaria, who lived in Seville.

Trade was intense between al-Andalus and the rest of the Islamic world, and with parts of India and the Far East. Muslim ships sailed across the Mediterranean carrying goods such as gems and silks, as well as foodstuffs. Spices and aromatics were a mainstay of the trade. Muslim, Jewish and Christian merchants grouped along religious and ethnic lines, each group forming a kind of club. Jewish traders controlled a major portion of the commerce, trading with Jewish communities around the Mediterranean. While Christians generally despised merchants, Jews and Muslims held them in high esteem.

The refinement of pleasure and the search for the most delicious combinations of foods became the preoccupation of a Muslim elite. A Kurdish lute player, Abul Hassan Ali Ibn Nafi, known as Ziryab, who came from the court of Harun al-Rashid in Baghdad and joined the Cordoban court, is credited with transforming the art of living in al-Andalus. Apart from introducing new music, he taught people how to dress, how to wear make-up, how to cut their hair short and how to dye their beards with henna. He also taught the refinements of cooking, as well as rules of etiquette, table manners and table setting. He established an order of serving different courses, starting with cold appetizers and followed by meat and poultry, pastas and rice dishes, then soups, pies, sweet puddings and pastries. Before that, all the dishes had been put on the table at the same time.

In 1031, the Caliphate broke up into separate small rival kingdoms and principalities called *taifas*, who fought among themselves. In 1086, when the Almoravids, a puritanical, fundamentalist Islamic Berber sect from Morocco, were called in to help fight off the Christians, they took over and reunited al-Andalus under their control. Another puritanical Berber dynasty, the Almohads from the Atlas Mountains of Morocco, succeeded the Almoravids, making the twelfth and thirteenth centuries a period of Berber influence and strict militant fundamentalist rule that frowned upon good living.

the *reconquista*

Within a few generations of the Arab occupation, the Christians began to fight back from their northern enclaves, pushing their frontiers southwards. This crusade, known as the *reconquista* (reconquest), in which the Christians fought to reconquer their land, lasted for more than seven centuries. They fought in a haphazard kind of way, grouping in separate kingdoms. Sometimes they fought among themselves, sometimes together, sometimes with the help of Muslim kings, sometimes for Muslim kings. By the time King Alfonso VI of Leon and Castile conquered Toledo in 1085, the Christians had recaptured the central plateau, and by the mid thirteenth century almost all of the Iberian peninsula, except for the enclave of Granada, had been repossessed. The marriage of Isabella I of Castile and Ferdinand II of Aragon in 1469 united the two most powerful Christian kingdoms. In 1492, their armies entered Granada. The Moorish king, Abu Abdullah Muhammad XII, or Boabdil, handed over the keys of the city. The spot where he took his sad farewell looking at the city from which he was banished for ever still bears the name of Suspiro del Moro ('the Moor's sigh').

The *reconquista* was a holy war, a crusade against the infidel. It was also a continuous process of colonization of the land. Conquered territories were resettled by Christians from the north, who brought their tastes with them – in particular the use of pork and pork fat, forbidden by Muslims and Jews, which came to symbolize the *reconquista*. Several features of the Muslim agricultural revolution were reversed. The land fell into the hands of nobles and the ecclesiastical authorities, who used most of it for the production of cereals and for grazing sheep. Some of the new crops, such as bananas, sugar cane and cotton, disappeared completely.

convivencia in the kitchen

The story of the Muslims in Spain and the cultural interactions between different communities – a part of Spanish history about which Spaniards were in denial and are still sensitive – has been opened up recently by scholars. For hundreds of years Spain was a land where Christians, Muslims and Jews coexisted. The rich variety, the sensual character and complexity of Spanish cooking today are in part the result of that long *convivencia*, or cohabitation, and the intermingling of the three cultures.

While much of the *reconquista* was over by the middle of the thirteenth century, the fact that an area had been reconquered by Christians did not mean that the entire culture or population changed, rather that a transfer of power had taken place. As the Christians moved south, there were usually not enough settlers to repopulate and cultivate the land, and Christians were not used to the types of agriculture that they found, so many Muslims were allowed to remain and work the land. In Valencia, the Muslim population was needed to continue to work in the rice fields and for silk work. The rural areas of the centre and south of the Iberian peninsula remained predominantly tenanted by Muslims, who lived in villages and were allowed to keep their faith, customs and laws. They were called Mudéjares. In the cities, Muslims were mainly employed as craftsmen and in the building trade.

Throughout the centuries of Muslim occupation there were continual wars and problems of coexistence, but there were also treaties and trade exchanges and long periods of peace. Christian knights served as mercenaries in Muslim armies and for *taifa* states, and Christian troops were contracted out to al-Andalus in exchange for gold. There were constant migrations of Christians who had kept their faith, from the Muslim south to the north. These Christians, called Mozarabs, spoke Arabic, wore Moorish clothes and cooked in the Moorish manner. In the parts under Muslim occupation, there was intermarriage (the Caliphs' wives and mothers were often Christian women from the north of Spain) and there were numerous conversions of Christians to Islam. Christians converting to Islam were called Muwallads. By the eleventh century, the majority of Christians in al-Andalus had converted to Islam while keeping their ancestral identity. Muwallads could become as much lords and masters as the Moors, especially if they came from the old Visigoth nobility. When territories were reconquered, they reconverted, sometimes en masse, and were reabsorbed into Christian society. Muslim converts to Christianity were called Moriscos.

There were many reconquered Christian towns in which Muslims lived among Christians and Jews. Intermarriage and sleeping together were taboo, but the communities fraternized despite condemnation by the Church. They sometimes lived in the same neighbourhoods, sometimes in the same house. They did business together. They ate and drank together, sang and played games together, and invited each other to their festivals and weddings. The Moorish cooking that had at first been rejected as the 'enemy culture' by Christians was eventually adopted by them. Its voluptuous character won over Castilian austerity.

Toledo in the time of Alfonso X, king of Leon and Castile, known as 'the Wise', was famously a tolerant world of cultural diversity where large Muslim and Jewish communities lived in their own quarters among Mozarab Christians, and Christians arrived from the north and from other countries. While the Castilian language was adopted, Arabic remained the lingua franca there for many centuries. The city is the centre of Spain's marzipan industry. There is a marzipan museum where this sweet delicacy is described as a product and symbol of the old inter-community harmony. There is controversy today among historians of Spain as to whether coexistence was ever happy and even fruitful. It was certainly fruitful in the arts, sciences and agriculture. In the kitchen it was responsible for a rich, exciting and delicious collection of dishes.

The direct Muslim influence in the kitchen continued throughout the land long after the fall of Granada and lasted into the seventeenth century. King Boabdil capitulated on terms that allowed Muslims who remained in Spain to retain their faith, language and property. But the terms were broken and they were soon forced to convert or to leave. As converted Moriscos they suffered discrimination. They rebelled and their revolts were brutally suppressed. To prevent organized opposition, in 1568, people of Muslim descent were forced to leave what had been the old kingdom of Granada and to disperse throughout Castile. Some 50,000, it is said, went to different parts of the land, travelling in groups, accompanied by soldiers, and were resettled in towns and mountain villages. They were artisans – weavers, dyers, masons, shoemakers – and they became muleteers and street vendors. Foods similar to those they would have sold are now familiar in tapas bars all over Spain. Among these are *pinchos morunos* (small spicy pork kebabs), *fritura de pescado* (deep-fried fish and seafood), *empanadillas* (little pies) and chickpea and spinach stews. *Churros* (long fluted pieces of fried dough) sold for breakfast from stalls are the same as North African fritters today. Vendors, who until recently went around villages by mule selling cheese, butter, honey and the like, now go with a van, but they still wear folk costume. Could it be a version of the old Moorish dress? Young Morisco girls worked in Christian homes as domestic servants. They cooked for families and their special dishes were appreciated. When wealthy and aristocratic Christian women remained unmarried it was the custom for them to become nuns and to take their servants with

them to the convent. Convents throughout Spain today specialize in Moorish-style pastries, which are most likely a legacy of the young Morisco maids. There were also prosperous Moriscos – silk merchants, skilled artisans, masons and physicians – living in cities, whose families had integrated into Christian society for generations. A report of 1588 from Seville described them as having great riches, dealing in food and controlling the greater part of the bread trade.

Priests were sent to teach the converted Moriscos to be good Catholics, while inspectors for the Holy Office of the Inquisition, established in 1478 to ensure that Christians remained true to orthadox beliefs and practices, knocked at their doors to make sure that they did not speak Arabic, sing Moorish songs, dance in their traditional manner, wear Moorish clothes or cook Moorish dishes. Inquisitors could enter a home at any time to check that the family cooked with pork fat and pork products. Perhaps this is the time when the Spanish custom of putting little bits of ham into every possible dish, including vegetable and fish dishes, took root, as converted Muslims and Jews, as well as 'Old Christians', were forced to show proof of their allegiance to Christianity by eating pork. Back in 1514, one Íñigo López de Mendoza, count of Tendilla, captain general of the Kingdom of Granada and viceroy of Andalusia, in a letter to the Catholic monarch, attacked the attempts of the Inquisition to force the Moriscos to abandon their customs. He wrote: 'What clothing did we use to wear . . . what sort of food did we eat, if not in the Morisco style? Did the kings cease to be Christians and saints because of this?'

In Aragon and Valencia, the nobility depended on Morisco agricultural labour and protected their peasants from the Inquisition, allowing them to observe their religion in secret. Until the beginning of the seventeenth century, Moriscos represented about one-fifth of the population of Aragon. In Valencia, they represented one-third. The more Castile tried to force cultural assimilation and integration, the more the Moriscos held on to their identity. In 1609, they were accused of conspiring against the crown with the Ottoman Turks and with North African pirates, who were mostly departed Moors. Except for a few, certified by the clergy as true Christians, the Moriscos were deported from Spain en masse. By the mid seventeenth century, all descendants of Muslims in the peninsula had officially been expelled from the country. Of course some remained. You can sometimes tell people's Morisco ancestry by their identifiable names that denote a trade, such as stonemason or ironmonger, and by the prefix 'al'. Alcaide is a common name in Spain (in Arabic it means 'the chief'). I met someone called Alcaide in Andalusia who told me that their family had owned a handwritten book of recipes in Arabic that was burnt by a great-aunt. The Inquisition might well have tried to eradicate the Moriscos' cooking from Spain, but its impact is striking today to anyone who knows anything about Arab and North African food.

a *hispano-moorish* cuisine

A new and unique culinary culture developed over the centuries in al-Andalus that mirrored the multicultural, cosmopolitan society of people drawn from various parts of the Muslim world together with Christians and Jews. The inhabitants of Granada, Toledo, Cordoba and Seville, and the Arab elites who set themselves up in the major cities in the south of al-Andalus and in the valley of the river Ebro, followed the fashions and manners of Baghdad, including the high style of cooking which derived from Persia. Settlers from Shiraz, in Persia, founded the city of Jerez. Their culinary ways, together with those of settlers from Syria, Palestine, Egypt, Yemen and North Africa, form the basis of medieval Andalusian cooking. The poorer migrants, Berbers from North Africa, who were made to settle in the harsh rural mountain regions and in the marsh areas of Valencia, used basic methods to cook mainly chickpeas, rice, pasta and couscous.

Forty-five years ago, I found a Spanish translation of a twelfth or thirteenth-century Arabic cookery manual of Al-Andalus at the British Library. Many recipes were similar to those in two culinary manuscripts of the same period, one from Baghdad, another from Damascus, which I had been cooking from. Like the Arab dishes, the medieval Andalusian recipes made use of a long list of spices including saffron, cinnamon, cumin and coriander, cardamom, mustard, nutmeg, cloves, allspice, aniseed and ginger; and of herbs, such as parsley, coriander and mint. Sweet dishes were scented with orange blossom and rose waters. The Muslims did not eat pork but they did drink wine, which is also forbidden by Islam. Some of the old Moorish dishes disappeared from Spain when the Muslims left. In the seventeenth century, eating couscous was seen as an un-Christian activity to be despised and for which a person might be obliged to do penance.

Arab cooking methods – the use of clay pots and of skewers and the ways of preserving in vinegar or in sugar syrup – were adopted throughout Spain. Moorish legacies in Spanish cuisine include meats cooked with fruits such as apples, pears and quinces, and marriages of artichokes and broad beans and of aubergines and courgettes. Stuffed vegetables filled with minced meat or rice or a mixture of the two, and sauces thickened with ground almonds and hazelnuts are other legacies, as are garnishes of raisins and pine nuts, and grilling meats on skewers. Meatballs, rice dishes, chickpea stews, rice pudding, fritters in syrup, almond pastries – all these, plus combinations of sweet flavours with savoury and of sweet and sour, are legacies of that old mixed society of diverse cultures and identities. You can hear the Arab influence in hundreds of Spanish food words such as *alboronía* (a vegetable dish with aubergine), *almíbar* (syrup), *alcachofas* (artichokes), *albóndigas* (meatballs), *arroz* (rice), *escabeche* (pickled in vinegar), *fideos* (from the Arab *fidawsh*, which are like very short spaghettini) and *aletría* (from *itria*, which are short macaroni). The tradition of salting and drying tuna roe to make botargo came from the Arabs, as did the technique of alembic distillation of alcohol for making spirits (the words 'alembic' and 'alcohol' are derived from the Arabic). The Arabs used spirits for medicinal purposes. Spanish alchemists (another Arabic word) and monks improved the techniques and the equipment used to make brandy, and these were eventually passed across to France. Today, many innovative chefs are inspired by the ancient cookery books to explore their medieval gastronomic roots. You might get couscous and *briks* (Moroccan savoury pastries) in some of the best Spanish restaurants.

Cooking techniques and tastes travelled in two directions. Versions of Spanish dishes are much-loved foods in North Africa, where the Muslims who were expelled from Spain settled. In cities like Fez and Tétouan in Morocco, where the similarities are striking, and also in Tunisia, these dishes are described as 'Andalusian'. A Morisco character in Cervantes' *Don Quixote* called Ricote tells Sancho Panza, his former neighbour, that his people, condemned by the expulsion to wander through the world in search of a new home, never stopped crying for Spain. Their traditional foods gave them comfort and started a culinary revolution in their new homelands.

JEWISH LEGACIES:
almond cakes and fried onion and garlic

Sitting on a bench in a little square lined with orange trees in the Barrio de Santa Cruz, the old Jewish quarter of Seville, I imagined my ancestors going about their lives in the labyrinth of narrow streets winding their way round whitewashed houses with wrought-iron balconies. When the Jews were banished from Spain in 1492, they were given the option of converting to Christianity and remaining as Conversos, as they and their descendants were called.

There was a Jewish presence in the Iberian peninsula even before the Roman Emperor Titus sent thousands of Jews there as slaves when he destroyed Jerusalem. During the Muslim occupation of Spain, large numbers of Jews migrated to al-Andalus from different parts of the Islamic Empire. They spoke Arabic, dressed like Arabs and cooked Arab foods with a special Jewish touch. They prospered economically and culturally. It was here that they rediscovered and reinvented Hebrew as a literary language and here that the most beautiful Hebrew poetry was written. When the fanatic Almohads took control of al-Andalus and tried to convert the Jews to Islam in the twelfth century, many fled north to the Christian kingdoms. That is how some typical Moorish dishes spread to all parts of the peninsula. The Jews settled in many cities, where they lived in quarters known as *aljamas* or *juderías*. They included artisans and physicians, scientists and scholars, merchants, moneylenders and royal tax collectors. Some were humble and poor. A few were bankers and courtiers who financed the wars against the Moors, and Christopher Columbus's voyage to the Americas in 1492. Many rose to high rank. In 1391, hostility against their perceived privileged status and relationship with the king ended in riots and massacres and the forcible baptism of thousands of Jews in many cities.

The Holy Office of the Inquisition was used to pursue those converts (Conversos) who kept up the Jewish faith in secret. In 1492, when King Ferdinand II of Aragon and Queen Isabella I of Castile gave Jews who had not yet converted the choice to either convert to Catholicism or leave Spain, in some towns the entire community left, in others the entire community converted. There were large numbers of Conversos in Castile, Aragon, Andalusia and Valencia. Within a century the majority had melted into the Christian population, but until the early nineteenth century they continued to be suspected of being secret Jews (Marranos). If denounced, they were interrogated and could be burnt at the stake in an auto-da-fé, or they could be imprisoned and have their property confiscated and their families would be stigmatized for generations. Inquisitors visited homes on Fridays to see if families put white tablecloths and candles on the table to celebrate the Sabbath. The dreaded Inquisitor General Tomás de Torquemada – himself a Converso – would stand on a hill above a city on Saturdays to identify the houses where there was no smoke coming out of the chimneys (Jewish laws prohibit any work, including cooking and lighting a fire, on the Sabbath). Records of the Inquisition show that food was used as evidence of Judaizing when women were brought to trial.

Because of the many religious rules related to food, cooking was central to the Jewish identity. So as not to use pork fat as Christians did for cooking, and to avoid clarified butter, which the Muslims used (their dietary laws forbid mixing meat with dairy products), Jews used olive oil exclusively for all their cooking. The smell of frying with olive oil became so strongly associated with Jewishness that even Old Christians of non-Jewish descent avoided it for fear of being mistaken for secret Jews.

The Jewish Sabbath dish *adafina*, a stew which was left to cook in a pot overnight in the ashes of a fire from Friday to Saturday, was regularly cited as a sign of Judaizing. It was made with meat, usually lamb and chicken, cut into large pieces – some of it minced and rolled into large oval balls – chickpeas, onions and vegetables such as cabbage, spinach or chard, or with aubergines. Sausages made of sheep's intestines stuffed with minced meat were added to the pot, as were hard-boiled eggs in their shells. These were called *huevos haminados*. To prove their true conversion to Christianity, Conversos put in ham, pork sausages and *morcilla* (Spanish blood sausage). The memory of *adafina* lives on in today's Spanish *cocidos* (page 303), especially those of Madrid, Asturias and Valencia, which contain chickpeas. In Asturias, there is a saying: '*Cocido de garbanzos, guiso de marranos*' (which means '*Cocido* made with chickpeas, stew of the Marranos' – secret Jews). The *pelotas*, big balls of minced meat or chicken with bread, almonds and pine nuts, sometimes wrapped in cabbage leaves, that go into the *cocidos* of Valencia, Murcia and Catalonia are similar to those small meatloaves added to the Sabbath cooking pots of North African Jews today.

Conversos ate pork ostentatiously. The word *marrano* also literally means 'pig'. In Majorca, families of Converso origin are known by the derogatory name *xuetes* (*xua* means bacon) because they cooked and ate large quantities of bacon out of doors for everyone to see. For some it felt like a betrayal of their ancestry. Antoni Campins Chaler, author of *En un fogón de La Mancha: La ingeniosa cocina de Don Quijote y Sancho* ('In a Fireside Kitchen in La Mancha: The Ingenious Cooking of Don Quixote and Sancho') (Grupo Cultural, 2004), sent me a story and a poem written in the fifteenth century by the Converso troubadour Antón de Montoro, known as 'El Ropero'. One day, when the troubadour went to the butcher he found only pork meat for sale and this inspired him to write the following verses in old Castilian addressed to Cordoba's *corregidor* (mayor), in which he says that the butcher who sold only pork caused him deep sorrow by obliging him to relieve his hunger by breaking his grandfather's oath:

*One of the stalwarts
of the king, a strong bulwark,
has given the butchers
reason to make me perjure myself,
not finding to my sorrow
anything to kill my hunger
they have forced me to break
my vows to my forebears.*

Translated by Edith Grossman

Almodrote de berenjena, a dish of mashed aubergines baked with cheese and eggs, which was made on Friday to be eaten cold on Saturday, was another food that compromised Jews. Other typical Sabbath dishes included aubergine fritters dipped in flour or batter, *fritadas* (omelettes with vegetables), and *empanada* and *empanadilla* (pies filled with minced meat or fish). Jews in Turkey continued to call these pies *empanadillas* up until the middle of the twentieth century, when they began to call them *borekitas* – a mark of integration into Turkish culture. *Boronía* was a dish of fried aubergines, courgettes and other vegetables. Sponge cakes, various almond pastries, marzipan and *membrillo* (quince paste) were traditional Sabbath sweets. Flourless cakes made with almonds, eggs and sugar, and flavoured with orange, were baked for Passover, when Jews could not use flour. Jews were known for their frequent use of minced meat – to make meatballs and as stuffings for vegetables and pies. Aubergines, quinces, fennel, onions and garlic were associated with Jews and were mentioned in plays and poems that satirized and outed Conversos, usually written by Conversos themselves. Spices such as cinnamon, saffron, cumin, caraway and coriander also held these associations. Jews were said to smell of onion and garlic, and their homes to smell of frying onion and garlic. Fried onion and garlic became the basis of the Spanish *sofrito*, the start of so many dishes in Spain, to which tomatoes were added later.

Blood purity laws (*limpieza de sangre*), which were only abolished in Spain as late as 1865, excluded people with any Muslim or Jewish ancestry from ennoblement and certain professions, and from high office in institutions such as the Church and state, or military orders. But wealthy and influential Converso families (many of the Jews who decided to stay and convert were the ones who had a lot to lose) were able to hide their ancestry by forging ancestry papers and paying witnesses. Fluent in many languages, some acted as diplomats and ambassadors. Their international connections with relatives and Jews of Spanish origin abroad enabled them to make easy transfers of money and to trade around the Mediterranean and across the Atlantic. Some amassed immense fortunes and managed to buy land and titles, to enter into the Church and state hierarchies, and to marry into the impoverished aristocracy. The nobility, the clergy and the kings came to depend on them for finance. Conversos financed the voyages of discovery and the military requirements of the empire. In the sixteenth century, two books appeared – the notorious *libros verdes* ('green books') – purporting to list the Jewish descent of noble families and providing evidence that a good part of the Spanish nobility, especially of Castile, had Jewish ancestry. In his *Don Quixote*, Miguel de Cervantes had Sancho Panza argue that since he was a peasant who could brandish his 'purity of blood', unlike the wealthy merchants, intellectuals and nobles who had Converso blood ties, he had the right to be made a duke.

Foods that were once associated with Jews are today common in many parts of Spain. Some of the pastries that nuns make in convents, such as the almond cake from Santiago de Compostela, are of Jewish origin. In the early days of the Inquisition, having priests and nuns in the family was a way that Converso families protected themselves from persecution. There were many nuns of Jewish origin; Saint Teresa of Ávila was one. That may be how Jewish pastries were taken up in convents. Another pastry that is of Jewish origin is the famous coil-shaped *ensaimada* of Majorca made with pork fat (*saim* means lard in the local Majorcan language). A Jewish equivalent today is made with butter or butter substitute. The roast baby lamb eaten in Castile and Leon with only a simple lettuce salad represents the ritual Passover lamb eaten with bitter herbs and lettuce dipped in salted water (symbolizing the bitter tears of the Jews who were slaves in Egypt).

Sephardi legacies (of Jews whose ancestors came from Spain) are celebrated now in Spain after centuries of silence and denial. Something of a recovery of a collective historic memory is going on with conferences and music festivals. '*Sefardí*' dishes appear on restaurant menus. A government-sponsored *Caminos de Sefarad* ('Sephardi Routes') links fifteen medieval cities with Jewish quarters and sites on a tourist itinerary. In Ribadavia in Galicia, where today's Ribeiro wine is produced and where the old Jewish community owned vineyards and produced wine, they re-enact a medieval Jewish wedding during the Festa da Istoria (historical festival) there in August. People confide that they believe they are of Converso origin because of their names or known family history, because they lit candles in a secret room on Friday nights, or their family hung their *jamón* (ham) outside or they always cleaned the house on Saturdays (it showed that they were contravening Jewish laws). And they are probably right, because widely publicized recent studies into the DNA of the Spanish population have established that at least 20 per cent have Jewish ancestry while 11 per cent have Berber ancestry.

FROM THE NEW WORLD:
red and yellow in the kitchen

Although Spaniards use very few spices and very little black pepper, these figure prominently in national lore. The Iberian trade in spices, which began with the Phoenicians and Romans and expanded hugely with the Moors, stopped when the Ottoman Turks' sea power and the activities of North African pirates made traffic difficult through the Mediterranean. This provided the Genoese sailor Christopher Columbus with the goal to set sail in search of an alternative route to India and the Spice Islands. In 1492, the Catholic monarchs Ferdinand and Isabella commissioned him to explore the western seas. He sailed away with three ships from Palos de la Frontera in Andalusia and discovered the Caribbean islands and the Americas. He was followed by conquistadors, who were mainly members of the lower nobility, and by adventurers, entrepreneurs and missionaries, who went out to conquer and colonize the New World. Peasants and artisans, mostly from Andalusia, Extremadura and La Mancha, were sent off with cargoes of grain and breeding stock – chickens, pigs, sheep, goats, cattle and horses. The colonizers took Christianity and the Castilian language to their new empire. They built churches and palaces and sent home gold and silver.

Around the same time, the Spanish kingdoms, with Castile at their head, acquired dominions in Europe through royal marriage. On Ferdinand's death in 1516, the thrones of Castile and Aragon passed to his grandson Charles V, also heir to the Habsburg Empire, who became Charles I of Spain; and the Spanish realms became partners in his dynastic rights to the Netherlands, the duchy of Burgundy and the kingdom of Sicily. Charles's son, Philip II, inherited parts of France, southern

Italy, Milan, Sicily and Sardinia, the Netherlands, a bit of Greece and a bit of North Africa, as well as most of South and Central America, the Philippines, Ceylon and several islands from Sumatra to the Azores. Then Portugal, with its Far Eastern and African empires and Brazil, was added to the territories ruled by Philip II. Spain was the supreme imperial power in the world and Toledo and Madrid became its centres of administration.

Spain's glorious period of supremacy was brief. From about 1540, the cost of running the enormous empire was crippling and constant wars to defend it drained her coffers. By the beginning of the eighteenth century, Spain was impoverished, parts of her empire were lost and the country was empty of people. Hundreds of thousands had died in wars and sea battles, while thousands had emigrated to the New World to escape poverty. Plague epidemics and the expulsion of the Moriscos contributed to the depopulation and falling agricultural production. Almost all of the Latin American empire was lost by the early nineteenth century.

From the point of view of gastronomy, the discovery of the New World was a fantastic success that was to revolutionize the diets of both the Old and the New worlds. The early colonizers found the native inhabitants of the Americas eating foods they had never seen before. Among these were maize, potatoes, sweet potatoes, tomatoes, beans and capsicum peppers, also Jerusalem artichokes, pumpkins, pineapples, papayas, guavas, custard apples, avocados and peanuts. They saw the locals roasting and grinding maize and making tortillas. They tasted a chocolate drink and also discovered the flavour of vanilla. They found turkeys and tobacco. On his return to Spain from his first voyage, Columbus made a triumphal show of the goods he brought back at the court of Ferdinand and Isabella. Among the exhibits were gold and silver jewellery, a variety of animals, fruits and vegetables, and ten native 'Indians'. Pietro Martire d'Anghiera, an Italian cleric at the Spanish court, wrote about chilli peppers at the time: 'Something may be said about the pepper gathered in the islands and on the continent … but it is not pepper, though it has the same strength and flavour, and it is just as much esteemed … When it is used, there is no need of Caucasian pepper.'

Many of the New World colonizers became farmers and used native Indians and black men shipped to the Americas from the West African coast as slave labour. They planted wheat and other cereals, as well as vines and sugar cane brought over from Spain. They also grew the local plants that were unknown in Europe. Franciscan and Jesuit missionaries were among the biggest landowning farmers. Potatoes, maize and beans, the mainstay of the native peoples, were found to be the cheapest way to feed the slaves working in the mines and fields. When Spaniards began to eat the foods themselves they wrote that potatoes tasted 'like cooked chestnuts when they are boiled' (they had probably eaten sweet potatoes) and that sauces were made with peppers and tomatoes. When the colonizers came back home to Spain they brought seeds, beans and tubers to grow in their own gardens. They also brought back wild turkeys they had domesticated.

The aristocracy adopted turkeys as food for special occasions, replacing the pigeons that had been the festive treat of the Muslim and Jewish communities. Turkeys became associated with Christmas. The aristocracy and the clergy also very quickly took to drinking chocolate. The clergy famously made chocolate to be drunk during Lent and on fast days. Beans were widely adopted. Black-eyed beans and broad beans were already cultivated in Spain so the new varieties were easily accepted. Dried haricot beans became the food of the peasantry and of the urban poor. They were stewed with bits of cured pork or sausage to give them flavour. But other new foods were slow to penetrate the Spanish diet.

Maize was first taken up in the north of the country, where it was used as animal fodder, while the rural poor turned it into flour to make bread, fried pancakes and a kind of porridge with milk. While peasants in the north grew potatoes for themselves to eat, the Church, the nobility, the judiciary and intellectuals throughout Spain despised them as 'poor food', good only for hospitals, military barracks and prisons. Records show that they were bought as part of the regular housekeeping of Seville's Hospital de la Sangre in 1573. Potatoes were not generally adopted in the Spanish diet until the beginning of the nineteenth century, after the French agronomist Antoine-Augustin Parmentier had popularized them in France.

At first, tomatoes were thought to be poisonous. They were cultivated in the early sixteenth century in Seville, where the warm climate allowed them to thrive, but they did not come into general use until the eighteenth century. The first cookbook to mention them, *Lo scalco alla moderna* ('The Modern Steward') by Antonio Latini, was published in Naples in 1692, a time when the Italian south was part of the Spanish Empire. Less than a handful of recipes in the book contain tomatoes, and all of these are labelled '*alla spagnola*' (meaning Spanish-style). A coulis of tomatoes with finely chopped onions and chilli peppers, oil, vinegar and salt is similar to descriptions of sauces that were found in the Americas and very like dressings and sauces you encounter in Spain today. Extensive use of the tomato began only in the nineteenth century. One complaint today about food in Spain is that tomatoes are used in almost everything. The *sofrito* sauce of fried onions, garlic and tomatoes is not only ubiquitous in Spain, where nowadays it most often also includes green peppers, but has become ever-present in all Mediterranean cuisines.

Varieties of peppers and chillies, both sweet and hot, spread quickly all over Spain. Chilli peppers were first grown in monasteries and the seeds were distributed throughout Spain by travelling monks. Dried and crushed, or pulverized as *pimentón*, peppers and chillies became the favourite and ubiquitous flavouring for Spanish dishes, together with garlic. Spices and black pepper had been in use all over Europe in the upper classes until they became rare when the trade was interrupted. *Pimentón* eventually replaced them all in the Spaniards' affections.

The revolution in the Spanish diet caused by the discovery of the New World was slow, but in the end the combination of ingredients from the New and Old worlds resulted in a very rich and particularly colourful cuisine. Before peppers and tomatoes arrived there had been nothing to eat in Spain that was red.

THE FRENCH INFLUENCE:
béchamel and crema pastelera

In the nineteenth century, the wealthy bourgeoisies of Catalonia and the Basque Country were in thrall to French haute cuisine. But French influence on the cooking of its Iberian neighbour dates back to much earlier. Since the Middle Ages, France and Spain had fought wars with each other and stolen colonies from each other, but their royals had intermarried and the two countries had traded together and influenced each other culturally. In 778, Charlemagne, king of the Franks, invaded Catalonia and set it up as a buffer state to keep the Muslims from the Iberian peninsula out of France, and Catalonia remained culturally part of the Frankish world until the eleventh century. On and off, the Kingdom of Navarre was under the control of French kings through marriage and inheritance. French Occitania was once a vassal of Catalonia–Aragon. The peoples of Languedoc, Provence and Catalonia all spoke similar languages. Troubadours from Provence came to the courts of northern Spain and sang of love and the joys of life. The old Basque nobility, their merchant and banking families, clergy and jurists, derived their wealth and titles from services to the king of France and Navarre. The northern part of the Basque Country eventually became part of France.

French pilgrims have made their way to the tomb of the apostle Saint James (San Jacobo) in Santiago de Compostela in Galicia since the ninth century. The oldest route, the *camino del norte* (the 'Northern Path') travels along the edge of the Bay of Biscay through the Basque Country, Cantabria and Asturias. The *camino francés* (the 'French Path') passes through Navarre, La Rioja, Castile and Leon. By the twelfth and thirteenth centuries, French shopkeepers, craftsmen and innkeepers had set up along the pilgrim routes. Whole quarters in towns such as Pamplona, Logroño, Burgos, Leon, Astorga and Lugo were inhabited by Frenchmen, who were called *francos*.

There was an early French presence throughout the Iberian peninsula. Over several centuries, religious orders, such as the Burgundian order of Cluny, established a network of monasteries. Expeditions of soldiers led by nobles came from France to help in the Spanish crusade against the Muslims. The Knights Templar, warrior monks led by French noblemen, helped the kings of Catalonia and Aragon and were rewarded with castles and a fifth of the lands conquered from the Muslims. In the mid seventeenth century, French labourers were invited to settle in Spain to make up for the disruption to agriculture caused by the forced departure of the Moriscos.

The first sovereigns of all the joint kingdoms of Spain came from foreign dynasties through royal marriage – the Habsburgs from Austria and the Bourbons from France. Throughout the Habsburg dynasty's rule in Spain (1506–1700), the king and queen each had their own separate kitchen. Foreign queens marrying into the Spanish court came accompanied by their own cooks. Philip IV's first wife, Isabella of Bourbon, brought French cooks; his second wife, Mariana of Austria, brought pastry cooks from Austria. Chefs at the palace came from France, the Netherlands, Germany, Portugal and Italy, but the majority were French. The seventeenth century, a Spanish Golden Age of great splendour and cultural efflorescence, was also a period of economic crisis, when the palace was forced to reduce its expenditure, and cooks made redundant were taken on by the high nobility.

Philip V became the first Bourbon king of Spain in 1700 and the Bourbon dynasty has held the throne, with a number of interruptions, up to the present day. Under the rule of the Bourbons in the eighteenth century, French influence pervaded the Spanish palace kitchens. Philip V was the grandson of Louis XIV of France. During Louis XIV's reign, the French had become accepted all over the world as the absolute arbiters in matters of style and taste. It was at that time that the haute cuisine we know today developed in the kitchens of the palace of Versailles and those of the French nobility who moved from the provinces to Paris, and Paris was enshrined as gastronomy's international capital. Philip V appointed chefs trained at Versailles for his Palacio Real (the royal palace) and a cookbook published in 1651 by François Pierre de la Varenne entitled *Le Cuisinier François* ('The French Cook'), which codified the new haute cuisine, was used in the royal and noble kitchens of Madrid. The recipes represented a refined sophisticated cuisine with elaborate techniques, expensive ingredients such as foie gras and truffles, rich butter and cream sauces, and plenty of wine and brandy. However, to appease the Spanish cooks, who felt displaced, there were also always a certain number of traditional Spanish dishes on the menu.

During and after the French Revolution, which began in 1789, French cooks who lost their employ crossed the border into Spain and found work with the high aristocracy and with the new industrial bourgeoisie that was emerging in northern Spain. In the nineteenth century, French winemaking families settling in Majorca, La Rioja and Cadiz brought their own particular cooking styles to those regions.

At the end of the nineteenth century, Mariano Pardo de Figueroa, writing under the pseudonym 'Doctor Thebussem', teamed up with several people, including a cook at the royal palace and a recipe writer, to discover, renovate, promote and popularize a truly Spanish national cuisine. It was a patriotic endeavour, a reaction against cosmopolitan and French influences. Together the authors wrote a book that featured recipes from fourteenth-century cookery books and from a book by the royal cook Francisco Martínez Montiño, first published in Madrid in 1611, entitled *Arte de cocina, pastelería, vizcochería y conservaría* ('Art of Cooking, Cake-making, Biscuit-making and Conserving'). But when they researched what people were actually cooking, they found that their battle was already lost. French chefs had opened cookery schools for the upper classes and their cooks, which taught from Antoine Carême's works and Auguste Escoffier's *Le Guide culinaire*, while new books destined for middle-class housewives featured mostly recipes translated from the French.

There was a new, enthusiastic fervour for all things regional and traditional in the early twentieth century, and efforts were made to recover old recipes and to record rural ones. A cookbook by Countess de Pardo Bazán published in 1913 is an example of that trend, but she too featured a great number of French recipes. In Catalonia, the prosperity generated by the industrial revolution brought about a cultural renaissance and the promotion of the Catalan language and local artists, but French cuisine remained all the rage for the aspiring classes. The great food writer Simone Ortega's book *1080 recetas de cocina* ('1080 Recipes'), published in 1972, the cooking bible of the Spanish middle classes for two generations, also contained a majority of French dishes.

Some of the classic French dishes have become Hispanicized, such as the béchamel sauce in which a chopped onion is cooked in butter or olive oil before flour and milk are added. The *croquetas* (croquettes) that you find in Spanish *tapas* bars today, the *leche frita* (fried cream) that you can buy in supermarkets, the *crema pastelera* (custard) that is much used in pastries, the crêpes you find in northern Spain, the *flan* (crème caramel) that is common throughout Spain, are all French dishes that have become an integral part of Spanish cuisine. As early as the eighteenth century, cooks for the elite started putting bouquet garni in their soups, stews and braises. The bunch of bay leaves, thyme and parsley tied with string took on a Spanish character when local wild herbs were included. In Catalonia, their bunch of savory, thyme and wild oregano wrapped in bay leaves is called *farcellets*. The ubiquitous combination of chopped onions,

carrots and celery or leeks called *mirepoix* that is sautéed at the start of many stews is a French touch, as are the practices of flambéing, of caramelizing the tops of puddings and baking in a bain-marie. Until the recent arrival of *nueva cocina* (Spanish nouvelle cuisine), anyone who aspired to cook grandly in Spain made French haute cuisine dishes and that is what people learnt at catering school.

THE ARISTOCRACY:
meat and game

In Sicily and southern Italy, there is a *cucina povera* ('poor food') of the peasantry and a *cucina nobile* of the nobility – an incredibly over-the-top, grand cooking style, which you encounter today in banqueting rooms, at wedding parties or on special saints' days. Feasting there is a matter of keeping up appearances (*la bella figura*) and gastronomic extravagance can reach incredible heights. Italians call it *spagnolismo* and say that it is a legacy of Spanish rule. So I was expecting to find an equally grandiose haute cuisine in Spain, a land that once had the greatest number of nobles of anywhere in the world and which once revelled in ceremony and stately court etiquette. But everybody I met in Spain told me there was no such thing, that today's creative *nueva cocina* by star chefs is the first Spanish haute cuisine.

Up until the beginning of the twentieth century, the high aristocracy, the royal entourage at the Madrid court, had French cooks and ate mainly French food. They gave ostentatious banquets, serving many different kinds of dishes buffet-style, in the French manner. But the vast number of landed nobility who lived in the countryside never ate grand dishes, nor did they have sophisticated tastes. They simply consumed a lot of meat while their peasant retainers ate foods based on bread, legumes and vegetables. The aristocratic culture of Spain was a culture of war. It was sober and austere. The *reconquista* in the Middle Ages created a social class whose raison d'être was war. For much of its history, Spanish society, and in particular that of Castile, was constantly in arms and the nobility was a fighting class. After the Muslims were finally vanquished at the end of the fifteenth century, Spain's armies and noble families fought against rebelling converted Moriscos hiding in the mountains; they fought to take and to keep colonies overseas; they fought in the Netherlands; they fought against England and France, and in Italy, Tunis and Algeria; they fought against Protestant heretics; and they fought at sea against the Turks and North African pirates. They also fought at home for the Spanish succession.

The nobility in most of the Christian states of the Iberian peninsula were either descended from the aristocrats of the Visigoth era or brought into being by their services to the sovereign. Private armies were recruited and maintained by nobles to serve their kings and queens. In recompense, they received immense domains containing entire villages, from land expropriated from the Muslims. The high nobility of grandees formed an exclusive caste at the top of a strict aristocratic hierarchy. Then came the *títulos* (those with titles) – dukes, marquises and counts. When the king needed financial help he created more *títulos* and distributed more land. A lower nobility of *caballeros* (gentlemen) and *hidalgos* (knights) was distinguished from the plebeian population, the *pecheros*, by the title 'Don'. Among them were foot soldiers who fought valiantly and were knighted, and younger sons of nobles who did not inherit land and served the crown in the hope of obtaining favours and property. City burghers, wealthy enough to maintain horses and fight as knights, entered the ranks of the lower nobility. Small armies of these *caballeros* and *hidalgos* followed the kings and the great lords. They were given small estates and were sent off to fight on far-flung fronts and to conquer the New World. The grandees and *títulos* kept buying up more land, revenues and fiefs, and came to control most of the land in the form of large estates. Some of the great old families are still in possession of their ancestral estates and palaces. Some have wineries (*bodegas*) and produce olive oil. You will find their

coats of arms on the *bodegas* – on the produce labels and on the buildings themselves.

Spain got its first capital city in 1561, when the Habsburg King Philip II chose Madrid to be his residence, seat of government and the centre of Spain's empire. When the nearby royal palace El Escorial was completed in 1584, the higher aristocracy of Castile and some of Aragon flocked to Madrid in search of royal favours and the pleasures of the court, but still kept their estates in the countryside. The noble lifestyle was expensive, with large households and numerous retainers to maintain. The residences of the high nobility were luxurious, with Flemish tapestries and family portraits on the walls. Their clothing was lavish; they wore satins and velvets, and silk brocades woven with threads of gold and silver. Thoroughbred horses and carriages were among the symbols of status and prestige. Court events

were expensive too: there were theatres and *fiestas* and bullfights to attend. Huge amounts of money had to be set aside for dowries. Aristocrats were exempted from paying taxes but were expected to give the king money when he needed it for his wars and to supply armed soldiers for his armies. Serving the king could bring grandees close to bankruptcy. In the sixteenth and seventeenth centuries, the nobility was in permanent financial difficulties and even the great lords were in debt. For a time they benefited from the silver and gold mined in the Americas and from the market for Spanish products there, until other countries took over the trade with the New World.

The life of the nobility was always in the rural world. In Castile and Aragon especially, the countryside was in the hands of the warlords, who controlled the rural economy and had the allegiance of thousands of vassals. Depending on where they had their estates, the great landowners produced and marketed wool, grains, olive oil or wine. Some produced cork. Others drew income from mills or from hunting preserves, or they bred bulls for the *corrida* (bullfight). Wool was Spain's main non-agricultural industry and sheep farming was mostly in the hands of the nobility. Part of the motivation for regaining land in the south of the Iberian peninsula from the Muslims was to access warmer winter grazing lands for the large flocks of sheep living on the *meseta*, the vast high central plateau that is dominated by long, cold winters. As owners of fields, roads and villages, the nobility also lived on rents and dues paid by peasants, usually in kind, sometimes under a sharecropping contract.

Spanish nobles consumed so much meat that many suffered from gout. Eating a large amount of meat was a vaunted sign of status, unlike today when eating small portions is a sign of distinction. Suckling pig, baby lamb and veal were favourite foods, as they are today. Chickens, capons, turkeys, geese, guinea hens and rabbits were also much consumed. The aristocracy loved to hunt, and game was plentiful in the wildernesses that belonged to them. Deer, wild boar, hares and birds such as partridges, pheasants, woodcock, pigeons, wild ducks and migrating quails were an important part of their diet. Apart from suckling pig, pork was eaten mostly as cured meat. Living in central Spain, away from the sea, the nobility ate hardly any fish apart from salt cod and occasionally the grander freshwater fish, such as salmon, eel and trout. Vegetables were considered poor food, but plenty of fruit was consumed – pears, apples, figs, cherries and oranges, also almonds and other nuts. Many noble families supported convents and monasteries financially, from which they received pastries and confectionery as gifts. They also drank wine and hot chocolate. Apart from the very high aristocracy that enjoyed French haute cuisine, the food was simply cooked, mostly roasted or stewed. Game was marinated to soften the meat and then cooked in wine and brandy. Lard was used for cooking. Aromatics and flavourings included garlic, saffron, cinnamon, cloves, bay leaves, oregano and parsley, and their condiments were oil, vinegar, mustard and honey.

The large numbers of lesser nobility were mostly poverty-stricken. Unemployed in peacetime and struggling to keep up appearances, they lived above their means trying to keep up the high standards required of the aristocracy, without soiling their hands and losing status and honour with work or trade of any kind. Their situation is humorously depicted in one of the first Spanish picaresque novels, *La vida de Lazarillo de Tormes* ('The Life of Lazarillo de Tormes'), published anonymously in 1554 and described as an autobiographical *novela de la hambre* ('novella of hunger'). It is the story of Lazarillo, a young lad who lives by his wits and serves many masters. In one chapter his master is a proud and impoverished nobleman who is starving but does not want the world to know this. Rather than lose face he goes around the town picking his teeth so that people will think he has just eaten meat. Not only is the nobleman not able to feed his servant but the servant has to find ways to feed the master, for whom he develops an affectionate respect.

The *hidalgos* (knights) who hung around the royal court in Madrid were held in popular ridicule for 'speaking loudly of their honour while having scarcely a ducat to their names'. 'On the *hidalgo's* table,' another saying went, 'there is much linen but little food.' In certain circles, the table settings and adornments were more significant in establishing social distinction than the quality of the food. This was the world satirized by Cervantes in his early-seventeenth-century masterpiece *Don Quixote*, where serving king and Church was the ideal, and the prevailing ethos was the cult of chivalry, bravado, honour and the love that conquers all. While the knight's servant, Sancho Panza (*panza* means belly), was always thinking about where he would get his next meal, Don Quixote gave food little thought and always managed to drag poor Sancho away from the table before he had finished eating, to set off on another mad adventure.

OF MONASTERIES AND CONVENTS:
Lenten dishes and pastries

The Catholic Church in Spain had a big influence on cooking traditions. For centuries it was one of the ruling forces, together with the nobility and the military. It was immensely rich and powerful and, like the nobility, was exempt from paying taxes levied by the crown. While the material fortunes of the nobility usually deteriorated, the Church always prospered, at least until the nineteenth century, when some of their lands were confiscated by a liberal progressive government. Bishops, abbots and cathedral chapters owned huge estates that were given to them by the king from lands reclaimed from Muslims. The Church, like the nobility, financed private armies. The clergy were at the top of the social hierarchy and were divided into a rich and powerful aristocracy recruited from wealthy noble families and a multitude of minor clergy who served them. A priest or a nun in the family gave it prestige.

The clergy were known for their appreciation of good food and their gargantuan appetites. Their rotund bodies, as depicted in the past, were cited to me as evidence. Monasteries were famous for culinary refinement. The peasants who worked the vast Church lands gave over to them much of their produce in lieu of rent and maintained the monasteries' vegetable and herb gardens. In the south of Spain, when monasteries took over Moorish palaces, the monks turned the interior patios into herb gardens. Monasteries were known for making wine, brandy and cheese, and for growing rare vegetables such as artichokes, spinach and asparagus, as well as a wide variety of herbs. Benedictine monks famously made chocolate. The high clergy were usually very well educated and had French and Italian connections. The food on their dining tables was more varied and refined than the mountains of meat produced by aristocratic kitchens. The lower clergy cooked their meat and game with the brandy and wine the monasteries produced and the herbs grown in the gardens. It is said that Charles V, king of Castile and Aragon, who was a renowned gourmand, chose to spend the years after his abdication in 1555 in the monastery of Yuste to the north-west of Madrid because of the food there. The monastery of Guadalupe in Extremadura, which provided daily meals for monks and pilgrims, also had a reputation for high gastronomy. The nineteenth-century chronicler Vicente Barrantes lists the New Year's fare prepared there for King Philip II and his entourage as including six baby deer, three large deer, two wild boar, 100 ducks, 100 partridges, 100 pigeons, 200 rabbits, four dozen hams, mountains of the best crystallized lemon peel and assorted confectionery, baskets of fruit and gallons of wine.

The style of cooking in monasteries and convents had nothing to do with their locality, because the clergy came from different parts of the country and their religious orders moved them around, together with their servants. Many spent long periods with their orders in the New World and came back with new produce from there. Certain grand dishes and several cookery books are associated with monasteries that became famous for their gastronomy. In the fourteenth century, the bishop of Tarragona's cook wrote *El llibre del coch de la Canonja de Tarragona* ('The Cookbook of the Diocese of Tarragona'). Another medieval Spanish cookbook, *El llibre de ventre* ('The Book of the Belly'), was written at the Ripoll monastery. The fourteenth-century Franciscan Catalan writer and theologian Francesc Eiximenis devoted a book to the art of good drinking and cooking, and to the courtesies and rules of etiquette of the table. The most famous culinary manuscript came out of the Benedictine monastery of Alcántara in Extremadura. It was discovered by the French General Junot when his troops sacked the monastery in 1807 during the Peninsular War – known as the War of Spanish Independence in Spain. He sent the manuscript to his wife, the future Duchess of Abrantès, who reproduced some of the recipes in her memoirs. Auguste Escoffier was later to comment that the manuscript was the only worthwhile French gain from the war. One of the most famous dishes described in it is pheasant stuffed with duck liver pâté and cooked in port wine with truffles (*faisán a la moda de Alcántara* – my recipe is on page 381).

Nuns came to convents from different parts of Spain, from the aristocracy and from the peasantry. There was a strict hierarchy. Rich or aristocratic women were superior, the others were the servants and labourers. Many convents were founded by noblewomen for women of their own class who were not married. If the daughter of a landowner fell in love with someone inappropriate, such as a labourer or retainer, she would be forced to become a nun. The convents received enough wealth in dowries and bequests so that their nuns could live in comfort. Some of the convents had dairy farms and produced all kinds of foods. Nuns in poorer convents baked cakes and pastries as gifts to show their gratitude to patrons who made their frugal existence possible. Cloistered convents today are famous for selling pastries (see page 488).

The Church had a hold on the Spanish diet through the Office of the Holy Inquisition, which was formally abolished only in 1834. Its role was to check on non-Catholic behaviour, and that included eating meat during fast days. At an eighteenth-century coach house converted into a hotel and restaurant in La Rioja, I was shown a handwritten document dated 1798 and signed by two government representatives – a tax collector and a Church inquisitor – who came to visit the inns in the village. They reported that the measures of grain were correct and that everything was in order. To keep out of trouble, people in town and country were obliged to abide by the rules of fasting and abstinence ordered by the Church during six weeks of *Cuaresma* (Lent), on every Friday and four times a year at the beginning of the seasons on Wednesday, Friday and Saturday. During those fast days dedicated to silence and prayer, meat was forbidden and vegetarian and fish dishes were eaten. Traditional Lenten foods were salt cod and cured herring, pulses such as beans, chickpeas and lentils, eggs and dairy products, as well as a variety of vegetables including carrots, potatoes and turnips, also leeks, spinach, peas and broad beans. Pastries and chocolate were allowed, to compensate for the lack of meat.

In his book *Spanish Society: 1400–1600* (Longman, 2001), the social historian Teofilo Ruiz quotes the fourteenth-century *Libro de buen amor* ('The Book of Good Love') by Juan Ruiz, which describes the struggle between Don Carnal (Lord Carnality) and Doña Cuaresma (Lady Lent). The former's armies, composed of succulent hams, pieces of bacon, cheeses, kitchen utensils, game and abundant wine, are routed by Lady Lent's host of dry salted fish, beans, chickpeas and other foods associated with vigils and fasting. Carnality was imprisoned and thus began the metaphorical withdrawal from the world during the forty days preceding Easter Sunday.

At the beginning of the twentieth century, several cookbooks were published dedicated to making Lenten and fast dishes agreeable. Each came preceded by an ecclesiastical permission and with an introduction for the faithful explaining the divine obligations to fast, and the idea that fasting combats passions. One such book is the Catalan *Ayunos y abstinencias* ('Fasts and Abstinence') by Ignacio Doménech and F. Martí, published in 1914. A long chapter on soups for institutions (the quantities are huge) gives recipes for substantial soups made with pulses and vegetables, and occasionally a little salt cod is added. They are flavoured with herbs such as bay leaves, thyme, oregano and parsley, and sometimes spices such as saffron and nutmeg. The recipes all have added stock cubes – the brands Maggi or Knorr (yes!). The authors give recipes from several Spanish regions as well as some foreign ones. For example, *cocottes de guindas à la Rothschild* is a pear compote with syrup, perfumed with vanilla and curaçao liqueur, and sprinkled with chopped pistachio nuts. The book was not written for the peasantry or for the urban poor.

PEASANT FOOD:
breadcrumbs and pimentón

The real food of Spain was the food of the peasantry, the *campesinos*. Until the mid twentieth century, 80 per cent of the population lived and worked on the land, which was owned by big landowners, for the most part the Church and the aristocracy. Nowadays 80 per cent of Spaniards live in towns and cities. Industrial farming methods have changed the old ways in the countryside and people have left the land to work in tourist industries. Supermarkets and exporters offer such a small price for agricultural produce that it is not worth farming on a small scale and producing a variety of crops. Agriculture has become specialized and industrialized and it is immigrants now – mostly North Africans but also Latin Americans and Eastern Europeans – who are the seasonal agricultural labourers. Huge areas are covered by a single crop, such as grapes in Castile and olives in Andalusia. Foreigners are buying up small farmhouses and cottages. Along the coasts, those who had a bit of land sold it to contractors who built golf courses, hotels and holiday homes for tourists. Anybody who had a little plot by the sea could become a millionaire. In the past, when families divided up their land, the eldest child would get the field; anything on the coast was not valued and was given to a daughter or the less beloved children.

Though few Spaniards want to work on the land today they still love to feel the connection. Families keep old farmsteads as holiday retreats, where they have vegetable gardens and fruit trees. In villages, people keep allotments. Spaniards are often sentimental about the human landscape of the land, the old traditional rural life that disappeared so quickly in just a few decades. The foods associated with it, including those that were once shunned as 'foods of the poor', are very popular today. That is, except with the young, who, as someone remarked to me, have gone from poor foods to fast foods.

In Spain, there was no middling peasantry as in France. Peasant life and conditions varied from one region to another, but the overwhelming mass of the peasantry were poorly paid salaried labourers. The rest, small tenant farmers, were obliged by the old sharecropping system inherited from feudal times that remained until the 1950s to pay crippling rents – sometimes in kind – to their landlords and to do unpaid work. In return they were allowed to cultivate a portion of the estate for their own benefit. In the distant past, the peasantry had also borne the burden of constant warfare in the form of taxation to fund the wars and had been expected to go to war with their warlord. In Andalusia, the peasantry was mostly composed of *jornaleros*, labourers contracted for seasonal work by the day. In the north, especially in Galicia and Asturias, there were small proprietors and peasant farmers living on estates as sharecroppers. They usually paid their landlords in kind, handing over animals and crops, leaving little for themselves. Their smallholdings were so small that they could barely support one family. Younger siblings had to emigrate in search of a living. In Catalonia and the Basque Country, there were some well-to-do farmers who paid rental dues and debts of allegiance to the lord of their lands. By the nineteenth century, landlords in those parts could be city merchants or industrialists who invested their new-found wealth in land because there was more status in owning land than in business.

Peasants ate what they grew. They grew the grains and legumes that their landlords required of them because these could be dried and sold at the market or exported. They grew vegetables for their own use in the small private patches they kept. Beans and vegetables from the New World had revolutionized the rural peasants' diet centuries before they were adopted by the Spanish middle and upper classes, who despised certain foods, such as potatoes and vegetables, as poor foods better suited to coarse palates. Potatoes, maize and beans replaced the grains and chestnuts that had previously been the mainstay crops for the peasantry. They used tomatoes and chillies as condiments and developed a great predilection for dried and pulverized chillies (*pimentón*), both sweet and hot, which they sprinkled on almost everything they ate. Already by 1560 it was said that there was not a vegetable garden in Spain that did not have chillies growing in it. They were easy to cultivate in a small space and could be dried and crunched into a powder that kept well.

Chickens were kept for their eggs, which were used to make dishes such as *tortillas* (omelettes) and to barter at the market for other foods like salt cod, sardines and anchovies, or for rice and legumes if families did not grow these themselves. In the woodlands, chestnuts and mushrooms were picked and snails gathered. Venison, wild boar and other game were reserved for the noble landlords by strict laws. But that did not prevent the Spanish peasantry from snaring rabbits and hares, poaching game birds and catching migrating birds, such as quails, in nets hung between trees. In the mountain hinterland, they fished in the rivers when they could. They never ate fresh fish from the sea because of the lack of transport and refrigeration. In the north of the country, families kept a solitary cow, which provided milk that could be turned into cheese and butter. Elsewhere, they made sheep's and goat's milk cheeses. Before roads began to be built in the 1960s, there was very little transport across Spain, and high mountains and harsh terrain made it difficult to go to market by mule or on horseback.

The culture of the pig had been important to the peasantry since the earliest times, and came to symbolize the Christian *reconquista* in the Middle Ages. By the middle of the eighteenth century, this was an all-important part of peasant life throughout Spain. Those who could afford to buy a pig fed it for nine months and fattened it intensively for three more on domestic leftovers of beans, maize, potatoes, turnips and cabbage, sometimes fruit and chestnuts or acorns. The pig would be killed in the coldest, driest, most windy months, usually November or December. Families salted the hams and hung them to dry in airy lofts – in wet, rainy parts in the north of Spain, they smoke-dried them in their kitchens – and made sausages by chopping the meat with fat and seasonings and stuffing it into the pig's scrubbed intestines. The fat was rendered to be used for cooking. These products, which they began to eat in the spring, were made to last until the next *matanza* (the name given to the event of the killing of a pig). They had to go a long way to feed a family for a year. Only tiny pieces at a time were used in stews and soups. Itinerant vendors went around villages 'hiring out' ham bones and *chorizo* sausages for people to put in their bean stews, shouting, '*Sabor! Sabor!*' ('Flavour! Flavour!') The women ran out of their houses or called from the windows. They were charged according to the number of minutes they kept the bone or sausage in the *potaje* (soup) and according to whether theirs was the first or the last kitchen to use it. Cured ham was a luxury, used as money to pay the doctor. On the big estates in Andalusia, the landowning aristocracy killed many pigs a year to feed their peasant labourers with *chorizos*.

The pig is still the king of the Spanish kitchen and it is used in its totality – you can see the feet, tail, snout and ears on every butcher's stall in Spain. Until the civil war in the 1930s, pork products were eaten almost exclusively by the peasantry. Today, salted and smoked cured pork products and all manner of sausages are a much prized part of Spanish gastronomy while *jamón ibérico* (see page 112) is the jewel in the crown. Until fairly recently, pork fat was the main cooking fat used in at least half of regional dishes, including savoury and sweet pastries. The rest were cooked with olive oil. During Lent and periods of abstinence, *bacalao* (salt cod), 'the pig of the sea', replaced cured pork in every kind of dish.

The only times when the rural poor ate fresh meat – apart from the small game they poached – was the pork offal eaten on the day of the *matanza*, and lamb or chicken during festivals, saints' days and at events such as funerals when the meals were paid for by the community or were offered by the rich. Banquets were given as charitable legacies by rich people in their wills. Carnivals and celebrations were dominated by food and drink. The way peasants ate and drank to excess on such occasions reveals their anxiety and obsession with food. Their preoccupation and their eating fantasies are reflected in mythical stories such as those about a land called Jauja (the Spanish version of Cockaigne) where the likes of partridges and hams flew through the air and landed directly into people's mouths. Paradise meant a stomach filled with foods and delicacies that in real life were eaten only by the rich. In *Don Quixote*, Cervantes captured the dreams of the perpetually hungry peasants in his description of Camacho's wedding feast, a real orgy of excess. A whole ox, its belly stuffed with twenty-four tiny suckling pigs, is roasted on a spit turning over burning wood. Hanging about on nearby trees are skinned hares, plucked chickens and a variety of game, waiting to be cooked, as well as sixty wineskins, each filled with eight gallons of wine. Loaves of white bread and whole cheeses are stacked up like a wall. Sweet pastries are dropped into cauldrons filled with boiling oil, then lifted out and plunged into a pot of honey. A variety of spices are displayed in a huge chest. Don Quixote's servant, Sancho Panza, asks a cook if he can dip a piece of bread in a simmering broth and the cook ladles out three hens and two geese for him.

The preservation of food was an important part of Spanish rural traditions. Provisions were made in the summer to last over the winter. Chestnuts and fruits were dried in lofts or on rooftops. In northern regions, maize was dried and stored in stone or wood buildings called *hórreos*. Tomatoes and fruits such as apples, grapes, apricots and plums were dried in the sun or in the hearth. Olives were pickled. Tomato sauces were bottled in jars, as were roasted and peeled peppers. Vegetables were preserved in brine and fruits in sugar syrup. People also made *escabeches* of fish, partridge and quails by preserving them in a vinegary marinade after cooking. All these are now commercially available delicacies that Spaniards keep in their larders.

In each region, two or three dishes emerged as the dominant ones that peasants ate every day, and these depended on what was available locally. Families made porridge, bread and flat *tortas* (unleavened flatbreads) out of barley, millet, sorghum, wheat and maize. They made soups and stews with broad beans, chickpeas, beans, dried peas and lentils. Bread was the most important food and the basis of many dishes. Chestnuts were the poor foods in Galicia, Asturias and the Basque Country. The wealthy only ate chestnuts preserved and sweetened (*confitadas*) – as marrons glacés or puréed with cream and sugar. In the wet regions of the north, peasants ate apples, pears and plums, walnuts and hazelnuts. In the Mediterranean regions, many more vegetables, such as aubergines, courgettes and pumpkins, and more fruits were available. In periods of economic crisis, maize was the main food of the poor. During the civil war, and for the period of rationing after the war, 80 per cent of the peasantry survived on maize. In Asturias, the exclusive consumption of ground maize – made into bread and as a kind of polenta with milk and butter called *fariñes* – was held responsible for an outbreak of the disease pellagra, referred to as *el mal de la rosa* (meaning 'sickness of the rose') because one of the symptoms is red skin lesions. It was only in the 1950s that people there started again making bread with wheat instead of maize flour. Wheat had been too expensive before. *Gachas* (page 29) is another typical peasant dish, a kind of gruel made from the flour of ground grass peas, beans, chickpeas or wheat, with oil and water.

The wool trade and the pastoral industry, especially in Castile, was all-important. Transhumance, the annual migration of sheep from grazing lands in the north to winter pastures in the south and then back, was practised. At one time a vast network of sheep tracks (*cañadas*) criss-crossed the whole of Spain. Shepherds packed their cooking pots on their mules and set off. They ate *migas* (see page 288) made from fried breadcrumbs flavoured with garlic and *pimentón*, and they fried cheese with honey. Although shepherds were not permitted to eat the sheep in their charge, there are many lamb dishes called *del pastor* ('of the shepherd'). Cervantes tells a story in *Don Quixote* about a boy, Andrés, who is accused of stealing sheep and is constantly beaten by his master, Juan Haldudo.

In the early twentieth century, peasants still worked simply to survive and landowners did not invest in the land. There were peasant revolts, land seizures, miners' revolts in Asturias and declarations of autonomy by Catalans and Basques. Anarchist and Marxist movements were born and a clandestine leftist network of underground trade unions developed. The boundaries between the cities and their hinterlands were fluid and there was a symbiotic relationship between the urban and rural worlds. People who lived in cities could be employed in agricultural work; and city elites – nobles, merchants and others grown wealthy in trades such as wool, textiles, furniture and mining – owned land in the country, often large estates, and lived there for part of the year. With the huge migrations from the countryside to industrialized cities and from the poor south to the richer north that started in the late nineteenth century, peasant dishes appeared in the cities, usually with some modifications. Some of these were festive saints' day special foods. These rural dishes were adopted as family meals by the middle classes, who simply added more meat. It was then that regional peasant foods began to be discovered and written about by food writers. One of the most influential writers was María Mestayer de Echagüe, whose two-volume *Enciclopedia culinaria: La cocina completa* ('Culinary Encyclopaedia: The Complete Kitchen'), published in 1933 under the pen name Marquesa de Parabere, featured many traditional Spanish recipes. Teodoro Bardají's *La cocina de Ellas* ('Cooking from *Ellas* Magazine'), which came out in 1935, is now seen as the precursor of modern Spanish cuisine. Bardají was born in 1882 into a family of cooks and as a boy was sent to Madrid as an apprentice. He worked in several of the top Spanish establishments and cooked for the Duke del Infantado for twenty years.

The civil war in the 1930s made people change their food habits. There was penury during the war and rationing after it, when everything was short. People speak with deep emotion about the horrors of the war. Some are still haunted by how desperately hard life was. Hundreds of thousands died fighting or of starvation, or were executed after the war on the orders of General Franco. In the country, people were better off than in the cities where produce was scarce, but breadwinners were all fighting and agriculture was neglected. In the victorious ex-Nationalist zones, where people had fought on Franco's side, they lived well. In ex-Republican cities they suffered most. Ignacio Doménech, who cooked for the aristocracy and was a prolific writer about gastronomy, was the only writer to produce a cookery book during the civil war period. He wrote in the prologue: 'The obsession in these last months of 1938 is food…Everywhere all that people can think of is food.' They dreamt of seeing markets full of fresh food and of feasts. Cervantes' Don Quixote remarked that 'there is no sauce in the world like hunger'. Today it is the fond memories of the old peasant life that are the 'sauce' which makes dishes taste delicious.

THE REGIONS

REGIONAL COOKING
in a land of multiple landscapes and stories

Spain is a land of breathtaking gastronomic diversity because of the contrasts of its extraordinarily varied geography and ecology and its dramatic patchwork history. Every region has its own special styles of cooking and the coastal regions each have three different traditions – one of the sea, one of the plain and one of the mountains. But unlike Italy, for example, cooking styles and dishes are not contained within regional boundaries.

You can divide the country broadly into three gastronomic zones: wet and mountainous northern Spain facing the Atlantic Ocean and the Cantabrian Sea; the dry Spain of the interior; and the Mediterranean coast and islands. But these are criss-crossed by other cultural zones. For instance, the great river Ebro and its fertile valley have brought Mediterranean crops and cooking styles from the coast deep into the northern interior; and the different northern regions that straddle the Pyrenees have similar mountain dishes.

You have to look into the past to understand Spain's complex gastronomic picture. Some dishes travelled from one region to another through internal movements of populations. In the Middle Ages, as the Christian kings reconquered Muslim territories in the south, they gave the land to aristocrats from the north who had helped them in battle, and northern peasants were

encouraged to move south to repopulate the land. These northerners brought with them their ways of making cured pork products and their dishes of beans and chestnuts. In the twelfth century, when the Berber Almohads tried to convert the Jews in al-Andalus (the name given to the areas of the Iberian peninsula governed by Muslims – see page 20) to Islam, the Jews fled to the Christian north en masse with their Judaeo-Moorish dishes. That is how their Passover almond cake was adopted as the iconic cake of Santiago de Compostela in Galicia, in Spain's north-west corner. In the sixteenth century, Muslim converts to Christianity were forced to leave Andalusia and to spread throughout the country. Many of them became vendors who sold their foods in the streets. That is why *pinchos morunos* – marinated and spiced pork kebabs – are favourites on the *tapas* circuit. Clergy, who famously had a powerful influence on the diet of the peasantry, were moved around the country by their religious orders. They spread their ways of making brandy and cheese, and nuns took their famous pastry-making traditions from one convent to another.

Certain foods, such as *migas* (see page 288), and lamb stews referred to as *del pastor* ('of the shepherd'), can be found across the country along the old routes of the seasonal transhumance of sheep to different pastures. A dressing of fried garlic, vinegar and *pimentón*, and dishes labelled *al ajo arriero* (*ajo* is garlic and *arriero* is a mule driver) can be traced along the old routes travelled by the mules that transported salt cod between seaports in the north and the interior. The muleteers also sold garlic, olive oil and *pimentón*. Some dishes that appear in different parts of the country arrived with Spanish returnees from colonies in the New World, Italy and North Africa.

In more recent times, Spaniards became familiar with the foods of other regions and there was a certain homogenization of cooking traditions. From the nineteenth century on, there was mass migration from the poorer south to the industrializing north and from the countryside to the cities. The many migrants from all over Spain who went to Madrid made that city a centre of culinary diffusion. Until just over a couple of decades ago agricultural labourers, sometimes with their entire families, travelled during harvest time from region to region to pick grapes, olives and fruit, and to cut wheat and maize. They needed feeding, and the landlords who provided their meals sometimes adopted their dishes. The Spanish Civil War in the 1930s made many children orphans, and there were many young peasant girls in need of work and a roof over their heads. Most middle- and upper-class families took on two maids, one to clean and to look after the children and one to cook. The cooks learnt the style of the house and also brought the culinary ways of their own *comarca* (terroir). Now markets all over Spain sell products from around the country and television programmes encourage people even in small villages to cook specialities from different regions. Everyone makes *tortilla*, *paella*, *gazpacho*, *croquetas* (croquettes), *fabada* (bean stew), *empanadas* (pies) and *flan*. These have become national dishes.

Because it proved confusing to give recipe titles in two languages for the regions that have their own language – Catalonia, Valencia, the Balearic Islands, the Basque Country, Galicia and Asturias – I have used the Castilian Spanish names for dishes throughout this book. In a few cases only, where the regional name has become well known, I have given the name of a recipe in the regional language instead.

THE NORTH:
seafood and milk puddings

Northern Spain, facing the Atlantic Ocean and the Cantabrian Sea, is the wet, green Spain of lush, wooded mountains and vast green pastures where cows graze. It is dairy land. People there make cheese and milk puddings – custards, flans, fried creams, cheesecakes and rice pudding. Recently, indigenous breeds of cattle that had been neglected in favour of good milk-producers have been reintroduced and are being raised for their meat. Pork fat, the traditional cooking fat, is now most often replaced by olive oil, while butter is used for pastries. Apples and pears, walnuts, hazelnuts and chestnuts grow here. Mountain forests have the widest variety of game, including deer and wild boar, rabbits, hares and birds. The rivers that rush down the mountainsides are full of trout, salmon and eels. The coast is dotted with fishing ports and villages where, despite the depletion of fish stocks, fishermen still bring in a huge variety of fish and seafood in their catches – including some of the best molluscs and crustaceans in Europe.

In this part of Spain the peasantry was poor but self-contained. They were tenant farmers and sharecroppers (*foreros*), who paid rent to the Church and the nobility who had owned the land since the early Middle Ages. In the nineteenth century, Church-held lands were expropriated and became common lands. Smallholdings (*minifundios*), with their little stone houses, each with a vegetable garden and vine trellises, are dotted around the mountains and valleys. Each family kept one or two pigs, a solitary cow for milk and cheese, and chickens for their eggs. They grew maize and rye, alongside beans and potatoes, cabbages, turnips, carrots, leeks, peas and broad beans. They cooked in the open hearth. To keep warm in winter, it was usual for animals to sleep downstairs while the family slept upstairs. In the northern regions, peasant families looked after their livestock with a particular kind of reverence. Pío Baroja, the Basque writer and radical Republican, wrote in the early twentieth century that in order to live well there, one had to be either a priest or a cow.

Transport was difficult over high mountain passes, and rural life was hard. Smallholdings were usually too small to sustain more than one family. In Asturias, the Basque Country and Catalonia, small farmsteads were passed to the eldest male on his marriage. In Navarre, parents chose the heir regardless of age or gender, while in Leon peasants practised equal inheritance. It was the custom for one of the remaining children to enter the Church, another to join the army and the others would leave. In the nineteenth century, the young emigrated in droves to the Americas. More recently, in Franco's time, it was to France, Switzerland and Germany. Nowadays Spaniards can find work in their own cities and emigrants are coming back.

The valley of the great river Ebro that cuts through the mountains of Navarre, La Rioja and Aragon has brought Mediterranean fruit and vegetables and Mediterranean styles of cooking, including the use of olive oil, to some of the landlocked northern regions. Cultural unity was created in the north by the pilgrim routes that run through the regions all the way to the shrine of Saint James in Santiago de Compostela in Galicia. Since the relics of the saint were found there in the ninth century, Santiago has been a place of Christian pilgrimage as important as Rome and Jerusalem. For a long time, the French were the main pilgrims and settlers along the way. That is one reason why the north of Spain became a zone of French influence quite early on. Then in the nineteenth century, French haute cuisine was adopted by the newly rich mining and industrial bourgeoisies and by the *indianos*, as the returning emigrants, grown rich in the American colonies, were called. That is why you find crêpe-like pancakes, béchamel sauces, quiche-like tarts, fried cream (page 477), flans and *crema pastelera* (custard – page 459) here.

The stream of pilgrims to Santiago encouraged the building of churches, cathedrals and monasteries along the way. The clergy were powerful landlords and had an important influence on what peasants grew. Monks who left for the Americas with their orders were the first to bring back maize, potatoes, beans and peppers, which became local staples. The north is known as a zone of heart-warming bean and potato soups and stews.

Whereas wine has always been the drink of the Mediterranean coast, on the Atlantic coast beer and cider were the traditional drinks until a decade or so ago, when fine wines started to be produced in the area.

galicia

Galicia has its own language, Gallego, similar to Portuguese, and is proud of its Celtic ancestry (bagpipes are a traditional musical instrument). Separated from the rest of Spain by high mountains, it was entirely isolated until fairly recently and was the poorest region. The only way out of poverty was emigration. That is why Galician dishes – boiled octopus (page 320), *caldo gallego* soup (page 167) and large crusty *empanada* pies (one filled with tuna is on page 195) – are among the most widespread dishes in cities all over Spain and as far away as Brazil, Mexico, Argentina, Venezuela and Cuba, where Galician emigrants opened restaurants and bars. Now many of them are returning because life has changed in Galicia with the advent of tourism. In cafes in Santiago de Compostela I heard groups of old men speaking with Latin American accents. They were visiting on holiday, whereas their sons are here to work. Many, especially those from Argentina, have opened *churrasquerías* (steak houses). The meat, fabulous veal from the indigenous blond Rubia Gallega cattle, is tender, juicy, marbled with fat and full of flavour. Galicians have also recuperated the indigenous Celtic pig that looks a bit like a wild boar. The enormous succulent capons of Vilalba that are fed on boiled maize, wheat and potatoes or on chestnuts soaked in milk or wine appear at markets all over Spain at Christmas time.

For centuries the cities of Galicia were under the lordship of bishops, and the countryside was shared out between the cathedrals, the abbeys and the local aristocracy. Together with Asturias, it was the region where peasants were more completely subject than elsewhere in the north. The rural population lived isolated in the hills and mountains in tiny farmsteads. They rented the land and gave part of their produce to the landlord in payment of rent. Families divided their land into ever-smaller holdings between their sons. Galicia, Asturias, Murcia and the Canary Islands are the only regions of Spain where maize is grown for human consumption as well as for animal fodder. In Galicia, they make bread with maize flour. Potatoes are the traditional staple, and apples and chestnuts are also used as vegetables. The long and pointed green peppers from around the town of Padrón, called *pimientos de Padrón*, which are sweet but occasionally burning hot, are served in bars all over Spain, fried and sprinkled with coarse salt. Families that kept a pig had to cure the hams and sausages indoors around the fireplace because of the wet weather (their attics would have been too damp). That is why Galicians acquired a taste for smoked products and why still today the ham and the pork fat used in some of the Galician dishes give them a peculiar strong, smoky flavour.

The Galician coast is known as the *costa del marisco* ('seafood coast') because of the magnificent seafood caught here. Vigo is the largest fishing port in Europe and Galicia has the largest fishing fleet. The region also has shellfish-farming and seafood-processing industries. *Pulpo a la feria* (page 320), boiled octopus dressed with olive oil and *pimentón* and served with boiled potatoes, is Galicia's festive signature dish.

The scallop shell is the symbol of Santiago de Compostela. Shells are encrusted into the ground marking the pilgrims' routes to the city. A relief in the shape of the shell is at the entrance to the great cathedral. The region is known for its almond *tarta de Santiago* (page 472), its marrons glacés and its cow's milk cheeses, which are rare in Spain. Most notable are the soft, creamy, mild-tasting Tetilla (the name means 'nipple' and the cheese is shaped like a woman's breast), San Simón, the strongly flavoured smoked version, Arzúa–Ulloa and Cebreiro cheeses.

The Rías Baixas – an area of breathtakingly beautiful estuaries and fjords – produces some of the best white wines in Spain. The prestigious dry Albariños, crisp, fresh, fruity and aromatic, are made from Albariño grapes that were brought here in the twelfth century by Cistercian monks from the Rhine and the Moselle valleys. Monterrey, Ribeiro, Rías Baixas, Ribeira Sacra and Valdeorras wines also use local grape varieties. Ribeiro is the most popular with Galicians, the one that evokes nostalgic memories when they leave. The vineyards of red Ribeiro grapes belonged long ago to Jews of Ribadavia, a former capital of Galicia. In one of the local *fiestas*, people celebrate the Jewish legacies by re-enacting a Jewish wedding in historic costumes of that time. *Orujo* is a spirit distilled from the residue of crushed grapes, and *queimada* is a hot drink made by setting light to *orujo* in an earthenware bowl with lemon peel, cinnamon, sugar and sometimes coffee beans. The ritual preparation is said to have pagan origins and to keep away evil spirits. They believed in witches here and amulets are still sold as protection against evil.

asturias

According to legend, in 718 the Virgin Mary appeared in a cave at the top of a high mountain in the Asturian village of Covadonga where the local leader, Pelayo, was taking refuge from the attacking Muslims. She gave him a wooden cross which he used to fight off the Muslim armies and he was crowned king of the first Christian kingdom of Spain. Asturias became a refuge for Christian nobles escaping Muslim occupation. In recognition of the place where the *reconquista* began and the role played by the nobles in the centuries-long war, the heir to the Spanish crown today has the title of Prince of Asturias, and Asturias is a principality.

This sensationally beautiful green and misty land of rugged, towering mountains, fast-flowing rivers and lakes is filled with little farmsteads (*caserías*) and apple orchards. It is renowned for a wide variety of beans, in particular for the large white ones they call *fabes*, which go into the famous *fabada* bean stew (page 298). The region is also famous for apple tarts, apple cakes, apple pancakes and apple puddings, and for apple cider that is hard, dry and still – made from a blend of sweet and acid apples. In the traditional cider houses, the cider is poured from on high so that it aerates as it splashes into glasses and on to the floor. Cider is used for cooking fish and chicken and in puddings. Asturias is also a region of walnuts and walnut cakes. Maize is used to make bread and there is a creamy maize polenta called *fariñes* (page 292).

You see cattle, sheep and goats foraging around farmsteads and in the high mountain Picos de Europa National Park. Not long ago, foreign breeds of cows that produced lots of milk predominated. Today the indigenous red Asturiana de la Montaña cattle are raised for meat. Game birds, especially woodcock (*becada*), are local delicacies, and wild boar and deer are hunted. A wide variety of fish and seafood caught around the rugged coast are a splendid part of the local gastronomy. Favourites are hake and monkfish, also crab and sea urchins. Salmon fishing in the many rivers makes Asturias the largest salmon-producing region of Spain.

In the nineteenth century, iron and coal were found here, and mining and heavy industry caused a mini industrial revolution. At the same time, jobless young men left for Latin America. The exotic, colourful Mexican-type colonial mansions of these returning *indianos* who came back wealthy from the New World – with domes and towers, pillars and balconies – are dotted around in elegant cities, and on mountainsides and seafronts. A palm tree in the front garden signifies that the original owner was a returnee from Cuba, Argentina, Uruguay, Mexico or Venezuela. The *indianos* adopted the French cuisine that was fashionable with the local nobility and new industrial bourgeoisie.

Asturias is the region of Europe that offers the widest range of cheeses. It is known as *el país de los quesos* ('the land of cheeses'). The most famous cheese is the strong-tasting blue Cabrales that is traditionally matured in mountain caves. Notable others are Los Beyos, Gamoneu, Peñamellera and Afuega'l Pitu. Asturias is the only region of Spain that does not produce wine.

cantabria

Tiny Cantabria has had a special relationship with powerful Castile ever since it sent men to help King Ferdinand III conquer Cordoba and Seville in 1236. The capital, Santander, became Castile's route to the sea for its wool exports to northern Europe and for its trade with the New World. The people of Santander also had early access to products such as olive oil, which their neighbours did not have. In the nineteenth century, the port on the beautiful Costa Esmeralda became the summer resort of the royals, which explains why some traditional local dishes have a touch of class, and why olive oil has long been used for cooking instead of lard, which was associated with the peasantry.

In the small communities dotted around the mountainsides of the region known as 'La Montaña' because of the steep Cantabrian mountains, families kept a few cows, sheep and goats. Cattle were jointly looked after by cowherds, while villagers took turns looking after everyone's sheep and goats. Nowadays rural tourism has become more important than agriculture. In the valleys where they once grew vines, wheat, chickpeas, potatoes and cabbages, many fields have been given over to grazing cattle. The young pink meat of indigenous breeds makes for splendid grills and for stews with beans and potatoes, as do local venison and wild boar. Cantabria is a region rich in wild foods – berries, chestnuts, walnuts, edible flowers and herbs. On the coast, fish and seafood are cooked in simple ways. Salmon, trout and eels are available from the rivers that fall from the mountains straight into the sea.

Like Asturias, Cantabria is an artisan cheese paradise with a wide variety of cheeses. The best known are the creamy blue Picón Bejes–Tresviso, made from a blend of cow, goat and sheep's milks, the fresh buttery Cantabria, the smoked Áliva and the semi-sweet or smoked Liébana. Cóbreces is made from cow's milk by the Cistercian monks in the Santa María de Viaceli monastery. Apple cider is the traditional drink of this region. They also make Chacolí, a light, acidy white wine, and the sweet red Tostadillo wine. The region is famous for its tinned-food industries, especially red peppers (*pimientos de Isla*) and anchovies preserved in salt and in oil.

the basque country

San Sebastian has for some years now been the prime destination of food lovers from all over the world, as the centre with the greatest concentration of trail-blazing innovative Michelin-starred chefs. Other gastronomic attractions are the lively bars offering both traditional and modern *tapas* – here called *pintxos* – and the famous men-only gastronomic societies where members take turns to cook and vie to outdo each other. It is here that Spanish *nueva cocina* was born. In the 1970s, top restaurants still served only French haute cuisine. They had done so since the late nineteenth century, when the beautiful seaside town was adopted as a retreat by the Queen Regent Maria Christina and became the fashionable belle époque resort of the Spanish upper classes. After the discovery of iron and the development of heavy industries, a wealthy Basque bourgeoisie emerged that could afford to eat out at expensive restaurants. There was also an old aristocracy whose ancestors had been ennobled by the kings of Castile in recompense for helping in the *reconquista* and the conquering of the New

World. French cooks had found employment here when they came to Spain in large numbers after the French Revolution. Spanish Basques also share a culinary heritage and cook similar dishes to the Basques on the other side of the border with France, and many speak French as well as their own Basque language, Euskara.

When Paul Bocuse, the godfather of French nouvelle cuisine, came to speak at a conference in Madrid in 1976, he invited two young Basque chefs, Juan Mari Arzak and Pedro Subijana, to go and work with him in Lyons. Back in San Sebastian, with a group of enthusiastic chefs, they developed the *nueva cocina vasca* (Basque nouvelle cuisine). It was the start of what was to become a national movement to renovate old traditional dishes and create new ones based on regional products, and was the first Spanish *alta cocina* (haute cuisine).

Basque culinary roots go back to a time before steel mills, factories, banking and tourism enticed people away from the land, to when this mountain region was a world of farmers, shepherds and fishermen, and when, as the Catalan traveller Mañe y Flaqué wrote about them 150 years ago: 'They look after their animals as if they were members of the family.' Rural life has not entirely disappeared. Capons and turkeys are reared for festive occasions. Indigenous cattle are bred for beef and for milk. Peas, green beans and cauliflower are traditional vegetables. Leeks and potatoes have a special place in the diet. A favourite dried bean is the red bean of Tolosa (page 302). The white *pocha* bean is harvested very young and cooked fresh. At least thirty varieties of wild mushrooms can be found in the fields and woodlands of the Basque Country. The pickled spicy green *guindilla* peppers of Ibarra are served as *tapas*. The elongated peppers from Guernica are used in many dishes, including the famous *piperada* (page 185). Many Basque dishes are similar to those of their neighbours in Navarre and La Rioja.

More than anything, Basques adore fish and seafood. Life on the coast was once all about fishing. Men went out in their boats at night. Their women ran to meet them on the beach in the morning with baskets on their heads, and went off to sell the catch at the market. For centuries fishermen had gone out on the high seas for long periods to catch whales and cod, which they dried and salted on the boats. There is now large-scale commercialization and mechanization of the fishing industry and fleets are depleted, but fresh fish and seafood are appreciated more than ever, as are tiny baby elvers from the rivers.

Local Basque wines include the slightly acid white Txakoli (or Chacolí) that is good with seafood and as an aperitif, and the carbonated red Rioja Alavesa. Cider, the traditional local drink, is sweeter and fizzier than Galician cider. The great Basque sheep's milk cheese, Idiazabal, is buttery, with an intense, piquant, slightly acid flavour. Shepherds made it during spring and summer when they grazed their sheep on the mountains and lived in small mountain huts.

The Basque language is said to be the oldest in Europe, and DNA tests have confirmed that Basques are of a very ancient race that have inhabited the western Pyrenees along the Bay of Biscay since time immemorial. They sought autonomy from Spain in the nineteenth century. The separatist movement was crushed during the Spanish Civil War but then rekindled after General Franco's death. There are still militant separatists who campaign for complete independence. Basques are as passionate about food as they are about politics and music. Theirs is a society of cooks and gourmets and also of singers. The members of a men's gastronomic club where I was a guest have their own choir.

navarre

The landscape in Navarre ranges from the misty, wet Pyrenees, with vast forests of pine, chestnut and hazelnut trees, to meadows with sheep and cattle grazing on the slopes; from a desert-like Bardenas Reales natural park near the town of Tudela to river valleys, vineyards, orchards, olive groves and vegetable gardens. Irrigation installed by the Arabs in the wide river Ebro valley allows the land to produce a succession of crops each year. There are wheat and sugar beet and a huge variety of vegetables. The region is famous for its asparagus, artichoke, cardoon and borage dishes, and for the small, white fresh beans called *pochas*. The little pointed red peppers of Lodosa, called *pimientos del piquillo*, that we can buy roasted and peeled in tins and jars have long been popular in bars and restaurants all over Spain, usually stuffed with fish or seafood or with minced pork. The region is also known for its crystallized fruit. Navarre has no coast but the rivers contain trout and salmon. The region shares produce and dishes with neighbouring La Rioja and Aragon. Typical dishes are an exciting mix of Mediterranean, French and Arab influences.

Navarre was inhabited by Basque tribes when Muslims conquered the Ebro valley in 714. In 824, a Basque chieftain, Íñigo Aritza, was made king of Pamplona, which later became the Kingdom of Navarre. The Christian kingdom coexisted with the small Muslim *taifa* kingdoms of Zaragoza and Tudela. Navarre passed by marriage to the counts of Champagne, then to the French crown in 1305, and remained on and off under a French king until it was annexed by Castile in 1515. Basque and French are spoken here, along with Castilian Spanish.

There are more heraldic crests and noble coats of arms on stone houses in Navarre than in any other part of Spain. During the heyday of the kingdom, 20 per cent of the population was of noble family. At the turn of the twentieth century, many wealthy *indianos* returned from the Americas to live in their ancestral villages. The noble heritage is reflected in the refined cooking: game cooked in rich wine sauces, to which sometimes chocolate is added, is a common dish in mountain villages. There is wild boar, rabbit and hare, and game birds such as quail, partridge and pigeon. The veal from local bull calves varies from pink to red with a fine marbling of fat, and makes for splendid grills over charcoal and in heart-warming mountain stews. The region is also famous for lamb and goat. *Chuletitas* (baby lamb chops) and roast suckling lamb are local specialities. Pork, both fresh and cured, is popular. Local sausages include the *chistorra* and a *chorizo* from Pamplona made with a mix of beef and pork. The *longaniza* of Navarre is made from *panceta* (streaky bacon). New products more recently introduced to the region are duck foie gras and duck confit.

In Navarre, they make two great cheeses with sheep's milk – the soft, aromatic, slightly sharp and piquant Roncal and the strong-tasting, aged or smoked Idiazabal, which is similar to the Basque cheese of the same name. Navarre wines are like those of La Rioja, with similar grapes and similar methods of production. Their rosés are delightful. Local Pacharán is made by macerating sloe berries and a few coffee beans in an anise-flavoured spirit.

la rioja

The great wine region of Spain is a land of rolling hills and valleys surrounded by mountains, with a climate that varies from cool and wet through warm and humid to dry. La Rioja is all about wine. Towns are packed with *bodegas* (wineries), some venerable and aristocratic, some small and family-run, some corporate and industrial, and a few that were built by world-famous architects. The Romans made wine here, then local monks took it up. The region is full of old monasteries in the mountains and forests. Some have been converted into hotels, a few into wineries. It is said that the Castilian language was born in one of the oldest monasteries, Yuso in San Millán de la Cogolla, where the first ever texts written in an early form of Castilian were found. There is a continuous history of Christianity in the area, which flourished even through Muslim rule, and the pilgrims' route to Santiago de Compostela passes through this region. It was a place of settlement for knights and nobles. They formed a wine nobility that has left many small palaces and mansions in the honey-coloured winemaking hamlets. You see noble heraldic shields everywhere, even on village houses.

Much of the broad river Ebro valley and the valleys of six of its tributaries, including the river Oja, from which La Rioja got its name, are covered with vineyards. The Riojan DOC (*Denominación de Origen Calificada* – the highest-quality Designation of Origin) covers an area that stretches over the border into parts of the Basque Country and Navarre. Until a little over fifteen years ago – before many other Spanish regions started producing really good wines – people all over Spain

knew only of La Rioja wines, apart from their own local wine. La Rioja became prominent when phylloxera devastated French vineyards in the second half of the nineteenth century and vintners from Bordeaux came to plant grapes free of the disease and to make their wines here. For years, French Cabernet and Merlot grapes were grown in La Rioja. When phylloxera destroyed the Spanish vineyards too and when French and Spanish vineyards were replanted with phylloxera-resistant rootstocks from America, the French went home and the Riojans went back to their indigenous Tempranillo, Garnacha, Mazuelo, Graciano and Viura grapes. But they kept the French methods of vineyard management and winemaking techniques, including the ageing of wine in oak barrels. They have now gone further and adopted new technology. Winemakers used to buy in their grapes, now they have their own vineyards. La Rioja is known for its excellent aged red wines. It also has good whites and rosés, and they make brandies and liqueurs.

As with all fine-wine areas, La Rioja is a gastronomic region. *Bodegas* offer both traditional and innovative *tapas* to accompany wine tastings. Grand restaurants serve innovative cuisine; family-run inns and unpretentious *casas de comidas* (eating houses) offer home cooking. Riojan home cooking has much in common with that of neighbouring Navarre, Aragon and Leon. It is simpler than that of many regions and relies on the quality of the local produce. In the valleys and plains of the river Ebro and its tributaries there are extensive wheat, potato and sugar beet plantations, as well as olive trees. Peaches, pears and cherries grow here too. Market gardens are full of the same vegetables as are found in Aragon and Navarre, including artichokes, asparagus, cardoons, borage, Swiss chard, aubergines and courgettes. Small and fiery red chilli peppers, *alegrías riojanas*, add a piquant flavour to dishes. Mediterranean cooking with olive oil coexists with French ways with butter and cream and the thickening of soups and sauces with a roux. As you would expect, there is a lot of cooking with wine and brandy. Traditional desserts are usually fruits poached in wine, and local pastries are made with walnuts or almonds.

The mountains have their own separate food culture. Pigs are kept. All kinds of cured pork products – *chorizo*, *salchichón* and a delicious sweet blood sausage made with rice – go into stews rich with the mottled *caparrones* and red beans. Wild boar, venison, partridge, hare and quail are hunted in the woodlands. Sheep, goats and cattle graze on the hillsides. A favourite way of cooking meat is grilled over smouldering vine prunings. They eat baby lamb chops (*chuletitas*) and large T-bone steaks (*chuletones*). Lamb and goat are spit-roasted. Potatoes and wild mushrooms are common side dishes. Trout and salt cod are also popular in Navarre. People serve the fresh, salty, slightly acidic Camerano goat's cheese as a *tapa* with caramelized onions.

aragon

When the Kingdom of Aragon was united with Catalonia through the marriage of the Count of Barcelona to Petronila of Aragon in 1137, the joint crown went on to acquire eastern Spain and a whole empire in the Mediterranean. In 1469, the union of King Ferdinand of Aragon and Queen Isabella of Castile brought the two most powerful kingdoms of the peninsula together and effectively led to the creation of a united Spain.

In this large, landlocked area that ranges from mountain glaciers and forests to rich pasture lands, arid desert steppes and verdant river valleys, there are at least two major Aragonese food cultures. One is typical of the fertile valley of the river Ebro that cuts through the mountains. It is a cosmopolitan Mediterranean style that makes much use of vegetables, fruits and olive oil. Wheat, barley and rye are important crops. Olives from lower Aragon produce sweet, fruity and aromatic extra virgin oils. Market gardens provide peppers, tomatoes, green and white beans, courgettes, sweet onions, asparagus, cardoons and borage. The fruits of Aragon – plums, pears, apples, cherries and especially peaches – are much admired in Spain. Among typical Aragonese desserts are peaches macerated in wine (page 457), and crystallized and chocolate-covered fruit. White truffles that once abounded in the wild are now being farmed. Some of the local dishes testify to the tastes of Muslims who, having converted to Christianity, were allowed to stay on in Aragon as Moriscos until the seventeenth century to irrigate the land and nurture the fruits and vegetables. The region is on the border with France and some dishes have a French touch and make use of butter and cream. The rivers provide freshwater crabs, trout and salmon.

Game, meat, cured pork and cheese belong to the Aragonese food culture of the mountains where cattle, sheep and goats graze on lush pastures. Lamb is the traditional meat in this old pastoral land, and popular foods such as *migas* made with breadcrumbs (page 288) remind you of the old transhumant life of shepherds. The town of Teruel is renowned for pork products made from its indigenous pigs. Hams here are cured with very little salt and have a delicate flavour and creamy fat. Their blood sausage is made with rice and onions. Partridge, quail, rabbit and hare, as well as big game like deer and wild boar, are hunted here. The local cheeses are made from cow's, sheep's and goat's milks. Tronchón is made in the mountains from sheep and goat's milks and was mentioned in Cervantes' *Don Quixote*. It is sold fresh and creamy, semi-cured and cured. Benasque, traditionally a sheep's milk cheese, is now made with cow's milk in the valley. Tauste from sheep's milk is semi-cured and is now also made like the very creamy Torta del Casar from Extremadura.

Aragon is an old wine-producing land. In the past, much of its traditional strong, highly alcoholic wines went over the border to France for blending. But the region is now producing some fine reds, whites and rosés with native and foreign grape varieties. Their Cariñena and Somontano wines have been reborn. Aragon is also known for fruit liqueurs and brandies made with berries, cherries and nuts.

CENTRAL SPAIN:
bread and chickpeas

The vast Spanish interior that encompasses Castile and Leon, Castile-La Mancha, Madrid and Extremadura is a high flat plateau, the *meseta*, bordered and divided into two by mountain ranges and crossed by great rivers. Before roads started to be built fifty years ago the interior was difficult to enter – travellers went by horse or mule – and empty of people. It is the 'dry' Spain with the typical continental climate of extremely cold winters, unbearably hot summers and hardly any rain, and with no sea to soften the harshness. The predominant vegetation is a treeless, wild entanglement of thorny scrub, but there are grasslands in the river basins, and the mountains are cloaked in dense woodlands. The Romans planted wheat and barley on the plains and grapevines on hillsides and in valleys, making it a land of bread and wine. Chickpeas, lentils and beans that need little water are the main traditional food crops. Agriculture consists mostly of small family farms that cultivate barley, wheat, grapes, sugar beet and other crops. Many farms also raise poultry and livestock, and almost all rural families have at least one or two pigs. Fruit and vegetables grow in irrigated areas by the rivers.

Although central Spain covers a huge area, there is little culinary diversity. Centuries of struggle against the Muslims had a profound effect on its culture and on its gastronomy. It was the frontier zone during the eight-centuries-long struggle between the Christian kingdoms of the north and the Muslim kingdoms of the south – the part of the Iberian peninsula constantly at war, where castles and fortified cities were won and lost, and where kings were always on the move. Conquered lands were given over to noble warlords and religious military orders on whom the kings depended for their military and financial support. In such a world, the ranching of sheep, cattle and horses that could be easily moved to new frontier settlements was the dominant activity. Because of the new settlers' inexperience in agriculture and the shortage of Muslim labour, newly acquired cultivated lands were given over to sheep farming, and wool production became by far the most important part of the economy, providing the Merino wool that was sold to Europe.

Because of the arid environment, flocks had to be moved from pasture to pasture, covering huge distances. The need for the migration of sheep and cattle from the north to reach the grasslands of La Mancha and Extremadura further to the south played an important part in the push to conquer more territory from the Muslims. In the thirteenth century, a sheep-breeders' guild, the Mesta, was formed by small sheep owners and a few great landlords and monasteries to organize the transhumance of flocks that migrated seasonally, and to arrange their protection from Muslim raids by knights and religious military orders. Great monasteries, many of which are now paradores (state-run hotels), are a reminder of the warrior monks – the Knights Templar and Hospitallers, the orders of Calatrava, Alcántara and Santiago – who fought in and then colonized the new frontiers for the Castilian kings. They, like the huge and ever-growing nobility, raised sheep, but they also had a strong interest in horticulture. The monks had vegetable gardens, orchards and vineyards, kept bees and made wine, honey and cheese.

Pork, forbidden in Muslim times, became the popular meat, and pig breeding was taken up in a big way, especially in Extremadura, around Salamanca in Castile and Leon and in the Andalusian interior. Pigs were left to forage on fungi and acorns in the holm oak forests, the *dehesas*. Families without land were allowed to bring their pigs to feed on royal or common lands.

The ascetic life and attitudes born under harsh frontier conditions and in an inhospitable climate changed little over the centuries. Life, especially for shepherds and peasants, was hard. The simple and austere food they survived on is still with us. It is mainly winter food. The elegantly sober dishes of roast lamb and pork – the grandest being suckling pig and baby lamb – were the status foods of the nobility and grandees. The wildlife, like the land, belonged to the nobility. The small game – partridge, pheasant, pigeon, quail, hare and rabbit – that inhabited the scrub and fed on wild herbs and berries, the deer and wild boar of the woodlands, were all theirs, but poachers had access to them too. Shepherds and peasants were left with the 'ignoble cuts' of meat – the feet, ears, heads, brains, tails, tripe. They cooked these with chickpeas, lentils and beans. While central Spain is characterized as the 'Spain of the roast' (*España del asado*), the festive peasant foods are stews, *platos de cuchara* (literally 'spoon dishes') that you eat with a spoon. These and the iconic foods of shepherds and peasants based on breadcrumbs (*migas*) are now extremely popular.

In the seventeenth century, when famine spread throughout the Iberian peninsula and wool was no longer in demand, sheep breeders took up cereal farming. Pasture lands were given over to grain, and sheep began to be bred for meat and cheese. They were reared on stubble and on barley, oats and vetch. Transhumance of livestock became unnecessary. But still today, in memory of the great sheep-walks (*cañadas*) and the rights granted to the Mesta in the fifteenth century, flocks cross the centre of Madrid once a year in the autumn.

An exotic culinary touch, a legacy of Muslims and Jews – their old quarters in cities like Toledo are identified in tourist guides and in museums – can be found in parts of central Spain. Christians met them at the market, bought their food and enjoyed their hospitality. Many remained after the expulsion of 1492 as converts to Christianity, and the Jews in particular melted into the population. The sautéed vegetable *pistos* and aubergine dishes, the boiled meat *cocidos*, the lavish use of garlic, the roast baby lamb in a clay dish accompanied only by a lettuce salad, the almond sweets, the cheese with honey, these are all part of the cosmopolitan culture the Castilians encountered when they moved into Toledo.

castile and leon

The ancient kingdom of Leon that once covered Galicia, Asturias, Cantabria and Castile in the north took over the torch of the *reconquista* from the Asturian kings. Castile was a province of that kingdom, and took its name from the great number of castles that were built to defend the land. It split from Leon in the early eleventh century and the two kingdoms were often at war and periodically united by conquest or royal marriage, until they were finally permanently reunited in 1230. The region of Castile and Leon today is studded with enchanting medieval cities, each with a Gothic cathedral and scores of Romanesque churches and monasteries, a reminder that their wars were about defending Christianity.

Castile and Leon, also known as Castilla la Vieja (Old Castile), is a vast, unending plain on the northern *meseta*, or plateau, a silent and austere landscape of rolling wheat fields and scrub, surrounded by mountains, with fertile valleys watered by the river Duero, its tributaries and lakes. The climate is dry, baking hot in summer, freezing cold in the long winter. But in the mountains of Leon, it is rainy and green.

Wheat is the main dry-land crop, and bread is the symbol of Castile, which was known as the bread basket of Spain. Bread was the basis of the foods of shepherds and peasants. Among these are the *sopa de ajo* (page 159), a soup made with bread and garlic, and an endless variety of *migas* (page 288), breadcrumbs with fried ham, *chorizo*, bacon and blood sausage. Communal bread ovens where people could bring their bread for baking were used well into the twentieth century. No other region produces as many and as wide a variety of pulses – white, red and black beans, lentils and chickpeas. The small *pedrosillano* chickpeas are the most common ingredients in their stews. Huge white *la Granja de San Ildefonso* beans (*granja* means farm) from around Segovia are the most prized beans, famously cooked with pigs' ears and feet and sausages (page 301). Soups and stews with beans or chickpeas and pork products – sausages, pigs' ears and feet – are everyday meals in the long winter months.

Castile and Leon is ranching pastoral country. The Morucha breed of cattle, originally raised around Salamanca for the plough and the bullring, is now primarily raised for beef, while Ávila is famous for the veal from its indigenous black cows. The two most typical breeds of sheep are the Churra and the Castellana. Their meat has a good distinctive flavour, and cheeses made from their milk include the intensely flavoured, slightly sharp and salty Zamorano and Castellano, and the Pata de Mulo (meaning 'mule's leg'). The Villalón and fresh, bland Burgos cheeses are made from a mix of cow's and sheep's milks, and the local Cabra del Tiétar is a goat's milk cheese. The region is also one of Spain's most important pig-breeding areas. The dry, cool air of the highlands means that the cured *jamón serrano* from white pigs requires only a light salt cure. Salamanca is famous for its magnificent ham and sausages from the small black Ibérico pig, also known as *pata negra* ('black foot'). The ham is called *de bellota* if the pigs are fed on acorns (*bellotas*) in the woodlands. The *morcilla* (blood sausage) of Burgos made with rice and onions is delicious. *Farinato* is a white sausage made with minced pork, breadcrumbs, lard and seasoning. The dishes that Castile and Leon is most famous for are roast suckling pig (*cochinillo asado* – page 407) and baby lamb (*lechazo*). It is said that baby lamb is at its meltingly tender best within the triangle formed by the cities of Segovia, Soria and Burgos, while suckling pig is at its best from the area between Segovia, Arévalo and Peñaranda de Bracamonte.

The region is also hunting and shooting country. Wild boar is found in the mountain forests, roe deer in the National Game Preserve. Partridge, quail, hare, rabbit and duck can be shot at game club reserves and in thousands of game estates. Partridge is the main Castilian game bird. Tender baby pigeons or squabs are an old local delicacy. You see curious old *palomares* (dovecotes) in wheat fields where the grains once provided ready seed for thousands of birds.

There is not much culinary diversity in this largest of regions. You find similar dishes in all the towns – roast baby lamb served with lettuce salad, bean and lentil stews, lamb with chickpeas (*olla podrida*), chicken with an almond and egg sauce (*gallina en pepitoria* – page 370), partridge and quail in *escabeche*, rabbit or chicken with garlic (page 364). Among many convent sweets, the *yemas de Santa Teresa* from Ávila (page 493) made from only egg yolks and sugar are the most famous.

Leon in the mountainous north, on the pilgrims' route to Santiago de Compostela, where dozens of hostels for pilgrims once lined the way, has more gastronomic variety and has some dishes similar to Galicia. La Maragatería is the mountain homeland of the mysterious Maragatos (they are whispered to be descendants of Moriscos). They were the muleteers who transported salt cod and other goods between the sea and the interior and spread a trail of dishes dressed with fried garlic, chillies and vinegar called *al ajo arriero* as far afield as Navarre, La Mancha, Extremadura and Andalusia. The Maragatos have a tradition of distinctive dishes, and cherries preserved in the spirit *orujo* is a speciality. Astorga was one of the first places in Europe where chocolate was manufactured and it is still made there now. The cheeses of Leon are La Armada and a blue cheese from Valdeón that is similar to the Asturian Cabrales.

Some of Spain's best wines are produced in Castile and Leon along the banks of the river Duero. The prestigious red Ribera del Duero wines are delicious young, and can age into splendid *gran reservas*. The majority of *bodegas* use the native Tempranillo grape. A few mix in a small percentage of other grapes such as Cabernet Sauvignon and Merlot. Other top-quality local wines are the fruity red Toro, the Bierzo, the Cigales rosés and the Rueda whites.

madrid

Madrid, in the centre of Spain, was a province of Castile-La Mancha until it became an autonomous community around the country's capital city. The countryside is an area of changing landscapes, with cereal fields, mountains covered by forests, rivers, lakes and valleys. There are vineyards and wine villages and an old tradition of winemaking. The purple-red Vinos de Madrid are very good fruity wines. A mature sheep's milk cheese called Campo Real is also produced here.

The fortress of Mayrit was reconquered from the Muslims in 1083 and the city was chosen in 1561 by the Habsburg King Philip II to be the seat of his court and the permanent capital of Spain. Quarters of the city reflect different periods of its history. The old medieval and Renaissance town centre is the Madrid 'de los Austrias' (of the Austrians), which was built during the reign of the Habsburgs. The eighteenth-century Madrid 'de los Borbones' (of the Bourbons) is luxurious with grandiose monuments and baroque and neoclassical palaces of the old aristocracy. Some have been turned into hotels. There is also a romantic nineteenth-century Madrid 'Isabelino' and a new ultra-modern Madrid.

As the capital of Spain, the city has attracted migration from all the regions. In the past the aristocracy came to be around the court. The inhabitants today are from all over Spain. Their presence is evidenced by the huge number of restaurants representing every region. Overseas immigrants, mostly from Latin America, now form about one-sixth of the population. On warm weekend days you can see them in Madrid's Parque del Oeste park, where they set up stalls selling their own typical home-made foods.

Madrid is a city of civil servants, bankers, service providers and painters. The old aristocracy is there too, so I was expecting a sophisticated cuisine. But the region shares dishes with the rest of central Spain and has only a few specifically its own. The most famous is the *cocido madrileño* (page 303) of boiled pork and chicken, with chickpeas, potatoes, cabbage, turnips, marrow bones, streaky bacon, chorizo and blood sausage. It is said to be a legacy of the wealthy Conversos who married into the Castilian aristocracy – *cocido* is a version of the old Sabbath dish into which the Jewish converts piled all kinds of pork meat. Another speciality is *callos a la madrileña*, a 'poor food' of tripe with tomato sauce. A Christmas dish that is now cooked throughout the year and is also found elsewhere in Spain is baked sea bream with slices of lemon embedded in cuts and a sprinkling of breadcrumbs and parsley (page 333). Cafes and vendors with stands in the streets of the city sell *churros* and an extra-thick hot chocolate (page 502).

castile-la mancha

The province of La Mancha covers most of the region of Castile-La Mancha in the southern plateau. It is the setting for Miguel de Cervantes' great novel *Don Quixote*, written in the early seventeenth century. The landscape is still as Cervantes described it: rolling plains and low hills, for the most part desolate, arid, treeless, covered with thorny scrub, but also in parts mountainous with vast oak and pine forests, green pastures, rivers and lakes. The climate is harsher, more extreme, than that of the northern plateau, with intensely hot summers, very cold winters and hardly any rain. Yet the region has always been an important agricultural zone that produces most of Spain's wheat, half of its wine and also olive oil. Old windmills that were used to grind flour, the kind that Don Quixote mistook for giants, dot the wide-open plains. Other dry-land crops grown here include barley and maize, chickpeas and lentils, beans and peas. La Mancha's aubergines are famously delicious; its purple garlic is considered the best in Spain; the famous local honey gets its flavour from the wild aromatic plants in the scrub; its saffron, the dried stigma of the *Crocus sativus*, is of the highest quality. Farmers in La Mancha also cultivate sugar beet, and sunflowers for their oil.

The area was reconquered from the Muslims in the twelfth century. Castile's frontiersmen, noble warlords and military monastic orders, were big sheep owners, and sheep-raising for Merino wool became the pillar of the region's economy. Today, sheep are reared for meat and cheese, and the local Manchego is Spain's most famous cheese. It ranges from fresh and creamy to mature and hard, slightly salty and piquant.

The wildlife of La Mancha includes deer, wild boar, rabbits and hares, partridges and quails. The marshlands in the river Guadiana basin are a stopping place for migratory water birds. In the province of Toledo, where the red-legged partridge breeds, the most appreciated item on restaurant menus is *perdiz* (partridge). There are trout, barbel and pike in the rivers.

Cooking in La Mancha is like that of the rest of central Spain – the main ingredients are meat, offal and giblets, bread and beans – and reflects the old medieval ascetic lifestyles. The grand status dishes, roast lamb, braised venison and wild boar, are elegantly sober. Quails and partridges are prepared in simple ways, sometimes in *escabeche* – in a vinegar marinade – so as to keep well. Only their *gazpacho* (nothing like the Andalusian soup), also known as *galiano*, is an over-the-top grandiose stew that includes rabbit, hare and pigeon all together in a pepper and tomato sauce served on a thin disc of fried unleavened bread with bits of fried dough to soak up the sauce. The *pisto manchego* (page 218) is a combination of sautéed onions, peppers, aubergines, courgettes and tomatoes to which potatoes, ham and eggs are sometimes added. Marinated aubergines from La Mancha can be found everywhere in central Spain at fairs and as *tapas* served in bars and inns. Marzipan pastries (page 491) are famously from Toledo.

La Mancha is the most extensive vine-growing region of Spain, perhaps of the world. Old photographs show peasants harvesting, carrying grapes in carts, treading them, dancing and laughing. They had a good time and it provided them with a living but the wine they produced was characterless. La Mancha now produces some really good wines at very competitive prices. Their whites, made with the old, much maligned Airén grapes, are now crisp, light and tasty. A number of fine reds are made with the indigenous Tempranillo grape (here also called Cencíbel), also with Monastrell and Garnacha Tintorera mixed with Cabernet Sauvignon, Syrah or Merlot. Valdepeñas wines are a reborn classic.

extremadura

Extremadura shares the southern plateau with Castile-La Mancha. It is a great area of production of *jamón ibérico*, an incomparable delicacy and Spain's greatest gastronomic treasure made from the small Ibérico black pig that feeds on acorns in the holm oak woodlands here. The hams are air-dried in the special microclimate of the Sierra de Montanchez for up to four years. Extremadura is also where my very favourite Spanish cheese is from, the creamy, almost liquid Torta del Casar, made from the milk of Merino sheep, which has a delicious slightly salty taste. You eat it with a spoon. You cut a piece off the thin crust on the top and put it back on like a lid. Other quality products from Extremadura include extra virgin olive oils, honeys and the spicy bittersweet smoked *pimentón de La Vera*.

The region was never an independent kingdom. The Romans found silver mines here and the Moors built fortified towns. When the area was reconquered in the thirteenth century it became a province of Castile. The land was given over to nobles from Castile, Leon and Galicia, and to the Knights of Santiago and Alcántara, the monastic military orders who organized its colonization. In the sixteenth century, because opportunities at home were limited in comparison with Castile, men of ambition left in great numbers for the Americas. The most famous conquistadors – Pizarro, Cortés, Balboa and others – as well as the majority of the early emigrants to the New World came from Extremadura. Many who returned there brought riches and built mansions and palaces. You can see them emblazoned with heraldic coats of arms. Extremadura is said to be the first place where chillies – brought back from the Americas by monks – were grown, in their monastery vegetable gardens. In the mid nineteenth century, farmers started to grow chillies on a large scale and to pulverize them into *pimentón*, the Spanish paprika that flavours *chorizos* and so many regional Spanish dishes.

In this land of rolling plains with fields of wheat, barley, maize and chickpeas, great wooded mountains and fertile valleys, sheep and pig farming were early on the most important parts of the economy. Nobles owned extensive estates of agricultural and grazing lands. They sold wool to Castilian merchants and rented out their pastures in the winter to northern stock raisers. Small landless farmers could rent common lands owned by towns and villages to graze animals and grow vines, fruits and vegetables. They also had access to royal lands, especially the mountain woodlands that provided the harvest of sweet acorns that fattened their pigs. Monasteries and convents owned vineyards and olive groves in the hills. While the cooking of the region is serious and austere, known for pastoral and peasant dishes, with lamb, pork and offal, the monasteries always had a reputation for fine cooking.

Apart from the Torta del Casar, other good cheeses of Extremadura are the Merino sheep's milk La Serena and the goat's milk Ibores, De La Vera and Cabra del Tiétar. Like almost all Spanish regions, Extremadura has an old winemaking tradition. Ribera del Guadiana was one of the first wine areas in Spain to use modern refrigeration equipment to combat the extremely high summer temperatures. Their new fruity reds made from Tempranillo grapes and whites from Pardilla grapes are extremely reasonable. In some villages such as Montánchez, the local Pitarra wine is fermented in clay pots called *tinajas* and kept in family cellars.

THE MEDITERRANEAN EAST AND SOUTH:
rice and vegetables

Mediterranean Spain is the Spain of deep blue seas, luminous skies and fragrant air. It is dry, with hot summers and mild winters, and occasional bursts of rain. People promenade and meet in open-air cafes. It is the Spain of the *alegría de vivir* ('joy of living'). Gastronomically it is the colourful, sensuous Spain of strong flavours and aromas. The lands around the Mediterranean Sea have been my world since I first holidayed in Alexandria, the Egyptian resort, when I was a child and it has been my 'patch' since I started writing about food. I feel at home here.

Catalonia, Valencia, Murcia and the Balearic Islands, and Andalusia too, share a culinary culture with other countries around the Mediterranean, most particularly with southern France, Italy and Morocco. Catalonia had a major role in creating and spreading that culture. For hundreds of years, the great seafaring mercantile nation was the undisputed 'Queen of the Mediterranean', and was the dominant partner in the Catalan–Aragonese kingdom that had an empire around the sea. Before Catalonia and Aragon were united by royal marriage in 1137, a count of Barcelona had acquired control over Provence and part of the Pyrenees through marriage to the heiress of Provence. The Catalans, in the name of the joint crown, took Valencia and the islands of Majorca and Minorca from the Arabs and received Sicily through marriage. The Pope granted James II sovereignty over Sardinia and Corsica, and the joint crown went on to possess Naples, Macedonia, parts of Greece, the North African island of Jerba and the French Roussillon and Cerdagne. It also established trading posts and 'consulates' in port cities as far away as Alexandria. The old 'Catalan lands', as they were called, which included Valencia and the Balearic Islands, were largely repopulated by Catalans when they were reconquered and the Muslims left. This explains why people speak a Catalan language in those places and why they have many dishes in common. You can also see why the Spanish *coca* is like Italian pizza and the Provençal *pissaladière*, why *samfaina* is like ratatouille, and why Spain's tomato sauce is an iconic symbol of Mediterranean cooking.

Despite the similarities, every region, province and village in Spain on the long sea coast and in the islands has its own take on the Mediterranean cooking style. It is a style rich in grains, vegetables, fruit and nuts, as well as fish, and olive oil is the main cooking fat. The Romans planted wheat, olives and vines, the Arabs introduced rice and a large number of vegetables and fruits, and many more varieties were brought from the New World to be grown here. Mediterranean vegetables include courgettes, aubergines, peppers and tomatoes, broad beans, spinach, asparagus, green beans, artichokes, pumpkins and many more. The fish stock in the Mediterranean Sea has been much depleted but the Spanish coast still boasts the most glorious fish and seafood dishes of any coast around the sea.

catalonia

Catalan cuisine is the richest, most complex and sophisticated of Spain. Their fish and seafood dishes are magisterial. They have a new foie gras industry and more wild mushrooms than anywhere else in Spain. Catalans are known for mixing savoury with sweet and sweet with sour, for pairing meat with fruit and seafood with meat. A dish of chicken and lobster or prawns (page 367) is an example of their *mar y montaña*, or 'sea and mountain', style of cooking. Raisins and pine nuts are common garnishes. Wine and brandy are much used and chocolate appears in both sweet and savoury dishes too. Catalans describe some of their dishes as *barroc i saborós* ('baroque and tasty'). Many dishes begin with a *sofregit* (*sofrito* in Castilian Spanish) of fried onion, garlic and just a little tomato. A *picada* – a garlic, parsley and almond or hazelnut paste – is often stirred in at the end of cooking to thicken stews and give another layer of flavour. A nutty sauce called *romesco* (page 152), made with garlic, tomatoes and special sweet dried red peppers, all blended to a thick cream, accompanies all kinds of dishes. *Alioli* (page 149) is a garlicky olive oil sauce. In Catalonia, a mix of olive oil and pork fat is the traditional cooking medium (they also sometimes use goose and duck fat), but now most people have dropped lard – for health reasons and because commercial lard is not as good as the one once lovingly produced by rural families for their own use. Catalonia's fruity extra virgin olive oils, in which Arbequino is the predominant olive, are among the finest of Spain. The *frutado* oil, made with green olives, has a hint of apple and a slight bitter almond flavour; the *dulce*, made with ripe black olives, is yellow, sweet and mild. Some of the olive trees in Catalonia are the oldest in Spain. There is one in Tarragona that is said to be more than 1,000 years old.

Apart from a narrow coastal plain and the wide valley of the river Ebro, where the produce and the cooking is Mediterranean, the Catalan interior is all high mountains with a gastronomic culture of the Pyrenees. Cows and goats are raised for butter and cheese, and intensive pig farming provides for a huge variety of *embotits* (sausages and salamis). The city of Vic is famous for its fresh *botifarres* (pure pork sausages), its salami-type *salchichón*, the spiced *longaniza* and *fuet* (for more details about sausages see pages 109–10).

Catalans have always been hard-working and proud of their industrial and trading activities, which resulted in a wealthy bourgeoisie that had no counterpart in Castile, where such work was not seen as compatible with an aristocratic lifestyle. The Catalan bourgeoisie aspired to live well and eat well. In the nineteenth century, the manufacture of cotton cloth from fibres from Latin American plantations started an industrial revolution here. Other industries included wine and brandy that were exported to Europe. Spaniards grown wealthy in Cuba – so-called *indianos* – came back to Catalonia to start manufacturing, and Andalusian peasants from the south came to work in the mills. Barcelona was the commercial and cultural hub of Spain. The Catalan language, which had not been taught at school since the time of the Bourbons, rediscovered its literary nobility and the glorious imperial Catalan medieval past was celebrated. But Catalan gastronomic traditions were neglected in favour of French haute cuisine. The dispossessed French aristocrats and cooks who flooded in from the start of the French Revolution in the late eighteenth century profoundly influenced the new Barcelona bourgeoisie into adopting French ways in the kitchen. Italians arrived at the same time and opened the first inns. Many French and Italian dishes were Hispanicized. Béchamel sauce made with fried onions and tomato paste, and Spanish *canelones* (cannelloni) are examples of those two trends. By the end of the nineteenth century, a large number of exclusive, flamboyant, French-style restaurants had opened in cosmopolitan Barcelona. Catalan chefs learnt French haute cuisine by working with French chefs and in catering schools. The wealthy Catalan elites expected their home cooks to make the exquisite and sophisticated dishes that became their '*cuisine bourgeoise*'.

It took until the late twentieth century, after General Franco's forty-year crushing of their culture and the expansion of industrialized food products, for Catalans to begin to value their own rural and popular home cooking. The great writer and gastronome Manuel Vázquez Montalbán was one of the first to begin chronicling 'the signs of resistance of Catalonia's gastronomic identity'. If it was a priority to save the language, it was also, he believed, important to save the cuisine. In 1977, he published *L'art del menjar a Catalunya* ('The Art of Eating in Catalonia'). But by 1994, it was clear that it was *nueva cocina* that was threatening Catalan cooking traditions. Although proud that the most innovative cuisine in the history of cooking, which put Spain on the gastronomic map and created demand for their products, was by their own superstar chef Ferran Adrià, Catalans also saw it as a tragedy because young chefs in thrall to Adrià only wanted to make mousses, gelatines and terrines of everything and to be on television. A group of food historians, gastronomes, nutritionists, sociologists and others got together with chefs to form the Fundació Institut Català de la Cuina (the Catalan Culinary Institute) in 1996, dedicated to researching the history and roots of Catalan cooking and to collecting and recording recipes from professionals and home cooks in every town, village and fishing port before they disappeared. The Institute is also encouraging chefs to revisit and update traditional Catalan dishes (to make them lighter and simpler). My friend Pepa Aymami has been involved in the project from the start. When I was staying with her in Barcelona she invited some of her collaborators on the committee of the Marca Cuina Catalana (Catalan Culinary brand) to lunch. They talked passionately about the food of Catalonia and its history.

Many Catalan dishes go back to the Middle Ages and the Renaissance, when there was a court cuisine and Catalans were rich from trading and benefited from their Mediterranean empire. For a long time their cooks were the most highly regarded and influential in Europe. Collections of recipes written in Catalan meant that medieval Catalan cuisine achieved wide fame in the fourteenth and fifteenth centuries. I had a taste of that medieval cuisine many years ago at the home of the late Rudolf Grewe, who was translating from ancient Catalan and researching the background of a now famous anonymous Catalan cookbook, the *Llibre de Sent Soví*, presumed to have been written in the early fourteenth century. When Rudolf came to London and consulted me about medieval Arab cooking, I cooked dishes for him from a thirteenth-century Arabic culinary manual known as *A Baghdad Cookery Book* (see page 27). And later, when I was in New York where he lived, he invited me to eat dishes cooked from the *Llibre de Sent Soví*. A giant crucifix bought from an old church hung on a big white wall over the table. He made a *sofregit* of slowly fried onions with garlic, an almond sauce – both quintessential cornerstones of Catalan cooking today – baby aubergines stuffed with a herby goat's cheese and fried fish *escabeche*, followed by chicken with the almond sauce. For dessert we ate fresh cheese flavoured with rose water and honey.

Another medieval Catalan cookbook, the *Llibre de Coch*, was written by Ruperto de Nola, head cook to Alfonso V, count of Barcelona and king of Aragon, who became king of Naples in 1443. Nola also later cooked for Alfonso's son, King Ferdinand. His sumptuous dishes symbolize the cultural apogee of the empire of the old Catalan lands. Some of his recipes claim to be in the styles of Genoa, Venice, Lombardy or France. Some are recognizably Arab in that they mix sweet with sour, savoury with sweet, and marry meat with fruits such as pears and quinces. They use ground almonds, rose and orange-blossom waters and sour pomegranate juice, and are garnished with raisins and pine nuts. Almond pastries and fritters with sprinklings of sugar and cinnamon are among the sweets. The book already contains a version of *crema catalana* (page 442). Many chefs today cite the *Llibre de Sent Soví* and the *Llibre de Coch* as sources of inspiration. A few have even based their menus on them. Chef and food writer Josep Lladonosa, who was for many years head chef at the famous restaurant Set Portes in Barcelona, was one of the first to use the old books and to popularize the old dishes.

All Catalans are extremely proud of their oils and their sausages, their cheeses and their wines. Among notable cheeses Garrotxa is a firm but creamy and slightly tangy goat's milk cheese covered by a light blue-grey mould; Montcerda is a semi-hard aromatic cow's milk cheese; Serrat, a sheep's milk cheese, has an intense piquant flavour; and Mató, made from cow's or sheep's milk, is soft, fresh and unsalted and great to eat with honey (see page 100). Catalan wines are among the most varied and exciting in Spain. Priorat's rich, complex and full-bodied fruity reds are outstanding. In the Penedès region, they make wonderful red and white wines and are famous for their cavas, made with local grapes by the champagne method into sweet, semi-sweet, dry, extra dry, brut and extra brut sparkling wines. Alella produces good dry and sweet white wines. The Conca de Barberà region is known for its rosés. Other wine-producing areas include Terra Alta, Montsant, Costers del Segre, Empordà, Tarragona and Pla de Bages. Rum, an anise-flavoured liqueur and *vin ranci* (a type of fortified wine like sherry) are all much used in cooking.

valencia

Valencia is a land of oranges and rice fields and of market gardens that produce vegetables all the year round. Roman legionnaires from southern Italy founded the city of Valencia in 137 BC. One of the Roman legacies is the outdoor stone oven that many people still have in their gardens today. Some local products, like dried salted fish and vegetable preserves, are said to have been introduced by the Phoenicians, Greeks and Romans. When James I conquered Valencia from the Muslims in 1238, he made it an autonomous kingdom within the Crown of Aragon and colonized it mainly with Catalans – that is why they have many dishes in common with Catalonia. A large part of the population remained Muslim, of mainly Berber descent. They were forced to convert to Christianity in 1502 but the nobility protected them because they depended on their labour. The mass expulsion from Spain of converts of Muslim descent in 1616 caused a catastrophic economic decline in the region.

Many village names in rural areas begin with Ben (which means 'son of' in Arabic) conjoined with names of Berber tribes – an indication of the spread of North African settlements that left a mark on the agriculture. Their Arab system of irrigation from rivers and springs allows the production of several crops a year on the coastal plain and in river valleys, and still today a weekly 'water court', the Tribunal de las Aguas, set up by the Arabs to resolve conflicts about water, meets at midday every Thursday in the centre of Valencia. The Arabs planted rice in the watery marshlands and lagoons (*albuferas*). You can see their type of traditional houses, *barracas* made from wood, reeds, clay and mud, where the workers slept on the bottom floor while the owner and his family lived in the floor above where the grain was kept.

Valencia has the widest repertoire of rice dishes in Spain – *paella* was born here. Their *fideuá* (page 287), a seafood *paella* made with pasta instead of rice, is relatively new. Here, fish and seafood are cooked on the grill or griddle and served with *alioli*, or simmered in soups and stews called *cassolas*, *sucs* and *suquets*. There are chicken and rabbit, wild game from the scrublands and ducks from the lagoons and marshlands. Vegetables are roasted or simply boiled and dressed with olive oil; they are stuffed or made into omelettes. Among the distinctive dishes of Valencia are pizza-type *coques* (pages 189–97), *empanadas* and *empanadillas* (pies). In the countryside and mountain hinterland, meat stews are special festive dishes made with lamb (there are no cows), chicken, pork products, chickpeas, beans and vegetables. What makes them different from stews in the rest of Spain are the oval-shaped meat or chicken dumplings – some are very large – called *pilotes*.

The usual dessert to finish a Valencian meal is fresh or dried fruit. Apart from Moorish convent pastries, people make sweets with fruits, especially oranges, sweet potatoes and pumpkins. Using a type of squash with flesh that falls apart into threads they make a sweet called *cabello de ángel* (meaning 'angel's hair'). They also have delicious ice creams flavoured with almonds and with *turrón* (page 450).

Every province has a special product. There is the black truffle from the Maestrazgo mountains and honey from the Marina Alta district. Jijona (or Xixona) is the world capital of *turrón* – a nougat made from ground almonds and honey; La Vila Joiosa is famous for its chocolate. A long, thin *llonganissa* pork sausage, *botifarra negra* (blood sausage), a white sausage called *blanquet*, peppery *chorizos* and a soft, paprika-flavoured spreadable *sobrassada* sausage paste are all mountain products. Local cheeses are bland, soft and fresh, made from goat's or sheep's milk or a mix of both – in particular Cassoleta, Servilleta and Blanquet. They are eaten with honey as a dessert.

Valencia's quality wines are from Utiel–Requena, Valencia and Alicante. There are white, red and rosé wines and sweet Moscatels. The Alejandría Moscatel wine is well known. Famous local drinks are the very refreshing tiger nut milk *horchata* (page 503) that I adore and *agua de Valencia* ('Valencia water' – page 501), which is cava or sparkling wine mixed with Cointreau and orange juice.

murcia

Murcia is a small mountainous region with fertile river valleys, a coastal plain and a saltwater lagoon called the Mar Menor ('Small Sea'). It has the same semi-arid Mediterranean climate as its neighbour Valencia and the two share an early history of Roman settlement and a long Moorish presence. But the Catalan influence on the cooking is missing here because the Castilians conquered the Muslim kingdom ruling the area in 1243, before the Catalans and Aragonese got there. The land was divided between military orders and knights from Castile and the north and, as in Valencia, Muslims stayed on to work the land.

Dishes here are less flamboyant than in Valencia or Catalonia. Murcia is known as the *huerta* (vegetable garden) of Spain and has more vegetable dishes than any other region. Vegetables are cooked with rice and put into omelettes, pies, soups, stews and salads. They are also stuffed. The region is famous for the very high quality of its rice, particularly in Calasparra (see page 260). Murcian rice dishes, like their game dishes with rabbit and hare, partridge and quail, are hearty, herby and flavoursome. Baby lamb and kid are cooked on grand festive occasions. A special Christmas dish, *caldo con pelotas*, is a stew of turkey or chicken with meatballs as big as an orange. The Mar Menor yields lobsters and prawns and a rich variety of fish. Fish baked in a salt crust (page 328) – a Phoenecian legacy – is one of the local specialities.

Murcia is full of orange and lemon orchards, and melons, watermelons, apricots, plums and pomegranates are grown here. In the almost-desert areas there are prickly pears. The region has industries making crystallized fruit, fruit preserves, marmalades, jams and honeys. Their goat's milk cheeses are soft, fresh and bland, or they are cured and have a slightly stronger flavour. Murcia al Vino is a matured cheese that has been soaked in wine. Three wines – Jumilla, Yecla and Bullas – that use a mix of local grape varieties and French ones are very pleasing.

the balearic islands

The undulating hills, rugged coastline and sandy beaches of the main Balearic Islands – Majorca, Minorca, Ibiza and Formentera – have been attracting people from all over the world since the mid nineteenth century. Until tourism expanded, most of the population lived in the interior, away from the sea, in fear of pirate raids. Now they are concentrated on the coast and in the big cities, where the work is.

Majorca grew rich on Mediterranean trade. The land was divided up between the nobles descended from the Catalans, who conquered the islands in 1229. Today their mansions in the hills and Mudejar-style town houses built around patios have been turned into hotels or become the holiday retreats of international celebrities. The old peasant houses dotted around the countryside have gone to painters, writers and hippies. In village squares where once women washed their laundry and where pigs were slaughtered, hordes of tourists sit in cafes. I stayed in Palma de Majorca with my cousin Steve Afif, who is an artist. I can understand why he lives there. It is a good life.

What surprised me is that researchers have recorded no fewer than 600 regional dishes in this archipelago of islands. Although the Balearics are small they are strategically placed and were an important trading centre. For centuries, settlers and occupiers have been coming and the islands have always been open to foreign influences. The gastronomy, like the culture, is primarily Catalan – they have *coques*, *suquets*, toasted bread smeared with tomato, *alioli* – and the Arab influence is important. You can feel the old Arab presence when you eat poultry stuffed with ground almonds and dried fruit, as you do when you see the old waterwheels and watermills.

The Balearic Islands are fantastically rich in produce of the land and the sea. A hundred years ago, the Catalan painter Santiago Rusiñol described the vegetation in these words: 'The fruit trees spread themselves...Everything grows, blossoms and fructifies as if to relieve its heart of some burden, and to bestow homage and gifts on the little houses around.' Apart from the usual wheat, grapes and olives, there are apricots, peaches, pomegranates, figs and carobs. Peasant dishes are based on vegetables. Aubergines are a favourite. Rabbit, hare and partridge inhabit the islands, quails stop off on their migration path and there are also sheep. But the most important dishes are with fish and seafood. Minorca's *caldereta de langosta* (page 354) is a stupendous lobster stew. As in Catalonia, olive oil and lard have an all-important role in cooking and pastry-making. Balearic olive oil is more astringent and bitter than the Catalan oils. Santiago Rusiñol described the oldest trees as 'twisting themselves into such intricate knots and rolling about in such hysterical convulsions that they could hardly be called trees'. They were, he said, more like epileptics. The main varieties of olives are Empeltre, Arbequina and Picual.

In 1708, the English occupied the island of Minorca and stayed for almost eighty years. They brought Friesian cattle over from England. The Minorcan bland, fresh cow's milk cheese Queso de Mahón is used to make cheesecakes. The matured variety has a delicious, slightly salty, strong flavour. *Flor de sal*, sea salt harvested by hand along the coast, is a new gourmet product of the island.

The great Majorcan speciality is *sobrassada*, an orange-coloured, semi-cured pork sausage that is a soft spreadable paste, flavoured with *pimentón* and other spices. There is a mild variety and a spicier hot one. The paste is pressed into pigs' intestines or into large bladders. The traditional meat used is from a special breed of fat black Majorcan pig with long ears called *porc negre* ('black pig' – this is not the Ibérico *pata negra* 'black foot' pig). *Sobrassada* is eaten on toasted bread, often with something sweet and fruity such as ripe figs, quince paste or honey. It is also fried with eggs. For the Majorcan peasantry, *sobrassada* was the main and for some the only source of meat.

The other food that Majorca is famous for is a fabulously light, melt-in-the-mouth, yeast-based puff pastry called *ensaimada* made with lard (lard is called *saim* in the local dialect). Locals eat small *ensaimadas* for breakfast and with drinks, and a huge, coiled, serpent-like *ensaimada* is often stuffed with custard. I could eat one every day. The Majorcan aristocracy sent their cooks to learn confectionery-making in France. They came back knowing about chestnuts in brandy syrup, meringues called *baisers* (meaning kisses in French) and almond cakes covered with chocolate. The island has the sweetest, tastiest almonds. Tourists organize their visits to coincide with the blossoming of the almond trees in January and February because the sight and fragrance are such a wondrous experience. The almonds go into Moorish-style pastries, and there is a famous local almond cake and an almond ice cream (page 45).

Majorca is the only one of the islands to produce wine. Binissalem and Plà i Llevant wines are made from native grapes – Manto Negro and Callet for red wines and Moll for whites. Majorcans also manufacture Palo de Mallorca, a celebrated *digestif* spirit made from cinchona bark, brown sugar, cinnamon and nutmeg. The English introduced gin in Minorca, where it is distilled from fermented grape skins and seeds and flavoured with juniper berries and aromatic herbs. The locals drink *pellofa*, gin with a dash of soda and lemon peel, or *pomada*, a mix of gin and lemonade. In Ibiza their hot *sangrí* is a punch with red wine, lemon or orange peel and a dash of nutmeg – it is poured over toasted bread. *Punys* is a drink of rum or brandy diluted with water, with added sugar and lemon peel.

andalusia

Orange trees line the streets of Andalusia, and the scent of jasmine is in the air. It is the home of bullfighting, flamenco and gypsies and where the *tapas* tradition was born. It was the Roman province of Baetica that produced grain, wine and olive oil for the Roman Empire. But it is the ghosts of al-Andalus that haunt the land, with its Moorish castles and palaces, its mosques and white-painted villages that the Arabs left behind. Ziryab, who came from the court of Harun al-Rashid in Baghdad and revolutionized the cooking at the medieval Muslim court of Cordoba, would be smiling to find that lamb with honey (page 398) and fish with raisins and pine nuts are on the menus of fashionable restaurants in Andalusia, and that the nuns make the greatest variety of Moorish pastries in all of Spain. No other region has so captured the allure of the old Muslim presence.

Andalusia has many faces. Most of the region is wild and mountainous, with huge *sierras* (mountain ranges) covered with scrub or chestnut and oak forests. The *sierras* are pig country, with the ideal conditions for curing pork in the cold, dry winter air. The prestigious cured ham, *jamón ibérico*, is produced here from the famous black *pata negra* pigs that feed on sweet acorns in the oak woods. Trevélez in Las Alpujarras mountains in the Sierra Nevada and the village of Jabugo in the Sierra de Aracena are both renowned for their exquisite *jamón*. Local mountain cheeses are mainly goat's milk cheeses from the Malaga breed of goats. Grazalema cheese, made from a blend of sheep's and goat's milks, is sweet and fruity.

Andalusia also has desert-like stretches and wetlands with freshwater lagoons where rice grows. Irrigation and a brilliant sun allow areas on the coast and the huge basin of the river Guadalquivir to produce a fantastic abundance of vegetables. Seville, on the banks of the river, was the gateway and port for goods arriving from the New World and was the first city to receive the new vegetables and fruits. Almond trees here are important to the confectionery and pastry production of Spain. Between the valley and the mountains, gently rolling hills are covered by seas of wheat and sunflowers, orange and lemon groves, and vineyards. They all eventually give way to olive trees as far as the eye can see and however far you travel. Olives and olive oil are the culinary symbols of Andalusia. The province of Jaén is the greatest producer of olive oil in the world. Their extra virgin oils made from Picual olives are fruity and fragrant. Three sensational Andalusian extra virgin olive oils, mainly from Picual and Hojiblanca olives, are the fruity, mildly bitter and slightly pungent award-winning Priego de Córdoba, the slightly bitter Sierra Mágina and the intense Sierra de Segura.

With two different waters on either side of the Straits of Gibraltar – the Atlantic Ocean in the west, the Mediterranean Sea in the east – where an immense exchange of water takes place, Andalusian fishermen bring in an extraordinary variety of fish and seafood, and the cooking of the sea represents some of the region's greatest dishes. Andalusians are famous for deep-frying fish and seafood (page 312), but they also have many other coastal specialities.

Socially, Andalusia has always been a region of great wealth and extreme poverty. The majority of the population was illiterate until the mid twentieth century. As land was reconquered from the Muslims, it was shared between warrior nobles from Castile, Galicia and Asturias, and the Church, and divided into large estates called *latifundios*. Peasant families from Asturias who migrated to work on the land brought with them the food culture of chestnuts and the food culture of the pig from the north.

Most of today's big estates date from the nineteenth century, when land held by the Church and the municipalities was put up for sale. At the same time, landowning families began to sell land to their workers who lived on the estates. All the members of peasant families worked and saved up to buy a plot. Generations spent most of their life economizing. Those who emigrated sent money from abroad.

The landless rural poor of southern Spain lived in small villages and were taken on as day labourers. They would hang around the village square to be picked for work. They often rebelled against their conditions. Their mass migration to the cities, to the industrialized north and abroad began in the nineteenth century. Some have come back to buy their dream bit of land and to plant olive trees. Today, tourism provides seasonal work and it is immigrant workers who do the labouring in the fields. The old life of the peasants has only recently disappeared and their *gazpachos*, *salmorejos* and *ajo blanco* (pages 157–60) have become famous around the world.

Sherry and locally brewed lager beers are the favourite aperitifs of Andalusia. Sherry, now called Jerez-Xérès-Sherry, is one of the best-known wines of the world. It is made in the area lying between Jerez de la Frontera, Puerto de Santa María and Sanlúcar de Barrameda in the province of Cadiz. It is fortified by adding grape-distilled alcohol. The juice of mainly Palomino grapes is fermented and then left to age in oak barrels. What is unique about sherry is the *solera* system by which wines from different harvests are blended and aged at the same time. For this, several rows of barrels are stacked in at least three layers, the one with the oldest wine at the bottom and the one with the newest at the top. Wine ready to be bottled is drawn off from the *solera*, which is the bottom row of barrels that contain the oldest blend. Then each barrel is topped up with wine from the row above.

Different styles of sherry are produced. For fino sherry, the driest and palest, a yeast called *flor* is allowed to grow on the surface to protect the wine from oxidation, and this also affects the taste. Pale, crisp and moderately dry manzanilla sherry is also aged with *flor*. Oloroso sherry is fortified to a higher strength in which the *flor* cannot survive. It is aged oxidatively for a very long time and becomes a dark-gold, rich and mellow wine with a caramel flavour. Amontillado sherry is aged first under a cap of *flor*, then exposed to oxygen, which produces an amber wine, lighter than oloroso with a slightly sweet nutty flavour. Sweet and medium sherries have had sweet wine added to them from Pedro Ximénez or Moscatel grapes that are dried in the sun.

Other Andalusian Designations of Origin (DOs) that produce dry fortified wines and sweet wines are Montilla–Moriles, Malaga, Sierras de Málaga and El Condado de Huelva. Sweet wines made from Pedro Ximénez grapes (also labelled PX) are dark coffee-black, intensely sweet and syrupy with dried-raisin flavours. Those made from Moscatel grapes are white and have orange-blossom aromas. The best are from Malaga.

Andalusia produces most of Spain's brandies (often called *coñac*), which are drunk as *digestifs* and are much used in cooking – they are sweeter than French cognac. An anise-flavoured spirit, *aguardiente de anís*, that can be either sweet or dry, is used in pastry-making. A variety of vinegars are made in Andalusia too. Dark brown sherry vinegar, *vinagre de Jerez*, is strong and complex in flavour. There are also sweet vinegars made from Pedro Ximénez and Moscatel grapes. A new product, Pedro Ximénez wine reduction, is the wine reduced to a dark, thick syrup. It is added to vinegar in dressings and drizzled over desserts and ice cream. Cooking with sherry characterizes Andalusian dishes. Every kind is used – fino, manzanilla, oloroso, amontillado, Pedro Ximénez.

THE CANARY ISLANDS:
of 'wrinkled' potatoes and hot sauces

The Canary Islands are different from the rest of Spain. The seven volcanic islands and six islets are in the Atlantic Ocean off the coast of Africa, near the border between Morocco and the Western Sahara. They were conquered by the Kingdom of Castile at the end of the fifteenth century and settlers from the Iberian peninsula occupied the land, which was inhabited by people of North African Berber origins called the Guanche. The settlers built cities and planted sugar cane and vines using native labour. The islands became a stopping point on the way to and from the New World and a place for foreign merchants to trade.

The main economy of the islands now is tourism. The fantastical landscapes that range from volcanic desolation to green jungle and the perpetually warm climate attract millions of holidaying Europeans and workers from the Spanish mainland, South America and Africa. Dishes with Spanish, North African and Latin American influences appear in the Canarian kitchen. The islanders were quick to plant products from the New World, like the potato (there are twenty different varieties here), maize, tomatoes and chilli peppers. They are famous for their *papas arrugadas,* or 'wrinkled' potatoes (page 238), and for their Moroccan-type spicy sauces – green, red and peppery *mojos* (pages 146 and 241) that accompany potatoes, vegetables, fish and seafood, and also meat. *Gofio*, a porridge of ground barley, wheat, chickpeas or maize, or sometimes a mixture, which was the staple of the Guanche, is an important part of the local cuisine.

The subtropical climate allows the cultivation of oranges and lemons, apricots, peaches and almonds, wheat, barley and maize. Huge plantations of extra-sweet dwarf bananas were introduced in the mid nineteenth century. More recently they have started to cultivate exotic fruits such as avocados, papayas, mangos, kiwis and pineapples in the islands. Palm honey is a rich, golden syrup made from the sap of local palm trees. Goats are the traditional main source of meat and of milk to make a variety of cheeses. Almogrote is a soft paste of matured goat's cheese with garlic, chilli pepper and olive oil.

The islanders make red and white wine. Their sweet Malmsey (Malvasia) wines were popular in England long ago – Shakespeare mentioned them often. A high-quality golden rum made from sugar cane and a honey rum called Ronmiel are also produced in the Canaries.

INGREDIENTS, UTENSILS AND BASIC TECHNIQUES

I hope the recipes in this book will inspire you and that you will get a lot of pleasure from cooking and eating Spanish dishes. Here are some general suggestions for achieving good results. Always buy good ingredients, the best you can afford – very fresh fish, good meat, if possible free-range organic chickens and eggs. Use sea salt and freshly ground black pepper, fresh herbs, unsalted butter and whole milk. Buy unwaxed lemons when you will be using grated zest or strips of peel. Most Spanish products are now available to buy in Britain but if you cannot find something just use a substitute, such as *prosciutto crudo* for *jamón serrano*, Hungarian sweet paprika for *pimentón dulce* and cayenne pepper instead of *pimentón picante*. Wash your vegetables and fruits.

Cooking is about pleasure, about pleasing yourself and pleasing others. You have to like what you cook. I have made all the recipes, sometimes several times, but when you follow them, you must also follow your own instincts and use your good sense and trust your taste. When you cook, you have to look and touch and smell, and you have to adjust seasonings and flavourings to your taste. The time needed to fry a chopped onion varies depending on its size, type and amount of juice, on the size of the pan, on whether the pan is heavy or light, on the heat. You have to decide how soft you want the onion and how golden. If your tomatoes are too acid, you will need to add a little more sugar. The garlic that you buy might have larger cloves than the ones I used, so put in as much as you like. Ovens vary and their temperatures are not entirely accurate. The cooking time also depends on whether a dish is cold from the refrigerator before it goes in. So look in the oven and take the food out a little before time or leave it in for a little longer if necessary. Spanish cooking does not have strict rules like French haute cuisine. In Spain, everyone feels they can have their own way of doing things in the kitchen and so should you. You will acquire skill by cooking the same dish over again – it might come out a little different each time – but do always feel that if something tastes good to you that is how it is meant to turn out.

INGREDIENTS

OLIVE OIL
aceite de oliva

Spain is the biggest producer of olive oil in the world and the biggest exporter. Much of its exports have been in bulk and the main market is Italy, where it is either consumed or repackaged in beautiful bottles and re-exported as Italian or Tuscan olive oil. But a variety of Spanish virgin olive oils are now enjoying a worldwide reputation for quality. Twenty have been awarded an official *Denominación de Origen* (Designation of Origin – DO) seal of quality. Olive trees grow everywhere in Spain except in the northern regions. Parts of the undulating Andalusian landscape, where once there were also fields of wheat, grapevines, barley, oats, chickpeas and all kinds of vegetables, are now entirely covered by a carpet of olive trees. The story of olive oil in Spain is ancient. A good deal of what I know about olive oil I learnt from my friend Alicia Ríos, who has written a book with Lourdes March on the subject called *La cocina del aceite de oliva* ('Cooking with Olive Oil') (Alianza, 2003). She is also a *catador*, or master taster, and an official ambassador of olive oil who organizes events and performances.

Olive trees have deep roots and need very little water. They thrive in a Mediterranean climate. It is claimed that some trees in Spain are 500, some even more than 1,000, years old. Could this be true? In Egypt, my Catholic nanny went on a pilgrimage and came back with a small branch from an olive tree under which the pregnant Virgin Mary is supposed to have stopped to rest. It is said that the Phoenicians introduced olive oil to Spain. The Greeks planted the first trees, but it was the Romans who planted olive trees on an industrial scale all over the Iberian peninsula. The oil was sent to Rome and throughout the empire for lighting, soap, cosmetic, medicinal and liturgical purposes; a top-quality *olio flos* was used for cooking and preserving foods. The Arabs brought more olive varieties and ways of cultivating them. The Spanish words *aceituna* for olive and *aceite* for oil come from the Arabic *al-zaitun* and *al-zait*. But an alternative Spanish word for olive is *oliva*, the olive tree is the *olivo* and the olive grove is the *olivar*, all derived from the Latin *oleum*. Oil mills are either called *molino* from the Latin or *almazara* from the Arabic.

When I was invited to take part in a conference on olive oil tourism in Seville in 2009, I talked about the time when in Seville and cities like Toledo and Cordoba you could tell who lived in each house as you walked through the narrow streets because of the smell of the cooking fat. The Christians used pork fat, the Muslims mostly clarified butter and the Jews only olive oil. Pork fat represented a badge of Christian identity. For a long time after the expulsions of Muslims and Jews in 1492, everyone was afraid of using olive oil for fear of being suspected of being a secret Jew.

Speakers at the conference discussed future olive oil 'routes', tourist visits to oil producers and olive plantations, harvest festivals, organized tastings, seminars and cooking demonstrations. We were treated to a trip around the countryside to visit nearby old *molinos*. Some were really ancient, massive conical stone grinders with a spherical millstone that had once been turned by a donkey – relics of another era which might not have changed much since Muslim and even Roman times. A beautifully designed modern museum in Úbeda took us through the different methods of making olive oil. Many people on the trip came from families that had produced olive oil for generations.

Until the Spanish Civil War, small family presses could be found all around the country. Franco's government encouraged the formation of large cooperatives that produced huge quantities of olive oil. The focus of the industry was to produce quantity without regard to taste. But according to José Ramón Guzmán Alvarez, forestry professor at the University of Cordoba, even before that the taste had never been good. Spanish olive oil always had a bad reputation. In an essay from 2007 entitled *'La génesis de los paisajes olivareros: siglos XVI–XX'* ('The Genesis of the Olive Grove Landscape: Sixteenth to Twentieth Centuries'), from which I gleaned much information, he explains that because the seigneurial landlords had exclusive milling rights until 1837, there were not enough communal mills around to provide for all the people who grew smaller quantities of olives. They would have to wait their turn for days and maybe weeks for their olives to be pressed, by which time their olives would have gone bad. The big landowners in Andalusia might have produced some good oil for their own personal consumption, but they could always sell low-grade oil in bulk for lighting and soap. They sold it to England as a lubricant for the factories that were operating during the industrial revolution.

You can see why the old traditional cooking of Spain was done with lard – lard tasted better than the alternative fats and it was hand-produced by families themselves. There were a few producers of decent olive oil at the end of the nineteenth century, especially in Catalonia, which had a prosperous bourgeoisie and French and Italian restaurateurs who liked to use olive oil as well as butter. Even there, though, dishes were never cooked only with olive oil. Lard would also be used, often mixing the two. Nowadays, from what I hear from young people in Catalonia, they have dropped the use of lard. The Catalan food historian and gastronome Néstor Luján has written that some people in Catalonia still think food lost much of its graciousness when olive oil became more common than lard. In the south of Spain and along the Mediterranean coast, olive oil had continued as the dominant cooking fat despite the historical prejudice associating it with crypto-Jews, yet it wasn't until the late nineteenth century that Spanish cookery writers began to extol its virtues over lard. Most of the recipes they featured in their books were French. By then, lard was associated with poor peasant food. It is still used in many traditional foods such as a *cocido* of boiled meats and *potajes* (hearty soups), where people feel it would be a sacrilege to use a substitute. Indeed, lard is now a sign of culinary tradition as opposed to innovation.

During the First World War, Italian demand for olive oil rose enormously and olive groves expanded all over the Andalusian hills. But it is in the last twenty or so years that domestic and world demand has increased phenomenally and spurred on the intensive monoculture of olive trees. The European Union gave subsidies to farmers planting olive groves and international campaigns boosted the consumption of olive oil by promoting the healthy aspects of the Mediterranean diet. Star chefs of the Basque Country and Catalonia started using olive oil rather than pork fat in their refined and sophisticated dishes and TV chefs advocated the healthy and gastronomic qualities of olive oil while sloshing great amounts into their pans. Enterprising oil producers started buying the latest state-of-the-art technology from Italy and putting all their efforts into creating the best conditions in every aspect of oil production, from growing and harvesting to pressing, blending and bottling. Many producers of top-quality oils own their own olive groves and use a combination of the best traditional practices and modern technology for extracting the oil. There has been a revolution in Spanish olive oil production just as there has been one in wine. It has resulted in extra virgin olive oils comparable in quality to the Iberian pig products.

about the oils

Olive oils can be light and delicate or assertive and strong, and their flavours and aromas can be simple or complex – experienced upfront and as an aftertaste. Flavours range from sweet to pleasantly bitter and pungent, through fruity, nutty, spicy and peppery. Fragrances may be elusive or intense – fruity, floral, nutty or grassy. Oils made from olives from the same tree can change from one harvest to another. Some harvests produce exceptional oil, some more ordinary. Blended oils hardly vary because blenders achieve consistency by adjusting their mixes. Their created styles marry complementary qualities of different varieties to follow local taste and tradition as well as the preferences, for lightness and mildness for instance, of the consumer countries newly converted to olive oil.

Oils vary depending on the type of tree and the soil in which it grows. They depend on the weather; on when and how the olives are harvested, if they are picked by hand, if the branches are beaten with poles or the trees shaken by machines into inverted umbrellas; on how ripe the olives are; on how quickly the oil is extracted and by what means; and on whether the oil comes from a single variety or has been blended. There are more than 260 varieties of olive tree in Spain, including sub-varieties that have changed in a different locality or through grafting. Arbequina, Picual, Hojiblanca, Empeltre and Cornicabra olives are the most extensively grown. Other varieties include Picuda, Nevadillo Blanco, Blanqueta, Sollana, Lechín, Chorruo, Pajarero, Farga, Morrut, Cornezuelo and Mollar. A few, like Manzanilla, are better as table olives for eating than being used for producing oil.

Methods of production that are now commonly used, called 'continuous' methods, separate the liquid from the solid olive paste gained by crushing the olives, then separate the oil from the rest of the juice by spinning the paste or liquid at high speed in a drum or centrifuge. 'Extra virgin' olive oils with a low acidity are the finest, with the richest flavours and aromas. When the group of English journalists I was with was invited to rate a few by a producer, small navy blue cups with glass covers were lined up. The dark colour of the glass ensures that you are not influenced by the colour of the oil in your tasting, because colour does not indicate quality or style (green oils are not better than yellow ones), although a dark green oil is more generally characteristic of a fruity, bitter, astringent oil produced from green olives that have not reached maturity, and a golden-yellow oil is usually made from sweet, ripe black olives late in the season. We were asked to cradle the cups in our hands to warm them before removing the cover and inhaling the aroma, then we were asked to taste the oil by dipping a piece of bread in it. In between each tasting we chewed on apple slices to clear the palate.

Oils labelled 'extra virgin' are obtained using only mechanical means and have not undergone any chemical treatment. Those sold simply as 'olive oil' come from second and subsequent extractions of oil from the olives, and have been processed chemically and refined to remove their acidity. I have tasted and brought home some fabulous extra virgin olive oils from Spain. Most memorable were a sweet and fruity Catalan oil made from Arbequina olives and a wonderful Priego de Córdoba oil made from a mix of Picuda, Hojiblanca and Picual olives that had a fruity aroma, slightly bitter taste and a piquant aftertaste. Of the twenty extra virgin olive oils with a DO seal of quality, ten are from Andalusia, five from Catalonia and the rest from Castile-La Mancha, Extremadura, Valencia, Murcia and Majorca.

I asked people in different parts of Spain what oils they used. In Seville, Cordoba and Jaén, the great olive oil-producing areas, they used extra virgin olive oil for everything. Top Spanish chefs said the same, except they do not use extra virgin oils for deep-frying. Otherwise, most Spaniards seem to use a cheap, bland refined olive oil for frying, braising and stewing, and for foods such as sweet oil-based biscuits and cakes where they do not want the strong flavour of extra virgin oils. Since high temperatures diminish the flavours and healthy qualities of extra virgin oils there is no point wasting them for deep-frying. Some people said they used sunflower oil because of the price. Many chefs told me that for mayonnaise they use a mix of sunflower oil and extra virgin olive oil because too much extra virgin would result in too overpowering a taste. A young scientist at the olive oil conference in Seville told me that 90 per cent of people in Spain use simply 'olive oil', not 'extra virgin olive oil', because they are not educated enough about quality – they are as untrained in appreciation and knowledge of quality oils as we are in non oil-producing countries. But everybody agrees that they use extra virgin olive oil raw as a dressing or to drizzle over a finished dish – a piece of bread, vegetables, fish, a soup, a bean stew. A passion for quality olive oil is a new phenomenon, as new as the great Spanish extra virgins that are now being produced.

TABLE OLIVES
aceitunas de mesa

On the tree, olives are first yellowish then pale green and gradually turn pink, purple and black as they ripen. In Spain, people prefer to eat them when they are green and their oil has not fully developed. Following the 'Sevillian' style of processing, the olives are washed, then treated in an alkaline solution for about five to seven hours to remove their bitterness, then washed again and left to ferment in brine. Every region has its own traditional way of flavouring their olives for local consumption, with garlic and herbs such as bay leaves, thyme, oregano and fennel. In Andalusia, they add a little vinegar. The manufacture of mechanically pitted olives stuffed with anchovies, almonds or roasted red peppers is a major industry.

The Manzanilla olives from Seville and south-west Spain are the most famous and popular green table olives in the world. Large and oval, pale green with tiny white dots, they are aromatic and mildly bitter. A whole family of olives – the black Cacereña, the green-and-black Carrasqueña, the Aloreña, the Campo Real, the Morona – stem from the Manzanilla either through adapting to different environments or through grafting. Other very popular green types are the Gordal Sevillana, as big as quail's eggs, fleshy and sweet, and the fruity and aromatic Hojiblanca of Cordoba. The small, very tasty, violet-green Arbequina olives are a speciality of Catalonia. Among the less common olives for eating are the green Cornicabra of La Mancha; the almost black, oily, strong-tasting and bitter Empeltre from Aragon; the oily and sweet Cuquillo of Valencia; the aromatic Picual of Jaén; and the Verdial from Huelva, which are darkened by oxidation.

SEA SALT
flor de sal

Sea salt is produced in salt pans (*salinas*) in Cadiz, Murcia, Majorca and Ibiza, as well as in the estuary of the river Ebro in Catalonia and the Canary Islands. In the last few years, Spain has seen, apart from industrial salt production, the growth of a high-quality gourmet product called *flor de sal*. This is the crunchy, irregular, crystallized flakes that form on the surface of special brine evaporation pools on beaches in hot, sunny, dry and windy conditions. Top layers are collected as they form by skimming them off the surface of the water by hand with a net at the end of a pole. *Flor de sal* has a distinctive taste of the sea and its high magnesium content makes it a particularly good flavour enhancer. When sprinkled over a finished dish it gives a pleasant taste sensation without being absorbed by the food.

VINEGAR
vinagre

Spain produces a whole variety of vinegars. There are red *crianza* vinegars aged in oak barrels and varietal ones made from single grapes such as Cabernet Sauvignon, Chardonnay and Garnacha. There is a white wine vinegar made from sparkling cava, a pale yellow sweet-and-sour Moscatel vinegar and a sweet, dark vinegar from Pedro Ximénez wine. Cider houses (*sidrerías*) in northern Spain make cider vinegar.

Vinagre de Jerez, a sherry vinegar made from sherry wines in wineries in Jerez, can be young or aged for at least six months in casks of American oak. *Vinagre de Jerez Reserva* is aged from two to five years. Some are amber coloured, some very dark, some strong and powerful (you only need a drop), some sweet. There are aged vinegars whose *solera* (see page 90) is 100 years old that can be drunk straight.

Apart from being used in dressings for salads, vinegar is an ingredient of cold soups such as *gazpacho* (page 158) and *ajo blanco* (page 160), and is added to hot soups and stews to cut the richness of pork fat. It is used to marinate food pickled in *escabeche* (page 357), and to deglaze the juices in a roasting tray or sauté pan. Adding an aged sherry vinegar mixed with a sweet Pedro Ximénez wine makes a sublime caramel-coloured sweet-and-sour pan gravy.

HONEY
miel

Bee-keeping is an important agricultural pursuit in many parts of Spain. Only about 70 per cent is in the hands of professionals and semi-professionals. The majority of professionals are migratory bee-keepers who 'follow the bloom' and carry their hives around from fruit groves to hills and mountain forests.

A study has identified thirty-six different types of Spanish honey. The most fragrant honeys are those that come from bees that feed on the nectars of orange and lemon blossoms (my personal favourites), from rosemary, thyme, lavender and heathers, and from oak and chestnut trees. There are also chestnut, blackberry, sage, alfalfa, clover, avocado, buckwheat and eucalyptus honeys. The most common, called *mil flores* ('a thousand flowers'), are blends from different wild flowers. The most important single-source varieties come from sunflowers. Honeydew honey is created from the sweet, sticky secretions of aphids that feed on plant sap. Some honeys and honey-producing areas have been awarded *Denominación de Origen* (DO) status.

CHEESE
queso

It is not the custom in Spain to offer round a cheese platter after dinner, but some top restaurants have now started to give tastings of artisanal cheeses at the end of the meal. Traditionally cheese is eaten as a *tapa* or *aperitivo* with a pre-dinner glass of wine, beer or cider. It is sometimes accompanied by sweet quince paste, called *membrillo* or *codoñate*, and is also served with grapes.

Enric Canut, the author of *Los 100 quesos españoles* ('The 100 Cheeses of Spain') (Salvat, 2000), who, with others, has rescued, helped to rejuvenate and continues to champion traditional artisanal Spanish cheeses, gave our little group of British journalists in Barcelona on a press trip a tasting of cheeses and a fascinating talk. The huge variety of traditional cheeses made in Spain is due to centuries-old customs and lifestyles – shepherds made cheese when they moved with their sheep from pasture to pasture and when they spent a lot of time alone with their goats in the mountains – and to the great diversity of *comarcas* (terroirs). Sheep's and goat's milk cheeses are the most common types. The harsh climate of the vast, semi-arid plains of the Spanish interior suits the foraging habits of sheep, while goats are happy even in rocky mountainous areas. Cow's milk cheeses are produced in the wet northern areas where they have green pastures, and in Minorca where Friesian cows were brought over from England during a period of British occupation of the island. What is peculiar to Spain is the blending of two, and sometimes three, types of milk.

In 1960, when Spain's economy was suffering under Franco, a decree was issued requiring cheese producers to process a minimum of 10,000 litres of milk per day. Cheese counters filled with industrially processed cheeses and most of the traditional ones became illegal due to the small scale of their manufacture. After 1984, when the decree was repealed, artisan cheese-makers could sell their produce openly. However, it is only in the last twenty years that many great artisan cheeses have become available outside their locality and have earnt a *Denominación de Origen* (DO) label of quality. A few Spanish cheeses are now also gradually becoming known abroad. You will find more information and the names of cheeses in the chapters about the regions.

A lovely Spanish custom of eating cheese with honey is worth adopting. In the past, vendors on mules would go around rural villages with barrels of cheese, honey and *arrope* (a sweet syrup made from boiled-down grape juice). They were called *mieleros* (honey vendors) and wore special clothes. Now the vendors travel around in vans but they still wear the same clothes. *Mel y mató* is a popular Catalan dessert of a fresh unsalted cheese made from cow's or goat's milk called *mató* (you can substitute ricotta, although it is not quite as good) and a dribble of honey (*mel* in Catalan). In other parts of Spain, a traditional shepherd's snack of fried or grilled cheese – a medium-young Manchego or cow's or goat's milk cheese will do – with scented honey has become popular.

BREAD
pan

Bread has always been an important part of a Spanish meal. In Cervantes' *Don Quixote*, there is a scene where Sancho Panza says that he has seen Dulcinea eating bread that was 'not very white', which implied that she was poor. Today the common traditional breads are big round loaves made with wheat flour. The *libreta* (named after *libra,* meaning 'pound', because it weighs one pound) is the finest and whitest, and the *hogaza*, a country bread, is rougher and not quite white. Bakeries (*panaderías*) and markets in Galicia, Asturias and the Basque Country sell maize and rye breads as well as the usual wheat loaves. Catalans and others in Mediterranean Spain eat dense, coarse-textured round loaves, which they cut in thick slices and dip in extra virgin olive oil, or rub with tomatoes. But the most common bread now throughout the whole of Spain is a crusty baguette-style loaf that is a bit denser than a French baguette. It is called *pistola* in Madrid and *pan de barra* elsewhere.

PASTA
fideos

Various types of dry pasta made of durum wheat, all of them short (about 2.5 to 4cm long), are called *fideos* in Spain – or *fideus* in Catalan. The name derives from *fidawsh*, an Arab word for pasta. Fourteenth-century Catalan cookbooks have recipes for *fideus* and for *aletría*, an alternative word for pasta that is derived from the Arabic *itria*. *Fideos* come in various thicknesses that are sized from 0 to 4. Size 0 is vermicelli-like and also called *cabello de ángel* ('angel's hair'). (For this you can use vermicelli nests – break them into small pieces in your hands.) There is also a thin spaghettini and a thicker spaghetti-type noodle, as well as a small, curved, macaroni-type pasta with a thin hole.

Fideos are cooked in a paella pan, like rice, or in a casserole or earthenware dish or in a pot and, also like rice, in Spain they are cooked in a stock or a sauce, not in boiling water. In Catalonia, they are sometimes first fried in oil – and are then called *rossejats*. Catalonia and Valencia have the greatest variety of pasta dishes. *Fideos* are a legacy of the Arabs. Italian-type pastas, such as cannelloni, penne and macaroni, in Spain date back to the nineteenth century, when a large number of Italian cooks came to work for the new wealthy Catalan and Basque bourgeoisies and later opened restaurants. Dishes with these types of pasta have become Spanish in style and flavour.

NUTS
frutos secos

Nuts of all kinds are an important part of the Spanish diet and are much used in both sweet and savoury dishes.

ALMONDS (*almendras*) are much used in Spanish cooking, especially in pastry and cake-making and to thicken sauces and stews. They are the main ingredients in marzipan (page 14) and *turrón* (a traditional nougat confection). To serve as a *tapa*, almonds are lightly fried and sprinkled with salt. Marcona almonds from Mediterranean Spain are large, round and flat, with a distinctive sweet taste.

HAZELNUTS (*avellanas*) grow in Catalonia, particularly around Tarragona. They are used in pastries, in the famous *picada* paste that is stirred into many savoury Catalan dishes at the end of cooking, and for making the iconic *romesco* sauce (page 152).

PINE NUTS (*piñones*) are mainly used in Spanish kitchens as a garnish.

WALNUT trees grow in northern Spain, where the nuts (*nueces*) are used to make cakes and pastries.

TIGER NUTS (*chufas*) grow in Valencia and are used to make the delicious, refreshing *horchata* (tiger nut milk), which is one of my favourite drinks (page 503).

CHESTNUT trees are part of many a Spanish landscape. In north-west Spain, chestnuts (*castañas*) were a main staple food before the arrival of potatoes and maize from the New World. They were worshipped by the Celts. In Galicia, it is said that to carry a chestnut in your pocket will keep away the *meigas* (witches). Peasants dried the chestnuts and made them into bread, and they are still eaten as a side vegetable, especially to accompany pork, game and turkey. In Galicia and Asturias, chestnuts are much used in soups and stews and in cakes. For a garnish they are boiled in water or milk. There are chestnut festivals across the chestnut-growing regions at the beginning of November.

SAFFRON

azafrán

The little red saffron threads that give a slightly bitter flavour, characteristic aroma and an intense yellow colour to *paellas* and many other Spanish dishes are the stigmas of a particular purple crocus, *Crocus sativus*. *Sativus* means 'cultivated' in Latin and saffron crocuses do not grow wild. Spanish saffron is of a high quality; the best is Mancha saffron grown in La Mancha. The Sierra saffron is a lower grade.

The crocuses' stigmas have to be removed by hand and dried quickly by very lightly toasting. Two hundred flowers yield only one gram of saffron. The plants do not reproduce themselves from seeds, like wild plants – their tiny corms (these look like bulbs, but they are not) have to be planted by hand. They remain dormant during the summer months and then the pale purple flowers come out in autumn. The crocus flowers must be harvested at dawn as soon as they open. The Fiesta de la Rosa del Azafrán – 'Festival of the Saffron Rose' – which takes place in Consuegra near Toledo in late October is a great tourist attraction, and there are other saffron feasts and festivals.

Spain was once the world's biggest producer of what has been described as 'the poor man's gold' – the poor man being the farmer. In the 1970s, about 6,000 hectares were under cultivation. But this has decreased so much that there are now only a total of some 150 hectares, of which about eighty-eight hectares are in La Mancha. A few hundred dedicated people continue the agricultural practices that began when the Arabs first brought the flowers to the Iberian peninsula. Saffron was a popular flavouring with the al-Andalus elites. The name, *azafrán* in Castilian Spanish, is derived from the Arabic. Iranian saffron, which is the biological progenitor of the Spanish variety, is its greatest competitor. Selling at less than half the price, and also of the highest quality, Iranian saffron now accounts for more than 90 per cent of world production. Some Spanish firms sell Iranian saffron and pass it off as Spanish. This has been in part responsible for Spanish growers giving up.

using saffron

Saffron threads keep for years if you store them in cool and dry conditions, out of direct sunlight. You must use very little – only a pinch or a few threads is enough to flavour a dish for six people. If you put in too much saffron the taste will be bitter and unpleasant. Some people count the threads and advocate variously 5 or 6 per serving or two pinches of 20 to 30 threads for a *paella* to serve six, but I would not be as prescriptive as that since the amount of saffron required also depends on the type of dish and size of serving as well as the quality of the saffron. I start with a tiny pinch and then add more to taste if necessary. By now I have an eye for how much to use.

You can simply throw the saffron threads, as they are, into a stock, sauce, soup or stew. It is said that if you heat them in a small frying pan, or wrapped in a piece of foil placed on a hot lid, then crush them with the back of a spoon, more flavour will be extracted. An alternative recommendation is to steep the threads for about 20 minutes in a little boiling water. I haven't noticed that these procedures make much difference. Although in dishes such as rice or pasta the colour is spread more evenly.

Saffron powder is much used in Spain because it is cheap and gives a good uniform colour, although it has lost most of its flavour and aroma in the grinding process and is adulterated with a filler. The powder is quickly absorbed and can be thrown into a dish a few minutes before serving. The amount to use is said to be about one-tenth of a teaspoon for four servings. A powdered colourant (*colorante*), containing a yellow dye, is also used to give a brighter yellow colour to rice. Only purists avoid it.

PEPPERS AND SPANISH PAPRIKA
pimientos y pimentón

Franciscan monks returning from the Americas in the sixteenth century were the first to bring back the seeds of various species of peppers of the Capsicum family to plant in their monasteries along the *camino de Santiago* (pilgrim route of St James) in northern Spain and also in Extremadura, where the monks of the Yuste monastery are believed to be the first to have grown the new plants. They called the peppers *pimientos*, which is like the word *pimienta* – for the peppercorns that had previously arrived from the Far East – because eating them produced a similar sensation. Fresh peppers were adopted quickly in peasant cooking all over Spain; then dried and crushed, or pulverized, peppers became the most loved and indispensable of Spanish flavourings.

The use of peppers is so characteristic of Spanish cooking that a great old friend of mine, whom I met again when I was testing recipes for this book, was afraid to eat anything at my house because he is allergic to peppers. Despite my assurances that I would not use them, he always insisted on taking me out to eat. There are many Spanish recipes without peppers, but they are ubiquitous in all kinds of dishes. Spaniards do not go in for hot, spicy food. Fresh, mild-flavoured peppers (they ripen from green, through yellow, to red) are eaten raw, roasted, fried, stewed or stuffed. Unripe green ones are favoured for the zing they bring to a dish, red ones are preferred for their sweetness. Intensively grown peppers from Murcia and Almería can be found in supermarkets all over Europe, but there are dozens of other types that are only known in their localities. A few peppers have started to become known outside Spain.

The small, elongated, green *Padrón* peppers (*pimientos de Padrón*, also known as *pimientos de Herbón*) of Galicia are mild, but the occasional one is extremely hot. They are deep-fried whole and eaten with a sprinkling of coarse salt. The uncertainty attached to biting into one that might be hot adds an element of excitement. A popular pepper typical of Basque cooking is the small, pointy, mild and gentle *pimiento de Gernika*. Traditionally, in the past, they were picked when ripe and left to dry hanging on long strings. Today they are eaten green and fresh – deep-fried or roasted – as a *tapa* or vegetable accompaniment to many dishes. The *pimiento Riojano*, conical-shaped with a pointed end, that grows in La Rioja is used mainly when it has ripened to be sweet and red, but it can also be used green, or half-green half-red, as in many local dishes. The peppers can be seen drying in garlands on village balconies. The small, sweet, bright red, triangular *piquillo* peppers, which come from Lodosa in Navarre, are sold roasted and peeled in tins and jars. They have become fashionable since innovative Basque chefs started stuffing them with meat and fish. Another pepper from Navarre, the *cristal*, which is smaller than the *piquillo* and with a sweet and delicate flavour, is also sold as a preserve.

By the nineteenth century, pepper-growing regions began to mill certain types of dried red peppers to a fine powder that they called *pimentón*. In 1893, the Spanish gastronome Ángel Muro wrote in his book *El Practicón* ('The Practitioner') that *pimentón* had become for almost all inhabitants of Spain a product of prime necessity, and that in Castile especially not a single food was put on the table that was not seasoned with it. Some have called it the 'Spanish vice'. Today, although many traditional regional dishes are flavoured with *pimentón*, now usually referred to abroad as Spanish paprika, some Spaniards hardly use it at all. My friend Alicia's mother in Madrid has always been very careful not to employ a cook from a region where there is traditional overuse of the spice because she doesn't like it.

Different varieties of peppers are left to ripen to a red colour, then are picked and sun-dried, to be used whole, in flakes or as pulverized *pimentón*. *Pimentón* comes in four varieties: sweet and mild (*dulce*), bittersweet (*agridulce*), hot (*picante*) and also smoked (*ahumado*). The sweet *pimentón dulce* is the most widely used because Spaniards generally prefer milder flavours. The hot *pimentón picante*, which is like cayenne or chilli pepper, is not much used except in Galicia, Extremadura and the Canary Islands. The *pimentón* from the valley of La Vera in northern Extremadura has a smoky flavour because tobacco farmers, who dried their tobacco leaves in barns heated by holm oak fires, used to hang peppers up to dry at the same time. The peppers absorbed the smell of the woodsmoke and their flavour became popular so the farmers moved their production from tobacco to *pimentón*.

Ñora peppers are always used dry. Small, round, dark burgundy in colour, mild and sweet with a delicate flavour, they are beloved of Catalans, Valencians and Murcians, who use them to flavour rice, pasta, fish, soups and stews. It is these that are also used to make sweet *pimentón dulce* in Murcia, so if a recipe calls for *ñoras* you can always substitute sweet *pimentón* if you cannot get hold of any *ñora* peppers. *Choricero* peppers from the Basque Country, Navarre and La Rioja have a similar flavour. A thick red *choricero* paste, made from the soaked pulp of the dried peppers, is sold in jars. *Guindilla* peppers are hot chillies. The Basque *guindillas del norte* are long and thin and small. When green they are semi-sweet and piquant; as they ripen to a red colour they vary from medium-hot with a sweet flavour to hot. They are eaten fresh, fried with garlic in olive oil. Green *guindilla* peppers are also sold preserved in white wine vinegar. Dried red *guindillas* are broken into flakes or pulverized to make *pimentón picante* or *pimienta cayena* (cayenne pepper).

FOIE GRAS AND TRUFFLES
foie gras y trufas

When the Chernobyl disaster in 1986 left radioactive clouds over Hungary and France those countries ceased to produce foie gras, and Catalonia, Navarre and the Basque Country started producing it instead. Now the Spaniards make some of the best goose and duck foie gras in the world and innovative chefs are fond of using it.

Wild black truffles (*trufas*) are found in mountain woodlands in northern Spain, and in Valencia, deep in the soil around oaks, hazels and pine trees. About 90 per cent of the crop goes to France. The rest is used by grand restaurants. Truffles never had a place in Spanish regional cooking. When the supply of natural wild truffles decreased, and prices and demand abroad increased, truffle cultivation started in areas where they had never grown before, such as the forests around the town of Sarrión in south-west Aragon. Here, a course on truffle cultivation given in 1987 by an agronomy engineering student, Francisco Edo Navarrete, was the initial inspiration for local people to start cultivating them. Locals are now using truffles in their cooking. Since truffles keep very well, they can use them all year round. Although cultivated truffles do not have the same powerful aroma as wild ones, they are still delightful.

SAUSAGES
embutidos, chorizos y morcillas

Romantic nostalgia in Spain has a smell. It is the smell of *chorizos* hanging in attics and kitchens. The taste and aroma of a piece of *chorizo* or *morcilla* (Spanish blood sausage) evokes powerful ancestral and family memories of the day of the *matanza* when the family pig was killed and everyone – father, mother, uncles, aunts, grandmothers – had a part to play in the preparation of hams and sausages for drying. They cut the pig's throat, drained the blood into a bucket, salted the hams, chopped the fat and the rest of the meat, and mixed in seasonings. They washed and scrubbed the intestines, cut them, stuffed them and tied them. It was hard communal work, but there was bonding and laughing, and a lavish feast at the end when the offals were eaten. The cured hams were a luxury that could also be used as payment for the doctor or midwife, but the sausages were made for family consumption. For some, the sausages were their only source of meat. Today the ritual of the family *matanza* is in decline, partly because of new hygiene laws that require a vet to test the health of a pig before its meat can be used.

Every region has its special ways of making sausages that were handed down in families for centuries; Catalonia alone has seventeen varieties and more sub-varieties of sausage. Now they are mass-produced in factories with curing plants where thousands hang from the rafters like stalactites in musty caves. But there are still family-run artisan concerns that do not compromise on quality and use traditional hand-crafted methods, and butchers still make their own sausages.

Ana Isabel Lozano, a young woman who lives in Madrid whom I got to know by email, wrote to me that her family continues to make *chorizos* and other sausages even though they no longer live in the country or keep a pig. They buy a pig from the butcher and have him cut it up. They give away half the meat to friends and the rest they eat throughout the year, some of it from the freezer. The family make the *chorizos* and sausages the way Ana's grandmother used to, enough so that they can have bits to put into all kinds of dishes throughout the year. They don't measure out exact quantities of ingredients, but make the sausage mixtures *a ojo* ('by the eye') or according to taste. They grind the meat in the food processor with fat and flavourings until it acquires a homogeneous reddish colour. They fry a little and taste it to see if there is enough salt and *pimentón* to preserve it, and then stuff it into tripe casings they buy from specialist shops. Every day at teatime they cut some semi-cured *chorizo* in slices, cook it in the microwave and eat it on bread.

Mass-produced Spanish sausages are available in Britain now and you can also find some artisanal ones. Here are the main broad types of Spanish sausages:

CHORIZO is a dry-cured sausage made simply with chopped pork meat and fat, with added salt, garlic and the *pimentón* (Spanish paprika) which gives it a reddish colour and distinctive flavour. There are hundreds of regional varieties – long ones and small ones, in mini links, thin and thick, in the shape of a horseshoe; with more or less fat, and more or less garlic; coarsely or finely chopped; with sweet *pimentón dulce* or hot *pimentón picante*, smoked or unsmoked; and with added herbs or other seasonings. *Chorizo blanco* is made without *pimentón*. Fully cured *chorizos* are ready to eat sliced as *tapas* and can also be added to a dish at the end of cooking. Soft, semi-cured *chorizos* must be cooked. They can be grilled or fried, whole or sliced, and can also be poached in wine or cider (try this – it is very good).

LOMO EMBUCHADO is loin of pork, trimmed of fat, salted and washed, then marinated in a paste of *pimentón*, garlic, oregano and olive oil (sometimes also wine), encased in a sausage skin and air-dried. When made from *ibérico de bellota* pork meat it is exquisite.

LONGANIZA is a thin sausage from Navarre and Aragon made with minced and marinated pork. It is fried or grilled.

SALCHICHA (called *botifarra* in Catalan) is a fresh, pure pork sausage. A curious sweet Catalan *botifarra dolça*, a pork sausage cured with sugar instead of salt and flavoured with cinnamon and grated lemon rind, is eaten as dessert with sweet fried or toasted bread. The Majorcan *botifarrón*, spiced with cinnamon, fennel seeds and black pepper, is pre-cooked and can be eaten as it is, with bread.

SALCHICHÓN is a salami-like sausage. The Catalan town Vic, north of Barcelona, once the venue of an important pig market, is the charcuterie capital of Spain and one of its specialities is *salchichón*. This sausage contains no *pimentón*, and is flavoured with just salt and pepper. One variety contains wine. Another speciality of Vic is a thin cured sausage called *fuet*.

MORCILLA is blood sausage (or black pudding) made with pigs' blood. In Burgos, Leon and Valladolid they mix in rice and onions. In Asturias, it is smoked and peppery. In Catalonia, it is called *botifarra negra*. When Catalans mix in rice and spices, they call it *botifarra negra d'arròs*. In Tolosa, they add minced leeks to the filling. In Leon, where the *morcilla* is smoked, breadcrumbs and onions are added. Other varieties include those made with pine nuts, and with flavourings such as nutmeg and black pepper or oregano and *pimentón*. A sweet *morcilla dulce* from La Rioja is flavoured with sugar, cinnamon, nutmeg, cloves, aniseed and black pepper. A special *morcilla* from Ronda in the province of Malaga is flavoured with cloves, oregano, cumin, coriander and black pepper.

SOBRASSADA, a speciality of Majorca, is a soft, sweetish, peppery, red, spreadable meat paste in a sausage skin – a mix of pork, creamy pork fat, salt and *pimentón*. There are some degraded commercial varieties but the good qualities are something to discover. The best is the *Sobrassada de Mallorca de Cerdo Negro*, made from the native black pigs with large floppy ears (they are not the Ibérico breed) that roam free and are fattened in their last three months on figs, pulses and barley.

CURED HAM
jamón

Pig-rearing in Spain is as old as antiquity. It was always part of the rural tradition, fulfilling for the peasantry the need for meat and providing flavour for otherwise bland food. The meat was dry-cured to last. Peasant families all over Spain kept at least one pig and lived off the ham and sausages it produced for an entire year. The hams were usually heavily salted to make sure that they did not spoil. The best ones were made in the mountain areas where a cold, dry climate was ideal for curing. The hams were hung to dry on rooftops and in attics with open windows to let in the air. In rainy regions, people dried them in their fireplaces, where they acquired a smoky flavour. In the nineteenth century, pork products were still seen as the food of the rural poor and lower classes. The upper classes found them 'indigestible'. It was during the civil war, when food was scarce, that they too came to appreciate them.

JAMÓN (dry-cured ham) is now the best-loved food and undisputed king of Spanish gastronomy. Consumption of cured ham and sausages has grown at a huge rate over the last two decades, triggering a rush of investment in modern production facilities and the latest technology that the European Union helped to fund. Domestic production grew into a huge industry and today Spain is the world's leading producer of dry-cured pork meat.

Two broad types of cured ham are made from different breeds of pigs. The most typical, representing the vast majority of all cured hams in Spain, is *jamón serrano* (*serrano* means 'from the *sierra*' or mountain range). It is produced from the meat of the European white (really pink) pig that is mostly cross-bred commercially. The other type of ham, called *jamón ibérico*, produced from the meat of the indigenous black Ibérico pig, amounts to only about 10 per cent of the total cured ham production. White pigs are quicker to fatten and more fertile, producing bigger litters than those of black pigs, which makes their hams cheaper.

JAMÓN SERRANO is produced all over Spain. Similar conditions to the mountainous *sierras* are created using technology that controls temperature, humidity and air flow in curing plants. Raw hams – the best are from the hind legs – are covered with a layer of humid coarse sea salt for about two weeks, during which time much of their moisture is drawn out and the meat acquires some saltiness. The salt is washed off and the hams are hung on racks to rest for a month. Then they are moved to a *secadero*, or drying room, where the temperature is gradually raised and the humidity lowered in a drying and ageing process that lasts about seven months, causing the fat to infiltrate the muscle and a distinctive flavour and aroma to develop. The hams are then transferred to the cooler *bodega* (cave) to mature for another two months. The best *serrano* hams come from Trevélez in the Sierra Nevada in Andalusia and from Teruel in Aragon.

JAMÓN IBÉRICO is produced from the Ibérico pig, which lives mostly in south-west Spain. It is descended from the Mediterranean wild boar and has a dark skin, long legs and a pointy snout. It is also known as *pata negra* ('black foot'). Ibérico pork products are protected by four official quality controls. One controls the breed of the pigs – there is 100 per cent pure Ibérico and a cross-breed with at least 75 per cent Ibérico. Three qualities are further graded according to the feed. The finest is *de bellota*, when the pigs are allowed to roam free in a *dehesa* or terroir of holm and cork oak tree woodlands to feed on acorns (*bellotas*). The next best quality, called *de recebo*, is produced from pigs that are pastured and fed on a mixture of grain and acorns. The third and least prestigious grade, variously called *de pienso*, *de cebo* or *de campo*, is from pigs fed entirely on grain.

The oak *dehesas* are protected natural parks mainly in the mountains of Andalusia and Extremadura and also in the province of Salamanca in Castile and Leon. Year-old pigs are taken there four months before slaughter, when the acorns start to fall from October on. Ibérico pigs know how to crack open the acorns, eat the inside and spit out the shell. During this time they put on a huge amount of weight and the fat infiltrates the muscles. The curing, ageing and maturing process of the hams is carried out according to centuries-old traditions with the help of the latest technology and takes more than two years. A particular flora forms on the hams that is supposed to add to their aroma.

JAMÓN IBÉRICO DE BELLOTA is the jewel in the crown of Spanish charcuterie and one of the great foods of the world. Place names such as Jabugo, Aracena, Cáceres, Badajoz, Huelva, Ciudad Real, Seville, Cordoba and Guijuelo are associated with the best hams. Believe me, *jamón ibérico de bellota* is irresistible – dark red, soft and silky, marbled with fat, with a deliciously sweet, barely salty lingering flavour and a beautiful aroma. Apparently, an added advantage of eating this ham is that the fat resulting from the acorn diet increases the ham's level of oleic acid, the unsaturated fat that lowers levels of 'bad' cholesterol and raises levels of 'good' cholesterol. It is the best ham I have ever eaten. On one occasion when I had the chance to eat as much as I liked I honestly could not stop eating it.

The ham is so good it must be eaten on its own accompanied only by bread and wine. It is at its best served at room temperature on a warmed plate. For carving, the entire ham is mounted horizontally on a wooden stand with the trotter held in a clamp. A long, thin, flexible knife is used to cut extra-thin bite-sized slices along the length of the leg.

Ibérico pigs have very small litters – the breeding, handling and curing are very labour-intensive and the process is seasonal. That is why the hams are so very expensive. Because whole hams last too long for today's small households and young people do not have the skill to slice them by hand, the majority of hams are sold boned and vacuum-packed, ready for slicing by machine, or packaged in slices. To experience the best qualities of texture, flavour and aroma of vacuum-packed slices, take them out of the refrigerator at least twenty minutes before you are ready to eat.

SPANISH WINES
vinos españoles

A winemaking revolution has turned the country with the greatest extent of land under vines in the world, which was known for producing cheap, undistinguished, anonymous wines to be sold in bulk, into the most promising and exciting country for quality wines. It surprised the world and it surprised Spain. Fifteen years ago, only sherry and Rioja wines were appreciated abroad and most Spaniards did not know much about wine. They only knew La Rioja and were used to drinking their own local rough, acid wines, and they used sherry for cooking. Small farmers made their own wine, usually in harsh conditions and in a primitive way. They dried grapes on their terraces or in their attics to make sweet wine, and distilled fermented grape skins and pips to make *aguardiente* (spirit). Large vineyards were owned by members of the aristocracy and by monasteries. In Franco's time, big *bodegas* (wineries) – some of them cooperatives run by the Church – bought grapes from peasant growers, whom they exploited, and produced oceans of cheap bulk wine for export. Today virtually every region of Spain makes wine with a distinctive character and many of them are astonishing. Asturias is the only region that does not make wine. Wine tourism is a growing industry and many areas promote wine routes with visits to wineries and vineyards. Spanish restaurants pride themselves on their wine lists. At a catering school I visited in Galicia, they also place great importance on training sommeliers.

I heard about what was happening in the wine trade mainly from three people who write about wine and food: Ana Lorente, editor of the magazine *Opus Vino*, Gaspar Rey, editor of the magazine *Cocina Futuro*, and Pepe Iglesias, author of *Comer con vino* ('Eating with Wine') among other works. Ana Lorente explained the phenomenon that has swept across the country over the last fifteen years as she drove my friend Alicia Ríos and I through the haunting Castilian landscape from Madrid to Segovia. As Spaniards became wealthy and discriminating in their tastes and when domestic and foreign demand for quality wines increased, it became worthwhile for wineries to invest and make a huge effort to achieve high standards. The official *Denominación de Origen* (DO) classification that aims to guarantee quality was a spur that rewarded their achievements and the European Union helped with subsidies.

There is enormous enthusiasm and competitive vitality in the trade. Old *bodegas* adopted state-of-the-art technology and sophisticated practices with the help of oenologists who learnt from French and New World winemakers. At first they started growing fashionable foreign grape varieties such as Syrah, Cabernet Sauvignon, Merlot and Chardonnay, and tried to emulate French styles. Then they went back to their native grapes – Tempranillo, Verdejo, Graciano, Monastrell, Garnacha, Prieto Picudo and many others – and focused on improving viticulture, from making the most of their *terruño* (land) and irrigating it, to training and pruning the vines and deciding when best to harvest. In Spain, there are hundreds of different native grape varieties and vines carpet many different terrains with different soils and climatic conditions: on the Mediterranean coast, on the Atlantic coast, on mountainsides and in river valleys, on vast dry plains and on volcanic islands. It is not surprising, then, that Spain has possibly the widest range of distinctive wines in the world. Most winemakers blend varieties and some include foreign grapes to achieve a characteristic colour, flavour and aroma, alcohol content and ageing properties. There are now seventy Spanish wines with a *Denominación de Origen* quality classification and fifty-five with the *Vinos de la Tierra* geographical classification. Some of these wines are mentioned in the chapters on the regions.

There are stars and heroes in the Spanish wine trade, pioneers who started the revolution twenty-five years ago and entrepreneurs who continue to create and improve. Previously little-known areas have produced superstar wines. A few wineries are rated as extraordinary. The map of Spanish wine changes so fast that wine writers find it hard to keep up with the ever-growing number of emerging wines. There is a lot to choose from in both cheaper everyday wines and the more expensive aged *reservas* and *gran reservas*. You will have to try what you find available in shops in Britain. In choosing wine to accompany a meal it is usual to start with a dry white and to continue with reds from the youngest to the oldest, from the lightest to the strongest.

KITCHEN UTENSILS
utensilios de cocina

In Spain, people kept their cooking utensils to pass on to their children, and in some families they still do. Migrating gypsies used to travel around the country sharpening knives, repairing pots and pans, making baskets. They would bang out a tune on a frying pan to announce their yearly arrival. There is a *Fiesta de Caldereros* ('Tinkers' Festival') that takes place in Tolosa in the Basque Country every February and commemorates the tradition with a re-enactment in gypsy dress. I love seeing Spaniards crushing garlic with a pinch of salt using a traditional pestle and mortar, grating tomatoes or passing sauces through a conical food mill and cooking in their clay dishes. But at home I have my own way of performing those tasks. Traditional Spanish utensils are good to use and look beautiful on the table, but you do not have to use them to cook any of the dishes in this book, except perhaps if you want to make a large *paella*.

The *PAELLA* PAN, the large, shallow, two-handled pan with slanting sides, is sold in many sizes. The wide and shallow shape allows for even evaporation of the liquid when cooking a *paella* and ensures that the different ingredients do not all disappear, buried in the rice. Huge *paella* pans can be bought for cooking outdoors over a wood fire or a large gas ring set on a tripod over a butane gas bottle. A heavier pan distributes the heat more evenly on a small domestic hob. According to my friend Lourdes March (see page 260), a specialist in rice and *paella*, the pan is often wrongly called a *paellera*.

The *CAZUELA* is a shallow, fired-clay dish with a glazed interior. It can be used in the oven and over direct heat on a gas burner (a few good brands can also be used on an electric hob). It distributes and retains heat well. A *cazuela* should last for a few years if treated properly. It might crack eventually but is but is cheap to replace. This is what you must do before you use it for the first time: soak it in water for at least 6 hours, then dry it and fill it almost entirely with water and bring it slowly to the boil over a low heat. Let the water simmer very gently until it has almost disappeared. When cooking on the hob, it is important to always start over a low heat and to turn the heat up gradually when the rim begins to feel warm. Very high heat is not advisable. You can make soups, stews, braises and rice dishes in a *cazuela*. *Cocottes* are clay dishes with straight sides and a lid. They are used like a casserole in the oven.

An *OLLA* is a tall metal stewing pot with a lid and curved sides. There are some made from clay. The *PUCHERO* is a cylindrical metal pot with a lid. Traditional stews are called *olla* and *puchero* after these pots, because the dishes would always originally have been made in them.

A *MORTERO* is a mortar with a pestle. The traditional Spanish mortar is made of heavy porcelain and has a beautiful yellow glaze. A marble one is equally good. They are much used in Spain for crushing garlic and parsley, almonds and fried bread, and to make sauces such as *alioli* and *romesco* (pages 149 and 152). Large wooden ones called *DORNILLOS* were used in Andalusia to make *gazpacho* out in the fields. A blender or the food processor, and an electric mixer, can do most of the same jobs very well.

A *PLANCHA* is a heavy metal two-handled flat griddle pan for grilling. It can also be a flat top plate that is part of the stove.

A *CHINO*, what we call a chinois, is a conical sieve with a wooden pestle used for straining sauces. Today in Spain it is more common to reduce sauces to a smooth cream by using an electric hand blender straight in the saucepan.

A SALAMANDER is a heavy metal disc mounted on a long handle. It is heated over a flame and used to caramelize the top of *crema catalana* and other desserts. A MINI BLOWTORCH is now widely available and as effective as a salamander.

BASIC TECHNIQUES

to CLEAN *and* COOK CLAMS *or* MUSSELS

Discard any clams or mussels that are chipped or broken, and those that feel too heavy or too light. Throw away any open ones that do not close when they are tapped on the sink or dipped in ice-cold water – this means that they are dead. They should be tightly closed. Store them in a cool place, such as the refrigerator, where they can breathe. Clam farms clean the clams through a process that scrubs and washes them but you will still need to wash them and maybe scrub them with a stiff brush in a bowl of cold water. Pull the beards off the mussels. Some sand will remain inside. After scrubbing and rinsing the shellfish, leave them for 20 minutes in fresh cold water – as they breathe they will push the sand out of their shells. Then lift them out and rinse in one or two more changes of water.

To steam the clams or mussels open, put them in a large pan with just a finger's depth of water over a high heat, and then put the lid on. Remove the pan from the heat as soon as the shellfish open (it will take about 2 to 5 minutes) – this means they are cooked. Discard any that remain closed.

Alternatively you can cook clams or mussels on a flat griddle over a high heat – they take about the same time to cook.

to CLEAN *and* PREPARE SQUID

Pull the head of each squid away from the body pouch and discard the soft innards that come out with it. Discard the insides of the pouch – the ink bag, if any, the icicle-shaped translucent cuttlebone and any soft innards. Keep the tentacles in their bunches but remove the eyes and the beak (the small round cartilage at the base of the tentacles) by cutting with a sharp knife just below the eyes – be careful that ink doesn't squirt out at you from the eyes. Rinse thoroughly.

to ROAST *and* PEEL PEPPERS

Choose fleshy round or elongated peppers. Put them on a sheet of foil on an oven tray and roast them in an oven preheated to 190°C/gas 5 for 30 to 45 minutes, until they feel soft when you press them and their skins blister and begin to blacken. Turn them over once.

Alternatively cook them under the grill, about 9cm from the grill, or on the barbecue, turning until their skins are blistered and charred all over. This will take much less time than in the oven.

Put the roasted peppers immediately in a strong plastic bag and twist it closed, or put them in a pan with a tight-fitting lid. Leave for 10 to 15 minutes to steam. This helps to loosen the skins further. When the peppers are cool enough to handle, peel them and remove the stems and seeds. Keep the juices that come out, straining to remove the seeds, as these can be used as part of a dressing.

NOTE: You can buy good-quality *piquillo* peppers in tins or jars to use as an alternative to roasted peppers in many recipes.

to USE DRIED *ÑORA* PEPPERS

There are several ways of preparing these sweet dried peppers for cooking. The old traditional way (before blenders came in) is to pour boiling water over the peppers in a little bowl and leave them to soak for 30 minutes, then cut them open, discard the stems and seeds and scrape the softened flesh from the skin with a spoon.

You can also simmer the peppers in a pan with just enough water to cover for 10 minutes then leave them to cool for 30 minutes. Remove the stems and seeds and blend them with the skin to a paste in the food processor.

Alternatively, simply remove the stems and deseed the *ñoras*, then fry them in a little oil.

ALTERNATIVES

- If you cannot get hold of *ñora* peppers, you can use *pimentón dulce* or sweet paprika, as it is *ñoras*, or other similarly sweet dried peppers, that are used to make sweet *pimentón dulce*.
- The thick red *choricero* paste sold in jars, made from the soaked pulp of dried *choricero* peppers, can also be used.

to MAKE FRESH BREADCRUMBS

Fresh breadcrumbs are used to make stuffings and meatballs. Use a loaf of dense country-style white bread, a day old or older. Slice off the crusts and cut the bread into thick slices, then into pieces. Turn the bread pieces into crumbs by pulsing them in the food processor. The breadcrumbs will keep for a couple of weeks in a plastic bag in the refrigerator.

to PREPARE SMALL ARTICHOKE HEARTS

With a small, sharp knife cut off the stalk and cut away or pull off the tough outer leaves, until you are left with pale inner leaves. Slice off the tough ends of these and open them out with your fingers, scoop out the prickly inner choke with a pointed spoon and discard it. Drop the artichokes into a bowl of water acidulated with 2 or 3 tablespoons of lemon juice or vinegar to prevent the exposed parts from darkening.

to PREPARE ARTICHOKE BOTTOMS

You need to use medium or large globe artichokes. Cut off the stalk at the base. Pull off the outer leaves and trim the base, cutting around it spirally to remove all the leaves. Scrape away and discard the chokes and drop the artichokes into a bowl of water acidulated with lemon juice or vinegar as you go.

to CHOP *or* CRUSH GARLIC

The flavour of garlic varies depending on how it is prepared – raw, fried, roasted or stewed. Many recipes in this book call for chopped or crushed garlic. In Spain, they crush garlic to a paste using a pestle and mortar. In most cases, though, when you are going to fry it to make a sauce, it is equally good to finely chop or crush the garlic.

To peel and chop garlic cloves, cut off the root ends, lay them on a board, place the flat blade of a large knife on top and carefully thump it with your fist. The papery skin will come away more easily. Chop the garlic cloves with an up-and-down movement, holding the tip of the knife against the board.

There are three good ways to crush garlic:

This is the Spanish way. Put peeled cloves in a mortar (preferably a porcelain one) with a pinch of coarse salt – this helps to achieve a smooth texture. Using the pestle, first pound then crush and mash the garlic to a creamy purée with a rotating movement.

Place your peeled cloves on a wooden board and chop them roughly using a large knife with a wide blade. Sprinkle on a pinch of coarse salt and proceed to crush the garlic with the flat blade of the knife held at a 45-degree angle, pressing down with force to squash it. Continue to crush the garlic with a back-and-forth movement until you have a purée to your liking. This method is favoured by chefs but leaves a lot of the flavourful juices on the chopping board.

Crush the peeled cloves through a garlic press. I know that some people are opposed to presses but there is nothing wrong with using one that works well. I still use the same press that I bought in Paris when I was a fifteen-year-old boarder in a *lycée* – I was sometimes invited to the homes of day girls and they all had garlic presses in their kitchens.

to PEEL *or* GRATE TOMATOES

In Jaén, in Andalusia, my friend Manolo peels tomatoes with a knife or turns them briefly under the grill, then pulls off the skin. In Catalonia, if people want peeled and finely chopped tomatoes for a sauce they grate them. They cut the tomatoes in half and grate the flesh through the large holes of a vegetable grater until they get to the skin, holding on to the skin to keep it intact before discarding it. This way the tomatoes are already very finely chopped.

Here is how I peel tomatoes. I pierce them with the point of a knife in two or three places, put them in a bowl and then pour on enough boiling water to cover them entirely. I leave the tomatoes soaking in the water for 3 to 4 minutes, until I can see the skin crack where I had pierced it. Then I quickly drain them and pull off the skin when they are cool enough to handle.

APPETIZERS AND TAPAS

aperitivos y tapas

One of the pleasures of life in Spain is the *tapas* tradition of visiting bars before lunch or dinner to meet friends over a glass of wine, beer, sherry or cider, accompanied by little plates of food. You go to meet, to chat and to have fun. My friend Alicia Ríos remembers a time, not long ago, when Spanish women would hurry back home after the church service on a Sunday morning to prepare lunch while the men got together at the local bars, waiting for the meal to be ready. Now the women go along for a drink too.

Some large cities like Seville, San Sebastian, Barcelona and Madrid have *tapas* zones – streets packed with *tabernas* (taverns), also known as *tascas*, where you eat and drink standing up, and bars and *cervecerías* (beer houses) where you can sit down – where it is usual to go on a *tapeo*, or *tapas* crawl, from one bar to another. The bars get so full that patrons spill out on to the street. In Basque cities the tradition of moving from bar to bar with friends is called the *poteo*, named after *potes*, the heavy wine glasses once used in the area, or *txikiteo*, after the coin that once represented the price of a glass of wine.

Tapas originated in Andalusia, and Seville is where the custom is said to have begun and where today a few little portions of food often replace a meal. The word *tapa* means 'cover' or 'lid'. It is said to have referred in early days to the pieces of ham or cheese that were laid across the narrow sherry glasses, called *cañas* by innkeepers, and handed to stagecoach drivers to keep them sober and, apparently, to keep insects out of the drink. The salty titbits also kept clients thirsty.

The world of *tapas* is complex. The simplest are *tentempiés* – nibbles such as olives, fried almonds, fried peppers *de Padrón*, bits of cheese, slices of *jamón* (ham), sausages. Standard *tapas* are potato omelettes cut into little squares, croquettes, baby eels sizzling with garlic, fried squid, prawns fried with garlic and parsley, small deep-fried fish, grilled blood sausage, *chorizo* cooked in wine or cider, boiled octopus with potatoes, meatballs in a sauce, mushrooms with garlic, oxtail stew, chickpea and bean stews, *empanadillas* (little pies). Some bars specialize in certain kinds of foods and every region has its own particular delicacies – in the north it is seafood, on the Mediterranean coast it is vegetables, in the south it is deep-fried fish.

Raciones are larger portions that are meant to be shared. *Cazuelas* are stews and foods with a sauce that are served in the small earthenware dishes that give them their name. In the north of Spain, *pinchos* are bite-sized offerings on toothpicks. When the toothpicks are wrapped in coloured paper like the barbed batons used in bullfights they are called *banderillas*. *Montaditos* are canapés on toast or in tartlets. Some bars in San Sebastian and Bilbao offer modern, creative upscale *pinchos* (*pintxos* in Basque) such as tartlets of foie gras with sautéed apple and Calvados, fried Moroccan *brik* (little savoury parcels wrapped in paper-thin pastry), and blood sausage *caramelos* wrapped like bonbons in filo pastry. It is usual for *pinchos* to be displayed on the bar counter for people to help themselves.

Tapas belong to the world of bars and taverns. At home people do not serve *tapas*. They offer *aperitivos* before a meal, food that you do not need to cook. In the past, during long formal meals at home and also in grand restaurants, platters of cured ham, sausage, olives and other bits of food were left on the table for people to nibble at between courses. The usual appetizers offered today with drinks before a meal, apart from bread with tomato (page 132), which is de rigueur in Catalonia and Majorca, are platters of charcuterie with bread. An alternative is a platter of preserved fish and seafood or a few cheeses. There can also be olives, fried salted almonds and pickled vegetables in brine or in olive oil.

It has become fashionable in some circles in Britain to entertain casually with four or five cooked dishes laid out like *tapas* on the table at the same time for guests to pick at. You will find inspiration for these throughout the book. But if you want to follow the Spanish way of serving appetizers, there are some ideas to try out on pages 127, 128 and 129.

SUGGESTIONS *for* CANAPÉS *for a* DRINKS PARTY

Some *tapas* bars specialize in bite-sized finger foods – *pinchos* and *montaditos*. Quimet I Quimet, a little bar *bodega* in Barcelona known as the culinary king of tinned foods, serves enchanting combinations of preserved products on small pieces of toasted brioche-type bread and little tartlet cases: mussels with caviar on a bed of tomato confit; anchovies, capers and chopped cornichons on olive paste; Manchego cheese with fig paste. Make up your own marriages of little delicacies and embellish them with a blob of mayonnaise, olive paste or *salsa verde* (page 223), or a trickle of extra virgin olive oil and a sprinkling of chopped parsley.

a PLATTER *of* COLD CHARCUTERIE

Choose two or more of the following. Serve the meats at room temperature, so take them out of the refrigerator about 20 minutes before they are to be eaten. Serve them with a sliced baguette, or other good crusty or country bread. For more information about the cured hams see pages 111–12; for more information about Spanish sausages see page 110.

JAMÓN SERRANO means ham from the mountains (*sierra*), where the climate is dry, cool and breezy enough to air-cure it.

JAMÓN IBÉRICO is dry-cured ham from the native Iberian black pig. The quality *de bellota* is the best in the world, with a fabulous taste and aroma and a soft, silky texture. It is also extremely expensive.

LOMO is dry-cured pork loin trimmed of fat and marinated in a paste of garlic, *pimentón* (Spanish paprika), oregano and olive oil, encased in a sausage skin.

CHORIZO is a brownish-red cured sausage flavoured with garlic and *pimentón*. There are infinite regional variations: thin and fat, sweet and spicy, coarse and smooth-textured, air-dried and smoked. (There are some *chorizos* that are semi-cured and need to be cooked – more about how to use them later.)

SALCHICHÓN is a hard salami-type sausage. The best is produced around the Catalan town of Vic, made simply with salt and pepper. Another type is made with wine and there is one made with local black truffles. *Fuet* from Vic is a thin *salchichón*.

SOBRASSADA, a speciality of Majorca, is a very soft red paste of pork and fat, flavoured with garlic and *pimentón*, in a sausage skin. It can be spread on a slice of dense bread and is good accompanied by *membrillo* (quince paste) or *fruta confitada* (crystallized fruit), or by sliced figs or grapes. Good *sobrassada* is delicious, but I have tried some that are not worth eating.

CECINA, salt-cured beef with lacy fat, has a strong meaty flavour. It should be sliced paper-thin. Once the food of the rural poor made from the cattle, goats, horses and mules that had died on the farm, it is now a great delicacy, produced exclusively from quality beef.

A PLATTER *of* SEAFOOD *from* TINS *or* JARS, *or* CURED SEAFOOD

Choose two or more of the following.

Serve SCALLOPS (*vieiras*), MUSSELS (*mejillones*), CLAMS (*almejas*) and COCKLES (*berberechos*) with a dribble of extra virgin olive oil, and, if you like, a drop of vinegar.

BOQUERONES are white anchovies marinated in vinegar and packed in olive oil.

TUNA (*atún*), ANCHOVY FILLETS (*anchoas*), MACKEREL (*caballas*) and SARDINES (*sardinas*) come in tins and jars in olive oil.

BABY ELVERS (*angulas*), PRAWNS (*gambas*) and BABY SQUID (*chipirones*) are best served warm. Heat a generous amount of olive oil. When it is sizzling, add crushed garlic and the elvers, prawns or baby squid and quickly heat through, turning them over once. If you like, add chopped flat-leaf parsley and serve sizzling hot.

OCTOPUS (*pulpo*) can be served with a dribble of extra virgin olive oil and a dusting of sweet or spicy *pimentón* or paprika.

MOJAMA is the salt-cured and dried loin of tuna. Cut it into thin slices and serve it with a dribble of extra virgin olive oil. Accompany with chopped tomatoes.

The salt-cured, pressed and dried ROES OF GREY MULLET (*huevas de mújol*) or of TUNA (*huevas de atún*) are served very thinly sliced on bread or toast with a dribble of extra virgin olive oil and perhaps a drop of lemon juice. In Britain we call it botargo and it is very expensive.

OTHER PRESERVED SPANISH DELICACIES *in* TINS *and* JARS

SNAILS (*caracoles*) are best served sizzling hot in olive oil with crushed garlic and finely chopped flat-leaf parsley.

There are many kinds of Spanish OLIVES (see page 98).

CAPER BUDS (*alcaparras*) and CAPERBERRIES (*alcaparrones*): those preserved in brine need to be washed, those preserved in salt must be soaked in water for more than 1 hour and the water needs to be changed three times.

PIQUILLO PEPPERS (*pimientos del piquillo*) – roasted and peeled small, pointy red peppers – are good cut into ribbons and mixed with chopped anchovy fillets, or stuffed with crab meat or tuna mashed with olive oil and lemon juice.

The fat, soft, WHITE ASPARAGUS (*espárragos blancos*) from Navarre are delicious with mayonnaise. They are white because they are made to grow covered by soil.

The small, green, mildly spicy *IBARRAKO PIPARRAK* CHILLIES (also called *guindillas de Ibarra*) come from Ibarra in the Basque Country.

BABY ARTICHOKES (*alcachofas*), WILD MUSHROOMS (*setas*), CARDOON STEMS (*cardos*), BORAGE STEMS (*borrajas*), CHARD (*acelgas*), GREEN GARLIC SHOOTS (*ajetes*), WHITE HARICOT BEANS (*alubias*) and BABY BROAD BEANS (*habitas*) – all these need only a dribble of olive oil and a little salt or a *vinagreta* (page 146).

COOKED *MORCILLA and CHORIZOS*

Morcilla and chorizos are made in every region of Spain (see page 110).

MORCILLA is blood sausage, also called black pudding, a sausage made with pig's blood. You must buy a Spanish one as others are quite different. Cut it into good slices and pan-fry the slices in olive oil, or grill them, for about 3 minutes on each side until crisp. Accompany them, if you like, with apple slices sautéed in butter or olive oil. In the north of Spain morcilla is often accompanied with apples.

CHORIZOS that are semi-cured and need to be cooked can simply be cut into pieces and fried in just a drop of oil since they release their own fat. They can be cooked whole or cut in slices in a pan of red or white wine, sherry or cider for about 20 to 30 minutes. They can also be wrapped in foil with wine or cider and baked in the oven. Another way is to grill the *chorizos*, then pour brandy or rum over them and set the liquor alight. It is called *chorizo al infierno* (literally meaning 'hell'). *Chistorra*, a long *chorizo*-type sausage from Navarre and the Basque Country, is grilled or fried or cooked in wine or cider.

CATALAN TOMATO BREAD
✻ *pan con tomate*

In Catalonia I was offered bread rubbed with tomato – it is *pa amb tomàquet* in Catalan – at all times of the day, and especially for breakfast and before a meal. The orthodox method is to rub the bread on both sides with tomato but I always got bread rubbed on one side only, which seems the best way as then you do not need a knife and fork and you can pick it up with your hands.

PER PERSON

✻ 2 thick slices of good country-style bread ✻ 1 large tasty ripe tomato
✻ mild extra virgin olive oil ✻ salt

Toast the bread lightly. Cut the tomato in half and rub one side of each slice with the cut side of a tomato half so that the toast has well imbibed the juices. Drizzle a little olive oil on top and sprinkle with a little salt to taste.

VARIATIONS

▓ *Pan con tomate* can serve as the base for slices of raw cured ham, slices of sausage, Pyrenean cheese, preserved anchovies or sardines.

▓ A Majorcan version called *pamboli amb tomàtiga* is topped with black olives and capers.

▓ An Andalusian variant is to blend tomatoes to a cream in the food processor and spread this thickly on toasted bread. You can blend the tomatoes without peeling, although locals will tell you not to.

SWEET ROASTED TOMATOES ❋ *tomate confitado*

These tomatoes have a deliciously intense flavour. Serve them hot or cold as an accompaniment to meat or fish. It is best to use plum tomatoes. Although they take a long time to cook, you can prepare the tomatoes in advance, even days before, as they keep well in the refrigerator.

SERVES 6–8

❋ 12 ripe but firm tomatoes ❋ olive oil ❋ 3 tablespoons sugar ❋ salt and pepper

Cut the tomatoes in half through their stem end and remove any hard green bits. Place a piece of foil on a baking sheet and brush it with olive oil. Arrange the tomatoes on the foil, cut side up. Sprinkle each with sugar, salt and pepper and a little dribble of olive oil. Cook in an oven preheated to 130°C/gas 1 for 3½ to 4 hours until shrivelled and shrunken.

ROASTED RED PEPPERS *with* ANCHOVIES
❋ *pimientos con anchoas*

Besides grapes, La Rioja is known for the vegetables that grow in the fertile plain of the Ebro river valley. The local red peppers (*pimientos riojanos*) have an intense colour and flavour. Their sweetness is brought out by the saltiness of the anchovies in this popular *tapa* that is served in the local wineries.

SERVES 6

❋ 5 round or elongated red peppers ❋ salt ❋ 3 tablespoons extra virgin olive oil
❋ 12 thin anchovy fillets or 6 fat ones, preserved in oil, cut in half lengthways

Place the peppers on a sheet of foil on a baking tray and roast in an oven preheated to 190°C/gas 5 for about 30 to 45 minutes, turning them over halfway through. Cook until they are soft and the skins slightly blackened in parts.

To peel the peppers more easily, put them in a couple of strong plastic bags and twist to seal. Leave for 10 to 15 minutes then, when cool enough to handle, peel and deseed the peppers, and cut each in half. Slice each half into 8 strips. Spread them on a flat serving plate, sprinkle with salt and the olive oil, and arrange the anchovies on top.

SALT COD FRITTERS
❋ buñuelos de bacalao

I have tried several versions of these fritters, some with a batter of flour and water or flour and milk, some just with potatoes and egg. These ones are fluffy and slightly moist. You may be able to buy *bacalao* (salt cod) desalted and vacuum-packed, or frozen. If this is not available, you can make the *buñuelos* with fresh cod fillet. See how to achieve something of the flavour of salt cod on page 348.

MAKES 24 SMALL FRITTERS

Boil the potatoes until soft, then drain and mash them.

Remove any skin and bones from the desalted salt cod and poach it for 2 minutes, then drain and, when cool enough to handle, shred it finely with your fingers. If you are using fresh cod simply poach it for 3 minutes or until it just begins to flake.

Mix the fish and potatoes in a bowl and add salt and pepper. Even salt cod might need some seasoning if it has been desalted excessively. Add the eggs, garlic, flour, baking powder or bicarbonate of soda, beer and parsley, and beat very well. Leave the creamy paste to rest for about 2 hours covered in the refrigerator.

Pour the oil into a wide frying pan until it is about 1.25cm deep. Heat until it sizzles when you drop in a small piece of bread and the bread does not brown too quickly. Take small portions of the mixture – about 2 tablespoonfuls' worth – and shape them into little cakes. Drop them into the oil and cook over a medium heat until the fritters are golden, turning them over once. Drain on kitchen paper.

❋ 1–2 floury potatoes (about 300g), peeled and quartered

❋ 250g desalted salt cod (see page 348) or fresh cod fillet

❋ salt and pepper

❋ 2 large eggs, lightly beaten

❋ 2 garlic cloves, peeled and crushed

❋ 2 tablespoons plain flour

❋ ½ teaspoon baking powder or bicarbonate of soda

❋ 4–5 tablespoons beer

❋ 2 tablespoons finely chopped flat-leaf parsley

❋ olive or sunflower oil for deep-frying

FRIED GOAT'S CHEESE *with* HONEY
❋ *queso de cabra frito con miel*

The combination of a slightly salty goat's cheese with fragrant honey is surprising and exquisite. I tasted it in Andalusia but it is also made elsewhere. Use a hard goat's cheese.

SERVES 4

Put a good layer of matzo meal on a plate. Turn the slices of goat's cheese in the egg yolks and use your fingers to cover them well with the yolks, being careful not to break them. Lay the cheese on top of the matzo meal and sprinkle with more matzo meal so that the slices are well covered.

Fry the cheese slices in medium-hot oil in a non-stick frying pan for 1 to 2 minutes on each side, turning them over very carefully with a spatula, until golden on both sides. Lift them out and serve immediately. Pass the honey round for people to help themselves to 1 heaped teaspoonful or so.

- ❋ about 75g fine matzo meal, for dredging
- ❋ 4 slices (about 200g) of hard goat's cheese about 1cm thick
- ❋ 2 large egg yolks, lightly beaten
- ❋ 2 tablespoons olive oil, for frying
- ❋ a pot of orange-blossom or other fragrant clear honey, to pass round

angelita garcía de paredes barreda

My ham croquettes kept failing – they burst and fell apart during the frying. Alicia Ríos told me her sister-in-law Angelita's *croquetas* always turned out well. I called her and she explained her recipe over the phone. It worked perfectly. Then I went to see her in Seville. Angelita García de Paredes Barreda is an eighty-four-year-old Franciscan missionary nun who, for many years, worked in different cities of the United States, helping out poor immigrants from South America, Puerto Rico and Cuba. She also spent time with an Indian tribe in Mexico. She stopped wearing a habit when she realized that people opened up to her more when she wore ordinary clothes. She is from an illustrious military family. Her ancestor Diego García de Paredes, from Trujillo in Extremadura, was a noble and daring officer who fought for the Castilian kings in Granada, Flanders and Italy in the late fifteenth and early sixteenth century. His son, also Diego García de Paredes, founded the city of Trujillo, a provincial capital in Venezuela, where he became the viceroy.

Angelita is one of ten children. Her father was a colonel in the Spanish army. Her grandmother was educated at the Irish Sisters of Loreto's Institute of the Virgin Mary in Gibraltar, where the bishop was a relative. The Irish order went on to open schools in Spain, where it was known as Las Irlandesas. Angelita and her twin sister attended first their day school and later went to their boarding school in Castilleja de la Cuesta, a small town in the province of Seville. When the girls had finished school, an English tutor, Miss Carol, a governess for the González Byass sherry family, used to come to the house every day for English conversation classes with them. Many of the Jerez elite had an English education. Some were descended from families who came from England in the eighteenth and nineteenth centuries. These families introduced the custom of tea with toast and biscuits and some English dishes.

Angelita showed me around Seville and its great cathedral, which is the largest Gothic cathedral in the world. We stopped at the little chapel that holds the sepulchre of her father's ancestors, the Jácomes, who

were a prominent family (Jewish converts to Christianity). Angelita's community of retired Franciscan nuns lives very frugally. She loves to cook and when it is her turn she manages to prepare inexpensive but exquisite meals – I know they are delicious because she described them to me. But the huge pile of recipes she gave me – some handwritten, some typed – reflects the grand style of her family as well as their Italian connection (her great-grandmother's family, on her mother's side, was from Rappallo and Ravena in Italy).

Angelita is highly educated and intellectual, she speaks four languages and is very sociable and cheerful. She joined me and some friends in *tapas* bars and restaurants and walked with us in the early hours of the morning through the city. The following is one of her recipes.

HAM CROQUETTES
❖ croquetas de jamón

Different types of croquettes – filled with ham, chicken, salt cod or even cheese – are served in every bar and restaurant in Spain. The one with ham is the *reina de las croquetas* (the 'queen of croquettes'). I have tried many different recipes that were very elaborate and difficult. This one is extremely simple and works perfectly well. It is creamy inside with a good strong flavour. Angelita García de Paredes, a Franciscan missionary nun in a convent in Seville (see page 138), gave me the recipe. She makes the béchamel in a particular way. It is much thicker than usual. When cold it firms up quite a bit, making it easier to roll, and when it is fried it becomes creamy inside with a thick, crisp crust. You can prepare the croquettes ready for frying the day before and keep them in the refrigerator.

MAKES ABOUT 30 *CROQUETAS*

❋ 75g unsalted butter ❋ ½ a large onion, peeled and finely chopped
❋ 200g *jamón serrano* or other raw dry-cured ham, finely chopped (this can be done in the food processor) ❋ a pinch of freshly grated nutmeg ❋ 725ml whole milk ❋ 150g plain flour
❋ salt, if necessary ❋ about 100g fine matzo meal or breadcrumbs ❋ about 125g medium matzo meal or breadcrumbs ❋ 2 large eggs ❋ sunflower or olive oil for deep-frying,
enough to cover the *croquetas*

In a large pan, melt the butter and gently sauté the onion over a low heat until it is soft. Add the ham and cook, stirring for a minute or so. Then stir in the nutmeg and about half the milk and bring to the boil.

Beat the flour with the remaining milk using an electric mixer until any lumps have disappeared. Then pour into the pan, stirring vigorously, and cook, continuing to stir constantly, for 8 to 10 minutes until the mixture has the consistency of a thick paste that comes away from the bottom of the pan. Add salt if necessary – it might not need it because the ham is salty. Chill for at least 2 hours or overnight.

» » »

To make the *croquetas*, cover a large plate with plenty of very fine matzo meal or breadcrumbs and a second plate with medium matzo meal or breadcrumbs. Beat the eggs lightly in a soup plate.

Two large spoons greased with oil are normally used to shape the *croquetas* into an oblong. Angelita uses a piping bag to squeeze out tubular pieces. But you may find it easier, as I do, to take lumps of the thick béchamel paste the size of walnuts and roll them into balls between the palms of your hands. You can rub your hands in oil if you do not want the paste to stick. As you make them, drop the balls into the fine matzo meal or breadcrumbs. Roll a batch of the balls in the fine meal until well covered all over, then roll them in the beaten egg, and then in the medium matzo meal. This will give them a nice thick crust.

To deep-fry the balls in batches in a frying pan, heat the oil until it is only medium hot (until a piece of bread dropped in sizzles immediately but does not turn dark quickly). Carefully lower the *croquetas* into the oil and fry over a medium-low heat for 5 to 6 minutes until lightly browned, turning them over once. If the oil is too hot they will burst. Lift them out with a slotted spoon and drain on kitchen paper. They are best eaten right away.

NOTE: The *croquetas* will keep for several days in the refrigerator and are good reheated – warm in the oven at 160°C/gas 3 for 15 minutes. They can also be frozen after rolling in the matzo meal and need to be defrosted before frying.

VARIATION

For *croquetas de bacalao* with salt cod, or for *croquetas* with fresh cod, boil about 200g desalted salt cod (see page 348) or fresh cod fillets in water or milk for 3 to 5 minutes, or until the flesh begins to flake when you cut it, then drain. When cool enough to handle, remove any skin or bones and shred the fish with your fingers, then mix into the hot béchamel instead of the ham. Add salt to taste and a pinch of nutmeg and proceed as above. These *croquetas* are traditionally shaped as an oblong or oval. See page 348 for how to get something of the flavour of salt cod using fresh cod.

STOCKS, SAUCES AND DRESSINGS

caldos, salsas y aliños

W ithin Spain, Catalonia and the rest of the Mediterranean coast is considered the 'zone of the sauces'. This part of Spain is known for cold sauces and dressings that make fabulous accompaniments to all kinds of dishes, especially meats, fish and cooked vegetables. With their subtle or strong flavours and soft or bright colours, they lift the simple grilled or poached foods people like to eat in the summer, and create an exciting spectacle for the table when they are passed around in little bowls.

Leaf salads are simply dressed with extra virgin olive oil and lemon juice or vinegar but other more substantial salads are dressed with *vinagretas* (vinaigrettes), usually embellished with tiny bits of chopped ingredients, such as tomatoes, herbs, capers, olives and onions, or hard-boiled eggs. Spanish *vinagretas* are usually less vinegary than the vinaigrettes of France. Spain now produces a wide variety of superb-quality extra virgin olive oils (see page 96–7) and wine and cider vinegars (see page 99) that are well worth discovering.

The people of the island of Minorca claim that mayonnaise was born there in the port town of Mahón and that the original name was *mahonesa* (still an alternative name for mayonnaise in Spain). Their story is that it was adopted by the French after the Duc de Richelieu took the city from the English in 1756. The recipe had already appeared in the fourteenth-century *Llibre de Sent Soví* (see page 82) as *ajada*. The sauce has a huge importance in the cooking of Mediterranean Spain, where it appears in many guises and accompanies many dishes.

Catalonia's iconic nut sauce, *romesco*, named after the pepper that is used to make it, was born in Tarragona at the end of the nineteenth-century, when it was called *salsa vermella* ('red sauce') – it is an orangey-red colour from tomatoes and red peppers. The Canary Islands, in the Atlantic Ocean off the coast of Morocco, have a range of splendid sauces, many of them based on garlic, herbs, peppers and olive oil, which they call *mojos*. In Catalonia and northern Spain, people make their own Spanish versions of béchamel sauce, some of which you will find within the recipes of this book, such as in ham croquettes (page 140), aubergine with béchamel and cheese (page 257) and fish and seafood in a saffron béchamel (page 344). The most symbolic Spanish sauce, though, is the fresh tomato sauce that became the signature tune of Mediterranean cooking.

STOCKS
caldos

Nowadays in Spain people buy ready-made meat, chicken and fish stocks. We too can buy good stocks and it is fine to use them as a base. Stock cubes can also be used to strengthen flavours. I have seen boxes of these kept under kitchen tables for use in Spanish restaurants. But a good home-made stock is still worth making if you have the time.

FISH STOCK
❖ *caldo de pescado*

It is not easy for us to find the types of rock fish here that give fish stocks their fabulous flavour in Spain, but we can still make an acceptable one. Use only the bones and heads of fresh white fish – fishmongers give them away. Do not use oily or blue fish such as salmon, sardines and tuna, as they give the stock an unpleasant taste. The best results I have had were with crustacean shells – prawn, lobster or crab shells – and best of all making stock with tiny whole prawns.

MAKES ABOUT 1.25 LITRES

❖ 1kg fish bones, skins, heads and/or crustacean shells, or 500g tiny raw prawns
❖ 1 onion, peeled and sliced ❖ 1 large carrot, peeled and sliced ❖ 1 celery stick, sliced
❖ 1 leek, sliced ❖ a small bunch of parsley stalks ❖ 1.5 litres water ❖ salt

Wash the fish bones and heads or crustacean shells thoroughly under cold running water. Put all the ingredients, except the salt, in a large pan and bring to the boil. Skim off any scum then simmer for no longer than 20 to 25 minutes (any longer and the flavour of the stock will become unpleasantly bitter).

Strain through a fine sieve, return to the pan and reduce a little for a more intense flavour, then add salt to taste.

CHICKEN STOCK
✳ *caldo de pollo*

I very often roast a chicken because it is my grandchildren's favourite food and then I use the carcass and juices to make a delicious and easy stock that can be used for clear soups, rice and vegetable dishes. The secret is slow simmering and adding salt only at the end, as otherwise it could turn out too salty after the stock has been much reduced.

MAKES ABOUT 1 LITRE

✳ 1 roast chicken carcass, with wings, plus the juices and fat from the roasting pan
✳ 1 carrot, peeled and sliced ✳ 1 onion, peeled and halved ✳ 1 celery stick, sliced ✳ 2 bay leaves
✳ a small bunch of parsley stalks ✳ 4–5 black peppercorns ✳ about 2.25 litres water ✳ salt

Put all the ingredients, except the salt, in a large saucepan, including the juices and fat from the roasting pan, and bring to the boil.

Skim off any scum and then simmer, covered, very gently over a low heat for 3 hours, skimming again every so often, and adding more water as necessary to keep the carcass covered. Strain the stock through a fine sieve into another pan and simmer again to reduce to about 1 litre, then add salt to taste.

Let the stock cool before ladling off the fat that floats to the top, or remove it with absorbent kitchen paper. Another way is to chill the stock in the refrigerator and lift off the fat when it solidifies. The stock can be refrigerated for 2 to 3 days.

NOTE: Do not remove the fat if you are using the stock to cook rice or to make a bean soup or stew.

SPANISH VINAIGRETTE ❊ *vinagreta*

My friend the Spanish food writer Lourdes March uses this *vinagreta* with boiled vegetables and grilled or poached fish. She sometimes adds capers, chopped olives or chopped roast peppers from a tin.

SERVES 6

❊ 7 tablespoons extra virgin olive oil ❊ 2 tablespoons white or red wine vinegar or sherry vinegar
❊ salt and pepper ❊ 1 tablespoon chopped flat-leaf parsley ❊ 1 small sweet, mild red or white onion,
peeled and finely chopped ❊ 1 hard-boiled egg, peeled and finely chopped

Using a fork, beat the oil and vinegar with the salt and pepper in a bowl, then add the remaining ingredients and mix well.

VARIATIONS

❊ Use the juice of ½–1 lemon instead of the vinegar and add the grated zest of ½ a lemon.

❊ Add 1 tablespoon of chopped fresh herbs such as tarragon and oregano with the parsley.

❊ Instead of vinegar, use a mixture of 1 tablespoon of sherry vinegar and 1 tablespoon of Pedro Ximénez or another sweet wine.

❊ CANARY ISLANDS

GREEN SAUCE *with* PARSLEY ❊ *mojo de perejil*

This is one of a range of wonderful garlicky sauces called *mojos* from the Canary Islands. You will find two more in the chapter on vegetables accompanying the recipe for 'wrinkled' potatoes (pages 241). This one makes a beautiful, fresh-tasting accompaniment to fish and meat and keeps well for up to 2 weeks in the refrigerator. It is difficult to give an exact measure for the parsley as the thickness and weight of the stalks in bunches varies. The large bunch that I used weighed 175g with the stalks.

SERVES 8 OR MORE

❊ a 175g bunch of flat-leaf parsley, stalks removed ❊ 5 garlic cloves, peeled and crushed
❊ 175ml mild extra virgin olive oil ❊ 2–3 tablespoons white or red wine vinegar ❊ salt

Blend all the ingredients to a creamy consistency in the blender or food processor.

TOMATO *and* ONION DRESSING ❖ *salmorreta*

Serve this simple fresh sauce with grilled or poached fish. The secret, according to Lourdes March, is that the tomato acquires a 'roasted' flavour.

SERVES 4

⁂ 1 large tomato (weighing about 200g) ⁂ ½ a large mild onion, peeled and cut into pieces ⁂ 1–3 garlic cloves, peeled and crushed (optional) ⁂ ½ a red chilli pepper, deseeded and finely chopped ⁂ 2 tablespoons chopped flat-leaf parsley ⁂ 6 tablespoons extra virgin olive oil ⁂ 2 tablespoons red or white wine vinegar ⁂ salt and pepper

Roast the tomato under the grill for about 20 minutes, turning it a few times until it softens a little and the skin comes off easily. Pull off the skin, quarter the tomato and remove the hard bit at the stem end. Blend the onion, garlic, chilli and parsley to a paste in the food processor, then add the tomato, the oil and vinegar, and blend thoroughly. Season to taste with salt and pepper.

VARIATIONS

- This dressing is also good made with raw tomato. You just blend it with the other ingredients, skin and all.

CATALONIA

TOMATO VINAIGRETTE ❖ *vinagreta de tomàquet*

This vinaigrette is wonderful with fish and seafood salads, and with boiled or steamed vegetables.

SERVES 6

⁂ 4–5 tablespoons extra virgin olive oil ⁂ 1 tablespoon red or white wine vinegar, or lemon juice ⁂ salt and pepper ⁂ 2 medium-sized tomatoes or 1 large tomato (weighing about 150g), diced or finely chopped

With a fork, beat the oil with the vinegar or lemon juice and salt and pepper in a small bowl or jug, then mix in the diced tomatoes.

VARIATIONS

- For a sweet-and-sour version, add 2 teaspoons of runny honey.
- Add 4 finely chopped spring onions and 1 tablespoon of chopped flat-leaf parsley or oregano.
- Instead of dicing them, cut the tomatoes in half crosswise and grate them on the large holes of a vegetable grater, leaving the skin behind.

MAYONNAISE

❋ *mayonesa*

Using extra virgin olive oil in this sauce makes it too strong for most tastes. Chefs I spoke to in Spain use sunflower oil or refined (not extra virgin) olive oil, or a mixture of sunflower and extra virgin olive oil. I use a mix of two-thirds sunflower oil and one-third mild extra virgin olive oil. But you should do it to your taste.

SERVES 4–6

Take the eggs out of refrigerator well before you need them – this will help prevent them curdling. Put the yolks in a warm mixing bowl with the salt and the lemon juice or vinegar and beat with a whisk or an electric mixer for 1 minute until smooth.

Drip the oil (first the sunflower, then the olive oil) into the egg yolks, drop by drop, whisking at the same time. When the mixture begins to thicken (within a minute and after about 4 tablespoons) you can add the oil a little faster, but not too fast as the egg yolks can only absorb the oil at a certain pace. Allow the oil to be absorbed each time before adding more. When all the oil is incorporated and you have a thick, smooth, firm mayonnaise, taste and add a little more salt and lemon or vinegar, if necessary, whisking all the time. If it is too thick add a tablespoon of cold water.

The mayonnaise can suddenly curdle. If it does, the mixture will become quite thin and the oil will start to separate and float to the top. If this happens you can easily save it by putting another egg yolk into another warm bowl, then start again whisking in the curdled mayonnaise, a teaspoonful at a time to begin with, until it re-emulsifies.

Cover with cling film and put the mayonnaise in the refrigerator until you are ready to use it.

* 2 large egg yolks
* ¼ teaspoon salt, or a pinch
* 2–4 teaspoons lemon juice or white wine vinegar, to taste
* 200ml sunflower oil
* 100ml mild extra virgin olive oil

GARLIC MAYONNAISE
❖ *alioli con huevo*

This creamy-white, garlicky sauce is a traditional accompaniment to fish and seafood, grilled meats and poultry, rice, pasta and potatoes. There are many versions of *alioli*. A tiny bit of honey is sometimes added, as are mashed tomatoes and purées of salt cod and of fruits such as quinces, apples and pears (see the recipe that follows). You can be inspired by these variations to try your own.

All i oli means 'garlic and oil' in Catalan and the authentic original sauce is an emulsion of garlic and oil alone. Garlic is mashed to a paste in a large mortar and extra virgin olive oil is added drop by drop, and stirred in vigorously with the pestle – always in the same direction – until it becomes a stiff sauce. Unless you are an old hand it is very hard to get this to work. All the people I asked in Spain said that these days nearly everyone makes *alioli* with egg yolks like the Provençal *aioli*, which is a garlicky mayonnaise. It is easier to make and they have come to prefer a lighter flavour. One Spanish chef I met does not use raw garlic – she roasts or boils it so that the flavour is gentler. The Catalan writer and gastronome Josep Pla famously wrote that the original *alioli* was to the milder garlic mayonnaise what 'a lion is to a pet cat'. Now it seems that even Catalans have come to love cats.

Follow the preceding recipe for mayonnaise but add pounded or mashed garlic to the egg yolks at the beginning. Use 3 to 5 garlic cloves, depending on their size and how garlicky you would like the *alioli* to be. Cut the cloves open and remove the green shoots in the middle, then pound and mash them to a paste with a pinch of salt using a pestle and mortar or as described on page 121. Add the paste to the egg yolks in the bowl and proceed as in the mayonnaise recipe.

VARIATIONS:

❖ For *alioli* made with bought mayonnaise to serve 4–6, put 200g good-quality commercial mayonnaise in a serving bowl and beat in 3–4 garlic cloves that have been crushed to a paste and 3 tablespoons of extra virgin olive oil. Add salt if necessary. It is cheating, but then many Spaniards cheat.

❖ For *alioli de miel* with honey, stir in 1 teaspoon of a runny aromatic honey such as orange blossom.

QUINCE *ALIOLI made with* BOUGHT MAYONAISE
✤ *alioli de membrillo*

In Catalan this is called *allioli de codony*, an alternative word for *membrillo* (quince). It is good when the quince has a strong flavour.

SERVES 6–8

✤ 1 small quince (weighing about 250g) ✤ 3–4 garlic cloves, peeled and crushed
✤ 4 tablespoons extra virgin olive oil ✤ 400g good-quality bought mayonnaise

Boil the quince whole in enough water to cover over a low heat until it is very soft. Depending on its ripeness and quality, this can take 30 minutes or even longer, but watch that it does not fall apart. (If you are cooking other food in the oven you can roast it instead, which will take even longer – start feeling it after about 45 minutes or 1 hour.) Cut the quince in half, remove the core, then peel it and mash the flesh to a smooth purée in a bowl. Beat the garlic and olive oil into the purée with a fork, then beat in the mayonnaise thoroughly.

VARIATIONS:

▩ Make an apple *alioli* like the quince *alioli* above but use 2 apples – Coxes or Granny Smiths – weighing about 300g, instead of the quince. Peel and core the apples and cut them into thick slices. Put them in a small pan with about 5 tablespoons of water and cook with the lid on over a low heat for about 15 minutes until they are soft. They will cook in the steam. Remove the lid and cook over a medium heat to evaporate any remaining liquid, then mash or blend them to a purée.

▩ For a pear *alioli*, use 2 pears instead of the quince, and follow the cooking instructions in the variation above.

TOMATO SAUCE
❊ salsa de tomate

The Catalan writer Josep Pla complained that the rural world had an ancestral obsession with putting tomatoes into everything and that they invaded every food and made Spanish cooking monotonous. Tomato sauce is certainly ubiquitous. An industrial form called *tomate frito* is a puréed tomato sauce with a flavour of fried onions and garlic. Pla also called garlic the 'Genghis Khan of the kitchen'. There are many versions of the sauce. This is a basic one without garlic. According to old Spanish cooking lore, tomato sauce should be made with enough oil to cover the bottom of the frying pan to a depth of 1cm. But I have seen it made with not too much oil and that is how I prefer it.

SERVES 6

❊ 1 large onion, peeled and finely chopped ❊ 4 tablespoons olive oil
❊ 1kg ripe tomatoes, peeled and chopped ❊ 2 teaspoons sugar, or to taste ❊ salt

In a large, deep frying pan, fry the onion in the oil over a low heat, stirring often, until soft and beginning to colour. Add the tomatoes and continue cooking, uncovered, over a low heat for about 25 minutes or until they have reduced to a thick jammy sauce, stirring occasionally so that they don't stick and burn at the bottom. Add sugar and salt to taste towards the end, because their flavours become concentrated as the sauce reduces.

VARIATIONS:

- Some people like to blend the sauce. This used to be done by passing it through a food mill, but now the sauce can be blended straight in the pan with an electric hand blender.
- Add 2–3 peeled and finely chopped garlic cloves with the onions.
- The Riojan *fritada* is a version of tomato sauce made with green peppers. It is now very widespread and accompanies meat, fish and vegetables, which are sometimes even cooked in the sauce. Add 1 deseeded and diced green pepper to the onions when they are slightly soft.
- For the Catalan *salsa de tomàquet*, omit the onion. Peel and chop the tomatoes, fry them in a little oil until they are reduced to a thick sauce, then add salt and, if necessary, a little sugar to counterbalance the acidity of the tomatoes. You can add a little crushed garlic at the start.

ALMOND, DRIED PEPPER *and* TOMATO SAUCE
✳ *salsa romesco*

Salsa romesco is always the star at gastronomic festivals in the ancient Roman port city of Tarragona on the Costa Dorada where it originated. It is made with a mild and sweet dried pepper called *romesco*, or *cuerno de cabra* ('goat's horn') because of its curved shape. Because these peppers are very expensive, the small, round, wine-red Murcian dried *ñora* (spelt *nyora* in Catalan) peppers, which are also mild and sweet but with a taste of their own, are more widely used today. You can substitute other mild dried peppers but you can also make a perfectly good *romesco* simply using *pimentón dulce* (Spanish sweet paprika), which is the same as the dried pepper in powdered form.

Romesco traditionally accompanies fish, vegetables or meat. A variant is *salsa salvitxada* that is served at *calçotadas* – the famous Catalan festivals held in early spring where a type of spring onion called *calçot* that is grown in a special way to become extra fat is grilled out on open fires. And the sauce is called *xató* when it is served as a dressing for a mixed salad of slightly bitter frizzy endive with salt cod or anchovies called *xatonada*. In the past, fishermen made *salsa romesco* with bread while people in the countryside who grew almond trees made it with almonds.

SERVES 4–6

✳ 2 dried *ñora* peppers ✳ ½ a head of garlic, in its skin ✳ 6 tomatoes (about 500g)
✳ 60g blanched almonds or hazelnuts, or 30g of each ✳ 2–3 teaspoons red or white wine vinegar,
or to taste ✳ 4 tablespoons extra virgin olive oil, or to taste ✳ salt

Cut the *ñora* peppers open and remove the seeds and stems, then put them in a bowl, pour on boiling water and leave them to soak for at least 30 minutes, until soft. Place the garlic cloves in their skins and the tomatoes on a large foil-lined grill tray and put them under the grill. Turn them occasionally, until the garlic feels soft and the tomato skins come off easily. It can take about 20 to 25 minutes for the tomatoes, very much less for the garlic. When they have cooled enough to handle, peel the garlic cloves, and remove the hard white bits at the stem ends from the tomatoes and peel their skins. Toast or fry the almonds or hazelnuts in a small frying pan over a medium heat, stirring and shaking the pan until they are lightly coloured. In the food processor, blend the drained *ñoras*, the peeled garlic and the nuts to a paste. Add the tomatoes and blend to a light, rough cream (the nuts give it a rough texture). Then mix in vinegar, oil and salt to your taste.

VARIATIONS

▩ Instead of roasting them, fry the garlic cloves in a little oil

▩ For a thicker version, add a slice of fried white bread, or make the sauce thinner with more olive oil. Use 2 teaspoons of *pimentón dulce* or sweet paprika instead of the *ñoras*.

▩ Add a piece of hot chilli pepper or a pinch of cayenne pepper.

SOUPS

sopas

Soups were the everyday foods of peasants and shepherds. Those based on fried bread and garlic sustained the shepherds of central Spain. The cold *gazpachos* of Andalusia were made by labourers in the fields. Spain's fish soups are said to be fishermen's soups, although I doubt that fishermen would have added the wine and brandy that go into most of them today. They are substantial and represent a main meal. You will find them in the chapter on fish.

Potajes, hearty vegetable soups with beans, chickpeas and lentils, are from the Castilian interior and from the mountains of northern Spain. They were the everyday meals that turned into festive stews when *jamón* (ham), *chorizos*, *morcillas* (Spanish blood sausages), pigs' trotters, spare ribs and ears were added. You will find some of these celebratory dishes in the chapter on bean and chickpea stews.

Delicate broths resulting from a *cocido* of boiled meats (page 303), with added vermicelli or rice, bits of ham or chicken and chopped hard-boiled eggs, are popular, as are cream of vegetable soups in parts of Spain where they have luscious vegetable gardens.

COLD TOMATO SOUP *with*
CHOPPED HARD-BOILED EGGS *and* HAM
❊ *salmorejo cordobés con huevos y jamón*

Salmorejo, a thick, dense, creamy version of *gazpacho* with more bread, is a Cordoban speciality. It is served at all flamenco song and dance (*cante*) events and festivals, together with a glass of wine. You find it in every bar and tavern in Cordoba, topped with chopped hard-boiled eggs and bits of *jamón serrano*. Some recipes use as much bread as tomatoes. In Antequera and the area south of Cordoba, they call it *porra* and add bits of tinned tuna with the topping. In Cordoba, I had a discussion about peeling tomatoes with a group of people on a bus. Most said you have to peel them but a couple who had food processors admitted they did not. I do not peel them.

SERVES 4

Put the bread into the food processor and turn it into fine crumbs, then pour these into a large serving bowl.

Wash the tomatoes and cut them into quarters and remove the hard white bits at the stem end. Blend in the food processor until the peel shows only as tiny specks of red in the pink cream. Add the rest of the ingredients, tasting to decide how much garlic, vinegar and sugar you want, and blend well. Then add to the breadcrumbs in the serving bowl and mix well. Cover with cling film and chill in the refrigerator.

Serve in bowls garnished with a drizzle of the olive oil and the chopped eggs and ham.

VARIATION

❊ For a *porra* that was the mainstay of the peasantry of Antequera, blend 500g bread soaked in water with 500g tomatoes, 1 green pepper, 4–5 crushed garlic cloves, 200ml extra virgin olive oil, and salt and vinegar to taste. Garnish with chopped egg, *jamón serrano* and tuna bits.

❊ 150–200g white bread without crusts, preferably one day old

❊ 750g tomatoes

❊ 2–4 garlic cloves, peeled and crushed

❊ 100ml extra virgin olive oil

❊ 1½–2 tablespoons red or white wine vinegar or sherry vinegar

❊ ½–¾ teaspoon caster sugar, or to taste

❊ salt and pepper

For the garnish

❊ 2 tablespoons extra virgin olive oil

❊ 2 hard-boiled eggs, peeled and chopped

❊ 100g *jamón serrano* or other raw dry-cured ham, chopped

COLD TOMATO SOUP
❊ *gazpacho rojo de tomates*

This famous Spanish cold soup is the best thing to have on a hot day in the summer, when tomatoes are sweet and full of flavour. It was born in the province of Seville, where tomatoes were first grown in Spain, and was the meal made by agricultural labourers when they worked in the vegetable gardens. They brought with them a *dornillo* (wooden mortar) in which they pounded the ingredients on the spot, some olive oil, salt and vinegar to dress them, and bread. Nowadays it is usual for the ingredients to be liquidized in the food processor or blender.

There are many versions. My friend Manolo el Sereno (see page 162), whom I stayed with in Frailes, makes his with just tomatoes and garlic and his own olive oil and vinegar. He makes quantities that he pours into large bottles so that he and his sister and any friends who happen to be around can have some at any time of the day. I have used the following recipe for years and you can make it hours in advance. I do not peel the tomatoes because if you use the food processor the skin all but disappears. In Andalusia they blend them with green peppers that taste a little peppery, but I like mine with the sweeter red pepper. If it is a very hot day, add an ice cube to each bowl when you serve the soup. The garnish is optional.

SERVES 4–6

Dry out the bread under the grill without browning it, turning the slices over once, then break it up into pieces. Wash the tomatoes, quarter them and remove the little white hard bits at the stem end.

Blend the pepper to a paste in the food processor. Add the rest of the soup ingredients and blend to a light cream. Add a little cold water to thin it if necessary – about 100 to 150ml. Pour into a serving bowl and chill in the refrigerator, covered with cling film, for at least an hour and for up to a day.

Check the seasoning and serve in soup bowls, accompanied, if you like, by the garnish ingredients below. Pass them around, each type on a separate little plate or in four piles on a large serving plate.

* 1 thick slice of white bread, crusts removed
* 1kg ripe plum tomatoes
* 1 green or red pepper, deseeded and cut into quarters
* 2–3 garlic cloves, peeled and crushed
* 2 tablespoons sherry or wine vinegar, or more to taste
* 6 tablespoons extra virgin olive oil, or to taste
* salt and pepper
* 1 teaspoon sugar, or more to taste

VARIATIONS

▒ Use ½ a cucumber, peeled and cut into pieces, and blend with the rest of the ingredients.

▒ *For the optional garnish:* have ½ a cucumber, finely diced, ½ a red onion or 4 spring onions, peeled, trimmed and finely chopped, ½ a green pepper, deseeded and finely diced, 1–2 slices of white bread, lightly toasted and diced.

GARLIC SOUP
✤ *sopa de ajo*

Versions of *sopa de ajo* can be found in Aragon, Extremadura and Andalusia along the routes that sheep once travelled in search of fresh pastures. Originally it consisted only of garlic and bread fried in pork fat or olive oil, with water poured over. The soup was responsible for the bad image of Spanish food received by travellers in the past who encountered platefuls of soggy bread in inns and taverns. In a grander form, with an added egg, it appeared on the menus of cafes in Madrid frequented by artists, writers and bohemians. I never felt like trying *sopa de ajo* until I tasted it in the restaurant of the elegant boutique hotel Orfila, a small nineteenth-century palace in Madrid that serves traditional foods in an exquisite modern style.

SERVES 2

Bring the water or stock to the boil in a saucepan.

In another pan fry the garlic in the oil, turning to brown the cloves lightly all over. Add the pieces of bread, stirring vigorously and turning them over for a few seconds until lightly browned. Stir in the *pimentón* or paprika, then pour in the boiling water or stock. Add a little salt and simmer for 5 minutes.

Just before serving break the eggs into the soup and simmer briefly until the whites coagulate.

VARIATIONS:

⚅ For a sophisticated Madrilenian version, use fine breadcrumbs and only the yolks of the eggs. They should still be almost liquid when cooked.

⚅ Fry chopped *jamón serrano* or other raw dry-cured ham in with the garlic.

⚅ In Malaga, they add a peeled and chopped tomato.

⚅ In Seville, they add ¼ teaspoon of ground cumin.

- ✻ 500ml water or chicken stock (page 145)
- ✻ 2 garlic cloves, peeled
- ✻ 2 tablespoons olive oil
- ✻ 1 slice of dense white bread or 100g French baguette, broken or cut into small pieces
- ✻ ½ teaspoon *pimentón dulce* or sweet paprika
- ✻ salt
- ✻ 2 large eggs

COLD ALMOND SOUP
with GARLIC *and* GRAPES
❊ *ajo blanco con uvas*

This splendid soup (*ajo blanco* means 'white garlic'), also called *gazpacho blanco*, is now widely popular in Spain. Proportions vary – some people put in as much bread as almonds. It is usually served with peeled and seeded Moscatel grapes or, less commonly, with small melon balls. You can use any sweet grapes (peeled or unpeeled). You can make the soup hours ahead or the day before. Bought ground almonds can be used but making your own with blanched almonds results in a finer taste. In Frailes, I helped my host Manolo (see page 162) make enough *ajo blanco* to fill a dozen washed-out super-size Coca-Cola bottles for a celebration of the Jaén Gastronomic Association, of which Manolo is president (I became an honorary member at the occasion). We made the soup with almonds picked from his trees, which we soaked overnight and then peeled (they pop out easily from the skins). We used the oil from his own olives, which he presses in an old converted washing machine. At the feast in Valdepeña de Jaén, our *ajo blanco* was served to 200 people in small plastic glasses followed by charcuterie, a great *paella* and pastries. A band of old men played flamenco and people got up and sang of the pain and the joys of those who worked on the land.

SERVES 6

Put the bread to soak for a few minutes in a bowl of water, then squeeze out the excess water.

Grind the almonds very finely in the food processor. Add the soggy bread, the garlic and the oil, and blend well. I also add 2 drops of almond extract – if you do, be careful not to add too much or the flavour will be unpleasant and the soup will be spoilt. With the food processor on, gradually pour in the measured water, enough to make a light, creamy consistency. Season to taste with salt and vinegar.

Transfer the soup to a large bowl, cover with cling film and chill in the refrigerator for 2 hours or longer. To serve, ladle into individual bowls and drop about 6 grapes into each.

VARIATION

❊ Loli Flores of Seville gave me her recipe for an *ajo blanco de piñones* made with pine nuts instead of almonds. Grind 250g pine nuts with 2 slices of crustless day-old white bread and 2 crushed garlic cloves in the food processor. Add 6 tablespoons of extra virgin olive oil, 2–3 tablespoons of white wine or sherry vinegar, some salt and 50ml water, and blend to a light cream. Serve chilled with Moscatel or other grapes.

❊ 75g white bread, without crusts

❊ 275g blanched almonds

❊ 3 garlic cloves, peeled and crushed, or to taste

❊ 100ml extra virgin olive oil

❊ 2 drops good almond extract (optional)

❊ 750ml cold water

❊ salt

❊ 2–3 tablespoons sherry vinegar or white wine vinegar, to taste

❊ 36 sweet white seedless grapes, or more

manolo el sereno
about peasant life in an andalusian *cortijo*

Manuel Ruiz Lopez, known as Manolo el Sereno, worked on an estate in Jaén, Andalusia, from the age of seven until he was drafted into the Spanish Army of Africa. His ten siblings were all placed in work when they were seven, the girls in families in the local town. Manolo's work was with the mules. Although in Castile and northern Spain oxen were the main work animals, in Andalusia mules were used much more. In the winter, Manolo and the other resident labourers slept with the horses, mules and donkeys to keep warm. He returned from the army to find work as the *sereno* (night watchman) in Frailes, a village in Jaén, deep in the interior of the Sierra Sur. His official job now is to measure the rainfall and the height of the river, and he is the president of El Dornillo, the gastronomic guild of the province. A *dornillo* is the huge wooden mortar that peasants took to the fields to make *gazpacho*.

When the travel writer Michael Jacobs (see page 375) chaired a panel on the Moorish influence on food in Spain at the Hay Festival Alhambra in Granada in 2008, Manolo and a group of friends arrived with olive branches, vegetables, fruits, herbs and utensils – an entire installation – as props for our panel. Then Manolo took me and my co-panellist Alicia Ríos back to stay in his house, which he shared with his disabled sister (she has passed away as I write). Downstairs it was a modest but comfortable traditional village house. Upstairs it was very grand. In the living room there was a shelf filled with books all inscribed to Manolo. Later he told us that he had never formally learnt to read and write and had depended on people he met to teach him. He now writes with the most beautiful hand, and his greatest joy is giving hospitality to authors. As the days went by I felt extremely lucky and happy to be a writer on the receiving end of his enormous

generosity. I stayed in a room with a super-glamorous en suite bathroom where Sara Montiel, a mega-star of the 1950s, once slept when she visited a few years ago for the showing of one of her films at the long-abandoned local mini cinema. Her photographs – including one taken with Manolo – are pinned on the walls.

Around Manolo's house is a plot with fruit trees; there are almonds, apricots, quinces, figs, pistachios, chestnuts and pears, plus a vegetable garden. He also keeps chickens and rabbits. Part of the plot is taken up by a space with stone tables and lighting – the kind you might get on a nightclub terrace – where he entertains friends.

I sat with Alicia, Manolo and his sister Carmelita around a little table covered by a heavy blanket, under which was an electric brazier, and asked him, in between eating, what life was like in a *cortijo* when he was a boy. A *cortijo* is the complex of farm buildings around a courtyard that is at the centre of the old Andalusian estates. Vegetables and fruit were cultivated in an area around the *cortijo*. The rest of the estate was given over to wheat and barley and other dry crops such as lentils, beans and chickpeas; some of it was grazing land for sheep and goats. In some estates, horses and fighting bulls were also bred. *Haciendas* were grander versions that combined a farm and a stately country house.

Landowners had overseers to manage their estates and *caseras* (housekeepers) to look after the house. They rented parts of their land to *labradores* (peasant farmers). The poorest, most arid and most distant bits of the estate went to *peletrines* (small sharecroppers). While the women cultivated their patch and kept chickens, the men got work ploughing with their own draught animals at the estate. Day labourers, *braceros* or *jornaleros*, men who lived in villages and towns sometimes far away, were employed on a seasonal basis. During harvest time they were put up on the estate. As many as a hundred slept together on the floor of a long barn. Entire families were put up in tiny outhouses. Women and children picked chickpeas, beans and lentils. Manolo was one of those who lived permanently on the estate as a servant. Sometimes he helped the woman who cooked for the labourers. They made *gazpachos*, *cocidos*, *potajes* and *ajo blanco* with bean flour instead of almonds. Every morning the men made *migas* (see page 288) with leftover bread. When *jornaleros* were working in the fields they organized feasts. They danced and sang and played flamenco music. Some *jornaleros* were gypsies.

Manolo is the most popular man in Frailes because, during his time as a watchman when he saw everything and knew everything that was going on, he helped everyone (he says he stopped burglars breaking into houses but let them off). He also worked at the pharmacy with his sister and assisted the doctor giving injections. Despite being eighty he is immensely strong. I thought he was short when I first saw him but most people in Frailes are smaller still. He took us visiting friends. The Rosales had *arroz caldoso* (soupy rice) with rabbit and chicken simmering in the fireplace and invited us to eat. Jose Velasco Serrano, who worked as a cook during the season in Palma de Majorca and now caters for hundreds of people at festivals, discussed recipes from the Balearic Islands. Beautiful Mercedes, a social worker who lives in a large new house with her teacher husband and two children, talked nostalgically of the times when she moved with her parents and siblings around the country to work the harvests, and of when they went grape-picking for the *vendimias* in La Mancha and in France. Many of Manolo's recipes and those of his friends are in this book.

Now the land in this part of Andalusia has been given over entirely to olive trees. It has been divided many times between the children of landowning families. And many of the small sharecroppers and labourers have bought bits of land from the old estates using their savings from family earnings abroad. They bring their olives to a cooperative for pressing. Their oil represents 60 per cent of the production of Jaén, an area that is the greatest producer of olive oil in the world. Many *cortijos* have been sold to English people, as have the little peasant houses and the barns where the work animals used to sleep. Manolo says Spain has changed more in the last twenty-five years than it has done over centuries. While older people still cook the dishes that were part of the old life, the young eat fast food and sandwiches – I saw them in the village square.

CLEAR BROTH *with* HAM *and* CHOPPED EGGS
❋ *sopa de picadillo*

The *caldo*, or broth (the literal meaning of *caldo* is 'hot'), is considered by some the best part of a big *cocido* of boiled meats (page 303). There is an old Spanish proverb *'El caldo de gallina, a los muertos resucita'* – which translates as 'Broth from an old hen can resuscitate the dead.' Another proverb claims that *'Caldo sin jamón ni gallina no vale una sardina'* – meaning 'Broth without ham and a hen is not worth a sardine.' Nowadays in Spain people can buy good broths or stock, and so can we. Either make the stock given on page 145 or buy a good-quality one. Do not use stock cubes for this recipe. Rice is often used but vermicelli cooks more quickly. Crush vermicelli nests into small pieces with your hand. In the variation, sherry gives the broth an intriguing flavour.

SERVES 3–4

Bring the stock to the boil in a pan, drop in the rice or broken vermicelli and simmer until tender – about 18 minutes for rice, a few minutes only for vermicelli. Add a little salt and stir in the ham.

Serve in bowls and pass around a bowl of chopped egg for everyone to sprinkle some on top.

VARIATION

❈ Add 175ml amontillado sherry at the same time as the vermicelli.

* 1 litre good beef or chicken stock
* 75g long-grain white rice or broken vermicelli (3 nests)
* salt
* 4 slices of *jamón serrano* or other raw dry-cured ham, finely chopped
* 1 hard-boiled egg, peeled and finely chopped

POTATO, CABBAGE *and* BEAN SOUP
✳ *caldo gallego*

Galicians make this soup with what they grow in their vegetable patches – beans, potatoes, cabbages and turnip tops. (They give the turnip roots to their pigs.) Their cabbages grow very long so they use them young and small for the soup and boil them for their animals when they are big and tough. Smoked salt pork fat, called *unto*, gives the soup a distinctive flavour. Because the climate was too wet to cure pork in the attics of the small farmsteads, peasant farmers used to cure it in their fireplaces. That is why a smoky flavour is one of the characteristics of many Galician dishes. A local journalist said that when he was young they all ate *caldo* every day. These days grand versions are made with chicken, veal or ham broths. I loved the one I ate at the Hostal de los Reyes Católicos, the parador hotel opposite the great Cathedral of Santiago de Compostela that has lodged pilgrims since 1499.

SERVES 6

Put the stock in a large pan with the bacon, potatoes and cabbage leaves. Bring to the boil, add salt and pepper, and simmer gently, covered, over a low heat for 30 minutes.

    Add the beans and cook for 5 minutes more.

※ 2 litres chicken or ham stock (you may use 2 stock cubes and, if you have one, a ham bone)

※ 150g smoked streaky bacon rashers, cut into pieces

※ 400g potatoes, peeled and cut into 2–2.5cm pieces

※ 250g green cabbage leaves (the pointed type imported from Spain or spring greens) or turnip tops, cut in 2–3 pieces

※ salt and pepper

※ 1 x 400g tin good-quality small white haricot beans, drained

BROWN LENTIL SOUP
❋ *potaje de lentejas*

Most regions of central Spain have a local lentil soup that can become a substantial stew when *chorizo* sausages are added. They use green or brown lentils of different sizes. The large, pale green lentils of La Armuña, Salamanca, are renowned for their fine taste and quality. When cooked, their skin melds in with the pulp. Amontillado sherry gives the soup a gorgeous flavour. A ham bone will give it extra richness, but a good beef or chicken stock will do very well. Lentils do not need soaking in advance but, depending on their provenance, they may need checking for tiny stones, and you do need to rinse them in cold water.

SERVES 6–8

Wash and drain the lentils, then put them in a pan with 1 litre of water. Bring to the boil, remove any foam and simmer for 15 minutes, adding salt when they have begun to soften.

In a large frying pan, heat the oil and fry the onion with the carrot, stirring over a low heat, until the onion is soft and golden. Add the garlic and the ham and stir well, then add the tomato and the *pimentón* and cook until the tomato softens.

Pour this mixture into the pan with the lentils, add the beef or chicken stock, the sherry, if using, and the bay leaves and cook, covered, for another 20 to 30 minutes, until the lentils are very soft. Add water as required (it will have become absorbed). You need a good amount of liquid – up to 800ml. Stir in the vinegar just before serving.

VARIATIONS

❅ For a substantial main dish add 8 good slices of cooked *chorizo* (boiled in water for 20 minutes) and 8 good slices of cooked *morcilla* (Spanish blood sausage, boiled for 10 minutes) at the end of cooking.

❅ Use a dry white or a sweet Moscatel wine instead of amontillado sherry.

❅ Other vegetables, such as green peppers, leeks, potatoes or mushrooms, can be added, cut into pieces, with the onion and carrot.

❅ Just before serving stir in 1–2 garlic cloves pounded with 1–2 tablespoons of chopped flat-leaf parsley.

* 400g large green or brown lentils
* salt
* 4 tablespoons olive oil
* 1 large onion, peeled and chopped
* 1 large carrot, peeled and chopped
* 3 garlic cloves, peeled and chopped
* 85g *jamón serrano* or other raw dry-cured ham, chopped
* 1 large beef tomato or 2 medium ones, peeled and chopped
* 1 teaspoon *pimentón dulce* or sweet paprika
* 500ml beef or chicken stock (you may use a stock cube)
* 125ml dry amontillado sherry (optional)
* 3 bay leaves
* 1–2 tablespoons red or white wine vinegar

SPINACH *and* CHICKPEA SOUP
❊ *potaje de garbanzos y espinacas*

This is a Castilian version of a thick soup that is eaten in many parts of Spain during Lent, when it is known as *garbanzos de vigilia* (meaning 'chickpeas of abstinence'). Bits of salt cod are sometimes added. At other times of the year pieces of ham or bacon may go in. It is surprisingly delicious and satisfying, with a rich texture and an intriguing flavour that comes from the mashed paste of fried bread, garlic and spices that is stirred in at the end. Versions of the soup are served in *tapas* bars in different parts of the country. It is a complex dish but not a difficult one. These days supermarkets usually sell young spinach leaves with very thin stalks. If you buy spinach at an open market you will need to pull off the hard stalks and wash the leaves carefully. If using fresh spinach you will need a large pan, as the leaves are very bulky and cook down to very little.

SERVES 6

Put the potatoes and chickpeas into a large pan with about 750ml of the stock, and simmer, covered, for 10 minutes. Put the fresh or frozen spinach leaves on top and cover the pan. Fresh leaves will soften quite quickly and collapse in the steam. Stir them in. Add vinegar and salt, and cook for 10 minutes more.

Heat the oil in a frying pan and fry the whole garlic cloves and the bread over a medium-high heat, turning them over until golden brown. Keep a careful watch, as they brown very quickly. Drain on paper towels then put in the food processor with the *pimentón*, cumin and ground chilli pepper, if using, and blend to a fine paste. Add the hard-boiled egg yolks and blend again. Gradually pour in the remaining 250ml stock and blend to a thin cream. Pour this into the soup, stir well and check the seasoning. Cook for another 10 minutes, then stir in the chopped hard-boiled egg whites and heat through.

Before serving, add some water if necessary to thin the soup a little – although it is meant to be thick.

- ❊ 3 medium potatoes (500g), peeled and cut into quarters
- ❊ 2 x 400g tins chickpeas, drained
- ❊ 1 litre vegetable or chicken stock, made with 1 stock cube
- ❊ 500g spinach leaves, fresh or frozen and defrosted
- ❊ 1 tablespoon red or white wine vinegar
- ❊ salt
- ❊ 4 tablespoons olive oil
- ❊ 4–5 garlic cloves, peeled
- ❊ 2 slices of bread (about 75g), crusts removed
- ❊ 1 teaspoon *pimentón dulce* or sweet paprika
- ❊ 1 teaspoon ground cumin
- ❊ a pinch of ground chilli pepper or cayenne (optional)
- ❊ 2 hard-boiled eggs, peeled, yolks reserved and whites chopped

CREAM *of* ASPARAGUS SOUP
❊ *crema de espárragos*

Cultivation of asparagus was introduced to Spain by the Arabs in the valley of the river Ebro in Navarre. Nowadays the main production is of the fat, all-white asparagus that are grown covered by earth without any exposure to the sun. This lovely soup is made with green asparagus that grow naturally.

SERVES 6–8

❊ 600g asparagus ❊ 1 or 2 floury potatoes (about 250g), peeled and cut into 2cm cubes
❊ 1 litre water ❊ 2 chicken stock cubes, crumbled ❊ 200ml whole milk, or more ❊ salt

Cut off the asparagus tips and keep them aside. Cut the remaining asparagus stems roughly into 4 pieces, discarding the hard white ends.

Put the potatoes in a large pan with the water and the stock cubes. Bring to the boil and cook for 10 to 15 minutes, covered, until the potatoes are tender. Add the chopped asparagus stems and cook for 10 minutes until they are soft.

Blend to a cream in the food processor and return to the pan, or use a hand blender in the pan. Bring to the boil, add enough milk to make a light cream and season to taste with salt. Drop the asparagus tips into the soup and cook for 2 to 3 minutes more until they are tender.

VARIATION
❊ Instead of 1 litre of water, use 500ml of water and 500ml of dry white wine.

VEGETABLE SOUP *with* PEAS
✳ *puré de guisantes*

Cream of vegetable soups are very popular in northern Spain and Andalusia. Some people still pass them through a *chino*, a conical sieve with a wooden pestle, but now they are usually blended. Butter and cream are used. I found this soup, based on peas, in *Tía Victoria's Spanish Kitchen* by Victoria Serra, translated by Elizabeth Gili (see page 223). It has a wonderful delicate flavour and appealing texture.

SERVES 4

✳ ½ a large onion, peeled and chopped ✳ 25g butter ✳ 1 tablespoon olive oil
✳ 1 medium floury potato (about 150g), peeled and cut into small pieces ✳ 1 large carrot
(about 170g), peeled and cut into small pieces ✳ 1 litre chicken or vegetable stock
(you may use 2 stock cubes) ✳ 250g fresh podded peas, or frozen and defrosted petits pois
✳ salt ✳ single cream, to pass around (optional)

In a large saucepan, sauté the onion in a mixture of the butter and oil, stirring often until soft.

Add the potatoes and carrots, then the stock. Stir well, and cook, covered, for about 15 minutes or until the vegetables are soft.

Add the peas and cook until they are tender – this should take 3 to 10 minutes depending on the peas. Then blend the soup to a creamy consistency. Add salt, taking into consideration the saltiness of the stock, and water if you like it thinner.

Pass the cream around for people to help themselves.

CREAM OF PUMPKIN SOUP
❊ *crema de calabaza*

I have collected many versions of this soup from several, mostly Mediterranean, regions, but this recipe is for one I tasted in Asturias.

SERVES 6

Remove the peel, seeds and any fibres from the pumpkin or squash. To remove the hard peel, cut into 5–6cm chunks, put them on a board and cut away by pressing down with a large, strong knife.

Chop the carrots, leek and onion (you can do this all together in the food processor) and sauté in the oil over a low heat until slightly browned, stirring and turning them over often.

Put in the pumpkin or squash and only enough of the stock to just cover. Add the lemon juice, salt and pepper and, if you like, a little sugar. Simmer for about 20 to 25 minutes until the pumpkin or squash is soft.

Let cool a little before blending to a cream in the food processor or with a hand blender. Add the remaining stock and bring to the boil, stirring. Serve very hot. Pass around the cream for those who might like some.

VARIATIONS

❊ A simple version is to cut the vegetables into pieces, boil them together, then blend the soup to a cream with 5 tablespoons of extra virgin olive oil.

❊ Just before serving stir in 1–2 garlic cloves pounded with 1–2 tablespoons of chopped flat-leaf parsley.

❊ For another easier version put about 400g cubed pumpkin flesh in a pan with 175ml water. Put the lid on and cook (it will steam) for about 20 to 30 minutes until soft. Add 300ml milk, season with salt and bring to the boil. Then blend to a cream and serve with a sprinkling of ground cinnamon.

❊ 1 slice of orange pumpkin (about 900g) or a medium-sized butternut squash (1kg)

❊ 2 carrots (about 250g), peeled

❊ 1 leek, white part only, trimmed

❊ 1 onion, peeled

❊ 5 tablespoons olive oil

❊ 1 litre chicken stock or water with 2 chicken stock cubes

❊ juice of ¼ lemon, or more to taste

❊ salt and pepper

❊ 1 teaspoon sugar (optional)

❊ single cream, for serving (optional)

EGG DISHES

huevos

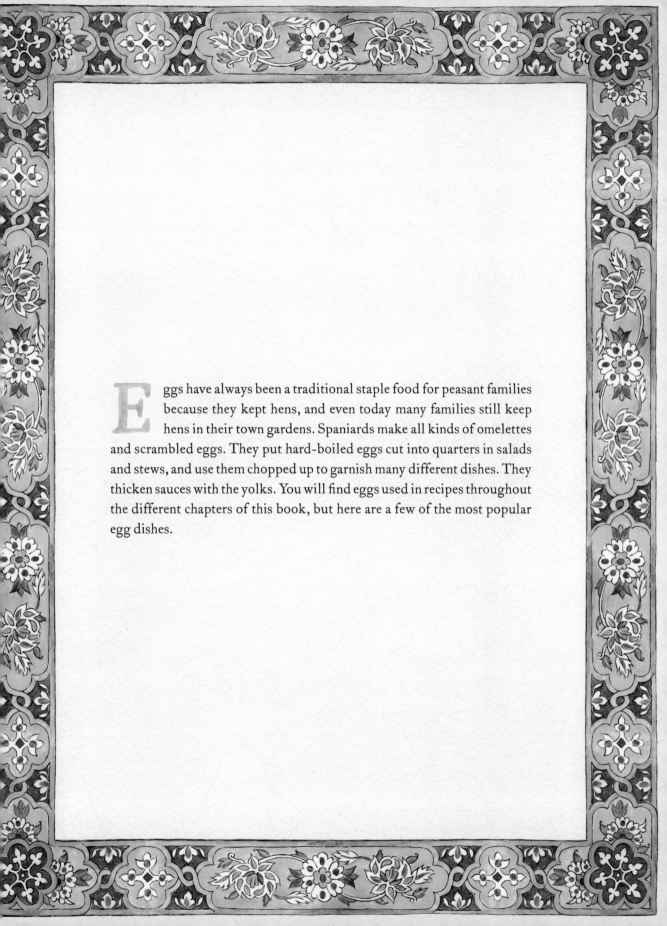

Eggs have always been a traditional staple food for peasant families because they kept hens, and even today many families still keep hens in their town gardens. Spaniards make all kinds of omelettes and scrambled eggs. They put hard-boiled eggs cut into quarters in salads and stews, and use them chopped up to garnish many different dishes. They thicken sauces with the yolks. You will find eggs used in recipes throughout the different chapters of this book, but here are a few of the most popular egg dishes.

POTATO OMELETTE
❊ *tortilla de patatas*

In Spain this omelette is also known as *tortilla española* (Spanish omelette) because you find it eaten everywhere, in every region, in *tapas* bars and at home. Some people like to make it with potatoes only, some add onions. Some like it moist, others firm and dry. Some people slice the potatoes, some cut them into small dice. I prefer my *tortilla de patatas* with onions, and slightly creamy. I will not pretend that it is easy to make. On the contrary, making *tortilla* is an art that has special methods and tricks, and requires skill and intuition. In trying to make a large one, I failed twice, partly because I do not have the strength to turn a heavy frying pan on to a large platter without most of the uncooked part spilling out. I called my friend Alicia Ríos in despair. She sent me five pages of 'secrets' for getting it right.

For years I had been making an Arab potato omelette by boiling the potatoes then slicing them, and finishing off the omelette under the grill. Alicia, said, 'No! No! No!' to that. The important thing for me, she said, was to make two small omelettes rather than one large one. She said to use a very light non-stick frying pan and a slightly concave saucepan lid, larger than the pan, to catch any liquid running out from the upturned omelette. The shape of the lid is important. I have been told that a particular lid for *tortilla* is something you hand down in the family.

With Alicia I met a young chef who taught at a catering school. He said that he used sunflower oil to cook *tortillas* because it is cheaper than olive oil. Alicia kept silent but when we were alone she said, 'No! Anyway with olive oil you can use it again and again so it works out cheaper than other oils.'

≫ ≫ ≫

SERVES 4

❋ 250g new or waxy potatoes, peeled and cut in 1.5cm dice ❋ 300ml olive oil
❋ 1 medium onion, peeled, halved and sliced thinly (optional) ❋ salt ❋ 6 large eggs

Dry the potatoes on a tea towel or some kitchen paper as soon as you have diced them.

Heat the oil in a smallish non-stick frying pan large enough to contain all the ingredients (I use one with a 16cm-diameter base) over a medium heat and put in the potatoes and the onion, if using. Cook over a low heat, with the lid on, for 20 to 30 minutes, until the potatoes feel tender when you prick them with the point of a knife. Do not let them colour. Move them occasionally with a fork. Then drain in a colander, keeping the oil for another time. Spread the potatoes and the onion, if using, on kitchen paper and sprinkle lightly with salt.

In a bowl, beat the eggs lightly with a fork, adding a little salt. Add the potatoes and the onion, if using, and mix gently.

Pour 1 tablespoon of the drained oil back into the frying pan and heat until it almost begins to smoke. Pour in the egg and potato mixture, and turn down the heat to low. Cook for 3 to 4 minutes until the eggs set at the bottom, shaking the pan occasionally with a gentle circular motion so that the omelette doesn't stick. Place a slightly concave lid larger than the pan on top and flip the pan over quickly, inverting the omelette on to the lid. Pour another tablespoon of the oil into the frying pan over a high heat, then slide the omelette gently back into the pan, uncooked side down, and lower the heat. Cook for 2 minutes more until only just set. Run a wooden spoon round the edge of the omelette to give it a tidy look and turn out.

Serve it warm or at room temperature.

VARIATIONS

❋ I have put the *tortilla* under the grill instead of turning it over and I can recommend this method to those who find it difficult to 'flip' a *tortilla*.

❋ In Navarre, there is a *tortilla al horno* cooked in the oven. Boiled potatoes cut into little squares are mixed with chopped parsley and beaten eggs and seasoned with salt and pepper. They are poured into a greased dish and baked at 160°C/gas 3 for 45 to 60 minutes. If it gets too brown, cover with foil.

❋ For a *tortilla de cebolla* with onions alone, fry 2 large thinly sliced onions in 3 tablespoons of oil until golden. Mix them in a bowl with 8 lightly beaten eggs, season with salt and pepper and proceed as above.

VEGETABLE OMELETTE
❋ *tortilla de la huerta*

Murcia is known as the vegetable garden of Spain. They grow all kinds of vegetables there that turn up in omelettes. This one makes a good vegetarian dish.

SERVES 2–3

❋ 1 red pepper, deseeded and cut into 2cm squares ❋ 1 small aubergine (about 200g), cut into 2cm dice ❋ 4 tablespoons olive oil ❋ 4 garlic cloves, peeled and crushed ❋ 3 tomatoes (about 250g), peeled and chopped ❋ salt ❋ 4 large eggs

Sauté the pepper and aubergine in 3 tablespoons of the oil in a wide frying pan over a medium heat, stirring and turning them over, for about 12 minutes or until they are tender. The aubergine will absorb the oil very quickly but will release it again as it becomes soft. Stir in the garlic and, within a few seconds when it just begins to colour, add the tomatoes and some salt. Cook, stirring, until the tomatoes are reduced to a jammy sauce.

Beat the eggs in a bowl with a little salt, then stir in the vegetables. Pour the remaining tablespoon of oil into another smaller non-stick frying pan with a base about 16cm in diameter. It should be small so that the resulting omelette is thick.

Pour in the egg mixture. Cook gently over a medium-low heat until the bottom is set. Put it under the grill to set the top and turn out.

VARIATION

❋ You can add chopped *jamón serrano* or other raw dry-cured ham, or bacon, at the beginning when you fry the vegetables.

CREAMY SALT COD OMELETTE
✤ *tortilla jugosa de bacalao*

In late winter and early spring it has always been a traditional custom to visit cider-makers in the hills of the Basque Country to taste the new vintage and stock up on provisions. Still today cider houses open for a few months of the year and offer local rural dishes in their tavern-like restaurants with communal wooden tables. Hard cider runs out of taps from enormous barrels as people line up to have their glasses replenished. A moist, creamy salt cod omelette is a speciality of the cider houses. Other specialities include *chorizo* cooked in cider and T-bone steak cooked rare on glowing embers. Basques are crazy about salt cod. If you do not have salt cod, the omelette can be made with hake fillets or fresh cod (see how to make it taste like salt cod on page 348).

SERVES 2

⁂ 8 thin spring onions or 4 fat ones, thinly sliced (remove the greener ends)
⁂ ½ a green pepper, deseeded and chopped ⁂ 3 tablespoons olive oil ⁂ salt
⁂ 125g salt cod, desalted (see page 348), rinsed and drained ⁂ 4 large eggs
⁂ 1 tablespoon finely chopped flat-leaf parsley

In a large non-stick frying pan, with a base about 25cm in diameter, sauté the spring onions and pepper in 1 tablespoon of the oil over a low heat, stirring until they are soft, and adding a little salt.

Put the desalted and drained cod in a pan of cold water and bring it slowly to the boil, then barely simmer for 3 minutes. Lift out the fish and, when it is cool enough to handle, remove any skin and bones and break it up into small pieces.

Beat the eggs well with a fork, adding a little salt, then add the spring onions, peppers, fish and parsley and mix well.

Clean the frying pan with kitchen paper and pour in the remaining 2 tablespoons of oil. Place over a high heat until it is almost smoking, then pour in the egg mixture, tilting the pan so that it spreads evenly, and reduce the heat to medium. The trick now is to stir for a few seconds only to allow some of the liquid at the top to touch the bottom of the pan and set. Shake the pan so that the omelette does not stick. After less than a minute, while there is still some liquid left, use a spatula to fold one side of the omelette over to the centre, then fold the other side to overlap. You will have an elongated oval. Cut the omelette in half and slide the pieces on to your plates. It should be runny in the middle.

VARIATION

⁂ Instead of the spring onions and green pepper, fry a chopped onion and a piece of chopped chilli pepper.

SCRAMBLED EGGS
with WILD MUSHROOMS
❋ *revuelto con setas*

This simple way of cooking wild mushrooms makes a sumptuous starter. The traditional wisdom is to clean off any soil from the mushrooms with a soft vegetable brush, or to wipe them gently with a damp cloth, but washing them under the cold tap and shaking off the water does not spoil their taste, while absorbing a little water makes them less porous to oil when they are cooking. Trim off the earthy base from their stems, rinse and dry them on a tea towel or with kitchen paper. Cut large ones in half or in quarters and leave small ones whole. Be ready to eat with your bread toasted when you start scrambling the eggs because they cook very quickly. They should be moist and creamy.

SERVES 4

❋ 4 tablespoons mild extra virgin olive oil ❋ 400g mixed wild mushrooms, such as ceps, chanterelles and morels ❋ salt and pepper ❋ 35g butter ❋ 8 large eggs, lightly beaten with a fork
❋ 4 slices of good country bread, lightly toasted

Heat the oil in a large frying pan. Add the mushrooms and cook for 7 to 10 minutes over a high heat to start with, then over a medium heat. Add salt and pepper and stir, turning the mushrooms over until they are tender and lightly brown in parts.

Heat a second large non-stick frying pan over a medium heat. Put in the butter and, when it is almost melted, add the eggs and sprinkle with a little salt. Let the eggs set slightly at the bottom before gently turning and stirring them with a wooden spoon or spatula, so that the liquid at the top runs underneath. Turn off the heat when there are still some runny parts – the eggs will continue to cook and will be done by the time you serve them.

To serve, spoon some scrambled eggs on to each piece of toast and cover with the sizzling mushrooms.

VARIATION
❋ You can use cultivated brown mushrooms instead of wild ones.

PEPPERS *and* TOMATOES *with* EGGS
❋ *piperada vasca*

When I was a girl in Paris, we often had French Basque *piperade* for dinner at my boarding school. The fried onions, peppers and tomatoes with eggs mixed in at the end tasted good but looked a mess. Modern Basque chefs roast the peppers and deconstruct the dish to make it more presentable and appetizing. It means more pans to wash but it is worth it. And you can more easily double the quantities. Serve it with slices of toasted or fried bread.

SERVES 2–3

Roast the peppers under the grill (see page 118), then peel and deseed them and cut them into strips about a finger wide.

In a large frying pan, fry the onion in the oil over a low heat, stirring often, until soft and golden. Add the garlic and the chilli pepper and stir for a few seconds, then add the tomatoes. Add the sugar and salt and pepper, and cook until the tomatoes have collapsed and most of the liquid has evaporated – about 10 minutes. Then stir in the strips of roasted peppers. You can do this in advance and reheat when you are ready to serve.

Just before serving, melt the butter in a small non-stick frying pan and add the eggs with a little salt. Let the eggs set slightly at the bottom over a medium heat before gently turning and stirring them with a wooden spoon or spatula. Turn off the heat when there are still some runny parts – they will continue to cook and be ready by the time you serve. They have to be creamy. Serve the *piperada* with the eggs on the side and the ham, if using, heated under the grill.

- ❋ 1 round or elongated red pepper
- ❋ 1 green pepper
- ❋ 1 large onion, peeled, halved and sliced
- ❋ 2 tablespoons olive oil
- ❋ 2 garlic cloves, peeled and sliced
- ❋ 1 small red chilli pepper, deseeded and chopped
- ❋ 3 medium tomatoes, peeled and chopped
- ❋ ½ teaspoon sugar
- ❋ salt and pepper
- ❋ a knob of butter
- ❋ 3–4 large eggs, lightly beaten with a fork
- ❋ 3 or more slices of *jamón serrano* or other raw dry-cured ham, for garnish (optional)

SCRAMBLED EGGS
with ASPARAGUS *and* PRAWNS
✳ *revuelto de espárragos con gambas*

This is a recipe made with the thin wild asparagus called *trigueros*, after the word *trigo* (meaning wheat), because they grow wild in wheat fields. I ate it in a restaurant in Jaén where they also had scape in the dish – these are the tender garlic shoots or stalks of the flowers of the garlic plant (*ajetes* in Spanish) that are harvested just as they begin to grow in a curl, before they straighten into a stem. They are also know as garlic spears. Theirs is a mild, garlicky taste.

Serve the *revuelto* with thin toast.

SERVES 4

Cut the asparagus into 3cm pieces and remove any tough ends. Boil them in salted water until they are soft (not crunchy), then drain.

Heat the oil in a non-stick frying pan over a medium heat and add the garlic. Before it begins to colour add the asparagus. Sauté for a minute, stirring and turning them over, and adding a little salt. Add the prawns and cook for 1 to 2 minutes, turning them over until they go pink. Pour in the eggs with the parsley, add a little more salt and stir for seconds only. The eggs should be slightly liquid. They will turn creamy off the heat.

- ※ 250g wild or thin asparagus
- ※ salt
- ※ 4 tablespoons olive oil
- ※ 4 garlic shoots (scape) cut into 2.5cm lengths or 4 garlic cloves, peeled and sliced
- ※ 250g raw peeled prawns or frozen ones, defrosted
- ※ 4 large eggs, lightly beaten
- ※ 2 tablespoons chopped flat-leaf parsley

VARIATION

▨ Instead of prawns, fry 4 slices of bacon, coarsely chopped, then add the garlic and drained asparagus, then the eggs.

SAVOURY PASTRIES

coques, empanadas y empanadillas

*E*mpanadas, large pies, are a symbol of Galicia, while *empanadillas*, small turnovers, are a speciality of the Balearic Islands and Valencia. Savoury pies feature prominently in medieval Arabic manuscripts of al-Andalus and are an Arab legacy. Pizza-type open tarts called *coques* (*coca* in the singular) came into the Spanish repertoire much later and are a speciality of Catalonia, Valencia and the Balearic Islands. They use a bread dough, or a variety of different pastry doughs made with olive oil, lard or butter, and sometimes eggs. You can also find puff pastry versions. All kinds of ingredients are used as toppings and fillings, from vegetables and preserved fish (anchovies, tuna, sardines) to *chorizo* and sausage, as well as olives and pine nuts, but hardly ever cheese. Sweet *empanadillas* and *coques* are associated with festivals. Creamy tarts belong to northern Spain.

OPEN PIE *with* ROASTED PEPPERS
and AUBERGINES
❋ *coca de recapte*

The most common *coca* in Catalonia, which is sold in bakeries, has a thin bread-dough base and a topping of roasted peppers and aubergines, onions and tomatoes. They say this *coca* was born in the area of Lleida and Taragona. It is usually eaten cold (although I like it hot too). *De recapte* here means 'what you have in stock' because you can add the kind of everyday topping ingredients that are normally on hand in Catalan kitchens – see the variations at the end of the recipe.

The recipe I give below uses ordinary dried active yeast. If you have the fast-action instant 'easy bake' type of dried yeast, use a 7g sachet and mix it with the flour and all the ingredients at the same time.

SERVES 8 AS A STARTER

For the pastry dough ❋ 400g strong white bread flour ❋ 1 teaspoon salt ❋ 2 tablespoons olive oil, plus a little more for the bowl and to brush the baking sheets ❋ 2 teaspoons dried active yeast ❋ about 200ml warm water (maybe a little more) ❋ ¼ teaspoon sugar

For the topping ❋ 2 aubergines (about 500g) ❋ 3 red peppers ❋ salt ❋ 5 tablespoons olive oil ❋ 2 large onions, peeled and chopped ❋ 5 tablespoons olive oil ❋ 2 tomatoes (about 200g), peeled and chopped ❋ 1 teaspoon sugar

Put the flour in a large bowl, sprinkle in the salt and add the oil. Put the dried yeast in a glass with about half of the measured warm water with the sugar and stir well. When it begins to froth, pour it into the flour, then gradually pour in the rest of the warm water, stirring it in first with a fork, then with your hand. Add just enough to have a soft ball of dough that sticks together.

Knead for 10 minutes until the dough is smooth and elastic – adding water by the tablespoon if too dry and a little flour if too sticky. Pour about ½ a tablespoon of oil into the bowl and turn the dough over in the oil to coat it well so that a dry crust does not form when it rises. Cover the bowl with cling film and leave the dough to rise in a warm place for 1 to 2 hours until doubled in volume.

For the topping, put the aubergines and peppers on a sheet of foil on a baking tray. Prick the aubergines in a few places with a pointed knife and put the tray in an oven preheated to 180°C/

» » »

gas 4 for 45 minutes, or longer. Take the peppers out of the oven when they are soft and their skins have blistered, put them in one or two strong plastic bags and twist to seal. Leave for about 10 minutes, then peel them, remove the seeds and cut them into small squares of about 1.5cm. Take the aubergines out of the oven when they feel soft when pressed. Peel them, put in a colander and press slightly to let the juices drain away. Then cut them into similar sized pieces. Mix the pepper and aubergine pieces together and dress with salt and 2 of the tablespoons of oil so that they are well coated all over.

Fry the onions in the remaining 3 tablespoons of oil in a large frying pan over a low heat until soft, covered to begin with and stirring often. Add the tomatoes, sugar and some salt, and cook over a medium-high heat, stirring occasionally, until much of the liquid has evaporated.

Punch the risen dough down, knead for a couple of minutes and divide it into two balls. Roll them out thinly, on a floured surface with a floured rolling pin, into oblong or oval shapes of about 28cm by 38cm.

Brush two large baking sheets with oil. Lift up each sheet of dough by wrapping it on the rolling pin and unwrapping it on to a baking sheet. Spread the onion and tomato sauce evenly over the dough then dot with the peppers and aubergines.

Bake both *cocas* in the preheated oven at 180°C/gas 4 for about 30 minutes, or until the crust around the edges is crisp and brown. When the one on the top shelf is ready, move the one on the lower shelf up and give it some more time.

VARIATIONS

- For *coca de cebes* of Valencia, with an onion topping, cut 4 large onions (about 1 kg) in half and slice them, then cook in 4 tablespoons olive oil in a wide pan, covered, over very low heat for 40 minutes or until very soft, stirring and turning them over often. It takes a long time because there are so many onions. Uncover towards the end to reduce the liquid and add a little salt and pepper. Spread all over the rolled-out dough. If you like, arrange 12 thin anchovy fillets, or 6 large ones cut in half lengthways, on top, and 12 black olives, pitted or not. Bake and serve as above.

- Cut the vegetables into 2cm-wide strips instead of squares and small pieces.

- Spread a tin of anchovy fillets in oil among the vegetables for the topping before baking, or a tin of tuna or of sardines, drained and broken into pieces.

- Arrange 8 fresh pork sausages, fried and cut into slices, on top.

- Add about 16 thin streaky bacon rashers, lightly fried.

- Scatter over 500g sliced and briefly sautéed mushrooms.

OPEN PIE *with* PEPPERS, TOMATOES *and* ONIONS ❖ *coca de trempó*

Lydia Larrey, a journalist from the Catalan newspaper *La Vanguardia*, called to ask me about pizza-type foods in Mediterranean countries. After we had talked, I asked her to email me her favourite *coca* recipe and she sent me this one. It is from her native Majorca, where it is sold in pastry shops. The name comes from the local salad of diced tomatoes, light green *rubio* peppers and onions, which is called *trempó* and is used as the topping. The dough contains no yeast. After I had made it I emailed Lydia and she confirmed that the *coca* was as it should be – with the pastry very thin and crisp.

SERVES 6 AS A STARTER

For the pastry dough ❋ 125ml olive oil ❋ 125ml lukewarm water ❋ ½ teaspoon salt
❋ 250–300g plain flour

For the topping ❋ 4 tomatoes (about 350g) ❋ ½ a large onion ❋ 1 green pepper, halved and deseeded
❋ 1–2 teaspoons sugar (optional) ❋ salt ❋ 3 tablespoons extra virgin olive oil

To make the topping, cut the tomatoes, onion and green pepper into small pieces. Put them in a bowl, season with a little sugar, if you like, and some salt and mix well. Leave to stand at room temperature for 1 to 2 hours, then drain thoroughly so that the pastry does not get too soggy. Dress with the extra virgin olive oil just before using.

To make the pastry dough, mix the olive oil, water and salt very well in a bowl, then gradually stir in the flour, mixing with a fork and then with your hand. Add just enough flour to form a smooth soft ball of dough that does not stick to your fingers. Wrap in cling film and leave to rest at room temperature for half an hour.

Divide the dough in half and spread it on to two large baking sheets, pressing it into a very thin layer with your fingers and the palm of your hand. Form a low rim around the edges if you like. Bake for 10 minutes in an oven preheated to 180°C/gas 4 to seal the pastry, then cover entirely with the topping. Bake for a further 45 to 60 minutes, until the pastry is crisp and the topping soft. If the topping is too dry and becomes brown before the pastry is crisp, cover the *coca* with foil.

Serve warm or at room temperature cut into pieces.

VARIATIONS

❊ Add black olives or capers to the topping.

❊ For a *coca de pimiento* with a red pepper topping, roast, peel and deseed 5 red peppers (see page 118). Cut them into thin strips and dress them with 2 crushed garlic cloves mixed with 3 tablespoons of olive oil, 1 tablespoon of vinegar, salt and a ½ teaspoon of ground cumin.

❊ Instead of the oil-based pastry you can use a bread dough, as in the *coca de recapte* recipe on page 190.

TUNA PIE
✳ *empanada de atún*

Angelita García de Paredes Barreda (see page 138) gave me this recipe and told me not to change anything without asking her first. This pie is good to eat hot or cold and keeps well.

SERVES 6 AS A STARTER

For the pastry, beat the egg lightly with a fork in a large bowl, then beat in the baking powder or bicarbonate of soda, oil, wine and salt. Gradually work in enough flour to make a soft malleable dough – stirring it in with a fork to begin with, then working it in with your hand. Roll the dough into a ball, wrap it in cling film and leave it to rest at room temperature for an hour.

For the filling, fry the onion and the pepper in the oil in a large frying pan over a low heat, stirring often, until soft. Add the chopped tomatoes, sugar and a little salt, taking into account the saltiness of the olives that will be added later. Cook over a medium heat for about 15 minutes until the sauce is thick and jammy. Remove from the heat and stir in the tuna, the olive pieces and the chopped hard-boiled eggs.

Grease a pie dish or tart tin, about 28cm in diameter, with oil. Divide the dough into two balls – one larger than the other. Roll out the larger one (keep the remaining dough wrapped in cling film) on a smooth surface. Do not flour the rolling pin or the surface – the dough will not stick as it is oil-based. Roll it out thinly so that it is large enough to come over the sides of the pan. Carefully transfer the sheet of dough to the pan by rolling it on to the rolling pin and unrolling it gently into the pan. Without stretching the dough, ease it into the corners. Trim the edges to 1cm over the rim and brush all over with egg white (you will not need it all) to stop it getting too soggy. Bake in an oven preheated to 180°C/gas 4 for 10 minutes, take it out and let it cool.

Spread the filling evenly inside the crust. Roll out the remaining dough and lay it carefully on top so that it covers the edges of the bottom crust. Brush with the egg yolk mixed with ½ a teaspoon of water and bake in an oven preheated to 180°C/gas 4 for 35 to 40 minutes until lightly browned.

VARIATIONS

▓ Use a strong, still cider instead of the white wine.

▓ Use bought puff pastry instead of the dough to make an *empanada de hojaldre* (a puff-pastry pie).

For the pastry dough

✳ 1 large egg

✳ 1 teaspoon baking powder or bicarbonate of soda

✳ 125ml olive oil, plus a little more for greasing the pie dish or tart tin

✳ 125ml dry white wine

✳ ½ teaspoon salt

✳ about 375g plain flour

✳ 1 egg white, lightly beaten

✳ 1 egg yolk lightly beaten with ½ teaspoon water, for the glaze

For the filling

✳ 1 large onion, peeled and chopped

✳ 1 red pepper, deseeded and cut into small pieces

✳ 2 tablespoons olive oil

✳ 1 x 400g tin chopped tomatoes

✳ 1 teaspoon sugar

✳ salt

✳ 250g tinned tuna in oil (drained weight), drained and crumbled

✳ 20–24 black olives, pitted and cut into pieces

✳ 2 hard-boiled eggs, peeled and chopped

LITTLE PIES *with a* TOMATO, PEPPER *and* TUNA FILLING ✳ *empanadillas de atún y pimiento*

Empanadillas are ideal to serve at parties and are good warm or cold. They come with a variety of fillings and different doughs. The filling here is the most common and the dough is easy to make and to work with. The pies can be fried, but I prefer them baked.

MAKES 16–20 EMPANADILLAS

For the dough, mix the oil, water or white wine and salt in a bowl, beating with a fork, then gradually work in enough flour to have a soft, smooth, malleable dough that does not stick. Begin by stirring the flour in with a fork, then work it in with your hands and knead briefly. You may use the dough right away or keep it for as long as a day, covered in cling film. But it must be kept at room temperature and not chilled in the refrigerator.

For the filling, grill the pepper, peel it and remove the seeds (see page 118), then cut it up into small pieces – about 1.5cm square.

In a large frying pan, fry the onion in the oil over a low heat until very soft, stirring often. Add the tomatoes and cook over a medium heat until the liquid has disappeared and you can see the oil sizzling, then season to taste with salt and pepper. Add the tuna, shredded with your fingers, and the roasted peppers, olives and parsley. Mix well and leave to cool.

To make the *empanadillas*, divide the dough into 4 or 6 pieces. Roll each piece out thinly and cut circles in the sheet with a 10cm round pastry cutter. You do not need to flour the surface or the rolling pin since the dough is very oily and will not stick. Collect the dough off-cuts and reserve them. Roll them into a ball at the end, then roll the ball out thinly and cut it into rounds. Do not waste any dough.

Fill each batch of pastry rounds one at a time. Paint around the edges with a little egg yolk (this helps to stick the pastry). You can use cotton buds or your little finger to do this. Put a generous tablespoon of filling in the middle and bring the two sides of the pastry up to meet over the filling, making a half-moon-shaped pie. Pinch the edges together, then lay the pies down and press around the edges with the prongs of a fork to seal the *empanadillas*.

Place the pies on a baking sheet lined with foil lightly greased with oil. Brush the tops with the remaining egg yolk mixed with a drop of water and bake in an oven preheated to 180°C/gas 4 for 30 minutes or until golden.

For the pastry dough

* 125ml olive oil, plus a little more for greasing the foil
* 125ml warm water or dry white wine
* ½ teaspoon salt
* about 375g plain flour
* 2 large egg yolks, lightly beaten

For the filling

* 1 round or elongated red pepper
* ½ a large onion, peeled and finely chopped
* 2 tablespoons olive oil
* 300g tomatoes, peeled and chopped
* salt and pepper
* 100g tinned tuna (drained weight)
* 14 green or black olives, pitted and cut into pieces
* 2 tablespoons chopped flat-leaf parsley

CREAMY LEEK TART

❋ *tarta de puerros*

Basques love leeks and you find them in many of their dishes. This tart makes an elegant first course that can be served hot or cold.

SERVES 8 AS A STARTER

To make the shortcrust pastry, cut the butter into small pieces and rub it into the flour and salt with your hands until it becomes like damp sand in texture. You can also do this very well in the food processor. Add the egg, mix well and work very briefly with your hand until the dough holds together in a soft ball, adding a little milk if necessary. Wrap the dough in cling film and refrigerate for 1 hour. Before using, let it warm up and soften so that it becomes easier to work.

Grease a 28cm tart tin or flan dish and line the bottom and sides with the dough by flattening lumps in the palm of your hands, then pressing them into place and smoothing the seams. Brush the dough with the egg white (you will not need it all) and prick it in a few places with a fork. Bake in an oven preheated to 180°C/gas 4 for about 20 minutes until the pastry is lightly coloured. Remove from the oven and let it cool.

For the filling, boil the leeks in salted water for about 10 minutes until soft. Then drain well and chop them not too finely in the food processor. Drain again to get rid of the water.

In a bowl, lightly beat the eggs with a fork, then beat in the cream followed by the chopped leeks. Add salt to taste and pour into the baked crust. If you are using a tart tin, place it on a baking tray. Bake in the preheated oven for 40 to 45 minutes, or until the filling is set and the top is golden.

For the shortcrust pastry

- ❋ 125g chilled unsalted butter, plus a little more for greasing the tart tin or flan dish
- ❋ 250g plain flour
- ❋ ¼ teaspoon salt
- ❋ 1 large egg, lightly beaten
- ❋ 1–2 tablespoons milk (if required)
- ❋ 1 egg white, lightly beaten

For the filling

- ❋ 500g leeks, trimmed, washed and cut into 5cm lengths
- ❋ salt
- ❋ 4 large eggs
- ❋ 250ml double cream

MEAT PIE
❖ *pastel de carne*

This meat pie is celebrated as an important part of the local culture in Murcia, with regional festivals dedicated to it. The pies are said to be of Arab origin (for me, cinnamon is the clue). In the late seventeenth century, an ordinance signed by King Carlos II regulated their content. Bakeries and pastry shops make them with two different types of lardy pastry – a shortcrust base and a puff-pastry top. The tops are crafted in a curious way with rolls of thin dough cut into narrow ribbons and coiled so that the pies come out of the oven with amazing crisp, golden, spiky pastry spirals. Some bakers add crumbled *morcilla* (Spanish blood sausage), some add chopped *chorizo* – very rarely there is a touch of something sweet like raisins. The artistry did not work in the same glorious way with my bought puff pastry so I made my second pie with a flat top.

SERVES 6–8

Roll out the shortcrust dough on a floured surface with a floured rolling pin, so that it is large enough to line a 25 to 30cm tart tin or oven dish greased with butter. Carefully transfer the sheet of dough to the tin or dish, easing it into the corners. Trim the excess dough by cutting round the edge with a knife.

Put the minced veal in a bowl. Add the garlic, salt, pepper, cinnamon and ham. Mix well and work with your hand to a soft paste. Spread it evenly inside the shortcrust dough in the tin or dish. Sprinkle with the chopped *chorizo*, arrange the hard-boiled egg wedges on top, and dust lightly with salt.

Roll out the puff-pastry dough on a floured surface with a floured rolling pin. Carefully lift it up by rolling it around the rolling pin, then unroll it over the filling in the tin or dish. Trim the edges with a knife so that the top pastry covers the bottom one and press the edges together. Brush the top all over with the beaten egg yolk mixed with a drop of water and cut a small steam hole in the middle using a pointed knife.

Bake in an oven preheated to 200°C/gas 6 for 50 to 60 minutes, but cover the pastry with foil after about 30 minutes, when the top is golden brown and the pastry puffed up.

Serve the pie hot or cold.

- 1 x 500g pack bought shortcrust pastry
- a small knob of butter, to grease the tart tin or oven dish
- 350g (about ⅔ of a 500g pack) bought puff pastry
- 1 egg yolk, lightly beaten, to brush the pastry

For the filling

- 750g minced veal, preferably slightly fatty meat from the shoulder
- 1 garlic clove, peeled and crushed
- salt and pepper
- 1 teaspoon ground cinnamon
- 100g *jamón serrano* or other raw dry-cured ham, finely chopped
- 50g *chorizo*, chopped
- 4 hard-boiled eggs, peeled and cut into thin wedges

VEGETABLE DISHES AND SALADS

entremeses de verduras y ensaladas

Vegetables and salads are served as *entremeses* (hors d'oeuvres) or starters in Spain. Salads can be very simple – a few tomatoes with a sprinkling of chopped sweet, mild onion; a bowl of crisp lettuce; sliced oranges with a few black olives; diced tomatoes, peppers and cucumbers – or they can be complex and represent a snack meal. An English friend of mine who has employed Spanish au pairs commented that they 'could never leave vegetables alone', and it is true. Spaniards do not cook vegetables as a plain boiled side dish; they turn them into something that can be enjoyed as a dish in itself. An enormous variety of vegetables grow in Valencia, Murcia, Catalonia, Andalusia and in the valleys of the great rivers of Spain. There are only a few Spanish vegetables that we cannot easily get hold of in Britain. These include a species of tiny, tender baby artichoke that can be eaten whole, and *pochas*, a type of white haricot bean that is eaten fresh and is grown on family farms in La Rioja and Navarre. Most of the vegetables in our supermarkets come from far away and have not ripened in the sun. Some, such as artichokes, peas and spinach, are now available frozen in a way that preserves their flavour and texture, so do not feel unhappy about using these frozen vegetables if fresh ones are unavailable.

Vegetables were once despised in Spain as 'food of the poor', belonging to the vegetable patches of the peasantry. It is only since the middle of the twentieth century that they have become truly appreciated. Now star chefs of the *nueva cocina* have elevated vegetables to a rank as high as foie gras and caviar in their menus – at least that is what they say. They do produce fantastic delicacies made with vegetables that are a modern take on what their grandmothers used to cook. Peasant families, where the old vegetable dishes originated, lavished a lot of love and attention on their preparation because that was virtually all they had to eat. They made them more appealing by adding chestnuts, sometimes almonds, pine nuts and raisins, or chopped hard-boiled eggs, but most often it was tiny bits of home-cured ham. This last custom came about at the time when agents of the Inquisition visited at mealtimes, obliging everyone to prove their Catholicism in an obvious way. During Lent (*Cuaresma*), and on the many religious days of abstinence from meat that occurred throughout the year, ham was not included in a dish as that could leave you open to accusations of heresy and to punishment. Monasteries famously devised special vegetable dishes to be cooked during Lent, to which they would add herbs, and sometimes substitute salt cod for ham. But Lent made little difference to the urban poor, who lived on bread and vegetables alone.

One of the best things that innovative Spanish chefs have done is to put grilled or roasted vegetables – the way that peasants prepared them out in the field – and lightly boiled vegetables on their menus, and this has made them suddenly trendy. *Bollit* (in Valencian Catalan) or *hervido* (in Castilian Spanish), the assortment of boiled vegetables that represents the traditional evening first course in Valencia and Murcia, has spread to other parts of the country. On my arrival in Madrid, Alicia Ríos (see page 219), with whom I was staying, served up a platter of hot steamed tiny artichokes, tender wide green beans and asparagus. I dressed the vegetables on my plate with sweet, fruity extra virgin olive oil and a sprinkling of sea salt. It was all I could wish for. New or waxy potatoes, and green vegetables such as courgettes, leeks, spring onions, chard and spinach are served in this way. Some people like to add a little vinegar with the olive oil.

If you are vegetarian, you will find a huge choice of dishes here. You will also find vegetable dishes in other chapters – combined with rice, as fillings for pies, as toppings for pizza-type *cocas*, and in soups and omelettes. They make perfect starters, and some also can be eaten as main dishes.

VEGETABLES *with a* TOMATO *and* HARD-BOILED EGG VINAIGRETTE

❧ *verduras de la huerta con salsa vinagreta*

There are many versions of Spanish vinaigrette (see the recipe variation at the end). *Vinagreta* adds glamour and flavour to a simple dish of boiled vegetables and makes it light and refreshing, as well as an elegant start to a meal. The vegetables can be served hot or at room temperature and can be prepared in advance. All kinds of vegetables may be used; you can substitute or add others, such as carrots, runner beans, green beans and cauliflower. The main thing is to give each vegetable the right cooking time. Leeks have to be very well cooked and soft while asparagus are best a little crunchy.

SERVES 4–6

Trim and wash the leeks, cut off the green ends and cut each of them into three pieces. Peel the potatoes and cut them in half. Trim the hard ends of the asparagus. Cut the artichoke hearts or bottoms in half. Put a large pan of salted water on to boil and throw in the leeks and potatoes. Simmer for 10 minutes, then add the artichokes. Cook for 5 minutes, then add the asparagus and cook for 5 to 10 minutes more until all the vegetables are done. Drain well and arrange them in a wide serving dish.

While the vegetables are still warm make the *vinagreta*. Beat the oil and vinegar or lemon juice with some salt and pepper in a bowl. Stir in the parsley, chopped tomatoes and hard-boiled egg and pour over the vegetables, turning them so that they absorb the dressing well.

VARIATION

❧ You may add ½ a chopped sweet, mild red onion and a few capers and chopped olives to the *vinagreta*.

* 4 leeks
* about 500g new or waxy potatoes
* 250g asparagus
* 3 fresh baby artichoke hearts (see page 120) or frozen and defrosted artichoke bottoms
* salt

For the vinagreta

* 7 tablespoons extra virgin olive oil
* 2 tablespoons white wine vinegar or juice of ½ a lemon
* salt and pepper
* 2 tablespoons finely chopped flat-leaf parsley
* 2 firm tomatoes (about 200g), chopped
* 1 hard-boiled egg, peeled and chopped

CREAM *of* TOMATO *with* TUNA *and* HARD-BOILED EGGS

❋ *sopeao*

Flame-haired Loli Flores, who was for many years a chef in Seville, remembers *sopeao* from the village of Mairena del Alcor near Seville, where she lived as a child with her mother, siblings, grandparents and great-grandfather. It was a one-dish summer meal. They served it with crusty bread to soak up the puréed tomatoes – the name *sopeao* is derived from the word *sopear*, meaning 'to soak up'. For a big party during the annual *Feria* (the Seville spring fair), the *sopeao* would be made in a huge, deep platter, into which pieces of pigeon and rabbit were added. It would be served in lettuce leaves and followed with melon or watermelon.

SERVES 4–6

There is no need to peel the tomatoes. Cut them into quarters and remove the little hard bits at the stem ends.

To make breadcrumbs, dry out the bread under the grill without browning it, turning the slices over once, then process to coarse crumbs in the food processor and remove. Now put the pepper in the food processor and blend to a paste, then add the tomatoes and garlic and blend to a cream. Add the sugar, salt and pepper, the vinegar and olive oil and blend again. Return the breadcrumbs and blend briefly just to fold them in. Taste and adjust the seasoning.

Pour into a wide platter and arrange the egg quarters or slices and the tuna, broken into pieces, on top.

- ❋ 1kg large ripe tomatoes
- ❋ 100g sliced firm white bread, crusts removed
- ❋ 1 green or red pepper, deseeded and quartered
- ❋ 2–3 garlic cloves, peeled and crushed
- ❋ 1 teaspoon sugar
- ❋ salt and pepper
- ❋ 2–3 tablespoons sherry vinegar or wine vinegar
- ❋ 125ml extra virgin olive oil
- ❋ 4–6 hard-boiled eggs, peeled and quartered or sliced
- ❋ 2 x 160g tins tuna in oil, drained

ORANGE SALAD
❀ *ensalada de naranja*

The Arabs introduced bitter oranges to Spain, and in the early sixteenth century sweet oranges arrived from China. Sweet oranges are used in a variety of salads. A tablespoon of sweet wine or port mixed with sherry vinegar in the dressing adds an intriguing touch to this one.

SERVES 4

❀ 2 oranges ❀ 1 small cos lettuce ❀ ½ a sweet, mild red onion, peeled and chopped
❀ 3 tablespoons extra virgin olive oil ❀ 1 tablespoon sherry vinegar
❀ 1 tablespoon sweet Pedro Ximénez wine or port ❀ salt

Peel the oranges so that no pith is left and cut them into slices crossways. Cut the lettuce into wide slices. Arrange the orange slices and lettuce in a platter and sprinkle over the chopped onion.

Just before serving, mix the olive oil, vinegar, sweet wine or port and a little salt, and pour over the salad, then gently toss together.

GRILLED VEGETABLES
❀ *verduras a la plancha*

Grilling vegetables on a *plancha* (griddle) was the way peasants cooked them in the fields, and now innovative chefs have made this cooking method fashionable. Asparagus, spring onions, peppers, tomatoes, tender baby artichokes, aubergines, courgettes and mushrooms are turned in olive oil and cooked whole or in slices on a lightly oiled griddle or on an oiled grill over dying embers. You can also do them under the grill or roast them in the oven at its highest setting. Turn the vegetables over once. If you watch them you cannot go wrong. Serve with a sprinkling of sea salt and a trickle of extra virgin olive oil or accompanied by any of the following: *vinagreta* (page 146), *salmorreta* (page 147), *alioli* (page 149), mayonnaise (page 148) or *mojo de perejil* (page 146). You will find these in the chapter on sauces and dressings.

ROASTED TOMATO SALAD
with OLIVES, EGGS *and* TUNA
✳ *mojete huertano*

This salad was both a festive peasant dish and a dish *de vigilia* – something that could be eaten on days of abstinence. The ingredients bathe in the juice of roasted tomatoes – you need ripe tomatoes with a fine taste. Serve it in soup bowls with spoons and accompany with good country bread. Some call it *pipirrana*.

SERVES 6

✳ 1kg tomatoes ✳ 6 tablespoons extra virgin olive oil ✳ 1 teaspoon sugar
✳ 2 tablespoons red or white wine vinegar ✳ salt ✳ about 24 black olives ✳ 3 hard-boiled eggs, peeled and quartered ✳ 1 x 160g tin tuna in oil, drained and broken into chunks

Turn the tomatoes under a hot grill until their skins are lightly browned and loosened and they feel soft. Peel them, cut away and discard the hard bits near the stem, then chop their flesh. Place the tomatoes with their juice in a wide serving dish, add the olive oil, sugar, vinegar and salt, and mix well. Then stir in the olives and arrange the hard-boiled eggs and tuna on top.

VARIATIONS

▩ Instead of roasting the tomatoes, simply peel them with a serrated knife and blend them to a purée.

▩ Add 6–8 medium-sized boiled new potatoes, peeled and sliced and sprinkled with salt.

▩ In Castile-La Mancha, 1 teaspoon of ground cumin is added to the dressing.

▩ Add a few anchovy fillets.

▩ Add 2 green or red peppers, roasted, peeled (see page 118) and cut into ribbons.

▩ For a quite different MOJETE MANCHEGO of roasted peppers and onions to serve 6, put 1 whole head of garlic, 6 red peppers and 7 white or red medium onions on sheets of foil on baking trays in an oven pre-heated to 180°C/gas 4 (with the onions on a lower shelf). Take the garlic out after about 20 minutes, the peppers after about 45 minutes and the onions after an hour or longer, when they are soft. Peel the peppers and cut them into strips (see page 118). Peel the onions, cut them in half then into thick slices. To make the dressing, peel the garlic cloves and blend them with 6 tablespoons of extra virgin olive oil, the juice of 1 or 1½ lemons, salt and 1 teaspoon of ground cumin. Pour the dressing over the peppers and onions, add a handful of black olives, and mix well.

ROASTED PEPPERS
and AUBERGINES ✳ *escalivada*

In Catalan, *escalivar* means 'to grill'. Another name for this dish is *rustifaci*, which means 'roasted'. It was usual in Catalonia to cook all kinds of vegetables over wood embers in the fields and on beaches. That is also how they were cooked at home in the fireplace. Some, like onions and potatoes, were wrapped in foil and left in the ashes. This way of cooking gives vegetables a delicious, smoky flavour, but today they are most often roasted in the oven. *Escalivada* has become popular throughout Spain, and is now usually made with aubergines and peppers alone. It is dressed simply with olive oil and a little salt.

SERVES 6

✳ 4 medium aubergines ✳ 4 fleshy (round) or elongated red peppers
✳ 6 tablespoons extra virgin olive oil ✳ salt

Put the aubergines and peppers on a sheet of foil on a large baking tray. Prick the aubergines in a few places with a pointed knife to prevent them from bursting and put the tray in an oven preheated to 180°C/gas 4. Turn the vegetables over once.

Take the peppers out after about 45 minutes, when they are soft and their skin has blistered. Put them in a plastic bag and twist to seal the bag. Leave the peppers to steam in the bag for about 10 to 15 minutes – this will make the skin come away more easily. When the peppers are cool enough to handle, peel them, remove the stems and seeds and cut them into strips. The strips can be thin or wide. I usually have 8 strips per pepper. Reserve the juices.

After a further 15 minutes (about 1 hour total cooking time), when the aubergines feel soft when you press them, take them out of the oven. Once they are cool enough to handle, peel and cut the aubergines into long, similar-sized strips to the peppers.

Arrange the vegetables in one layer on a serving plate, alternating peppers and aubergines, and sprinkle with the olive oil and a little salt.

VARIATIONS

❀ Cook the peppers and aubergines under the grill or on a barbecue over glowing embers. Keep turning them until they are soft and blackened all over, then continue as above.

❀ Put 4 whole small to medium-sized onions in the oven on another baking tray. They take a bit longer than an hour to soften. Peel and cut them into wedges, and add them to the peppers and aubergines.

❀ Garnish the finished dish with black olives and chopped flat-leaf parsley, if you like.

❀ In a version of *escalivada* from Aragon called *frigolla*, you put 4 tomatoes in the oven with the peppers and aubergines. They are done in about 10 minutes, when they feel slightly soft. Peel and cut them into wedges, and add them to the other vegetables.

RATATOUILLE-*like* VEGETABLES
✳ *samfaina*

Samfaina is like the ratatouille of Provence. It is served as a hot accompaniment to fish, chicken and meat, and is also good as a cold starter to serve with bread. Many countries around the Mediterranean have a similar dish. In Catalonia, they cut the vegetables up small and cook them until they are very soft and jammy, and do not usually include courgettes. I too prefer it without courgettes. Catalans say that the dish originated with them, and that is very likely since they were the first in the Mediterranean to put aubergines, which were introduced by the Arabs, together with the peppers and tomatoes that arrived from the Americas.

SERVES 4

✳ 1 large onion, peeled, halved and sliced ✳ 6 tablespoons olive oil ✳ 1 red or green pepper, deseeded and cut into 1.5cm squares ✳ 4 garlic cloves, peeled and chopped ✳ 1 aubergine, cut into 1.5cm cubes ✳ 1 courgette, cut into 1.5cm cubes (optional) ✳ 2 tomatoes, halved crossways and grated (see page 121), or peeled and chopped ✳ salt

In a wide frying pan, sauté the onion in the oil, covered, over a low heat, stirring often, for about 7 minutes until soft. Add the pepper and cook, covered, for another 7 minutes or so, stirring occasionally until it is softened. Add the garlic, stir for 2 minutes, then add the aubergine and the courgette, if using. Cook, covered, for 20 minutes, stirring and turning the vegetables often until they are slightly browned. Now add the tomatoes, season with salt and continue to cook, uncovered, over a medium heat for 10 to 15 minutes, until the vegetables are so soft they have almost lost their shape and much of the liquid has disappeared.

COURGETTES *with* ONIONS *and* OREGANO
❋ *zarangollo*

Cooking courgettes with onions and herbs until they are very soft gives them a delicate flavour and pleasing texture. This is good hot or cold.

SERVES 6

❋ 1 large onion, peeled, halved and sliced ❋ 3–4 tablespoons olive oil ❋ 1kg courgettes, thinly sliced ❋ salt ❋ 1 tablespoon chopped fresh oregano

In a very large frying pan, fry the onion in the oil over a very low heat, stirring often, for about 15 minutes until soft and golden. Add the courgettes and cook for about 30 minutes over a low heat, turning them over occasionally, sprinkling with salt and covering the pan with a lid or a large piece of foil. Add the oregano and cook for 10 minutes more. The vegetables cook in their own steam.

VARIATION

❋ Lightly beat 5 eggs and, when the courgettes are done, stir the eggs in and cook briefly, stirring gently, until they set to a creamy consistency.

SAUTÉED PEPPERS *and* TOMATOES
✻ *fritada de pimientos y tomates*

Also known as *chilindrón*, *fritada* is a speciality of the valley of the river Ebro in north-east Spain. It is served hot as a garnish for meat, chicken or fish, or cold as a starter.

SERVES 4

✳ 1 large onion, peeled, halved and sliced ✳ 3–4 tablespoons olive oil ✳ 2 red peppers, deseeded and halved, then cut into 8 strips ✳ 2 garlic cloves, peeled and sliced ✳ 500g tomatoes, peeled and chopped ✳ salt and pepper ✳ 1 teaspoon sugar ✳ a drizzle of extra virgin olive oil

Fry the onion in the oil in a large pan over a medium heat until soft, stirring occasionally. Add the peppers and cook, stirring, until the peppers have also softened. Add the garlic and, when it begins to colour, add the tomatoes, salt, pepper and sugar. Cook for 20 to 25 minutes over a low heat until the peppers are soft and the sauce has reduced to a jammy consistency. Serve at room temperature with a drizzle of the extra virgin olive oil.

VARIATIONS

▨ Roast and peel the peppers (see page 118) and cut them into squares, then add them when the tomato sauce is almost done.

▨ For *pimientos en chilindrón con jamón*, fry 4 slices of *jamón serrano* or other raw dry-cured ham, cut into small pieces, with the onion.

▨ For a wonderful light meal to serve with bread, break 4 eggs over the vegetables at the end and cook until they set.

SALAD *of* ROASTED PEPPERS *and* TOMATOES
✣ *pipirrana*

Pipirrana, also called *mojete*, is part of a large family of salads based on chopped or creamed tomatoes. They were the food of agricultural labourers from Andalusia, Murcia and Castile-La Mancha, who made *pipirrana* in the fields over an open fire. On festive occasions, tuna, hard-boiled eggs and black olives would be added. Roasting the tomatoes gave the sauce a sweet intense flavour.

SERVES 4

✳ 3 round or elongated red peppers ✳ 500g tomatoes ✳ 1–2 garlic cloves, peeled and finely chopped ✳ 3 tablespoons extra virgin olive oil ✳ salt and pepper ✳ 1 teaspoon sugar

Place the whole peppers and tomatoes on sheets of foil on two baking trays and roast on the top shelf in an oven preheated to 240°C/gas 9. Take the tomatoes out after about 15 minutes, when they have softened a bit and their skins have loosened. Once they have cooled enough, peel and chop the tomatoes, removing the hard white bits at the stem ends.

Turn the peppers over and roast them for a further 15 minutes, or until they are soft and the skins have blistered and are black in parts. Put them in a plastic bag, twist it shut and leave for 10 to 15 minutes, then peel them, remove the stems and seeds and cut the peppers into strips about 1.5cm wide. Collect their juices to add to the dressing.

Sauté the garlic in 1 tablespoon of the olive oil in a large frying pan for seconds only until the aroma rises. Add the roasted tomatoes, salt, pepper and sugar, and cook over a high heat for about 8 minutes until the sauce has reduced, then take off the heat and mix with the peppers. Serve cold, drizzled with the remaining olive oil and the juices from the peppers.

VARIATION

✣ *Asadillo* in Castile-La Mancha is a similar salad of roasted red peppers, simply dressed with fresh tomatoes blended to a cream in the food processor (no need to skin them) with extra virgin olive oil, a little crushed garlic, salt and a pinch of sugar.

SAUTÉED VEGETABLE MEDLEY
❋ *pisto manchego*

I was surprised to find that this Mediterranean ratatouille-type dish is typical of the centre of Spain. Castilians adopted the old Moorish dish of fried onions, aubergines and courgettes, called *alboronia*, after they conquered Toledo, where Muslims, Jews and Christians went on to live in the city together. Peppers and tomatoes were added later. Some versions are made without aubergines. Some people peel the aubergines and the courgettes. Some add potatoes or have eggs cooked on top at the end. I prefer to cook the aubergines separately. The best *pisto* that I have ever eaten was made by Rosemary, my friend Alicia's young Bolivian maid, in Alicante. She learnt how to cook at the home of the Spanish architect Antonio Lamela, who built the modern centre of Madrid and whose family created the bourgeois style in the exclusive Salamanca *barrio* (district) of the city. She swam with us early in the morning, then started cooking fabulous dishes for the large company of family and friends. This is her slightly adapted recipe.

SERVES 6

In a large frying pan or *paella* pan, fry the onions in about 5 tablespoons of the oil, stirring often, over a medium-low heat until they begin to soften. Add the peppers and, when they begin to soften, add the courgettes. Season with salt and pepper and cook, turning the vegetables over gently, until they are soft. Then add the tomatoes and sugar and cook until the liquid has evaporated.

In another large frying pan, fry the aubergines in the remaining oil over a high heat, stirring and turning them over with a slotted spoon or spatula. They will absorb a lot of oil but then gradually release most of it. After 10 to 15 minutes, when they are well cooked and soft, lift them out and drain on kitchen paper, then add them to the rest of the vegetables. Mix gently and cook all together for a couple of minutes more.

VARIATION

❈ Rosemary also sometimes makes *pisto* with potatoes and she flavours it with 1 teaspoon of chopped oregano. For this, peel and boil 4–6 medium-sized new potatoes until tender, then cut them into 1.5cm cubes and add them to the pan at the same time as the aubergines.

- ❋ 2 large onions (about 500g), peeled and coarsely chopped
- ❋ 10 tablespoons olive oil
- ❋ 3 red peppers or a mix of red and green (about 500g), deseeded and cut into 1.5cm squares
- ❋ 3 courgettes (about 500g), cut into 1.5cm cubes
- ❋ salt and pepper
- ❋ 5–6 tomatoes (about 500g), peeled and diced
- ❋ 1–2 teaspoons sugar, or to taste
- ❋ 1–2 aubergines (about 500g), cut into 1.5cm cubes

alicia ríos ivars

When I arrived from Madrid's Barajas airport for one of my research trips for this book, Alicia had a vegetable feast waiting for me. Alicia is a friend of many years. She was my main mentor in Spain as I worked on this book, arranging invaluable contacts, taking me to visit people, answering endless questions and sending me recipes and articles. I stayed with her in Madrid, where I used her extensive library of culinary books. You will find her name throughout the book. She is tall and thin and dresses in toreador style, fashioned from the exotic silks and colourful cottons she collects on her travels. When she came to London after university in the 1960s to improve her English she cooked at Cranks and other vegetarian restaurants to earn extra money. Alicia taught philosophy and psychology before opening a restaurant where she also did the cooking. She is a food historian and olive oil specialist and is known internationally as a food artist who creates collective performances.

Alone, or with Ali&Cia, the Eat Art group she founded with her architect niece Barbara Ortiz, she has created edible hats, edible greenhouses, libraries, a Berlin Wall and, most spectacularly, edible cities and islands in different parts of the world. For the edible cities, the group invite local communities to think of ways to construct a section of their city using their own traditional foods. With columns of spring rolls, palaces built out of Indian sweets, parks made from green rice and skyscrapers from bagels, stuffed vine leaves and sushi, the final edible map reflects the ethnic mix of the population. In the end, with background music, the public is invited to eat the result. On 28 April 2007, I was in Trafalgar Square with my children and grandchildren and we watched fourteen volunteer teams from community centres and social clubs, led by Alicia and Barbara, bring together their models of different parts of London created with samosas, pakoras, pizzas and the like. Because of the huge crowds we did not get to eat any of it.

Alicia has a summer house in Calpe on the Costa Blanca in the province of Alicante. Her little *casita* (cottage) is next to her mother Pepa's house. Her maternal grandfather had land in Alicante and her parents were so taken by a rock in the sea called el Peñón de Ifach — her father was an internationally renowned geological scientist from Zaragoza — that they built three little houses overlooking it on the seafront so that their three daughters would always have a home there. The houses used to be the only ones near the little fishing village of Calpe. Now, one has been sold and the two left are the last Spanish enclave in a world of high-rise buildings and an English, German and now also Russian ex-pat population.

I stayed at the *casita* with a group of Alicia's friends. She had attached hundreds of plastic flowers on strings hanging from the ceilings and strewn many more over the floors and on the beds. Margarita, Pepa's companion, young Rosemary from Bolivia and Ana, whose husband is a local fisherman, prepared sumptuous meals for us every day. Many of their recipes can be found in this book.

MEDLEY *of* SPRING VEGETABLES
❋ *menestra de primavera*

This marvellous combination of green vegetables in a soupy sauce is one of the great vegetable dishes of Spain, a speciality of the regions crossed by the river Ebro. In the 1837 edition of the *Diccionario de la Real Academia Española* ('Dictionary of the Royal Spanish Academy of Language') it was cited as a soup. Although some modern chefs cook the vegetables al dente, I prefer them in the traditional way – cooked for a longer time, soft, in a delicious soupy wine sauce slightly thickened with a little flour. You can vary the proportions. It makes a perfect first course but can be served as a side dish, in which case it is enough for six. Tiny bits of ham lend a traditional Spanish touch. Make it with fresh vegetables in the spring, but you can also have a very good dish using frozen ones.

SERVES 4–6

Bring the stock to the boil in a large pan and put in the broad beans. Simmer for 5 minutes, then add the artichoke hearts or bottoms. Simmer for 5 minutes, then add the asparagus. Simmer for a further 5 minutes, then add the peas. Cook until the vegetables are only just tender, adding a little salt.

At the same time, make the sauce. In a smaller pan fry the onion in the oil over a low heat, stirring, until soft. Add the garlic and chopped ham or streaky bacon and stir for 1 minute. Add the flour and stir until it acquires a little colour, then gradually add the wine, stirring vigorously.

Cook, stirring, for a few minutes, until the sauce thickens a little, then add 2 ladlefuls of the stock from the vegetables. Stir vigorously and cook for about 8 to 10 minutes. Pour the sauce over the vegetables, shake the pan and cook until the vegetables are very tender.

* 600ml chicken stock (you may use 1 stock cube)
* 250g podded broad beans, fresh or frozen and defrosted
* 4 artichoke bottoms or baby hearts, fresh (see page 120 for preparing them) or frozen and defrosted, halved
* 250g asparagus, trimmed of hard ends
* 250g podded peas, fresh or frozen and defrosted
* salt
* ½ a medium onion, peeled and chopped
* 2 tablespoons olive oil
* 1 garlic clove, peeled and chopped
* 2 thin slices of *jamón serrano* or other raw dry-cured ham, or streaky bacon rashers, chopped
* 1½ tablespoons plain flour
* 250ml medium-dry white wine

ARTICHOKES *with* GREEN SAUCE
❋ *alcachofas con salsa verde*

This recipe is inspired by one in *Tía Victoria's Spanish Kitchen* by Victoria Serra, translated by her daughter-in-law, Elizabeth Gili. The book was lent to me by Elizabeth herself, a beautiful blue-eyed woman in her nineties who had studied philosophy. Her husband, Joan Gili, a Catalan, had come to London in 1934. He ran a Hispanic bookshop in Cecil Court off Charing Cross Road and, with Stephen Spender, translated several of Spanish poet and dramatist Federico García Lorca's books. He was a founding member and later president of the Anglo-Catalan Society. Nostalgic for his family's cooking, he wrote to his mother for recipes and eventually encouraged her to write the book, which was published in Spain as *Sabores* by his father, the publisher Luis Gili.

I used frozen artichoke bottoms. If you want to use fresh artichokes, see page 120 for how to prepare them.

SERVES 4

Boil the artichokes in salted water for about 10 minutes until just tender and drain. In a small frying pan, fry the bread and the whole garlic cloves in the 2 tablespoons of olive oil over a medium heat, turning to brown them all over. Then drain on kitchen paper.

Pour the vinegar on to the fried bread and blend in the food processor with the cooked garlic. Add the parsley, the extra virgin olive oil and some salt and blend to a creamy sauce.

Serve the artichokes at room temperature, spooning a little of the sauce on to each one.

- ❋ 9 artichoke bottoms or baby hearts, fresh (see page 120) or frozen and defrosted
- ❋ salt
- ❋ ½ a slice of white bread, without crusts (about 30g)
- ❋ 1–2 large garlic cloves, peeled
- ❋ 2 tablespoons olive oil, for frying
- ❋ 1 tablespoon white wine vinegar
- ❋ a 25g bunch of flat-leaf parsley, chopped
- ❋ 3 tablespoons extra virgin olive oil

ARTICHOKES *in* ALMOND SAUCE
❈ *alcachofas en salsa blanca*

I loved a delicate dish of cardoon stalks in an almond sauce that I ate in Navarre. At home I had trouble finding cardoons, so I was happy to hear that artichokes are also cooked in the same way. You may be able to find cardoons preserved in jars. In Spain you can buy them frozen. If you have fresh cardoons, see the instructions on how to prepare them in the variation I give below. I use frozen artichoke bottoms, which I buy in Middle Eastern shops. In France you can find frozen hearts – I hope they will become available in this country soon. It is the kind of dish you can easily make for a lot of people if you have frozen artichokes.

SERVES 8

❋ 500ml whole milk ❋ 500ml chicken stock (page 145) ❋ 2 tablespoons olive oil
❋ 2 tablespoons plain flour ❋ 2 garlic cloves, peeled and crushed ❋ 75g ground almonds
❋ salt ❋ 2 x 400g bags frozen artichoke bottoms, defrosted

Bring the milk and stock to the boil in a saucepan. Heat the oil in a large saucepan. Add the flour and stir vigorously with a wooden spoon over a low heat for 30 seconds without letting it brown. Stir in the garlic, then gradually add the milk and stock mixture, a little at a time, stirring vigorously until there are no lumps. Continue to stir over a low heat until the sauce thickens, then stir in the ground almonds and add salt to taste.

Add the artichoke bottoms to the sauce and cook for about 15 minutes over a gentle heat until they are tender. Serve hot.

VARIATIONS

❋ Instead of artichokes use cardoons, fresh or preserved in jars. Fresh cardoons are often sold with the prickly outer parts on the stems removed. Only the inner part of the stalks or hearts are eaten. If they have not already been trimmed, you will need about 1.75kg of cardoons. Tear off the leaves and cut the stalks into 8–10cm lengths. Cook in boiling salted water acidulated with the juice of ½ a lemon for about 20 minutes. Drain and refresh in cold water, then peel off and discard the tough skin and strings from the stems. Drop the bare inner stalks in the sauce and cook for 15 to 25 minutes until tender.

❋ Ribs of Swiss chard are also cooked with the same sauce.

BRAISED PEAS *and* ARTICHOKES
❊ *guisantes y alcachofas*

Being a favourite vegetable in Catalonia, broad beans are more often used than peas in this extraordinarily aromatic dish, but this version with peas is delightful. Serve it with toasted bread drizzled with extra virgin olive oil.

SERVES 6

❊ 1 large onion, peeled and chopped ❊ 2 tablespoons olive oil ❊ 100g *jamón serrano* or other raw dry-cured ham, or streaky bacon, cut into small pieces ❊ 3 garlic cloves, peeled and crushed ❊ 2 medium tomatoes, peeled and chopped ❊ 1 teaspoon sugar ❊ 100ml brandy ❊ 1 cinnamon stick ❊ 2 sprigs of thyme or oregano ❊ 3 sprigs of mint ❊ 400g frozen artichoke bottoms, defrosted, or 6 fresh baby artichoke hearts (see page 120) ❊ 500ml chicken stock (you may use ½ a stock cube) ❊ salt ❊ 400g young fresh peas or defrosted frozen ones

In a wide saucepan, sauté the onion in the oil over a low heat, stirring occasionally, until it is soft and just beginning to colour. Add the ham or bacon, and cook, stirring, for half a minute if it is ham, or 2 minutes if it is bacon. Add the garlic and cook, stirring, for seconds only until the aroma rises, then stir in the tomatoes and sugar. Cook for about 10 minutes over a medium heat until reduced to almost a paste.

Pour in the brandy, add the cinnamon stick, the sprigs of thyme or oregano and the mint. Put in the artichokes, cover with the stock, add salt and cook, covered, over a low heat for 10 to 15 minutes until they are tender. Then add the peas and cook for a further 5 to 10 minutes or until the peas are soft.

Serve hot or at room temperature.

VARIATIONS

❊ Instead of peas use broad beans, fresh or frozen, and put them in at the same time as the artichokes. Cook until the vegetables are very tender.

❊ For another version, instead of the brandy, add 4 tablespoons of Moscatel or other sweet white wine, *aguardiente* or grappa.

PEAS *and* BROAD BEANS *with* HAM
✣ *guisantes y habas con jamón*

I love the Catalan way of making a grand dish with a symphony of flavours out of ordinary vegetables, which are cooked until they are soft, not crisp. Serve them with toasted bread and a drizzle of extra virgin olive oil. The dish is often made with broad beans alone; sometimes tomatoes are added. Adding Catalan sausages or *chorizos*, as in the variation, turns this into a main dish.

SERVES 6

Cut the ham or bacon into small pieces and sauté in the oil over a medium heat in a casserole or large saucepan, stirring, for half a minute if it is ham, for 3 to 4 minutes until lightly browned if it is bacon. Add the garlic and stir for seconds only until the aroma rises.

Add the beans, the stock or water, the sprigs of marjoram or oregano and mint, and the bay leaf. Simmer, covered, for 10 to 20 minutes until the beans are tender (the time depends on how young the beans are). Add salt and some pepper.

Add the peas and spring onions, the rum, brandy or anise-flavoured spirit, and cook, covered, for 7 to 10 minutes more until the vegetables are soft.

VARIATIONS

✻ Omit the peas and use double the quantity of broad beans.

✻ Add 2 peeled and chopped tomatoes at the start, after sautéing the ham or bacon and the garlic.

✻ Omit the rum, brandy or anise-flavoured spirit and the sprigs of marjoram or oregano and mint, and instead add a cinnamon stick at the start and 3 tablespoons of roughly chopped fresh mint towards the end of cooking.

✻ Boil 400g semi-cured cooking *chorizos* in water for 20 minutes, then drain, cut into slices and add them to the peas and broad beans at the end of the cooking.

✻ Boil 400g *morcilla* (Spanish blood sausage) in barely simmering water for only 10 minutes, cut into thick slices and add them when you are ready to heat through and serve.

* 125g *jamón serrano* or other raw dry-cured ham, or streaky bacon, thinly sliced

* 4 tablespoons olive oil

* 5–6 garlic cloves, peeled and chopped

* 500g podded broad beans, fresh or frozen and defrosted

* 500ml chicken stock (you may use 1 stock cube) or water

* a sprig of marjoram or oregano

* a sprig of mint

* 1 bay leaf

* salt and pepper

* 500g podded peas, fresh or frozen and defrosted

* 6 spring onions, trimmed and thinly sliced

* 5 tablespoons rum or brandy, or an anise-flavoured spirit

WILD MUSHROOMS ✣ *setas*

My Catalan friend Pepa Aymami had a huge crateful of wild mushrooms (*setas*) spread out on towels over the garden table on her terrace in Barcelona. You could smell the forest. She cleaned off bits of earth with a brush and cooked the mushrooms in a huge pan over a high heat with a little sweet-tasting extra virgin olive oil, a sprinkling of salt and only just a touch of crushed garlic, so that it would not mask the mixed flavours and aromas of the mushrooms.

Wild mushrooms grow in breathtaking varieties in the Basque Country and Catalonia, where people are crazy about them. Catalans have identified a hundred edible species – about fifteen of them of gastronomic quality. The most prized are ceps, chanterelles and morels. During the mushroom season in September and October market stalls are full of them. People go mushroom-hunting in the mountains. There are organized tours where you learn to identify the edible ones and you get to cook and eat them. The regions have several mushroom festivals during which restaurants dedicate their menus to them. The mushrooms are grilled, sautéed, baked or scrambled with eggs, and cooked with game and meat and in sauces and stews.

Wild mushrooms grow in other parts of Spain, especially in the wet north-west, but people have always been afraid of picking them there – until the enthusiastic Catalans and Basques arrived. They did not value them because they were wild and free, and they were afraid because it is said that every year three or four people die of food poisoning from eating wild mushrooms they have picked.

MARINATED MUSHROOMS *with* LEMON
✳ *champiñones marinados*

These mushrooms lose their juices and absorb the scent of grated lemon zest in the marinade. They keep well in the refrigerator and make a good little appetizer to pick at with bread and olives.

SERVES 6–8

✳ 500g button mushrooms ✳ juice of 1 lemon ✳ grated zest of ½ a lemon
✳ 5 tablespoons extra virgin olive oil ✳ salt and pepper ✳ 2 tablespoons chopped flat-leaf parsley

Wipe the mushrooms and rinse them briefly, if necessary. Trim the stems, then cut them into halves or quarters. Heat them in a wide, dry, non-stick frying pan, over a medium heat, for 10 to 12 minutes, turning them over until they release their juices and these evaporate. Mix the lemon juice and lemon zest with the oil and some salt and pepper in a wide, shallow bowl. Put the hot mushrooms in the bowl with the marinade and mix well. Let cool, then cover and refrigerate for at least 5 hours. They keep for several days. Serve at room temperature with a sprinkling of parsley.

MUSHROOM FLAN ❊ *pastel de hongos*

The region of Navarre has had a long relationship with France. That is one reason why people cook with a lot of cream there. They also farm dairy cows. If wild mushrooms such as ceps and chanterelles are unavailable or too expensive, use chestnut (*cremini*) or button mushrooms for this dish.

SERVES 4–6

❊ 500g mushrooms ❊ ½ a large onion, peeled and chopped ❊ 3 tablespoons olive oil ❊ salt and pepper ❊ 3 large eggs ❊ 250ml double cream or crème fraiche ❊ 1–2 garlic cloves, peeled and crushed ❊ 3 tablespoons chopped flat-leaf parsley ❊ a knob of butter, to grease the baking or flan dish

Clean and, if necessary, rinse briefly and trim the stems of the mushrooms, then cut them in half, or into quarters if large.

In a large frying pan, fry the onion over a medium-low heat in the oil until it is soft and just beginning to colour. Add the mushrooms, salt and pepper, and cook, stirring, until the mushrooms have released their water and it has evaporated.

In a large bowl, beat the eggs lightly with a fork, then beat in the cream or crème fraiche with the garlic and parsley. Fold in the mushrooms and onion, season with a little more salt and pour into a wide buttered baking or flan dish.

Bake in an oven preheated to 200°C/gas 6 for 45 minutes to an hour, until set and golden. Serve warm.

MUSHROOMS *with* GARLIC
✻ *champiñones al ajillo*

I find Spanish terms for mushrooms a bit confusing. All mushrooms are *hongos*, wild ones are referred to as *setas*, and cultivated button mushrooms as *champiñones*. The easiest mushrooms to cultivate and the most common are the *champiñones de París*, so-called because they were first cultivated near Paris in Napoleon's time. These are ordinary button mushrooms. They are highly regarded in Spain. As they do not have the rich flavour and aroma of wild fungi, this way of preparing them with plenty of garlic, a rich virgin olive oil and sometimes a little lemon juice or wine suits them well. They are a popular *tapa* all over Spain, served with crusty bread to mop up the garlicky oil.

SERVES 4

Wipe any earth off the mushrooms and, if necessary, rinse them briefly and trim the stems. Cut them in half, or into quarters if they are large. Heat the oil in a frying pan and sauté the mushrooms with the garlic and the chilli flakes, if using, over a medium-high heat, stirring and turning them over, and adding salt and pepper. The mushrooms will absorb the oil at first, then will release it with their juices. Add the lemon juice or white wine, if using, lower the heat and cook, uncovered, until the mushrooms are very soft and the juices have almost evaporated and the oil sizzles through. In all, the cooking may take about 15 to 20 minutes.

Stir in the parsley and serve hot or cold.

* 250g button mushrooms
* 4 tablespoons extra virgin olive oil
* 4–5 garlic cloves, peeled and chopped or sliced
* ½ teaspoon chilli pepper flakes (optional)
* salt and pepper
* 1 tablespoon lemon juice or 4 tablespoons dry white wine (optional)
* 2 tablespoons chopped flat-leaf parsley

SPINACH *in a* BÉCHAMEL *with* HARD-BOILED EGGS
❈ *espinacas con béchamel*

This makes a lovely vegetarian main dish. The Spanish-style béchamel is light and creamy and has a special taste and aroma. I love it.

SERVES 4 AS A STARTER OR 2 AS A MAIN DISH

Remove any thick hard stalks from the spinach. Wash the leaves thoroughly and drain well. In our supermarkets we can buy baby spinach leaves with very thin small stalks – you do not need to take these off. Put the leaves in a large pan, with only the water that clings to them after washing and draining, and put the lid on. (If you have bought ready-washed spinach in a bag, add about 5 tablespoons of water to the pan.) Put the pan over a high heat until the water begins to boil, then lower the heat and steam for 2 to 3 minutes only, until the leaves wilt into a soft mass. Drain well and cut up coarsely.

Heat the milk in a pan with the sherry or wine until warm. In another saucepan, sauté the chopped onion in the butter over a very low heat until the onion is soft. Add the flour and cook, stirring, for 1 to 2 minutes over a medium heat, then gradually add the warm milk and sherry or wine, a little at a time, stirring vigorously all the time to avoid lumps forming. Add salt and nutmeg and cook, stirring, for 15 to 20 minutes over a gentle heat until the sauce thickens to the consistency of a light cream.

Add the spinach to the creamy sauce and mix well. Cook for 3 to 5 minutes and adjust the seasoning. Serve hot in little bowls, and top each with a quartered egg.

VARIATIONS

❈ Use chicken stock instead of milk for the béchamel and add 2 beaten egg yolks at the end of cooking the sauce, with the spinach.

❈ Substitute 175ml brandy for the sherry or wine.

❈ 750g fresh spinach (weight without hard stalks)

❈ 500ml whole milk

❈ 175ml dry sherry or white wine

❈ ½ an onion, peeled and finely chopped

❈ 75g butter

❈ 3 tablespoons plain flour

❈ salt

❈ a pinch of freshly grated nutmeg

❈ 4 hard-boiled eggs, peeled and cut into quarters

SPINACH *with* RAISINS *and* PINE NUTS

✢ *espinacas con pasas y piñones*

This way of preparing spinach is also known throughout the rest of Spain as *espinacas a la catalana*. It can be served as a starter or as a side dish. You will need a very large saucepan if you use fresh spinach, since the leaves are rather bulky before they collapse into a soft mass. It is fine to use frozen leaf spinach – see the recipe variation.

SERVES 4

Soak the raisins in water for 20 minutes and then drain. Remove any thick stalks from the spinach. Wash the leaves thoroughly and drain well. In our supermarkets we now get baby spinach with very thin little stalks – you do not need to take these off. Put the spinach leaves, with only the water that clings to them after washing and draining, in a large pan with the lid on. (If you have bought ready-washed spinach in a bag, you will need to add about 5 tablespoons of water to the pan.) Put the pan over a high heat, covered, then lower the heat as soon as the water begins to boil. The leaves will cook in the steam and wilt into a soft mass in just 2 to 3 minutes. Then drain well.

In a large frying pan, sauté the pine nuts very briefly in the oil over a low heat, shaking the pan or stirring constantly, until they just begin to colour. Add the drained raisins and spinach and mix well. Season with salt and pepper, and cook for 5 minutes, stirring occasionally.

* 2 tablespoons raisins
* 750g fresh spinach (weight without hard stalks)
* 2 tablespoons pine nuts
* 4 tablespoons olive oil
* salt and pepper

VARIATIONS

* If you want to use frozen leaf spinach, defrost it and cook it in a little water for a few minutes until soft.
* You can use Swiss chard instead of spinach.

RED CABBAGE *with* APPLES, RAISINS *and* PINE NUTS
❊ *lombarda a la madrileña*

Red cabbage is the main ingredient of this winter dish that is served on New Year's Eve in Madrid. The sweet-and-sour flavour goes well with game and roast pork. The cabbage is sometimes cooked with apples only, sometimes just with raisins and pine nuts. Cook the dish in a large casserole or pan with a tight-fitting lid.

SERVES 8

Soak the raisins in water for 20 minutes and then drain. Remove the outer leaves and cut the cabbage into quarters through the core, then cut away the hard core and shred the cabbage.

Put the cabbage in a large casserole or pan with 4 tablespoons of the oil, the apples, garlic, raisins, vinegar, sugar, salt, pepper and water. Mix well and cook with the lid on, over a very low heat, for about an hour or until the cabbage is very soft, stirring every so often.

Very briefly fry the pine nuts in the remaining ½ tablespoon of oil, stirring and shaking the pan until they just begin to colour. Stir them into the cabbage and serve the dish hot.

VARIATIONS

- Sauté 100g bacon, cut into small pieces, in the oil before you put in the pine nuts.
- Fry a chopped onion in the oil before you put in the pine nuts.
- Flavour with ½ a teaspoon of ground cloves and ½ a teaspoon of ground cinnamon, adding these at the same time as the apples and other ingredients.
- Use red wine instead of the water.

- 4 tablespoons raisins
- 1 red cabbage (weighing about 1kg)
- 4½ tablespoons olive oil
- 2 Golden Delicious or other dessert apples, peeled, cored and cut into 1.25cm pieces
- 2 garlic cloves, peeled and crushed or finely chopped
- 5 tablespoons red or white wine vinegar or cider vinegar
- 2 tablespoons sugar, or to taste
- salt and pepper
- about 125ml water
- 4 tablespoons pine nuts

HARICOT BEANS *with* CHESTNUTS
❊ *judias blancas con castañas*

Chestnuts were once a staple food in Spain. Peasants dried them for use throughout the year. For this dish they would have soaked both the beans and dried chestnuts the day before. This easy version is delicious. With a little more liquid it can be eaten as a *potaje* (soup); with the *chorizos*, as in the variation, it becomes a substantial main dish.

SERVES 4

In a wide saucepan, fry the onion in the oil slowly over a low heat, stirring often, until soft. Add the garlic and stir for a moment or two until the aroma rises. Add the chestnuts, barely cover with water, put in the cinnamon stick and cloves and season with salt and pepper. Simmer, uncovered, for about 15 minutes until the chestnuts are tender and the liquid a little reduced. Then stir in the beans and cook for about 5 minutes longer.

Serve hot or warm, with the extra virgin olive oil drizzled over.

VARIATIONS

❊ To thicken the sauce, take out a few chestnuts, mash them with a fork then return them to the pan.

❊ Try adding a pinch of saffron threads and 1 teaspoon of sugar with the cinnamon stick and cloves.

❊ To make this a main dish, boil 500g semi-cured cooking *chorizos* in water for 20 minutes, then drain, cut them into thick slices and add them at the same time as the beans.

❊ Use fresh chestnuts. To peel them see page 374.

- ❊ ½ a large onion, peeled and chopped
- ❊ 2 tablespoons olive oil
- ❊ 3 garlic cloves, peeled and crushed
- ❊ 250g chestnuts, frozen and defrosted or vacuum-packed
- ❊ 1 cinnamon stick
- ❊ 2 cloves
- ❊ salt and pepper
- ❊ 2 x 400g tins good-quality haricot or butter beans, drained
- ❊ 1½ tablespoons extra virgin olive oil

ROUGHLY MASHED POTATOES
with OLIVE OIL *and* SPRING ONIONS
❊ *patatas aliñadas*

I love this potato dish, which I first ate in a bar in Seville. It is a speciality of Malaga, where potatoes are still sometimes called by their early names – *papas* or *batatas*.

SERVES 6

Bring the potatoes to the boil in a large pan of salted water and cook for about 25 minutes until soft. Drain, keeping about 125ml of the reserved cooking water. Mash the potatoes coarsely. Stir in the olive oil, salt and pepper to taste and enough of the reserved cooking water to have a soft, slightly moist texture. Then stir in the spring onions and the parsley.

Serve at room temperature.

- 750g floury baking potatoes, peeled and halved or quartered
- salt and pepper
- 6 tablespoons extra virgin olive oil, or more
- 6–8 spring onions, chopped
- 2 tablespoons chopped parsley

WINTER VEGETABLE MEDLEY
❊ *menestra de invierno*

This winter dish from Asturias is soupy and heart-warming. Hard-boiled eggs, cut in half, are often served as an accompaniment.

SERVES 4

In a large saucepan, boil the carrots, leeks and potatoes in enough salted water to cover for 20 minutes, then add the cauliflower florets and boil for another 10 minutes.

Meanwhile, in a large frying pan fry the onion in the oil over a medium heat until soft, then add the garlic and the ham or streaky bacon and stir for 1 to 2 minutes. Add the flour and stir for another minute.

Drain the vegetables; keep 500ml of the cooking water and discard the rest. Add this water to the onion and ham mixture, a little at a time to begin with, stirring vigorously so that lumps do not form, then pour the sauce into the large saucepan over the vegetables and cook for 10 minutes or until the vegetables are very tender.

- 1 large carrot, peeled and cut into bite-sized pieces
- 1 large leek, trimmed and cut into 2cm-wide slices
- 4 new potatoes, quartered
- salt
- 250g small cauliflower florets
- ½ a large onion, peeled and chopped
- 2 tablespoons olive oil
- 2 garlic cloves, peeled and chopped
- 3 slices jamón serrano or other raw dry-cured ham, or streaky bacon rashers, cut into pieces
- 1½ tablespoons plain flour

'WRINKLED' POTATOES *and* *their* RED *and* GREEN SAUCES
❋ *papas arrugadas y mojos canarios*

My daughter Anna brought back a little booklet entitled *Papas arrugadas y mojos canarios*, which was subtitled 'The best recipes from the Canaries', from a family holiday in Lanzarote in the Canary Islands. Their hotel had held cooking demonstrations of the famous Canarian 'wrinkled' potatoes and accompanying green and red sauces. Potatoes (they call them *papas*) are the most popular food on the islands. Twenty varieties, most of them ancient ones, are grown there and the favourite way of cooking them is boiled in their skins with a huge amount of salt until all the water has evaporated. The potatoes come out wrinkled and covered with a white powdery film. I ate them in an Irish pub in Seville. They had a firm but tender texture and an intense potato flavour. Amazingly they were not too salty because the salt in the water has the effect of drawing out their juices rather than being absorbed. I cooked 'wrinkled' potatoes at home several times – on two occasions they turned out to be inedible because they were too salty when the skins had been too thin, so look for good skins. Serve the potatoes in their skins, hot or warm. They can be reheated in the oven before serving. You are supposed to pick up the potatoes with your fingers and to dip them into the sauces, in shared dishes on the table, as you take bites. The friends who ate at my house preferred to put blobs of sauce on their plates or to spoon some on their cut-open potatoes.

SERVES 6

❋ 1kg small to medium-sized waxy potatoes in their skins, washed ❋ 4 tablespoons coarse sea salt

Put the potatoes in a large pan where they fit in one layer. Add just enough cold water to cover and the salt. Boil hard, uncovered, over a medium-high heat, letting the water bubble, for 25 minutes or until the potatoes are very tender and the water has evaporated. (Watch that they do not burn.) Then leave them over a very low heat for a few minutes, moving them and turning them over in the dry pan until they are wrinkled and covered with a fine powder of salt.

Serve hot or warm with one or both of the following two sauces.

» » »

GREEN SAUCE *with* CORIANDER LEAVES
❧ *mojo verde de cilantro*

This sauce, which accompanies the 'wrinkled' potatoes on page 238, is also great with fried, grilled or poached fish. It keeps well in the refrigerator.

SERVES 6

❊ ½ a green pepper, deseeded and cut into large pieces ❊ leaves of a large bunch of coriander (75g weight with stalks) ❊ 2 garlic cloves, peeled and crushed, or to taste ❊ ¼–½ teaspoon ground cumin ❊ 1½ tablespoons white wine vinegar ❊ salt, to taste ❊ 125ml extra virgin olive oil

Blend all the ingredients, except the oil, to a paste in the food processor, then add the oil and blend again to a light creamy consistency.

SPICY RED SAUCE
❧ *mojo picón*

This popular spicy *mojo* is a garlic and chilli pepper sauce, also called *mojo colorado*. In the Canaries, they make it hot or sweet with their own special dried chilli peppers that are soaked in boiling water, then pounded with plenty of garlic. The one I ate in Seville was made with ordinary *pimentón* (Spanish paprika), which is very simple for us to reproduce.

TO SERVE 4

❊ 4 garlic gloves, peeled and crushed, or to taste ❊ ¾ teaspoon hot *pimentón picante* or cayenne pepper ❊ 2 teaspoons *pimentón dulce* or sweet paprika ❊ ¼ teaspoon ground cumin ❊ 6 tablespoons extra virgin olive oil ❊ 2 tablespoons white or red wine vinegar ❊ salt

Mix the garlic, hot and sweet *pimentón* (or cayenne and paprika) and the cumin in a bowl, then beat in the olive oil and the vinegar with a fork and add salt to taste.

POTATOES *with* FRIED ONIONS, GARLIC AND EGGS

❋ *patatas a lo pobre con huevos rotos*

Manolo el Sereno, my host in the Andalusian village of Frailes, took me to an artisan sausage and ham maker called Embutidos Luque in Fuensanta de Martos in the province of Jaén, where I tasted, among others, one of their new *chorizos* that is made with olive oil instead of pork fat. Hams and sausages hung from the ceiling like stalactites in a cave. Huge piles of salted pigs' ears and feet were waiting in boxes. We went on to the family restaurant Estrella, where three ladies, Loli Luque Peragón, Yolanda Luque Garrido and Igna López Fernandez, cooked half a dozen local dishes for us. When we had finished eating we visited the kitchen and they gave me the recipes. This potato dish is one of theirs. I made double the quantity in my *paella* pan for a family lunch in the garden. When I explained that the potatoes were called *a lo pobre*, meaning 'of the poor', my six-year-old granddaughter Nell said, 'But we are not poor!'

SERVES 4

Boil the potatoes in salted water for 15 to 25 minutes until tender, then drain.

In a large frying pan fry the onions in the oil over a low heat, covered with a lid. Stir often until they are soft and their juice has evaporated so that the oil is sizzling. It can take about 25 minutes.

Cut the potatoes into slices just under 1cm thick and put them into the pan of onions. Cook over a medium to high heat, uncovered, turning them over with a spatula until both the potatoes and onions are golden, adding salt to taste. You can cook them in advance up to this stage, then reheat and continue just before you are ready to eat.

Beat the eggs lightly with a little salt and pour over the potatoes. Stir over a medium heat until they scramble to a creamy consistency. Serve hot, sprinkled with the parsley.

* 500g waxy potatoes, peeled
* salt
* 1½ large onions, peeled, halved and sliced
* 4 tablespoons olive oil
* 6 large eggs
* 2 tablespoons chopped flat-leaf parsley

VARIATIONS

❊ Add 1 green pepper, deseeded and cut into small pieces, to the onions after they have cooked for 10 minutes.

❊ Fry 250g sliced semi-cured cooking *chorizos* and about 8 rashers of streaky bacon in a little oil and serve them with the potatoes.

❊ Sprinkle 2–3 teaspoons of wine vinegar over the potatoes when they are in with the onions.

STUFFED ARTICHOKE BOTTOMS
✳ *alcachofas rellenas*

I ate delicious stuffed baby artichokes at the Bar el Choto in the village of Frailes in Andalusia. The cook, Caridad Zafra, described the stuffing for me. I cannot get small artichokes with leaves tender enough to eat, so I made the dish with frozen artichoke bottoms instead, which I buy from a small Iranian store near me. They come from Egypt and are sold in 400g bags of about 10. I baked them instead of deep-frying them.

SERVES 6–8

To make the stuffing, coarsely blend the bread, parsley leaves, ham and garlic in the food processor. Then mix in the eggs and add salt if necessary. You may not need any salt because of the saltiness of the ham.

Spread a heaped teaspoonful of the mixture into each artichoke bottom and arrange them in a wide baking dish. Pour in enough chicken stock so that the liquid does not entirely cover the artichokes, and bake in an oven preheated to 190°C/gas 5 for about 30 minutes, until the artichokes feel tender when you cut into them with a pointed knife.

- ✳ 75g white bread, without crusts
- ✳ a large bunch of flat-leaf parsley (about 44g with stalks)
- ✳ 6 slices of *jamón serrano* or other raw dry-cured ham
- ✳ 3 large garlic cloves, peeled and crushed
- ✳ 2 large eggs, lightly beaten
- ✳ salt, if necessary
- ✳ 2 x 400g bags frozen artichoke bottoms (about 20), defrosted
- ✳ about 500ml chicken stock (you may use 1 stock cube)

TOMATOES STUFFED *with* TUNA
tomates rellenos de atúnrotos

These tomatoes can be served hot or cold. I like them best cold and with chopped olives in the filling.

SERVES 4–8

- 8 small to medium tomatoes (about 650g)
- 1 large onion, peeled and finely chopped
- 2 tablespoons olive oil
- 2 garlic cloves, peeled and chopped
- 200g tinned tuna in oil (drained weight)
- 3 tablespoons coarsely chopped black olives (optional)

Cut a circle around the stem end of each tomato and cut out a lid. Remove the centre and seeds with a pointed teaspoon (eat these with a drop of extra virgin olive oil and a little salt – do not throw them away) and turn the tomatoes upside down so that the juices run out.

In a frying pan, fry the onion in the oil over a medium-low heat until soft, stirring often. Add the garlic and stir until it begins to colour. Take off the heat and stir in the tuna and the olives, if using.

Using a teaspoon, stuff the tomatoes with this mixture and replace the lids. Arrange them snugly in a small baking dish. Pour in about 4 tablespoons of water and bake in an oven preheated to 200°C/gas 6 for 20 minutes or until soft.

STUFFED TOMATOES *with* MEAT
❋ *tomates rellenos de carne*

These tomatoes can be served as part of a hot main dish.

SERVES 4

Cut a circle around the stem end of each tomato and cut out a lid. Shave the inside of the lid to leave more room for the stuffing. Remove the centre and seeds with a pointed teaspoon. (Do not throw these away – make Catalan tomato bread on page 132 or simply eat with a little olive oil and salt.) Arrange the tomatoes in a baking dish.

For the filling, fry the onion in the oil over a medium heat until golden. Add the minced pork and cook for about 8 minutes, stirring, turning it over and breaking it up, until the meat is no longer pink. Season with salt and pepper and let it cool a little. Put it in the food processor with the ham and the quartered hard-boiled egg and blend to a smooth paste. Taste and adjust the seasoning.

Stuff the tomatoes with the paste, pressing it in firmly, and cover with the lids. Bake in an oven preheated to 200°C/gas 6 for 30 minutes, or until the tomatoes are soft. Keep an eye on them and remove them from the oven before they start to fall apart.

* 4 large beef tomatoes (about 1kg)

* ½ a large onion, peeled and chopped

* 2 tablespoons olive oil

* 150g minced pork

* salt and pepper

* 4 slices *jamón serrano* or other raw dry-cured ham, chopped

* 1 hard-boiled egg, peeled and quartered

PEPPERS STUFFED *with* RICE *in* *a* TOMATO SAUCE ❈ *pimientos rellenos de arroz con salsa de tomates*

I prefer to use the sweeter-tasting red peppers for stuffing, but others prefer the more peppery green ones which can also be used. The most common filling is a mix of minced pork and rice, but this one with rice alone makes a beautiful dish for vegetarians. It is best to use a short-grain or 'round' rice, which becomes soft and sticks together when cooked. Choose peppers with a good base so they can stand up in a baking dish.

SERVES 6

Make the tomato sauce first. You do not need to peel the tomatoes. Cut them into quarters and remove the hard white bits near the stem end, then blend them to a cream in the food processor. Heat the garlic and chilli in the oil in a wide frying pan over a medium heat, stirring, for 30 seconds, then add the creamed tomatoes, the sugar and some salt. Cook over a medium-high heat, stirring occasionally, for about 25 to 30 minutes until the sauce is reduced and thick.

For the rice filling, in another frying pan fry the onion in the oil over a medium heat, stirring often until soft and golden. Add the tomatoes, sugar, a little salt and the oregano, and cook until the liquid has almost disappeared. Then add the rice, stir well, and add the stock. Stir in the saffron, a little more salt and some pepper. Bring to the boil and simmer, uncovered, over a low heat for about 15 minutes until most of the liquid has been absorbed but the rice is still underdone.

Retaining the stalk, cut a circle around the stalk end of the peppers and keep these to use as lids. Remove the cores and seeds with a pointed spoon and shave the inside of the lids to make more room for the filling. Using a teaspoon, fill the peppers with the rice without pressing it down too much so that there is a little room for it to expand. Replace the lids and place the stuffed peppers snugly in a baking dish.

Pour the tomato sauce around the peppers, cover with a sheet of foil and bake in an oven preheated to 200°C/gas 6 for about 1 hour. Remove the foil and continue to bake, uncovered, for another 15 minutes, or until the peppers are soft and have browned on top. Look at them occasionally to make sure they don't fall apart. Serve hot.

For the tomato sauce
- ❈ 1kg ripe tomatoes
- ❈ 6 garlic cloves, peeled and chopped
- ❈ ½–1 red chilli pepper, deseeded and finely chopped
- ❈ 3 tablespoons olive oil
- ❈ 2 teaspoons sugar
- ❈ salt

For the stuffed peppers
- ❈ 1 large onion, peeled and chopped
- ❈ 4 tablespoons olive oil
- ❈ 3 medium tomatoes, peeled and chopped
- ❈ ½ teaspoon sugar
- ❈ salt and pepper
- ❈ 2 teaspoons chopped oregano
- ❈ 250g (round) short-grain Spanish rice or risotto rice
- ❈ 600ml hot chicken or vegetable stock (you can use 2 stock cubes)
- ❈ a good pinch of saffron threads
- ❈ 6 medium-sized red or green peppers, or three of each

rosa tovar larrucea

I went shopping with Rosa at Madrid's San Martín market and watched her cook lunch for friends in her charming attic flat. Rosa Tovar Larrucea was born in Salamanca. Her mother was from a Basque ship-

owning family. Her father, a university professor, was a gourmand who acquired a varied palate because his notary father moved the family between northern Castile, Cantabria, Castellón, Alicante and Madrid. He always had little stories to tell about the dishes that his wife put on the table and passed his fascination with the history of food on to his daughter.

In 1985, Rosa founded a catering company making pastries and frozen sauces. Now she teaches cooking in schools in Madrid, Guadalajara and Salamanca. She teaches all kinds of people, including professional chefs, pastry cooks and butchers. Young people in Spain want to learn new technology, the latest international trends, quick and easy dishes, traditional ones to make at weekends, and about healthy eating and organic foods. Her cooking represents the way traditional foods can be updated and become lighter, healthier and more pleasing without losing their character. She has written several books, including *Arroces*, about rice, and *3.000 años de cocina española* ('Three Thousand Years of Spanish Cooking') with Monique Fuller. Some of the recipes that she has emailed me have gone into this book, including the two for stuffed aubergines.

BAKED AUBERGINES STUFFED *with* ALMONDS
❈ *berenjenas al horno con almendras*

This surprising recipe with almonds and a gentle sweet-and-sour flavour is from Rosa Tovar. She says it is of Jewish origin – many foods are in Majorca, where there was a large community of converts from Judaism. Use a wide casserole that you can put on the hob and also in the oven. Otherwise use a large frying pan with a lid to steam the aubergines, then transfer them to a baking dish and fill them.

SERVES 4

Trim the stem ends of the aubergines and cut them in half lengthways. Pour the water into a wide casserole or a frying pan that has a tight-fitting lid and stir in the sugar, vinegar and 2 tablespoons of the olive oil. Put in the aubergine halves, cut side up, and cover with the lid. Bring to the boil over a medium heat, then reduce the heat and cook in the steam for 5 to 8 minutes, until the aubergines have softened but are still holding their shape.

When cool enough to handle, hollow out the aubergines with a large pointed spoon, leaving just a little pulp to form a thin wall with the skins. Leave them in the casserole – or if you used a frying pan transfer them to a baking dish with any remaining liquid. Chop up the aubergine pulp coarsely.

In another frying pan, fry the onion in the remaining oil over a medium heat until soft and beginning to colour. Add the chopped aubergine pulp and cook, stirring and mashing with a fork, for a few minutes over a medium heat until it is very soft and the liquid has evaporated. Add the breadcrumbs, ground almonds and the eggs, season with salt and pepper and mix well.

Fill the aubergine shells with this mixture and bake in an oven preheated to 180°C/gas 4 for about 20 minutes, or until the stuffing puffs up (it will collapse when you take it out of the oven). Serve hot, sprinkled with the parsley.

VARIATIONS

❈ You can mix 2 teaspoons of rose water or 1 teaspoon of chopped oregano into the filling.

❈ You can use the same filling to stuff courgettes. They need to be fat ones. Cut them in half lengthways and cook them in salted water very briefly until they soften a little, before hollowing them out with a pointed spoon or an apple corer. Then fill and bake as the aubergines.

* 2 medium-sized elongated aubergines (about 500g)
* 150ml water
* 1 teaspoon sugar
* 1 tablespoon red or white wine vinegar
* 4 tablespoons olive oil
* ½ a large onion, peeled and chopped
* 4 tablespoons fresh white breadcrumbs (see page 120)
* 50g ground almonds
* 2 large eggs, lightly beaten
* salt and pepper
* 1½ tablespoons chopped flat-leaf parsley

AUBERGINES STUFFED *with* MEAT
✳ *berenjenas rellenas de carne*

Aubergines are favourite vegetables in the Balearic Islands. This dish, which can be served as a starter or main course, is not at all greasy because the aubergines are not fried. The recipe is Rosa Tovar's (see page 250). She softens the aubergines by steaming them in a pan with a little water before filling them. Use a wide casserole that you can put on the hob and also in the oven. Otherwise use a large frying pan with a lid to steam the aubergines, then transfer them to a baking dish and fill them.

SERVES 4

Trim the stem ends of the aubergines and cut them in half lengthways. Pour the water and 1 tablespoon of the oil into a wide casserole or frying pan and put in the aubergine halves, cut side up. Season with salt and pepper, cover with a tight-fitting lid and place over a medium heat. When the water begins to boil, lower the heat. The aubergines should cook in the steam in about 5 to 8 minutes. Check that they have softened slightly with the point of a knife. Add a little extra water if it dries up too quickly. When they are done, leave the aubergines in the casserole – or if you used a frying pan transfer them to a baking dish with any remaining water.

In a small bowl, mix the breadcrumbs with the milk. Hollow out the aubergines with a large pointed spoon, leaving just a little pulp to form a thin wall with the skins. Chop up the pulp coarsely.

In a frying pan, fry the onion in the remaining oil over a medium heat, stirring until it just begins to colour. Add the garlic, stir for 30 seconds, then add the tomato and cook for 3 to 5 minutes. Add the minced pork and season with salt and pepper, the cinnamon and cumin. Stir, turning over the meat and breaking it up, for 5 to 8 minutes until it changes colour. Add the chopped aubergine pulp and the breadcrumbs soaked in the milk. Cook, stirring, until any liquid has evaporated.

Add the egg and mix very well. Spoon the mixture into the aubergine shells. Sprinkle with the grated cheese and bake in an oven preheated to 180°C/gas 4 for 20 minutes. Serve hot.

* 2 medium-sized elongated aubergines (about 500g)
* 150ml water
* 3–4 tablespoons olive oil
* salt and pepper
* 4 tablespoons fresh white breadcrumbs (see page 120)
* 4 tablespoons whole milk
* 1 medium onion, peeled and chopped
* 2 garlic cloves, peeled and chopped
* 1 medium tomato, peeled and chopped
* 250g minced pork
* ½ teaspoon ground cinnamon
* ¾ teaspoon ground cumin
* 1 egg, lightly beaten
* 50g grated cheese – use Manchego, Mahón or even mature Cheddar

AUBERGINE FRITTERS *with* HONEY
❋ *berenjenas con miel*

I have eaten several versions of these aubergine fritters, which are a speciality of Cordoba, and loved them all. The combination of savoury and sweet is sensational. In the town of Priego de Córdoba in the mountains, which is on the '*Ruta del Califato*' (a tourist route through old Muslim southern Spain) and where there is an old Moorish quarter, the aubergine slices were very thin and crisp and served with a dribble of honey. I learnt a new way to avoid them absorbing too much oil, from the chef at the Rio restaurant. It is to soak the aubergine slices first in milk, then to drain them and cover them in flour. They are best eaten as soon as they are cooked but are also very good reheated in the oven.

SERVES 4–5

Peel the aubergines and cut them into slices about 7.5cm thick crossways. Put them in a large bowl with the milk. Place a small plate on top to hold them down. Let them soak for 1 to 2 hours, then drain and discard the milk.

Preheat the oil in a large saucepan. Cover a plate with plenty of flour mixed with a little sprinkling of salt. Turn the aubergine slices in this so that they are entirely covered with flour and shake them to remove the excess. Deep-fry in oil that is sizzling but not too hot (when you throw in a piece of bread it should not brown too quickly), turning the slices over as soon as one side is brown. This will take around 3 to 4 minutes in total. Cook the aubergine slices in batches, trying to keep the temperature of the oil as constant as possible. Then lift them out and drain on kitchen paper.

Serve hot with a thin dribble of honey, letting everyone help themselves to more.

VARIATION

❋ In Cordoba, I ate aubergine slices dipped in batter before being fried. The batter was crisp, the aubergine slices were moist, and they were served with cane sugar molasses.

* 2 aubergines (about 600g)
* about 600ml whole milk (enough to cover the aubergine slices)
* olive or sunflower oil, for frying
* plain flour, for dredging
* salt
* orange-blossom honey, or other clear aromatic honey

AUBERGINE *with* BÉCHAMEL *and* CHEESE
❋ *berenjenas con queso*

The sixteenth-century Sevillian soldier and madrigalist Baltazar de Alcazár dedicated a poem to aubergines. He wrote: '*Tres cosas me tienen preso / de amores el corazón, / la bella Inés, el jamón / y las berenjenas con queso.*' ('Three things hold my heart a prisoner of love – the fair Inés, ham and aubergines with cheese.') He was of Jewish descent and was proclaiming his love of ham, the most Catholic of foods, and at the same time his loyalty to an ancestral dish of aubergines and cheese that, according to the archives of the Inquisition, was considered a sign of Judaizing. I have learnt from people in Spain to steam the aubergines, which gives them a meltingly soft texture. Even the skin becomes very soft. The sauce is light and creamy and there is a crunchy garlicky crust on top.

SERVES 4

Steam the aubergine slices for 4 to 5 minutes until they are very soft. Use a steamer with a basket – some baskets fit into any large saucepan with a tight-fitting lid. The water at the bottom should be boiling but should not touch the aubergine slices. Then gently lift them out and arrange them in one or two layers in a lightly oiled baking dish. Sprinkle very lightly with salt.

For the sauce, heat the milk to scalding point in a saucepan. In another pan melt the butter, add the flour and stir vigorously with a wooden spoon over a low heat for 3 to 4 minutes. Then pour in the hot milk, a little at a time, stirring vigorously over a low heat until the sauce is thick and smooth. Let it cook gently for 10 minutes, then stir in the cheese. If necessary, add a little salt. Pour this béchamel sauce over the aubergines in the baking dish.

Mix the breadcrumbs, parsley, garlic and olive oil with a little salt and sprinkle over the top. Bake in an oven preheated to 190°C/gas 5 for 20 minutes, then lightly brown the top very briefly under the grill.

- ❋ 1 large aubergine or 2 medium ones (about 500g), cut into 1.5cm slices
- ❋ 1 tablespoon olive oil, plus more to oil the baking dish
- ❋ salt
- ❋ 300ml whole milk
- ❋ 50g butter
- ❋ 2 tablespoons plain flour
- ❋ 75g coarsely grated mature Manchego or mature Cheddar cheese
- ❋ 4 tablespoons fresh breadcrumbs (see page 000)
- ❋ 3 tablespoons chopped flat-leaf parsley
- ❋ 1 garlic clove, peeled and crushed

RICE AND PASTA

arroces y pastas

In Spain, rice dishes are traditionally served as a starter, but many are so rich and complex with so many ingredients that they are a meal in themselves. You can eat a different, equally delicious, rice dish every day of the year. Any rice dish with chicken could also be made with rabbit, duck, quails or partridges. Seafood rice can be made with different types of fish and seafood. You can put pork ribs, meatballs, different sausages, pigs' feet and ears into meaty rice dishes. And vegetables in season always have a place in Spanish rice dishes.

It was the Arabs who first introduced the grain to Spain in the early Middle Ages and Berber peasants were brought in from North Africa to grow it. The Berbers remained to work the rice fields well into the seventeenth century, and many villages still bear the names of their tribes (see page 83). *Arroz*, the Spanish word for rice (it is *arròs* in Catalan and Valencian), comes from the Arabic *roz*.

People eat rice all over Spain and now many regions grow it. Andalusia and Extremadura are very big producers and the colder regions of Aragon and Navarre also cultivate rice. But the historical rice-growing regions where it is a staple are the Mediterranean regions of Catalonia, Valencia and Murcia. Their high-quality indigenous Spanish grains are protected by the Designations of Origin: *Arroz del Delta del Ebro*, *Arroz de Valencia* and *Arroz de Calasparra*. Rice is classified commercially by the size of the grain and the relationship between length and width. Indigenous Spanish rice is medium and short grain. Long grain was introduced recently, mainly for export, but now also sells at home for cooking plain white rice, and new-style dishes such as rice salad. Some varieties of short (or round) grain result in a sticky rice that falls apart and is best used for stuffing vegetables and some puddings. The special quality of Spanish medium-grain rice is that it has a higher starch content than the long grain, and this allows it to absorb maximum flavour from the stock in which it is cooked and from the other ingredients. It can absorb twice its volume of liquid while still remaining as separate grains.

In her book *El libro de la paella y los arroces* ('The Book of *Paella* and Rice Dishes') published in 1985, the celebrated Spanish food writer and broadcaster Lourdes March uses medium-grain rice for all the traditional Spanish recipes except for stuffed vegetables and puddings. But that was before the rise of Bomba, an ancient Spanish strain of tiny round rice that was nearly extinct, which became famous and much in demand a decade or so ago after it was acclaimed by celebrity chefs and written about by foreign journalists. Bomba is said to be the rice for 'people who cannot cook *paella* or haven't the time to watch it' because it keeps a firm shape and does not easily overcook, due to its ability to absorb up to three times its own volume in liquid without falling apart. It has become the rice of choice for chefs and gourmets. It is more than twice the price of other grains because the yield of the very tall plant is low. It was neglected in Franco's time when high production was required. The three Designations of Origin produce Bomba rice now, as do other regions too.

At home people still cook with the medium grain they are used to (it is considered sacrilegious to use long grain for *paella*) – the major types of medium-grain rice are: Senia from the marshlands surrounding the Albufera lagoon in Valencia; Bahía and Montsianell from the flatlands of the river Ebro in Catalonia; and the hybrid Balilla X Sollana from the mountains of Murcia along the banks of the river Segura near the town of Calasparra. Calasparra became famous for its Bomba rice because the sowing and harvesting is done by hand in the small terraces where machinery cannot get to, and the irrigation water comes from cold mountain springs, while Moorish-type canals, dams and waterwheels continue to regulate the flooding and draining of the rice paddies much as they did in the early Middle Ages. In the last twelve years Catalonia and Valencia have been cultivating a high-quality Bomba. These regions are very active in agricultural research to improve varieties and methods of sowing, harvesting and processing (hand labour, they say, is for tourists). What makes a grain different is the type of terroir – the environment and climate – in which it grows: flat, humid lands; cold mountain climates; or dry lands.

The main thing about cooking Spanish rice dishes is knowing how to handle the grain – how much water it needs, how long to cook it. I have learnt much of what I know from Lourdes, who is a long-time friend. In Spain, rice is never soaked or washed before cooking. Stock is almost always used, hardly ever water, and the stock has to be boiling when it comes in contact with the rice. Different amounts of liquid are required for different types of dishes. For dry rice dishes (*arroces secos*), cooked *al horno* in earthenware casseroles in the oven, you need to add about twice the volume of stock as of rice, which works out at 250ml of stock per 100g of rice. Rice cooked in wide, shallow *paella* pans needs more liquid because much of it evaporates. Moist *arroces melosos*, with a so-called 'honey' texture (*miel* means honey), are cooked in large saucepans with two and a half times the volume of stock as of rice, while the *arroces caldosos* (soupy rice dishes) need three times the amount of stock by volume. You add all the stock

at once (unlike when making risotto) and you stir only once with a wooden spoon then leave the rice alone. You do not keep stirring throughout the cooking because that would break some grains and release the starch that gives Italian *risotti* their creamy, slightly sticky texture, something that is not desirable in a Spanish rice dish.

None of the cooks that I watched making rice ever measured their base ingredients. They all took handfuls of rice, saying '*un puñado*' (a handful), and added stock *a ojo* ('by the eye'). It makes sense because qualities of rice vary. Even the same type of grain from the same field can behave differently from one harvest to another and it differs if it is new or has been hanging around in a shop for ages. It can absorb different amounts of liquid and can take more or less time to cook. The amount of liquid needed also depends on the size and shape of the pan or baking dish, the amount of rice in it, and the heat of the oven or hob. In making soupy rice the amount of liquid matters less than the cooking time, which is all-important. If you cook it for too long the rice will be soggy and may fall apart. In making *paella*, where the amount of liquid matters, there is no foolproof method to know the exact quantity needed. Cooking *paella* is an art and the skill is gained through experience. You have to watch that the rice does not get too dry, adding a little more boiling stock or water if necessary, and also watch that the rice does not overcook.

The general rule is to allow 100g of uncooked rice per person. The recommended amount of salt needed for rice is generally given as 1 teaspoon for 400g of plain rice, but as in Spain rice is always cooked in stock you have to take into consideration the saltiness of the stock and, of course, salting has to be a matter of taste. If you cannot find a Spanish rice – they are often labelled simply *paella* rice – an alternative that you can use is Arborio or Carnaroli risotto rice. Do not use long grain.

paella

Paella is a dish with a strong emotional charge in Spain. It is a Sunday dish, and its preparation is a convivial, social affair that takes place when possible in the open air in the countryside or in the garden. According to my friend Alicia Ríos, cooking *paella* has become a man's job, one that does not bring their virility into question. On the contrary, it is a way of showing off their skill.

Paella valenciana is the iconic food of Valencia, which became the first emblematic national dish of Spain. What was simply *arroz a la valenciana* became known, as it spread around Spain, as *paella valenciana* after the large, shallow double-handled pan with a slightly convex base that is used to cook it in (*paella* means frying pan in the Valencian–Catalan language). The first *paella* was born in the rice fields around the Albufera lagoon. It was a communal meal that the labourers cooked for themselves over a wood fire. They put in what they had at hand – eels, snails, green beans or whatever vegetables were in season, sometimes also chicken, rabbit or fresh butter beans. Eventually every village in Valencia and neighbouring Murcia put all kinds of meats, poultry, fish, shellfish and vegetables into their *paellas*. With the beginning of mass tourism, *paella*

was adopted by seaside resorts and city restaurants where it was transformed. *Paellas* became gargantuan, baroque dishes, with a huge number of ingredients, that usually did not taste as good as they looked.

The fashion now in Valencia and also in Madrid is to make *paella* with a very thin layer of rice in the pan – ideally, they say, the thickness of only three grains and definitely no thicker than one finger's width (*un dit*) or 1cm. That is why you need a very wide pan. *Paella* pans come in many sizes, some large enough to feed a hundred people at a festival. You can cook a *paella* for 2 to 3 people in a large 30cm-diameter frying pan. Otherwise you need to use a *paella* pan (see page 116). For 4 people you need a 40cm pan, measured across the top, for 6 people a 45cm pan. However, you may choose to have a thicker layer of rice, as is common in the north of Catalonia where it can be up to 4cm thick.

There are two passionately held beliefs about the best way to cook *paella*. One method is to start by making a *sofrito* of fried onion, garlic, tomatoes and any bits of pepper, with meat or seafood, then to stir in the rice and coat it with the reduced oily sauce before adding the flavoursome stock. The other is to pour in the stock when the *sofrito* is ready and bring it to the boil before adding the rice. It is perfectly fine, and often better, to cook some of the meats or seafood of a *paella* separately and to put them on top of the rice at the end to heat through. But it is important not to crowd the pan with too many ingredients. The rice is all-important because it is the rice that carries the wonderful flavours of the stock and the *sofrito*, and it should not be covered up and hidden. I am afraid I am sometimes guilty of overcrowding a *paella* with seafood because I know my guests want a lot of it.

An important piece of advice from Lourdes March is to always have boiling hot stock or water at hand in case you need to add some more. Often, at the end of cooking, the rice at the top is a bit hard while underneath it is well cooked. Her tip in that case is to cover the finished dish with a damp cloth as it rests for 5 to 10 minutes. Rice needs to be cooked for 18 to 20 minutes. The grains should be dry and separate when done and the bottom layer should have a caramelized crust called the *socarrat*.

Count Ybarra (see page 414), from whom I learnt much about Spanish cooking, also had some tips. The rice should never reach higher than the level of the rivets for the handles in the pan. The stock should be boiling hot. Start cooking on a high heat and then as soon as 'crab holes' appear, lower the heat. If you are cooking a large *paella* on your domestic hob, put all the burners on and move the pan around so that the rice cooks evenly and all the way to the edges. In Spain, when a *paella* is cooked outdoors, a wide, built-in charcoal grill or a special large gas ring with several concentric circles joined to a butane cylinder gives the required spread-out heat. When you hear crackly noises it means that the famously desirable *soccarat* is forming. Use medium-grain Spanish or '*paella*' rice. If that is not available use Italian Arborio or Carnaroli risotto rice. Most people in Spain add a pinch of yellow colouring (see page 104) instead of, or as well as, saffron threads to give the rice a bright yellow colour. Try the two.

SEAFOOD *PAELLA* ❖ *arroz a la marinera*

This *paella* looks stunning. You can vary the quantities of seafood and also put in crab, crayfish or lobster that you boil separately. In Catalonia, where the tradition of mixing meat and seafood is very old, they also add pieces of chicken, pork, rabbit, duck and sausage into their seafood *paellas*. Today this has become common in other regions, where seasonal vegetables such as green beans, peas, artichokes or peppers also go in. It is called *paella mixta*. Serve this *paella* with garlic mayonnaise or *alioli* (page 149) if you like.

SERVES 4

❋ 1 large onion, peeled and finely chopped ❋ 5 tablespoons olive oil ❋ 2 garlic cloves, peeled and crushed ❋ 2 tomatoes (about 200g), peeled and chopped ❋ ½ teaspoon sugar ❋ salt ❋ 1 teaspoon *pimentón dulce* or sweet paprika ❋ a good pinch of saffron threads ❋ 4 small squid, cleaned (see page 118), the bodies sliced and tentacles left whole ❋ 400g medium-grain Spanish rice or risotto rice ❋ 750ml fish or chicken stock (pages 144–5), plus more if needed ❋ 250ml dry white wine ❋ 12 large raw king prawns in their shells ❋ 16 or more mussels or clams (cleaned – see page 118)

Fry the onion in the oil in a 40cm *paella* pan over a low heat until soft, stirring often. Stir in the garlic, and before it begins to colour add the tomatoes. Add the sugar, salt, *pimentón* or paprika and saffron, stir well, and cook over a medium heat until the tomatoes are reduced to a jammy sauce and the oil sizzles. Add the squid and cook, stirring for a minute or so, then add the rice and stir until all the grains are coated. (You can do all this up to 2 hours in advance – no longer, because of the squid.)

Bring the stock and wine to the boil and pour on the rice, then add salt (the broth can taste a bit salty but it will not be salty when it is absorbed by the rice). Stir well and make sure the rice is evenly distributed in the pan, then do not stir again. Cook the rice over a low heat for 18 to 20 minutes, moving the *paella* around on the hob so that it cooks evenly. Lay the prawns on top of the rice after 10 minutes and turn them over when they turn pink on the bottom side. Add a little more hot stock towards the end if the rice seems too dry and you hear crackly frying noises from the bottom of the pan before it is done, and cover the pan with a large piece of foil. Steam the mussels in a pan with a tight-fitting lid with a finger's depth of water. As soon as they open they are cooked. Throw away any that have not opened and arrange the ones that have on top of the rice.

VARIATIONS

▓ Add 4 small, quartered artichoke hearts or bottoms, a good handful of peas or broad beans – fresh or frozen and defrosted – runner or string beans cut into short lengths and roasted red peppers, cut into strips, with the rice

▓ In Alicante they use the pulp of 1 or 2 dried and soaked *ñora* peppers, which they grow there (see page 107), instead of *pimentón*.

SEAFOOD *PAELLA without* SHELLS
❊ *arroz a la marinera del señorito*

When my friend Alicia Ríos sent an email to her friends asking for their favourite recipes, María Ortells sent this seafood *paella*, a speciality of Alicante, which is different from other seafood *paellas* in that everything is peeled and removed from its shells so that you do not need to use your fingers to eat it. Presumably, that is the way local young noblemen (*señoritos*) liked it. It has caught on in the rest of Spain, where it is also called *arroz limpio* (literally 'clean rice') or *arroz de marisco pelado* ('peeled seafood rice'). It is less dramatic to look at than other seafood *paellas* but equally delicious and less messy to eat.

In Alicante they use dried *ñora* peppers (see page 107), but *pimentón* will do. The *ñoras* are soaked in boiling water for half an hour, then drained, cut open and the seeds discarded. The pulp is scraped from the skin with a spoon. You only get about 1 teaspoon of pulp from each *ñora* pepper. Nowadays our supermarkets sell shelled raw (grey) king prawns and frozen ones. I can also buy frozen baby squid (less than 9cm long), already cleaned, from the fishmonger. If the squid you buy has not been cleaned see page 118 for instructions. You can use mussels instead of clams, or small scallops. If you cannot make or buy good fish stock you may use good chicken stock (see pages 145–5).

Serve this *paella* with garlic mayonnaise or *alioli* (page 149).

SERVES 6

❊ 6 baby squid, cleaned and cut into slices about 1cm wide ❊ about 24 clams ❊ salt
❊ 1 large onion, peeled and chopped ❊ 5 tablespoons olive oil ❊ 4 garlic cloves, peeled and crushed
❊ 2 tomatoes, peeled and finely chopped ❊ a good pinch of saffron threads ❊ pulp of 2 *ñora* peppers
or 1 teaspoon *pimentón dulce* or sweet paprika ❊ 500g medium-grain Spanish rice or risotto rice
❊ 1 litre fish stock (page 144) ❊ 250ml dry white wine ❊ about 18 raw peeled king prawns
❊ 1½ lemons, quartered ❊ 2–3 tablespoons chopped flat-leaf parsley

» » »

If you need to prepare and clean the squid see page 118. Scrub the clams under the cold tap and put them in a bowl of cold water with a little salt for 30 minutes. Throw away any with broken shells or that do not shut when knocked sharply. Drain and put them in a pan with about 1cm of water. Put the lid on and bring to the boil. The clams will steam and open very quickly, which means they are cooked. Throw away any that do not open. Take them out of their shells when they are cool enough to handle and throw away the shells. Strain the water left in the pan and add it to the fish stock.

In a 45cm *paella* pan, fry the onion in the oil over a low heat until soft, stirring often. Then stir in the garlic and a few seconds later the tomatoes and a little salt. Cook over a medium heat until the sauce is jammy and the oil begins to sizzle. Add the saffron and the *ñora* pulp (see the recipe introduction) or the *pimentón* or paprika. Add the squid, stir well, then add the rice, turning it over gently so that it gets well coated with the sauce.

Bring the stock and wine to the boil in a pan and pour over the rice. Add a good amount of salt (the rice will need it but the amount depends on the saltiness of the fish stock) and stir well, spreading the rice out so it is evenly distributed in the pan. Do not stir the rice again during the cooking. Bring to the boil and cook over a high heat for 3 minutes, then reduce the heat to low and cook for another 10 minutes. Occasionally, rotate the pan over the hob, so that it heats evenly.

Put the prawns on top of the rice and cook for another 8 minutes, or until they turn pink and the rice is done. Add the clams 3 minutes before the end of cooking to heat through. Add a little boiling water if it becomes dry too quickly. Leave to rest for 5 to 10 minutes, covered in foil.

Serve with the lemon quarters and sprinkled with parsley.

VARIATIONS

- I often use scallops instead of the clams, and monkfish, cut into 2cm cubes, sautéed in oil.
- You can also use mussels instead of the clams. To clean them see page 118.
- For a soupy *arroz caldoso marinero del señorito*, add 1.75 litres of fish stock and no wine. Cook for just 20 minutes and serve at once or the rice will fall apart. It is very good.

andresito's banquet in alicante

We were twenty around the table, wearing straw hats with fresh flowers pinned on. We sat eating for hours, laughing and dancing in between courses – conviviality and *alegría de vivir* ('the joy of living') are in the spirit of Mediterranean Spain. We started with marinated anchovies, tiny sweet tomatoes, green olives and *pan con tomate* (page 132); then came little pizza-like *coques* with tomatoes, peppers and aubergines (pages 190–1), and broad beans and artichokes cooked with pancetta. The main course was chicken and baby lamb chops cooked over embers on the outside grill, and we finished with fruit and pumpkin fritters. A giant pumpkin filled with honey and cognac was baked in the outside bread oven. Nearly all the ingredients for the meal came from the estate.

Our host, Andresito – Andrés Bertomeu – a handsome stocky man with a little pointed beard, had cooked all the dishes with his wife. The rest of us were the house guests of Alicia and her mother Josefa in their neighbouring *casitas* (country houses) by the sea. Andresito was born on the estate of Alicia's grandfather in Benissa, Alicante, a province of Valencia. His grandparents and parents were peasant retainers. Alicia's grandmother died when she had just given birth to Josefa, and Andresito's grandmother, who had recently lost her own baby, breastfed her.

Andresito's father planted fruit trees, tended vines and grew vegetables on the estate. As a young boy Andresito boarded with the Franciscans, where poor children got a free education, but he ran away from the convent after only two years, and that was the only schooling he had. At twelve he started working in the fields with his father, and as a teenager he worked in construction, building houses for tourists. After army service he started his own construction company with builders, painters, electricians, plumbers and eventually a secretary who spoke several languages. Now he is a contractor and property multimillionaire with an estate of his own, a grand house with a central courtyard and swimming pool, vegetable gardens, and every kind of fruit tree imaginable. There are geese, ducks and turkeys running around. He is an example of the many Spaniards who have done well from the tourist boom. Anybody who owned the tiniest bit of land by the sea became a millionaire.

Andresito now lets his wife, María, run the business (her father was the village butcher) while he paints, cooks, collects old recipes, interviews locals and writes nostalgically about what life was like before tourism in the mountain interior and by the sea. Villages were small. Church bells rang to announce births, deaths and weddings. People travelled by mule and cart. They did not have electricity, so they kept food cool in the

» » »

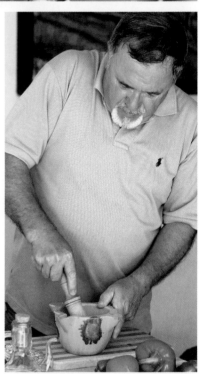

wells. His grandmother never bought meat or fish. She cooked chicken only once or twice a year. When a woman gave birth, the villagers boiled a hen, gave the woman the broth and the men ate the meat. People ate wild rabbits, hares and wild ducks. They caught small birds in nets and hunted game. Bullets were expensive so they reused them. They went out at night with oil lamps to find snails in the vineyard. They ate rice every day. The *paella* of the interior was made with wild things – rabbit, duck, snails, water rat, the vegetables in season. Andresito's father kept a pig or two. The family cooked the meat, cut into pieces, slowly in its own fat and kept it in jars. Once in a while they would bring out a small piece from a jar and divide it between them. His mother always said she did not want any. There was a man who kept goats and a few cows. The villagers came to him with bottles and clay jars to be filled with milk. Labourers walked to the fields at sunrise and returned home at sunset. They took their food with them and carried their wine in goatskin bags. Bread was the mainstay of the diet and they used it instead of cutlery to pick up morsels of food.

On our way to Andresito's estate we passed through small mountain towns and villages, many of them walled, named after Berber tribes and with Arabic prefixes of 'Ben' and 'Al'. There had been a large population of Moriscos (see page 26) here. When they left en masse in the early seventeenth century, Alicante was repopulated mainly with people from Majorca and Ibiza, who took over their land and houses. The descendants of Moriscos who remained can be recognized today by the surnames that their forebears took when they converted to Christianity – such as Ferrer (iron worker), Fuster (carpenter) and Zapatero (shoemaker). The festival of *Moros y Cristianos* that is celebrated throughout the whole of Spain at different times of the year is an extraordinary event in Alicante, where it takes place in April, with a procession and a dramatic re-enactment of battles between Moors and Christians in imagined medieval costume. Even after the expulsion of the Moors, the area continued to have connections with North Africa, and it shows. When the French were in Algeria, the people of the coastal town of Denia went there to work in the vineyards. More recently, Moroccans have been coming to Alicante to work in the construction industry.

Tourism has not entirely destroyed the old life. The young, like Andresito's sons, eat pizza and fast foods, but in the villages in the interior people still cook traditional foods. Many families now live in small towns but keep a *casita* with a small plot, where they have fruit trees and grow vegetables and vines.

CHICKEN, RABBIT, SNAIL *and* BEAN PAELLA
❋ *paella valenciana*

I have a fabulous memory of the original and 'real' *paella valenciana* that I ate more than twenty years ago when I was on reconnaissance for a BBC television series. It was fantastic and exquisite, cooked out in the open in a field in a giant *paella* pan. This is Lourdes March's recipe from her *El libro de la paella y los arroces* ('The Book of *Paella* and Rice Dishes'). She uses fresh *garrofones*, a type of fresh white butter bean, but you can use tinned beans or those that come in jars. The snails bring a taste of the rosemary they feed on. If you can't find them you can substitute a sprig of rosemary. It will not be the *paella* they cook in the Valencian countryside, but it will be near enough.

SERVES 6

Heat the oil in a 45cm *paella* pan and fry the chicken and rabbit or pork pieces over a high heat, turning to brown them lightly all over. Add the runner or string beans, then the tomato and the *pimentón* or paprika. Add the water, bring to the boil, then turn down the heat. Add salt and simmer for about 45 minutes, or until the meats are very tender. Much of the water will have evaporated.

Take out about two cups of the water and keep to one side. Add the snails or rosemary, the saffron and the butter beans. Turn up the heat and add the rice, stirring to spread it out evenly in the pan. Add as much of the reserved water as you need to cover the rice. Cook for 10 minutes, then turn down the heat for another 8 to 10 minutes until the grains are tender but firm, adding a little of the reserved water if it looks too dry and you hear crackly frying noises before it is done. The best part is said to be the crunchy and slightly brown bits at the bottom called the *socarrat*.

VARIATION
- Artichoke hearts or bottoms can be used instead of the runner or string beans.

- 150ml olive oil
- 750g chicken thighs and drumsticks
- 500g rabbit or lean pork, cut into chunks
- 250g runner or string beans, trimmed and cut in half
- 1 medium tomato, peeled and chopped
- 1 teaspoon *pimentón dulce* or sweet paprika
- about 2 litres water
- salt
- 12 small land snails, cleaned, or tinned snails
- a sprig of rosemary (optional)
- 2 pinches of saffron threads
- 200g tinned butter beans (drained weight), drained
- 500g medium-grain Spanish rice or risotto rice

RICE *with* MUSHROOMS
✤ *arroz con setas*

Here is a homely dish made with cultivated mushrooms that are available all year round. It is easy and delicious. The rice absorbs the flavour of the mushrooms and the almost-caramelized onions, as well as the chicken stock and sherry. I like to put in the larger quantity of mushrooms suggested below, but you might prefer the lesser amount, which is more common. Use white button mushrooms or the brown cremini mushrooms. The brown ones have a stronger flavour.

SERVES 4 AS A STARTER

Wash the mushrooms briefly or wipe them, trim the earthy base if necessary and slice them. Heat the oil in a wide casserole or pan. Put in the mushrooms and sauté over a medium-low heat, adding salt and pepper and turning them over occasionally until they have given up their juices and the oil they absorbed – about 8 to 10 minutes. Take them out, leaving the oil and juices behind.

Put in the onion and cook uncovered, stirring often, over a high heat for about 3 minutes to evaporate the juices, then lower the heat and cook for about 20 minutes until golden brown and jammy. Add the garlic and cook, stirring, for a minute or so. Return the mushrooms to the pan, add the rice and stir so that the grains are well coated with the oily juices. You can prepare the dish in advance up to this stage.

About 30 minutes before you are ready to serve, bring the stock and sherry to the boil and pour them over the reheated mushrooms and rice. Add salt and stir well, then cook, covered, over a medium heat without stirring again for about 10 minutes. Reduce the heat to low and continue to cook, covered, for another 10 minutes or until the rice is tender, adding a little boiling water if the rice seems too dry. Cover and leave to rest for 5 minutes before serving.

VARIATION

※ If you are lucky enough to have wild mushrooms, you can use them, cut in half or quartered if they are large, instead of the cultivated ones.

- ※ 300–500g mushrooms
- ※ 5 tablespoons olive oil
- ※ salt and pepper
- ※ 1 onion, peeled and finely chopped
- ※ 2 garlic cloves, peeled and chopped
- ※ 250g medium-grain Spanish rice or risotto rice
- ※ 600ml chicken or vegetable stock (you may use a stock cube)
- ※ 125ml dry oloroso sherry

BLACK RICE *with* BABY SQUID
❋ *arroz negro*

Catalans call this *arròs negre*. It has an unusual, delicate flavour and looks dramatic. When fishermen on the Costa Brava and along the Mediterranean coast used the ink from their squid and cuttlefish, there was only ever enough for a pale grey rice, and they made it darker by caramelizing the onions. Nowadays you can buy cuttlefish ink in sachets from fishmongers and shops, and chefs like to produce an intensely black rice. This recipe is from the *Corpus de la Cuina Catalana*, an inventory or archive of traditional Catalan recipes by the Catalan Culinary Institute (see page 81). I have added white wine as some people do. If you cannot make or buy good fish stock you can use chicken stock.

You can now also buy frozen baby squid – not more than 9cm long and already cleaned. If you need to clean fresh squid, see the instructions on page 118.

SERVES 6–8

❋ 2 medium onions, peeled and chopped ❋ 6 tablespoons olive oil ❋ 3 tomatoes (250g), halved and grated (see page 121) or peeled and chopped ❋ salt and pepper ❋ 500g baby squid (cleaned) ❋ 500g medium-grain Spanish rice or risotto rice ❋ 1 litre fish or chicken stock (pages 144–5) ❋ 250ml dry white wine ❋ 4–5 sachets of squid ink (4g each) ❋ a handful of chopped flat-leaf parsley ❋ about 350ml (300g) garlic mayonnaise or *alioli* (page 149), to serve

Fry the onions in the oil over a medium heat in a 45cm-diameter *paella* pan, stirring often until soft and golden. Add the tomatoes, season with a little salt and pepper, and cook until most of the liquid has evaporated and you can see the oil sizzling through.

Cut the body of the squid into rings 1.25 to 1.5cm wide. Put them into the pan with the tentacles and cook on a medium heat, stirring and turning them over, for 5 to 8 minutes. Add the rice and stir so that the grains are well coated with the sauce (you can prepare the dish in advance up to this stage).

Bring the fish or chicken stock and wine to the boil in a pan. Squeeze the contents of the ink sachets (I used 4 and liked it that way – 5 gives a more intense black colour) into a small bowl and beat in a little of the stock to dilute the ink thoroughly, then pour this into the pan and mix very well.

Heat the contents of the *paella* pan and pour in the boiling ink-stained stock. Add salt and stir, spreading the rice evenly around the pan. Then do not stir again but move the pan so that the rice gets an even heat on the hob. Cook over a medium heat for 10 minutes, then lower the heat for 8 to 10 minutes more, or until the rice is tender. If it gets too dry before it is done, pour in a little boiling water. Serve sprinkled with parsley and accompanied by *alioli* or garlic mayonnaise.

VARIATION

❋ For *chipirones en su tinta con fideos*, instead of adding rice, add 3 dry vermicelli nests broken into small pieces, and cook until done al dente.

CREAMY RICE *with* ARTICHOKES, BROAD BEANS *and* PEAS
❊ *arroz meloso con alcachofas, habas y guisantes*

Vegetable rice dishes in Murcia are called *a la huertana*, meaning 'of the vegetable garden'. Loli Flores, who gave me this recipe and many others, lives in Seville, where she was a chef for twenty-six years. One of her daughters (she has six children) is the chef/owner of a truly vegetarian restaurant called Habanita – no bits of ham, no pork fat or chicken stock – which is something that is very rare in Spain. We had a great meal there.

Use fresh vegetables when they are available, but defrosted frozen ones will do very well. See how to prepare artichokes on page 120.

SERVES 6

❊ 5 tablespoons olive oil ❊ 2 bay leaves ❊ 2 medium onions, peeled and chopped
❊ 1 green pepper, halved, deseeded and chopped ❊ 3–4 garlic cloves, peeled and chopped
❊ 1 litre vegetable stock (you can use 2 stock cubes) ❊ 4 artichoke hearts or bottoms, quartered
❊ 250g broad beans, fresh or frozen and defrosted ❊ 250g peas, fresh or frozen and defrosted
❊ 350g medium-grain Spanish rice or risotto rice ❊ salt

In a large pan, heat the oil with the bay leaves. Add the onions and the pepper and sauté over a medium heat, stirring often, for about 20 minutes until soft, then add the garlic and stir for half a minute.

In another pan bring the stock to the boil. Add the artichokes and broad beans to the fried onions and pepper, and pour in the vegetable stock. Simmer, covered, for 10 minutes then add the peas. Bring to the boil again, throw in the rice, stir and add salt. Simmer over a low heat for about 15 to 18 minutes until the rice is tender. It should be *meloso* – that means not dry and not soupy, but in between.

RICE *with* CHICKEN *and* RED PEPPERS
❖ *arroz con pollo y pimientos*

This is a very special and unusual rice dish in that the rice is cooked in a glorious mix of creamy onion sauce with chicken stock and sherry, and is flavoured with a touch of saffron. I roasted the chicken and mixed the juices and melted fat from the roast with the chicken stock.

SERVES 6

Put the chicken in a baking dish, season with salt, and rub it with 1 tablespoon of the oil. Lay it breast side down, pour in 200ml of water, and roast in an oven preheated to 190°C/gas 5 for 45 minutes. Then turn the chicken breast side up, add a little more water if it has dried out and roast for another 30 minutes, or until the chicken is brown and the juices run clear when you cut in between the leg and the body of the bird with a pointed knife.

Roast, peel and deseed the peppers (see page 118) and cut each into 6 pieces.

In a wide casserole or heavy-bottomed pan – preferably one that you can bring to the table – sauté the onions in the remaining 4 tablespoons of oil over a low heat. Put the lid on and stir occasionally until they are very soft and begin to colour, then cook, uncovered, over a medium heat until the onions are a golden brown. Add the garlic and stir until it is lightly coloured. This can all take 45 minutes because there are so many onions. Add the sherry and cook for 1 minute more. Blend with a hand blender or in the food processor and return this sauce to the casserole.

Take the chicken out of the baking dish. Boil the chicken stock and pour it into the baking dish, mixing it thoroughly with the roast chicken juices and melted fat. Pour this mixture into the onion sauce in the casserole. Add saffron and some salt – rice needs a good amount, but how much depends on the saltiness of the stock – and stir well.

Cut the chicken up – cut each leg and breast into two pieces – and keep covered. Pick the small pieces of meat off the carcass and wings and add them to the stock.

Half an hour before serving, bring the onion and stock mixture to the boil, pour in the rice and stir well. Cook without stirring again, uncovered, over a medium heat for 10 minutes, then lower the heat, lay the chicken pieces and red pepper slices on top, cover with foil and cook for another 10 minutes, or until the rice is tender and the chicken is heated through, adding a little more hot stock or water if it seems too dry before it is cooked.

- ❋ 1 x 1½kg chicken
- ❋ salt
- ❋ 5 tablespoons olive oil
- ❋ 200ml water
- ❋ 2 red peppers
- ❋ 3 large onions, peeled and sliced
- ❋ 4 garlic cloves, peeled and sliced
- ❋ 250ml dry amontillado or oloroso sherry (I used amontillado)
- ❋ 850ml chicken stock, plus more if needed (you may use 1½ stock cubes)
- ❋ a good pinch of saffron threads
- ❋ 500g medium-grain Spanish rice or risotto rice

BAKED RICE *with* CURRANTS *and* CHICKPEAS
✤ *arroz al horno con pasas y garbanzos*

In their splendid book *The Heritage of Spanish Cooking* (see page435), Alicia Ríos and Lourdes March say that in the Valencian mountain interior rice dishes are based on the broth of a *cocido* of boiled meats (page 303). In Spain today you can buy good *cocido* broth. If you cannot buy good beef or chicken stock, use stock cubes. Use a *cazuela* (see page 116) or a large shallow casserole that will go on the hob and in the oven. If you do not have one of these, start the dish in a deep saucepan, then transfer it to an oven dish. A head of garlic, the so-called 'partridge', is placed in the centre. Serve the rice with meatballs, or with fried pork ribs and sausages or blood sausages.

SERVES 8

※ 200g dried chickpeas, soaked in water for 6 hours or overnight ※ salt ※ 1 whole head of garlic, unpeeled ※ 5 tablespoons olive oil ※ 150g currants or raisins, soaked in water for 30 minutes, then drained ※ 1 large tomato (200g), peeled and chopped ※ 1 teaspoon *pimentón dulce* or sweet paprika ※ 1.25 litres meat or chicken stock (you may use 1½ stock cubes) ※ 500g medium-grain Spanish rice or risotto rice

Drain the chickpeas. Put them in a pan with fresh water and simmer for 1 hour, until they are soft, adding some salt when they have already begun to soften.

Wash the head of garlic and dry it. Heat the oil in a *cazuela* or large pan. Put in the garlic and half the currants or raisins, and stir over a low heat for 2 to 3 minutes. Add the tomato and the *pimentón* or paprika and stir well. Then add the chickpeas, the stock and some salt. Bring to the boil, add the rice and stir well. If you are using a pan, pour everything into a round baking dish about 36cm in diameter.

Move the head of garlic to the centre of the rice and sprinkle the remaining currants or raisins over the top. Bake in an oven preheated to 200°C/gas 6 for 30 minutes, or until the rice is tender. When serving, give everyone a garlic clove for them to squeeze out the soft inside.

BAKED RICE WITH AN EGG CRUST
❊ *arroz con costra*

This baked rice dish is unusual in that it has an egg topping. The chicken drumsticks, spare ribs and sausages make it a hearty and flavourful meal in itself. You will need a wide casserole or a *cazuela* (page 116) with which you can start cooking on the hob, then continue in the oven. Otherwise, start in a saucepan and transfer to a baking dish (see note).

SERVES 6

Heat the oil in a large, wide casserole or *cazuela* over a medium heat. Put in the spare ribs or chops, sausages and drumsticks and cook, turning to brown them all, over a medium-high heat. Take out the sausages and ribs or chops as soon as they are lightly browned and put to one side, but cook the drumsticks for at least 15 minutes, turning them often, before removing.

Add the tomatoes to the pan and season with salt, pepper and *pimentón* or paprika, then stir in the rice and chickpeas, if using, with a wooden spoon.

Bring the stock to the boil in a saucepan and pour it into the casserole. Return the spare ribs or chops, the drumsticks and the sausages, cut in half, to the casserole and stir to distribute the rice and meats evenly. Add salt, bring back to the boil and simmer over a low heat, without stirring, for 5 minutes.

Put the casserole, uncovered, in an oven preheated to 200°C/gas 6 and bake for 15 minutes or until the rice is almost tender. Take it out of the oven, season the beaten eggs with a little salt and pour them evenly over the top. Bake for another 15 minutes or until the eggs are firm.

NOTE: If you do not have a wide casserole, brown the meats in a frying pan; fry the tomatoes in a saucepan, add the stock and the rice, then pour into a large baking dish. Arrange the meats on top and continue as above.

- 3–4 tablespoons olive oil
- 6 pork spare ribs or thin loin chops
- 3 pure pork sausages
- 6 chicken drumsticks
- 2 tomatoes (about 200g), peeled and chopped
- salt and pepper
- 1 teaspoon *pimentón dulce* or sweet paprika
- 400g medium-grain Spanish rice or risotto rice
- 200g tinned chickpeas, drained (optional)
- 1 litre beef or chicken stock (you can use stock cubes)
- 5 large eggs, lightly beaten

RICE *with* PORK, CHESTNUTS *and* RAISINS
❋ *arroz con cerdo, castañas y pasas*

The meatballs take time but they are worth it. Use fresh peeled, frozen or vacuum-packed chestnuts. You can start the dish in advance and put the rice in half an hour before you are ready to serve. Instead of frying the meatballs you can turn them under the grill until they are brown all over.

SERVES 4

Heat the oil in a *cazuela* or a wide ovenproof casserole with a lid and sauté the spare ribs – in batches if necessary – for 10 to 12 minutes over a medium heat, turning them once to brown them lightly all over. Then remove them from the pan.

Sauté the onion in the same oil over a low heat until it begins to colour. Add the garlic and stir for a moment or two until the aroma rises. Add the tomatoes and cook over a high heat until they are reduced to a jammy sauce. Then stir in the saffron, the *pimentón* or paprika and the currants or raisins. Pour in the stock, return the spare ribs to the pan, add a little salt and cook, covered, for about 20 minutes until the spare ribs are tender.

For the meatballs, soak the breadcrumbs in the milk for a few moments. Put the minced pork in a bowl with the egg, the soaked bread-crumbs and the parsley. Season with the cinnamon, salt and pepper, and work to a soft paste with your hands. Cover a platter with flour. Roll the meat paste into 16 to 20 balls the size of large walnuts and roll them in the flour to coat them all over. Fry them in batches for 8 to 10 minutes in a large frying pan with about 1.5cm depth of oil, over a medium-high heat, turning them over once to brown them lightly all over. Remove the meatballs with a slotted spoon and drain on kitchen paper.

Half an hour before serving, bring the stock with the spare ribs to the boil and add salt. Put in the chestnuts and the rice, stir very well, and bring to the boil again. Do not stir again. Cook over a high heat for 3 minutes, then reduce the heat to low and cook for another 7 minutes. Now place the meatballs on top of the rice, cover with a lid or with foil and cook for 10 minutes, or until the rice is done. The meatballs will have cooked further in the steam.

* 4 tablespoons olive oil
* 8 pork spare ribs
* 1 medium onion, peeled and finely chopped
* 2–3 garlic cloves, peeled and crushed
* 300g tomatoes, peeled and chopped
* a good pinch of saffron threads
* 1 teaspoon *pimentón dulce* or sweet paprika
* 50g currants or raisins
* 1 litre chicken stock (you may use 1½ stock cubes)
* salt
* 300g chestnuts, fresh peeled (see page 374), frozen and defrosted or vacuum-packed
* 400g medium-grain Spanish rice or risotto rice

For the meatballs

* 6 tablespoons fresh breadcrumbs (see page 120)
* 4 tablespoons whole milk
* 500g minced pork
* 1 large egg, lightly beaten
* 2–3 tablespoons finely chopped flat-leaf parsley
* 1 teaspoon ground cinnamon
* about ¾ teaspoon salt
* pepper
* plain flour, for dredging
* olive oil or sunflower oil, for frying

PASTA *with* PEAS, CHICKEN
or RABBIT *and* PORK CHOPS
❊ *fideos en cazuela*

This heart-warming pasta dish is from the Catalan interior. Small, curved macaroni are cooked in an aromatic stock and the meats, sautéed separately, are added towards the end along with the marvellous nutty, fragrant thickener called *picada*. You will need a *cazuela* or a wide casserole to make this in.

SERVES 5–6

Heat 3 tablespoons of the olive oil in a large frying pan and sauté the chicken or rabbit pieces over a medium heat, turning them and sprinkling with a little salt and pepper, until lightly browned and cooked through. Take them out and put them on a plate. Sauté the pork chops in the same oil over a medium heat until lightly browned and cooked through, adding salt and pepper and turning them over, then transfer them to the plate as well. Prick the sausages with the point of a knife so that they don't burst, then sauté them in the same pan over a medium heat, shaking the pan and turning them over until done. Take the sausages out, put them on the plate and cut into thick slices.

Fry the onion, pepper and garlic in a wide casserole in the remaining 2 tablespoons of oil over a low heat until soft, stirring often. Add the tomatoes, sugar, a little salt and the bay leaf, and cook over a medium-high heat for about 10 minutes. Meanwhile bring the stock to the boil.

Add the pasta to the casserole and stir well. Read the instructions on the pack to see how long the particular pasta requires as cooking times vary. Pour in the boiling stock and add the peas and some salt. Bring back to the boil and simmer over a low heat for about 3 to 4 minutes, leaving the pasta still slightly underdone. Taste the pasta with a little of the sauce when it begins to soften and add extra salt if necessary.

Blend all the *picada* ingredients to a paste in the food processor, then dilute the mixture by adding about 100ml of the stock from the casserole. Stir this into the pasta, together with the rabbit or chicken pieces and the sausage slices. Lay the pork chops on top, cover the casserole with foil or a lid, and cook until the pasta is done and the meats are cooked through and hot.

- 5 tablespoons olive oil
- 2 chicken thighs or 300g skinless boneless rabbit, cut into 2–3cm pieces
- salt and pepper
- 6 tiny pork chops
- 4 thick pork sausages (about 200g)
- 1 large onion, peeled and chopped
- 1 red or green pepper, deseeded and diced
- 2 garlic cloves, peeled and finely chopped
- 3 tomatoes, peeled and chopped
- ½ teaspoon sugar
- 1 bay leaf
- 1 litre chicken stock (you can use a stock cube)
- 400g small macaroni-type pasta
- 100g peas, fresh or frozen and defrosted

For the picada

- 40g almonds or hazelnuts, lightly toasted
- 2 garlic cloves, peeled
- a pinch of saffron threads
- 3 tablespoons roughly chopped flat-leaf parsley

SEEFOOD PASTA
✳ *fideuà* or *fideuada del señorito*

In Valencia I ate a seafood pasta cooked in a *paella* pan with short, thin, curved macaroni. Another I had in Catalonia with a vermicelli-type pasta was especially memorable. They were both delicious, with glorious-looking seafood. This recipe, called *fideuada del señorito* (literally 'of the young gentleman'), is less messy to eat because the seafood is peeled or out of its shell but if you want to make a spectacular one see the recipe variation at the end.

SERVES 6

Heat 4 tablespoons of the oil in a 40 to 45cm *paella* pan. Put in the monkfish, sprinkle with salt and cook over a medium heat for 3 to 4 minutes, turning the pieces over. Put in the squid and cook, stirring, for about 3 minutes. Then put in the prawns and scallops and stir, turning them over, until the prawns are pink and the scallops just seared, about 1 or 2 minutes. Transfer all the cooked fish and seafood to a platter. Keep the liquid aside to add to the fish stock for extra flavour.

Heat the remaining oil in the *paella* pan, stir in the garlic and when the aroma rises and before it begins to colour, add the tomatoes. Add the *pimentón* or paprika, saffron and a little salt, and cook for 10 minutes, stirring occasionally, until much of the liquid has evaporated and the oil is sizzling through.

Meanwhile, bring the stock and the liquid from cooking the seafood to the boil. Add the pasta to the sauce in the *paella* pan and cook, stirring, so that it is well coated. Pour in the boiling stock and arrange the monkfish and seafood on top. Cook until the pasta is al dente – this can take from 2 minutes to about 10 minutes, depending on whether you are using vermicelli or spaghettini – adding a little more stock or boiling water if the liquid dries up before the pasta is done. It should still be moist.

Serve sprinkled with parsley and garnished with lemon quarters. Accompany with *alioli* or garlic mayonnaise.

VARIATIONS

✳ Substitute dry white wine or dry oloroso sherry for 250ml of the stock.

✳ Have 6 langoustines, 12 king prawns in their shells and 18–24 clams or mussels, instead of the squid and scallops. Cook them separately – boil the langoustines for 4 minutes, steam the clams or mussels open (see page 118) – and arrange them all on top of the pasta.

✳ 6 tablespoons olive oil

✳ 400g monkfish fillet, cut into 2cm cubes

✳ salt

✳ 4 baby squid, cleaned and the bodies cut into rings

✳ 12 or more raw peeled king prawns

✳ 12 bay scallops

✳ 4–5 garlic cloves, peeled and crushed

✳ 3 tomatoes, peeled and chopped

✳ 1 teaspoon *pimentón dulce* or sweet paprika

✳ a good pinch of saffron threads

✳ about 1.25 litres fish or chicken stock (pages 144–45)

✳ 500g *fideus* size 1 or 2, vermicelli nests or thin spaghettini, broken into 3–4cm pieces

✳ 3 tablespoons chopped flat-leaf parsley

✳ 1½ lemons, quartered, to garnish

✳ about 350ml (300g) garlic mayonnaise or *alioli* (page 149), to serve

FRIED BREADCRUMBS ❖ *migas*

Migas, fried breadcrumbs, is the legendary food of shepherds that was adopted by agricultural labourers along the old transhumance routes that criss-crossed Spain (these were the routes that sheep took when they travelled seasonally to reach new pastures – see page 49). It was cooked on little braziers (*braseritos*). The dish has recently become very fashionable. I ate *migas* in restaurants around the country and at a glamorous party in Madrid. Spanish supermarkets sell it vacuum-packed, ready to heat through.

Depending on the region, the breadcrumbs are fried in olive oil or lard, or a mixture of the two. In Castile-La Mancha, Aragon and Andalusia, they are cooked in olive oil. Also depending on the region, they are eaten with a wide variety of accompaniments, such as fried bacon and chorizo, or blood sausage, and sometimes also eggs. There are people who eat *migas* with bits of *jamón* (ham) and those who eat it with grapes and chocolate. In Granada they eat *migas* with anchovies, melon and orange slices. Some like to eat the breadcrumbs with a sprinkling of sugar. In the valley of the river Duero, they eat *migas* like pasta, with a sauce made from fried onion, garlic, a chilli pepper and sweet *pimentón dulce* (Spanish paprika). In Aragon they make the sauce with bacon, *chorizo* and sweet and hot *pimentón*; in Navarre with fried onion, garlic and *jamón*.

My friend Cuqui Gonzales de Caldas described how in Andalusia olive pickers made *migas* during the harvest. One man, the '*miguero*', fried the breadcrumbs in olive oil in a huge communal pan and all the harvesters served themselves from the pan, and ate it with olives, raw turnips and fried or grilled sardines. To finish, they had more *migas* with oranges. Cuqui's mother, who came from Osuna in Andalusia, made the dish for the family.

FRIED BREADCRUMBS *with* BACON
❋ *migas con tocino*

This is comfort food for the stomach and for the soul. There is an art to tearing up bread into very small pieces with your fingers and Cuqui Gonzales de Caldas showed me how to do it at our table at the Sol y Sombra bar in Seville. It reminded me of a man in a Paris restaurant I saw tearing up bread into piles, who I thought had an obsessive condition until I saw him later in a park feeding birds.

SERVES 2

❋ 250g dense country bread, crusts left on ❋ 125ml warm water ❋ salt
❋ ½ teaspoon *pimentón dulce* or sweet paprika ❋ a pinch of *pimentón picante* or hot paprika (optional)
❋ 3–4 tablespoons olive oil ❋ 5 garlic cloves, peeled ❋ about 8 rashers of streaky bacon

Cut the bread in very thin 5mm slices, then into strips, and again into dice as small as a chickpea and put them in a bowl. Mix the water with some salt and the *pimentón* or paprika. Sprinkle this on the diced bread, turning it with your hand so that the pieces dampen evenly. Leave for a few hours or overnight, covered with a cloth.

When you are ready to eat, heat the oil in a large frying pan (non-stick if you like). Fry the garlic and bacon over a medium heat, turning them once. Take out the garlic when it is golden brown and discard it. Remove the bacon on to a plate when it is crisp and has released most of its fat. Throw in the damp bread and fry over a high heat for about 15 minutes, turning it over continually and breaking it up with a spatula into ever smaller pieces, until the biggish crumbs are crisp, golden and crunchy but also soft and slightly damp inside. The fat will be soaked up very quickly, but you can continue to cook, turning the crumbs over in a dry pan. Cut the bacon up into small pieces and return them to the pan to heat through at the end.

josé luis alexanco's porridge
❉ about *gachas, fariñes, farinetas*

In a primitive kitchen off his studio and art gallery outside Madrid, the painter, sculptor and typographer José Luis Alexanco cooked us *gachas* and other foods of the rural poor of Castile-La Mancha. Then, feeling happy and satisfied, we went on a tour of his huge white gallery to see his stunning artwork. *Gachas* is a gruel or porridge made from the finely ground flour of the legume *almorta* (*Lathyrus sativus* or grass pea), which was both fodder for animals and eaten by shepherds and peasants. The excessive consumption of *gachas* during the Spanish Civil War and the period after was blamed for a neurological disease that caused weakness or paralysis of the legs. What was once referred to as '*gachas de los años difíciles*' (*gachas* of the tough years) is now a popular dish, served with vegetables or with pork products such as bacon, *chorizo*, *salchichón* (salami-type sausage) or *morcilla* (Spanish blood sausage).

José Luis fried lots of garlic with mushrooms and asparagus tips in plenty of olive oil. He removed them and poured in the *gachas*, stirring until the flour acquired a light golden colour. Then he gradually added water, stirring all the while. As he stirred the bubbling porridge, he talked about the lives of the peasants of La Mancha – those who had to give more than half their produce to their landlords; those who waited every day in the village square to be picked for odd jobs; the women who dyed all their clothes black when somebody in the family died and never again wore anything else. His maternal grandmother kept a goat for milk and cheese, and chickens for their eggs, and she dried her own tomatoes. In the winter she cooked *gachas* and *caparrones* (mottled brown-and-white beans) in the fireplace on a wood fire. His paternal grandfather was the butcher in Ojacastro in La Rioja. His pigs tasted better than the pork you get today because they were fed differently. He only slaughtered under a full moon, and he never mixed the meats of a male and a female swine in his sausages.

In other regions, chickpea flour, wheat flour and maize flour are used to make *gachas* in a variety of ways, sometimes with fried onion and croutons, sometimes with tomatoes and snails or with salt cod. In Andalusia, they are made from wheat flour and coloured and flavoured with *pimentón* and saffron. In Murcia, *gachas* are flavoured with caraway seeds and cloves. In the Canary Islands, they make *gachas* from a mix of maize and wheat flours and call the dish *gofio*. Sweet *gachas* are made with milk and are sometimes flavoured with grated orange peel and cinnamon, or with vanilla. Honey, raisins and almonds can be sprinkled on top. In Asturias, Galicia and Aragon, *gachas* are made from maize flour and are also called by the local names *fariñes* and *farinetas*. Grass pea flour is not easy to find outside La Mancha.

SPANISH POLENTA
✳ *fariñes*

Asturias and Galicia were the only regions, along with the Canary Islands and Murcia, where people ate the maize they grew. In the past, they dried it and kept it in elevated stone or wood grain stores, then ground it into a fine meal. The rest of Spain would only feed maize to their animals. However, in the hungry years during the Spanish Civil War and after, many people started making maize bread and eating *fariñes*, a maize-meal porridge that is like polenta. Some Spaniards nostalgically remember the way their grandmothers used to make it, cooking the porridge for an hour or so, stirring it continually. Now we can use instant (pre-cooked) maize meal sold as polenta, which cooks in a few minutes. The standard box of polenta contains 375g of maize meal that makes enough for 4 to 6 portions.

In northern Spain, rural families had milk and butter from their cow and pork products from their pigs. For a treat they served *fariñes* with fried bacon, *chorizo* and *morcilla* (Spanish blood sausage). If you want to use these, slice and fry them in a little oil so that they are ready at the same time and serve them on top of the *fariñes*.

SERVES 4–6

✳ 1.5 litres water ✳ 2 teaspoons salt ✳ 1 x 375g box instant polenta or maize meal ✳ 50g butter

In a very large pan, bring the water to the boil. Add the salt, lower the heat and gradually stir in the contents of the pack of polenta or maize meal with a wooden spoon. Stir vigorously and continuously for 5 to 8 minutes, until the polenta pulls away from the sides of the pan. Then stir in the butter. Serve immediately.

VARIATION

❈ Serve the *fariñes* in soup bowls and pass around very hot milk for everyone to pour some on top and let it seep in.

BEAN AND
CHICKPEA STEWS

ollas

*C*ocido, *olla*, *puchero*, *pote and escudella* are all general terms for stews that rural families would have kept on the simmer in huge pots hanging in the fireplace or sitting on a tripod over burning coals. Based mainly on legumes, with vegetables and tiny bits of ham or sausage thrown in, they represented for the peasantry in every region of Spain the main meal of the day almost every day. On grand festive occasions great quantities were made with a variety of meats and cured pork, including pigs' ears, tails, snouts and trotters. These stews still appear at festivals where cooks compete for excellence awards.

Beans were characterized in traditional lore as 'the meat of the rural poor'. In the Basque Country not very long ago *babazorro*, or 'bean eater', was an insult meaning country bumpkin. In the hunger years during the Spanish Civil War when there was no meat in the cities, people ate beans, chickpeas and lentils. In the post-war days of rationing in the 1940s, pulses were part of the one-dish meal – the *plato único* – that people in the cities ate once a day. They ate it at two thirty in the afternoon at news time, when children came home for lunch and everybody listened to the radio together.

I have never been to a country that has as great a variety of pulses, and as much respect for and pride in them, as Spain. You can see displays in shops and markets of more than twenty types of beans, lentils and chickpeas, sometimes with a card giving their provenance, sometimes down to the name of the village where they were grown. Beans – small and huge, round, flat, white, black, red, pale green and speckled – grow in many different parts of Spain. Apart from black-eyed beans and broad beans, they all came from the New World. By the sixteenth century, farmers were selling them dried at markets. Generally referred to as *alubias* or *judías*, they also have regional names such as *garrafones*, *judiones, fabes, mongetes* and *caparrones*. Every region has its beloved favourites. Some beans, such as the *judiones de la Granja de San Ildefonso*, the *judías de El Barco de Ávila*, the *alubia de La Bañeza-León*, the *faba Asturiana* and the *Galician faba de Lourenzá*, are covered by a Protected Geographical Indication (PGI). The pale green *lenteja de la Armuña* lentils, the brown *lenteja Pardina de Tierra de Campos* lentils and the *garbanzo de Fuentesaúco* chickpeas also have the same protected badge of guaranteed quality that links the pulses with the soil and location.

People wonder why the word *alubia* for bean comes from the Arabic and why *judía*, the other general word for them, literally means 'Jewish', given that beans first arrived in Spain after Muslims and Jews were officially expelled from the country in 1492. One possible explanation is that cooking with black-eyed beans was early on associated with Arabs, who called them *lubia*. The Jews cooked black-eyed beans at their New Year as a symbol of plenty and fertility (in my family we still do) and broad beans at Passover in memory of what they ate when they were slaves in Egypt. The Jewish Sabbath meal-in-a-pot, *adafina* (see page 30), contained chickpeas. The Jews who converted to Catholicism and stayed behind after the mass expulsion substituted the new beans in the parts of Spain where chickpeas were not available. The general formula of the Spanish *cocido*, the boiled stew that exists in every region in different forms, follows the pattern of the *adafina*, including the way the broth was eaten first with vermicelli or rice.

Despite the prestige and traditional importance of pulses in the Spanish diet, consumption and production have dropped dramatically since the 1980s as people have little time to cook and are concerned with putting on weight. Pulses represent hearty traditional fare and rarely feature in modern innovative dishes, except as accompaniments or garnishes served with baby kid, partridges and quails, or in salads. Some of the beans had almost disappeared because they were too expensive to grow. Efforts are now being made to restore them as a crop. And pulses are sold ready-cooked and vacuum-packed. Although they are not eaten very often, these substantial dishes that are affectionately called *platos de cuchara* – 'dishes that you eat with a spoon' – are loved everywhere in Spain with special nostalgic intensity. Whereas once everything – meats, sausages, beans, vegetables – would have been put into the stew pot at the same time, the inspiration of modern chefs now sees the addition of ingredients according to how much cooking they need. Or they are cooked separately so as to get rid of some of the fat from the pork products before reuniting them at the end.

I happened to see on YouTube a video of the *gran pucherada* that took place on 23 October 2007 in San Severino in the Basque Country. The main event of the festival was a competition of bean dishes – *alubiadas*. Dozens of men (I did not see any women) were lined up behind their *pucheros* – tall, cylindrical metal pots, each sat on a tripod with a compartment of glowing embers burning underneath. These pots, still in use in the area of Las Encartaciones in the Basque Country, were famously used by railwaymen who worked on the old coal-fired steam trains and utilized burning coals to cook stews during their long journeys. The background song about beans and *txakoli* – the wine the revellers were drinking – that played as they cooked made me dance in front of my computer.

For us outside Spain, *pucheradas*, *alubiadas* and the like might not bring the same joy to our hearts as they do in Spain but they can provide a great meal in a pot to enjoy with friends in the winter. If we cannot buy the same pulses we can always find an equivalent. In Spain, I was told that beans should be young, a year old at most, and that I should look at their age – the date when they were harvested – because the soaking and cooking times depend on their age as well as on their type. Beans that are less than a year old do not need soaking. Here we do not have the privilege of knowing the harvest date. We only know the sell-by date that is written on the packet, so we have no way of telling exactly how long they will take to cook. You just have to bite into one every so often. I am also told that if the water in your area is hard it will lengthen the cooking time. That is why some people advocate using bottled water. A Spanish trick which is supposed to stop the beans from falling apart is to 'scare' (*asustar*) them by pouring a little cold water on them from time to time during the cooking. I am not sure whether this practice works and Spain is the only country I know that does it. Some people now use pressure cookers to cook their beans, but as beans can so quickly overcook and fall apart they often end up making bean purées.

about soaking beans

❧ Soak the beans in plenty of water for 6 to 10 hours.

❧ A quicker method is to boil the washed beans in plenty of water in a large saucepan for 2 minutes, then remove from the heat, cover the pot, and let the beans soak for 1 hour.

BEANS *with* CURED PORK *and* SAUSAGES
✳ *fabada*

I ate *fabada* at Casa Fermín in Oviedo, Asturias. Luis Alberto Martínez Abascal and Maria Jesús Gil García served a stupendous avant-garde Asturian tasting menu. At the end, when I could hardly eat any more, I asked for a taste of a traditional *fabada*, and it came.

Fabada is the iconic festive dish of Asturias that has become popular all over Spain. The special Asturian large white beans called *fabes* (*faba* in the singular) that are used to make it have a delicious nutty flavour and a buttery texture with a thin skin that melts in the mouth. The best qualities from special farms are referred to as *del cura* ('of the priest'), *del peón* ('of the farm labourer') and *del colmillo* ('of the sharp tooth'). They are expensive and hard to find outside Spain but you can use other large white beans.

We heard more about *fabada* from Jaime Rodriguez, our host at the guest house where we stayed in the mountains (see page 476). The family had kept cows and our rooms were where the cows had slept. They used to make *fabada* with smaller white beans that are easier to grow and cheaper than the *fabes* which grow entwined round maize stalks and need careful nurturing. They ate *fabada* three or four times a week with tiny pieces of home-cured bacon, *chorizo* or *morcilla* (Spanish blood sausage).

The grand version made years ago for weddings has plenty of cured pork meats and sausages, blood sausages, pigs' feet and ears, sometimes also spare ribs or *cecina* (cured beef). The following recipe has the most common combination of ingredients. Pork products in Asturias are all smoked because families cured them in their smoky fireplaces as it was wet outside and damp in their lofts. I prefer them unsmoked. By tradition all the ingredients are cooked together but many people now cook the meats separately, as I do, to eliminate some of the fat.

» » »

＊ 500g *fabes* or white haricot beans, soaked (see page 297)
＊ 1 small onion, peeled ＊ 1 whole head of garlic, unpeeled ＊ 2 bay leaves
＊ salt ＊ a pinch of saffron threads (optional) ＊ 250g *lacón* (fatty dry-cured ham from the shoulder)
＊ 100g pancetta, salt-cured pork belly or bacon, in one piece ＊ 250g semi-cured cooking *chorizos*
＊ 250g *morcillas* (Spanish blood sausages)

Drain the beans and put them in a large pan with enough fresh cold water to cover them by about one fat finger. Bring to the boil, skim off the foam that floats at the top, and put in the onion, garlic and bay leaves. Simmer gently, over a very low heat, with the lid slightly tilted. Shake the pan occasionally so that the beans do not stick to the bottom. The cooking time depends on the type and age of the beans. It can take between 1 and 2 hours, so start trying them as you near 1 hour to see if they are soft, and watch if they begin to break. Add cold water 2 or 3 times to keep the beans covered all the time. You should end up with a soupy stew. When they have begun to soften add some salt. Add saffron, if you like, at this stage too.

As soon as you start cooking the beans, put the *lacón* and pancetta, pork belly or bacon to boil in another pan in plenty of water. Simmer over a low heat for 1 hour, put in the *chorizos* and cook for 15 minutes, then add the *morcillas* and simmer for 10 minutes more. Take them all out, cut the sausages into thick slices and transfer them to the pan with the beans, when the beans are tender. Heat through. Some like to present the two dishes separately.

VARIATION
▓ If you do not have *lacón*, get a larger piece of pancetta, pork belly or bacon.

WHITE BEANS *with* SAUSAGES, PIG'S FOOT *and* EAR
✴ *judiones de la granja de san ildefonso*

On our way to Maracaibo, the best restaurant in Segovia, Ana Lorente, editor of the wine magazine *Opus Vino*, took us to visit the Palacio Real de la Granja de San Ildefonso in the hills near Segovia, north of Madrid, where the most prestigious beans of Spain, the *judiones de la Granja*, are from. The palace is like a little Versailles. It was built by Philip V, grandson of Louis XIV of France, and was the summer residence of the Bourbon kings in the eighteenth century. They came here with their court, cavalry, servants and cooks. In the tourist shops around the palace they sell the large, oval, cream-coloured beans. The name *de la Granja* ('from the farm') is after the farm that was run by the monks of El Parral from whom the king first bought the site. The monks are said to have planted the beans, and the gardeners at the palace continued to grow them to feed the horses. At Maracaibo we were served some of the most fabulous food I have eaten in Spain. Afterwards they sent me their recipe for the dish made with these large, delicious beans with a nutty flavour and buttery texture. The pig's ear and foot give it a rich gelatinous quality. It is worth making for a lot of people.

SERVES 12

Singe off any remaining hairs over a flame and scrub the pig's ear and foot under cold running water, then boil them in water for 20 minutes and drain.

Drain the beans, put them in a very large pan and cover with fresh water. Bring to the boil, remove any scum, and put in the drained pig's ear and foot, the pancetta or fatty bacon, the onion, garlic and bay leaves. Simmer, covered, over a very low heat, adding a little cold water from time to time to keep the beans covered. Add some salt when they have begun to soften. *Judiones de la Granja* need 2½ to 3 hours to become very tender. Other beans would need less time, so if you use other beans boil the pig's ear and pig's foot in water for 1½ hours before adding them to the beans with their water at the start of cooking.

Half an hour before serving, cook the *chorizos* in a pan of boiling water for 20 to 30 minutes, and in another pan boil the *morcillas* for 10 minutes – not longer or they can burst. Take the sausages out, cut them into thick slices and put them in with the beans to heat through. Serve with a drizzle of olive oil.

* 1 pig's ear
  (if you can get one)

* 1 pig's foot (ask the butcher to cut it in half)

* 1kg *judiones de la Granja* or large white beans, soaked (see page 297)

* a 250g slab of pancetta or fatty unsmoked bacon

* 1 large onion, peeled and chopped

* 4 garlic cloves, peeled and chopped

* 2 bay leaves

* salt

* 500g semi-cured cooking *chorizos*

* 500g *morcillas* (Spanish blood sausages)

* extra virgin olive oil, for drizzling

TOLOSA RED BEAN STEW
❖ *alubias rojas a la tolosana*

Like many rural bean dishes, this one is a *potaje* (soup) that is transformed on festive occasions into a grand meal with pork ribs and all kinds of cured pork meats, blood sausages and *chorizos*. But even then the consistency has to be soupy. By tradition the dish is accompanied by boiled cabbage and small, elongated, mild green peppers called *guindillas* pickled in vinegar.

The red beans of Tolosa that grow in symbiosis with maize in the steep vegetable gardens of small farmers in the Basque hills have become legendary. They are celebrated during a *Semana de la Alubia* ('bean week') in Tolosa with cooking competitions and communal meals. The beans are dark purple, almost black, and deliciously creamy with a thin skin. The important thing is to cook them so that they are very tender without their skins splitting.

SERVES 6

Drain the beans and put them in a large pan with the onion, garlic and 3 tablespoons of the olive oil. Cover with fresh cold water, bring to the boil, remove any foam and simmer over a very low heat for 1½ hours, or until they are very tender. Keep adding cold water to cover, and watch that their skins do not split. Add salt when they begin to soften.

In another large pan cook the spare ribs and bacon or lardons in plenty of water over a low heat for 1 hour. Add the *chorizos* and simmer for 20 minutes, then add the *morcillas* and cook very gently, for no more than 10 minutes or they might burst.

Boil the cabbage separately in a third large pan of salted water. It will be tender in 3 to 4 minutes. Take the pieces out, then plunge them again in the same water brought to boiling point just before serving.

Serve the beans in soup bowls – there should be a good amount of liquid. If you want to thicken it, take out a few beans, mash them and stir them in again. Cut the bacon into pieces and the sausages into thick slices and put them on top. Serve the cabbage with a drizzle of the remaining olive oil and accompany with the *guindillas* served in a bowl.

VARIATIONS

❖ *Caparrones*, also known as *alubias pintas*, are the small mottled beans that grow in La Rioja, where they are celebrated as the king of beans. They are so important in Riojan cooking that many homely inns and restaurants call themselves Mesón los Caparrones. Cook them in the same way as the red beans of Tolosa. Or you can substitute borlotti or pinto beans. Some people add a handful of rice 20 minutes before they are ready to serve.

* 500g red beans, soaked (see page 297)
* 1 small onion, peeled
* 2 garlic cloves, peeled
* 6 tablespoons extra virgin olive oil
* salt
* 8 spare ribs
* 250g fatty bacon, in one piece, or lardons
* about 500g semi-cured cooking *chorizos*
* about 500g *morcillas* (Spanish blood sausages)
* 1 smallish green cabbage, cut into 6 chunks through the stem
* a jar of *guindillas* (mild green chillies preserved in vinegar)

BOILED MEATS *and* CHICKPEAS
with VEGETABLES
✳ *cocido madrileño*

Every region has its own version of *cocido*. It is the most basic and complex one-dish meal of Spain, served as two or three courses – the broth (or *caldo*) is served first with added vermicelli or rice. Sometimes likened to the French *pot-au-feu* and the Italian *bollito misto*, Spanish *cocido* is heavy with its own history and emotional associations. It is said to have evolved from the Jewish Sabbath dish *adafina* (see page 30), and that pork was added to the dish in the early period of the Inquisition. In some *cocidos* a large meatball, called the *bola* or *pelota*, is added to the broth – such as in the much-loved Catalan *escudella i carn d'olla*, said to be the soul of Catalan cooking, and in the Murcian *cocidos*. The *cocido* from Madrid, made with the local chickpeas, is the most famous. If you search for '*cocidito madrileño*' on the internet you can see comedy acts about it and you can hear a popular song from the 1950s that translates into something like this: 'Don't talk to me about Roman banquets, about the menu at the Plaza in New York, or about pheasant, foie gras or lobster . . . my sustenance and my pleasure are the touch that a loving woman gives to the *cocidito madrileño*.'

When the Congressional Club in Washington published their first international cookbook in the early twentieth century, they included a recipe for *cocido* signed by the Spanish king, Alfonso XIII. The recipe was from the head chef of the queen's kitchen, Candido Collar. In restaurants in Madrid, *cocido* is on the menu on Wednesdays. At home a simple version can be cooked any day of the week (*paella* or cannelloni is eaten on Sundays). A grandiose version is often prepared for festive occasions.

Cocido is very complex – it is an 'event' – but it is not difficult to make, simply a matter of many things boiling at the same time in several large pans. Leftovers from a *cocido* are eaten over several days – typical dishes made with them include croquettes (page 140) and a hash called *ropa vieja* (literally meaning 'old clothes').

» » »

SERVES 6

※ 500g beef from the knuckle or shin ※ 2 pieces of marrow bone – beef, veal or ham
※ a 200g whole piece of fatty bacon or fresh belly of pork ※ 4 chicken thighs
※ 350g dried chickpeas, soaked overnight ※ 1 medium onion, peeled and studded with 3 cloves
※ salt and pepper ※ 3 carrots, peeled ※ 8 small new potatoes, peeled ※ 2 celery stalks
※ 250g green or Savoy cabbage, cut in quarters through the core ※ 250g wide runner beans (optional)
※ 3 turnips, peeled and halved (optional) ※ 200g semi-cured cooking *chorizos*
※ 200g *morcillas* (Spanish blood sausages), preferably the type made with onions
※ 100–150g vermicelli, broken into small pieces ※ 4 tablespoons olive oil
※ 2 garlic cloves, peeled

Optional to serve with ※ a small baguette, cut into slices and toasted
※ extra virgin olive oil ※ a choice of pickles, such as gherkins, onions and *guindillas*
(mild green chillies pickled in vinegar) ※ tomato sauce (page 151)

Put the beef, marrow bones, bacon or belly of pork and chicken thighs into a very large saucepan or stockpot. Add enough water to cover everything by about 4cm. Bring to the boil and simmer for a few minutes before removing the scum that forms on the surface. Add the drained chickpeas and the onion studded with cloves, and cook over a very low heat for 2 to 3 hours until the meats are very tender. Add salt – you will need a good amount – after an hour or so. Occasionally skim off any scum that comes to the surface and keep adding water to ensure the meats are well covered. You want plenty of broth to serve as soup at the end.

Half an hour before you are ready to serve, boil the vegetables – the carrots, potatoes, celery stalks and cabbage, plus the runner beans and turnips (if using) – in salted water in another large pan for about 20 minutes. Drain, pouring the cooking water over the meat to add to the broth.

At the same time, boil the *chorizos* in water for 10 minutes in a third pan, then add the *morcillas* and simmer very gently for another 10 minutes (be careful as the *morcillas* will fall apart if you cook them for too long).

To serve the soup as a starter, strain at least 2 litres of the broth into another pan, reserving the rest to keep the meats moist. Skim off the fat, bring to the boil, add the broken vermicelli, season to taste with salt and pepper, and cook for 5 minutes until the noodles are soft.

Reheat the chickpeas, meats and sausages in the broth left in the first pan, and arrange them in a deep platter. Cut the meats into pieces and the sausages into thick slices. Serve the drained vegetables on another platter. Reheat the cabbage separately by frying it in the oil over a medium heat with the whole garlic cloves for flavour. You can serve the vegetables as a course on their own before the meats and chickpeas or lay everything out on the table and let people help themselves.

Serve the marrow from the bones on toasted slices of baguette. Put a bottle of extra virgin olive oil and plates of pickles on the table for everyone to help themselves. If you like, serve with a fresh tomato sauce.

FISH AND SEAFOOD

pescados y mariscos

Spaniards adore fish and seafood. Despite the depletion of their stock through overfishing, there is still a huge variety caught in the waters of both the Atlantic and the Mediterranean. Hake, monkfish, tuna and bream are favourites. Turbot, skate, sole, red mullet, sardines and anchovies are popular too. The list of splendid molluscs and crustaceans caught off the coasts sounds, in Spanish, like a magic incantation – *sepia, pulpo, percebes, vieiras, zamburiñas, almejas, berberechos, mejillones, bueyes, centollos, changurros, nécoras, quisquillas, camarones, gambas, carabineros, cigalas, langostinos, langostas, bogavantes, santiaguiños, navajas, lapas, bígaros*. Prawns and clams are much used. Sometimes they seem to be thrown in as an adornment.

Fish and seafood dishes, including soups, stews, omelettes and rice dishes, are invariably said to have originated in what fishermen once cooked for themselves on boats, or what their wives prepared for them at home. And older fishermen claim that until the 1960s, when mass tourism arrived, they fished for their own consumption, since they could hardly sell their catch. Even including lobsters, seafood was considered a poor food because the elites and aristocracy had only ever valued meat in the past. Because of the high mountains and lack of transport in the Spanish hinterland, before roads were built in the 1960s, fresh seawater fish was hardly ever consumed inland. The only fish available in the interior was from the rivers – trout, salmon and eels – or preserved salt cod (*bacalao*). As meat was strictly forbidden by the Church on days of abstinence, which amounted to a good part of the year, salt cod became the substitute for meat.

To understand just how important and appreciated the products of the sea have become in Spain, you only need to visit a food market in any big town and see the queues of people at the fish stalls. They watch the fishmonger in anticipation as he or she (the women who sell fish are dressed in elegant white blouses, coiffed and bejewelled) cleans, fillets and prepares the fish and seafood with art and tenderness. After Japan, Spain is the country that consumes more fish and seafood per head of population in the world.

Many of those old dishes that fishermen cooked in the past must have acquired glamour and sophistication somehow. Did they really use all that wine and brandy as people do today? Would they have made those fantastic sauces you will find in the recipes in this chapter? But they certainly would have lavished time and love on what was their main staple. Rural folk were once very suspicious of strange-looking creatures from the sea, but today it is the crustaceans and molluscs thrown together pell-mell in a soup or *paella* that lure tourists into quayside and coastal restaurants. Josep Pla, the greatest writer in the Catalan language, complained in the 1960s about the new spectacular dishes that were, he said, a 'diabolical combination of fish of all categories ... a disorder against nature ... not the integrated symphony that it should be'. In the past fishermen threw anything they did not sell from their catch into their soups and stews, but what Pla was complaining about was the kind of dishes that seaside restaurants were inventing to attract custom.

Those spectacular dishes that are a feast for the eyes may also be difficult and messy to eat. When you come to cook them you can choose versions referred to in restaurant menus as '*del señor*' or '*del señorito*' that do not entail using your fingers to crack open shells and pull out morsels. You will find these in the chapter on rice.

GRILLED FISH *and* SEAFOOD
parrillada de pescados y mariscos

The favourite way of cooking fish and seafood on every Spanish coast is *a la parrilla* (on the grill over embers) or *a la plancha* (on a large flat griddle). Cook one type of fish or seafood alone, or have a selection for a great *parrillada* (mixed grill). Serve it simply sprinkled with salt, extra virgin olive oil, lemon juice and chopped parsley, or accompany with one or more of the following dressings and sauces: *salmorreta* (page 147), *vinagreta* (page 146), *alioli* (page 149), *mayonesa* (page 148), *salsa romesco* (page 152), *mojo de perejil* (page 146), *mojo verde de cilantro* (page 241) or *mojo picón* (page 241). Grilling is not a very precise way of cooking; experience helps, but you have to use your intuition. Here are some guidelines.

FISH STEAKS

Use monkfish, tuna, swordfish, hake, turbot, cod, halibut or haddock. Brush with olive oil and sprinkle with salt. Place on a well-oiled grill about 5cm from the glowing embers, or on a medium-hot well-oiled flat griddle. Cook for 2 to 4 minutes on each side, depending on the thickness of the steak. The fish is cooked when the flesh begins to flake away from the bone when you cut it with the point of a knife.

NOTE: The best way to cook tuna is to marinate it in olive oil for 30 minutes, then sear it on the outside at a high heat (close to the fire), leaving it underdone on the inside.

FISH FILLETS *or* WHOLE LARGE FISH SPLIT OPEN *along the* BACKBONE

Keep the skin on. Use sea bass, bream, hake or turbot. Brush with extra virgin olive oil and season with salt. Cook on the skin side only, not too close to the fire if on the barbecue, or on a medium-hot well-oiled griddle. Do not turn over. The fish will cook through.

WHOLE FISH

Have them scaled and cleaned but keep the heads on. You can use small or medium-sized bream, red mullet, sardines or flat fish such as sole. Brush with extra virgin oil and season with salt. Cook for 2 to 5 minutes or longer on each side, depending on the size. Cut into the fish with the point of a knife to see if they are done.

MUSSELS *and* CLAMS *in their* SHELLS

Clean and test to make sure they are alive (see page 118). Put them on the hot griddle or on a flat baking tray over the fire. They will open within moments and be done. Throw away any that remain closed.

KING PRAWNS *in their* SHELLS

Sprinkle coarse sea salt on a moderately hot griddle and lay the prawns on top. Turn them over quickly when the cooked side turns pink, in about 3 to 5 minutes, and serve as soon as they are pink on both sides.

LOBSTER

One way of killing a lobster is to place the lobster in the freezer for an hour to put it to sleep, then lay it on its back on a chopping board and chop its head off and cut it in half lengthwise with a large serrated knife. Lay the lobster halves, shell side down, on a medium-hot grill, cover with foil and cook for around 15 minutes. When the flesh is white and opaque in the thickest part the lobster is ready. Provide nut crackers and lobster picks to remove morsels from the jointed claw sections. The green stuff, the tomalley, is the lobster's liver and is considered a delicacy, but some people prefer not to eat it because any contaminants, such as mercury, are concentrated there. The red bits are the roe in a female. They, too, are considered a delicacy.

SMALL SQUID

To clean and prepare squid see page 118. Cut the bodies open to make flat pieces. Using a sharp, pointed knife, score the inner sides with parallel lines 1.25cm apart, without cutting right through, and criss-cross with more parallel lines. Turn them in olive oil and place them, scored side down, on a very hot grill or griddle, together with the oiled tentacles. Cook for 1 to 2 minutes, then turn the pieces over. They will curl up immediately and will be done. Alternatively, cut the bodies into slices and put on an oiled griddle, then throw on some finely chopped garlic and finely chopped fresh chilli.

FRIED FISH *and* SEAFOOD
pescados y mariscos fritos

Andalusians are the world's best at frying fish and seafood. In Cadiz, *freidurías* (bars or kiosks selling fried fish) are open throughout the day for people to eat on the spot, or to take their cooked fish home.

Fry one type of fish or seafood, or a medley of small fish that may include red mullet, sole, anchovies, whitebait, baby hake, baby squid and king prawns. Large fish can be cut into steaks or fillets or into chunks. If you have squid, clean and prepare them as described on page 118 and cut them into rings. Peel the raw (grey) prawns – leave their tails on if you like.

Serve with lemon wedges and one or more of the following sauces: *alioli* (page 149), *mayonesa* (page 148), *salsa romesco* (page 152), *mojo verde de cilantro* (page 241), *mojo de perejil* (page 146), *salmorreta* (page 147) or *vinagreta* (page146).

Deep-frying fish and seafood is an art, but here are some rules to help you achieve success:

- Use olive oil for deep-frying – refined olive oil called simply 'olive oil', not extra virgin olive oil. There must be enough to generously cover the fish.
- When you are ready to fry, heat the oil until it is hot but not smoking. The temperature should remain constant so adjust the heat as necessary.
- Use a large, tall pan so that there is no risk of the oil bubbling over.
- Fry fish of about the same size together since their cooking times will be the same as it depends on their thickness.
- Season the fish with salt inside and out and cover entirely, but lightly, with flour. Shake off any excess flour.
- The smallest fish must be fried very quickly at a high temperature so that they are crisp and brown but still moist inside.
- Larger fish take longer and need a lower temperature so that they have time to cook inside before the skin gets burnt.
- Fish steaks or fillets are best first dipped in seasoned flour, then in lightly beaten egg, for extra protection, or they can be dipped in batter.
- When fish fillets are battered they are called *buñuelos* (fritters). The art is to have a batter that fries crisp and dry and is not at all greasy.
- When frying, turn each fish only once, lift it out and drain on kitchen paper.
- Prawns, squid and fat mussels are usually dipped in a batter before frying (see page 315). This is called *en gabardina*, literally 'in a raincoat'.

PRAWNS *with* GARLIC ❖ *gambas al ajillo*

This is a popular *tapa* served in bars all over Spain. It is very garlicky and a little hot with some chilli. The amount of garlic and chilli is up to you. Prawns have the flavour of the sea and there is no need for extra salt. If you cannot get fresh raw prawns, you can use frozen raw ones, defrosted. Serve the dish sizzling hot, with a warmed baguette cut into slices to soak up the garlicky oil.

SERVES 4 AS AN APPETIZER

❋ 4–5 tablespoons olive oil ❋ 500g medium or large raw peeled prawns
❋ 1 teaspoon red pepper flakes or ½ a fresh red chilli, deseeded and finely chopped
❋ 4 garlic cloves, peeled and finely chopped ❋ 2 tablespoons chopped flat-leaf parsley

Heat the oil in a large frying pan and put in the prawns and the pepper flakes or chopped chilli. After a few seconds, turn the prawns over quickly, as soon as one side becomes pink, then stir in the garlic. Stir over a medium heat for a minute or so, until the prawns are pink all over and the garlic has just begun to take colour. Serve immediately, sprinkled with the parsley, in a heated *cazuela* (small casserole dish) or bowl.

BATTER *for* DEEP-FRYING

Here is a batter for coating either 250g raw peeled prawns, to make *gambas en gabardina*, or 250g squid rings, to make *calamares en gabardina*. You can also use it for coating fish fillets to make *buñuelos de pescado* (fish fritters). For deep-frying see page 312.

SERVES 4 AS A APPETIZER

❋ 75g plain flour ❋ a pinch of salt ❋ 125ml cold water

Make the batter quickly, just as you are about to fry, when the oil is being heated. Put the flour in a bowl and sprinkle in a little salt. With a fork, beat in the cold water – the water should be as cold as possible. Do not over beat or the batter will be chewy. It can be slightly lumpy.

Mix the prawns, squid or fish in the batter so that they are well covered all over.

Working in batches, drop the pieces one by one into the hot oil. To test that the temperature is right, first drop in a little batter – if it floats back to the surface quickly the oil is ready, if it touches the bottom the oil is not hot enough, if it turns brown it is too hot. The oil should never be allowed to smoke.

WHITE HARICOT BEANS *with* CLAMS
✤ *alubias con almejas*

On the Cantabrian coast, in the north of Spain, clams are large and meaty. You can make this dish with good-quality white haricot beans from a jar or tin. They acquire a delicate flavour from the wine and a taste of the sea from the brine in the clams.

SERVES 2

Wash the clams and throw away any that are not closed, then soak them in cold salted water for 1 hour so that they release any sand they have inside.

Heat the oil in a wide casserole or pan with a tight-fitting lid. Put in the onion and stir over a low heat until it becomes very soft and is beginning to colour, then add the garlic and stir for another minute or so.

Add the beans, the wine and a little salt, mix gently and cook for 2 to 3 minutes. Place the clams on top, put the lid on, and cook over a medium-high heat for 3 to 5 minutes until the clams open. Throw away any that do not open and serve sprinkled with the parsley.

VARIATIONS

※ Fry ½ a small chopped chilli pepper in with the onions.

※ Some people add a little *pimentón dulce* or sweet paprika.

- ※ 650g clams
- ※ salt
- ※ 3 tablespoons olive oil
- ※ 1 large onion, peeled and chopped
- ※ 3–4 garlic cloves, peeled and finely chopped
- ※ 1 x 500g jar or tin small white haricot beans, drained
- ※ 125ml fruity white wine or cava
- ※ 2 tablespoons chopped flat-leaf parsley

BABY SQUID *in their* INK *with* PLAIN RICE
❉ *chipirones en su tinta con arroz blanco*

When cuttlefish or squid sense predators they squirt out an ink stored in sacs in their bodies to fend off attack. However, there is hardly enough ink to cook with inside the fresh squid you can buy. Many fishmongers and some supermarkets now sell frozen packs of baby squid less than 9cm long, ready to cook, and some also sell little sachets of concentrated squid ink. We can even buy good enough ready-made fish stock in supermarkets so this dish is an easy one to make. Frozen squid is now generally sold cleaned and packed with the tentacles inside the bodies. Defrost and drain the squid, take the tentacles out of the bodies, and cut the bodies into rings about 1cm wide. If you are using fresh squid, see how to clean it on page 118. Serve with fried or toasted bread, or with plain white long-grain rice, basmati rice or vermicelli noodles, and with *alioli* (page 149) or garlic mayonnaise.

SERVES 4

Sauté the onion in 2 tablespoons of the oil in a saucepan over a low heat, keeping the pan covered. Stir occasionally and cook for about 20 minutes, until the onion is soft and golden. Add the garlic and cook for a few moments only, stirring until the aroma rises and it just begins to colour, then add the tomato. Cook for 5 to 8 minutes, stirring often, then add the wine and the fish stock, the sugar and some salt and pepper. Simmer over a low heat for 10 minutes, then add the squid ink. Some people blend the sauce with a hand or other blender, but I like it as it is.

Fry the squid rings and tentacles in a large frying pan in the remaining oil over a high heat for 1 to 2 minutes, stirring and turning the pieces over. Drop them into the ink sauce with their juices and cook for 5 minutes, or until tender.

Serve hot over the plain rice, sprinkled, if you like, with parsley.

For the ARROZ BLANCO (PLAIN WHITE RICE) *to serve with*
Bring a large pan of salted water to the boil. Throw in 300g long-grain or basmati rice and boil for 12 to 18 minutes until tender. The time depends on the type and quality of the rice. Drain quickly in a strainer, return to the pan and stir in 50g butter, cut into pieces so that it melts in more evenly. Add salt if necessary.

* 1 large onion, peeled and chopped
* 4–5 tablespoons olive oil
* 2 garlic cloves, peeled and crushed
* 1 large or 2 medium tomatoes (about 200g), peeled and chopped
* 250ml dry white wine
* 350ml fish stock (page 144)
* ½ teaspoon sugar
* salt and pepper
* 1 or 2 4g sachets of squid ink
* 750g baby squid, frozen and defrosted or fresh prepared (see page 118)
* 2 tablespoons chopped flat-leaf parsley (optional)

BOILED OCTOPUS *with* POTATOES
❊ *pulpo a la feria*

This is the way octopus is cooked and served at fairs and festivals in Galicia. It is *polbo á feira* in Galician and *feira* means 'fair'. It has also become a popular *tapa* throughout the rest of Spain, where it is known as *pulpo a la gallega*. Octopus needs to be tenderized before it can be cooked. This used to be done by bashing it against a wall or the ground. In Spain, it is also the custom to plunge the octopus into boiling water for 10 seconds and lift it out three times before cooking. Nowadays it is tenderized perfectly by freezing. In Britain, octopus is commonly sold frozen – already cleaned and tenderized.

If the octopus has not come already cleaned, cut halfway through the muscle that attaches the tentacles to the inside of the head and discard all the contents of the head cavity. This involves pulling or cutting out the ink bag, the hard oval 'beak' and the gelatinous innards. Cut out the mouth, eyes and any cartilage around them with a sharp knife. Turn the head inside out and wash it well under cold running water. Remove any scales that may be left on the suckers and wash the octopus body well under running water.

SERVES 6

❋ coarse sea salt, to taste ❋ 1.25kg frozen octopus, defrosted ❋ 500g waxy potatoes
❋ up to 6 tablespoons extra virgin olive oil, for drizzling ❋ 1 tablespoon *pimentón dulce* or
sweet paprika, or a little *pimentón picante* or cayenne pepper, or a mix of the two

Bring plenty of lightly salted water to the boil in a large pan. Throw in the octopus and simmer, covered, for 30 to 45 minutes or until tender. To know if it is tender, cut a piece of tentacle with kitchen scissors and try it. It should not be rubbery.

Peel and boil the potatoes until tender. Cut them into slices about 1cm thick and arrange them in a wide, shallow baking dish. Drizzle with oil and turn to cover them all over. Heat through in an oven preheated to 160°C/gas 3 for about 10 minutes before serving.

Lift the octopus out of the water. If you are not serving the dish right away, keep the water in the pan and put it on the boil again before serving so that you can throw in the octopus to heat through. Cut off the head with the scissors and throw it away – it is not as good as the tentacles. Cut the tentacles into bite-sized pieces with the scissors and spread on top of the potatoes in the baking dish. Sprinkle generously with olive oil and some coarse salt and dust with sweet or hot *pimentón*, or paprika or cayenne pepper, or a mixture of the two. A traditional way of serving is on a round wooden platter.

BAKED CRAB *with* CIDER
❋ *centollo a la sidra*

In Asturias, this is the filling used for their famous spider crab called *txangurro*. It is spectacular to bake it in the crab shell as they do, but easier, although less dramatic, to enjoy it in a ramekin. Use cooked crab meat. Cider is the drink of Asturias – *sidrerías* (cider houses and bars) can be found everywhere in the region. Asturian cider is hard and dry. I used a vintage cider that was only slightly sweet and it went beautifully with the fish and crab meat.

SERVES 4 AS A STARTER

❋ 1 medium onion, peeled and chopped ❋ 2 tablespoons olive oil, plus extra to oil the ramekins ❋ 1 small tomato, peeled and chopped ❋ salt ❋ a pinch of cayenne pepper or chilli powder ❋ 250g hake or cod, or other white fish fillet, without skin or bones ❋ 250g cooked white and dark crab meat ❋ 175ml dry cider ❋ 2 tablespoons chopped flat-leaf parsley ❋ 2 tablespoons breadcrumbs (see page 120) ❋ 15g butter, cut into small pieces

In a large frying pan, sauté the onion in the oil over a low heat, stirring occasionally, until soft. Add the tomato, salt and cayenne or chilli powder, and cook over a medium heat for about 8 minutes.

Put in the fish fillet and cook for 5 minutes or until it begins to flake, turning it over once. Then flake the fish, and add the crab meat, cider and parsley to the pan. Mix gently and cook for 1 minute more. Oil 4 ramekins and spoon in the crab mixture. Sprinkle the tops with the breadcrumbs and dot with butter, then put the ramekins under the grill until lightly brown.

If you prepare the ramekins in advance you will have to reheat them in an oven preheated to 200°C/gas 6 for 6 to 8 minutes before putting them under the grill.

RAW MARINATED TUNA *with* TOMATOES
❋ *atún marinado*

Off the coast of Cadiz, in Andalusia, tuna are caught when they migrate from the Atlantic to the Mediterranean to spawn in the warmer water in the spring and early summer. They are caught by a technique called *almadraba*, introduced to Spain by the Phoenicians and practised by the Arabs, in which the fish are led through a maze of nets into a central area. When the last net is raised the larger adult fish are impaled on hooks by fishermen who jump into the water. The fish are hauled on to boats where flaked ice is shovelled over them while they are still flapping. Due to overfishing, the practice has now been drastically reduced, but tuna remains a favourite fish of this coast. You need the freshest, best-quality tuna for this dish, which makes a most delicious first course.

SERVES 8 AS A STARTER

❋ 2 thick slices of tuna steak (about 500g)
❋ juice of 1 lemon ❋ 9 tablespoons extra virgin olive oil
❋ salt and pepper ❋ 500g tomatoes ❋ 6 spring onions ❋ 1 tablespoon red or white
wine vinegar ❋ ½ teaspoon sugar (optional) ❋ 1–2 tablespoons chopped flat-leaf parsley

Cut the raw tuna slices into small bite-sized cubes.

In a glass or plastic bowl mix the lemon juice, 6 tablespoons of the olive oil and a little salt and pepper, and turn the tuna pieces in this marinade to coat well. Cover with cling film and leave in the refrigerator for about 6 hours, turning the pieces over in the marinade again at least once in that time.

Just before serving, dice the tomatoes, and trim and thinly slice the spring onions. Mix together and dress with the remaining 3 tablespoons of olive oil, the wine vinegar and a little salt. Add the sugar, if the tomatoes are not sweet enough. Serve on a shallow platter mixed with the marinated tuna. Sprinkle with parsley.

PAN-GRILLED FISH *with* GARLIC *and* CHILLI DRESSING
❖ *pescado a la bilbaína*

This method of cooking fish keeps the flesh moist and juicy. It is also called *a la Donostiarra*. You can also cook it on the barbecue. Use hake, bream, cod, monkfish or any firm-fleshed white fish. You need thick fillets with the skin left on, and the oil must be a good extra virgin. The dressing is simple and tasty. Serve with boiled potatoes.

SERVES 2

Season the fish with salt. Grease a heavy frying pan or flat griddle with 1 tablespoon of the oil and heat to just below smoking point. Place the fillets skin side down in the pan or griddle, and cook over a medium heat for 2 to 4 minutes on each side, depending on the thickness of the fillet. Do not overcook – the flesh should just begin to flake when you cut it.

For the dressing, very gently heat the remaining 3 tablespoons of oil with the garlic and chilli in a small pan until the garlic is only just lightly golden and crunchy (do not let it brown). Take off the heat and add the vinegar to taste and the parsley.

Serve the fish very hot, with the dressing poured over.

VARIATION

❋ Have the fishmonger cut open 2 small breams like a book and remove the backbone. Cook them as above, skin side down only, and pour the sauce over them as you serve.

* 2 x 175–200g thick fish fillets, skin left on
* salt
* 4 tablespoons extra virgin olive oil
* 5 large garlic cloves, peeled and sliced
* ½–1 small dried or fresh red chilli, deseeded and finely chopped
* 2–3 teaspoons white wine vinegar
* 1 tablespoon chopped flat-leaf parsley

WHOLE BREAM BAKED *in* COARSE SALT
✤ *dorada a la sal*

Bream cooked encased in a sea-salt crust is deliciously moist and flavourful. You can cook sea bass and grey mullet in the same way. It is a traditional fishermen's cooking method in areas where there are salt pans. They bury the fish in damp salt crystals inside wooden boxes and take them to be cooked in the local bread oven. I had trouble producing a firm crust that comes away cleanly taking the skin with it, as many recipes tell you it should do. José María Conde de Ybarra (see page 414) told me that the salt must be wet enough to stick together and that you need thick layers three fingers deep on top of and below the fish. I found it easier, and without using too much salt, to make a crust that comes away relatively cleanly by mixing the salt with egg white. If the skin does not come off with the crust it does not matter. The scales will come off.

Ask the fishmonger to gut the fish through a small incision, so that the salt does not get inside, and to keep the scales on – this is very important. You must use coarse sea salt that draws out moisture from the fish, not fine salt, which would be absorbed by the fish. The dish is served with new boiled potatoes and *alioli* or garlic mayonnaise.

SERVES 2

Line a baking dish large enough to hold the fish with a sheet of foil. In a bowl, mix the salt thoroughly with just enough egg white so that it feels like wet sand. Using about a third of this mixture, make a bed for each fish on the foil, and place the fish on it. Then cover the fish entirely with a thick layer of the rest of the salt mixture, moulding it firmly around the fish with your hands so that it is completely covered, and making sure that the opening in the belly is closed so that the salt does not get in. You can leave the tails uncovered.

Bake in an oven preheated to 200°C/gas 6 for 25 minutes. The top layer of salt will form a hard crust. To serve, crack open the crust along the centre with a heavy knife and carefully remove it. The skin may come off with the salt crust but, if it does not, brush off any remaining salt, then peel away the skin. Gently lift off the top fillets and transfer them to your plates. Then pull out the backbone and lift off the remaining fillets.

Serve with a drizzle of olive oil, accompanied by lemon wedges and the *alioli* or garlic mayonnaise.

- ✻ 2kg coarse sea salt
- ✻ 3 large egg whites
- ✻ 2 x 400–500g whole bream, gutted but not scaled

To serve with

- ✻ extra virgin olive oil, for drizzling
- ✻ 2 lemon wedges
- ✻ 150g *alioli* (page 149) or garlic mayonnaise

gaspar rey i grifé

Gaspar Rey I Grifé died just as this book was going to press so, very sadly, I had to change my text at the last minute and speak of my good friend and mentor in the past tense.

Gaspar was the founder, editor and main writer of *Cocina Futuro*, a Spanish magazine for and about chefs, caterers and restaurateurs. He travelled around the country wherever something of interest was happening and kept up with the latest trends in what chefs were doing all over Spain. Gaspar was a cultured and worldly Catalan who left Spain in the 1960s because he found it oppressive under Franco. The Madrid he left was like a small provincial city. The oil was rancid, the wine rough and acid, and the people did not care. Chefs were never seen out of the kitchen. After he came back to live in Madrid in 1994 he got a lot of joy from witnessing, and from being in a position to encourage, the transformation of Spanish products and gastronomy.

A friend gave me Gaspar's telephone number when I decided suddenly to go to Asturias, and I called him. Long before we had met he gave me contacts in many regions and phoned people to ask them to help me. He was a unique guide to what was going on in the kitchens of Spain. He took me to some of the best restaurants in Madrid and Toledo and gave me his insider's views on wine; on small farms that are recovering old products like black tomatoes; on new products like foie gras and seaweed; on food fashions; and on the techniques of *nueva cocina* chefs – all enthralling. We also discussed methods of cooking fish.

pepe iglesias

I recognized Pepe Iglesias at Oviedo airport from the cartoons on his website that show a round figure with a wide smile emerging from a casserole with a pen and notebook, and the same figure, formed of vapours from a bottle of wine like the djinn that appears out of Aladdin's magic lamp. Pepe's full name is José Juan Iglesias del Castillo y Díaz de la Serna. I was with Jane Kramer, who was writing about me for the *New Yorker* magazine. We had decided only days before to go to Asturias and a couple of telephone calls to friends led me to Pepe, the 'ambassador' of Asturian gastronomy. He took time off to drive us over the rugged mountains, along the fast-flowing rivers and through the woodlands of the fantastically beautiful Picos de Europa. We stopped at a little shepherds' village where we saw sheep and goats and tasted Cabrales, a

strong, cave-ripened blue cheese, and drank the local natural cider. We visited the sanctuary of Covadonga in Cangas de Onís, where, according to legend, the Virgin Mary appeared to the chief Pelayo in the eighth century and helped him to fight off the Muslim armies, thus assuring Asturias of its independence. Pepe talked to us in French about food and life and gave us a running commentary about the Roman, Gothic, Baroque and pre-Romanesque architecture of the region. We ate in his favourite restaurants. There are great chefs in this part of Spain doing their own exquisite takes on Spanish regional cuisines.

Pepe was born and raised in Madrid 'among the pots and pans' of his parents' restaurant, El Horno de Santa Teresa. When they died in a tragic accident in 1976, he abandoned his veterinary studies to take over the running of the restaurant. In 1990, he retired for a more peaceful life to the beach of Salinas near Aviles in Asturias, where he shares a house with his doctor wife, María. He is a restaurant critic and food and wine writer. People are always sending me recipes they have cut out from Spanish magazines and newspapers that turn out to be his. He has written twenty books, including one on Masonic cookery about the history, rituals and table traditions of the Freemasons, and *Comer con vino* ('Eating with Wine') about matching food to wine. But he is most famous for his virtual *Enciclopedia de Gastronomía* where he gives recipes and publishes articles and chats about food and wine. His website is http://www.enciclopediadegastronomia.es. When I ask him for a recipe he sends me half a dozen. The following is one of his.

WHOLE ROASTED BREAM *with* POTATOES
✳ *besugo al horno con patatas*

This is the great festive and Christmas Eve dish of Madrid that is now popular in other parts of Spain. I ate it in Asturias when I was with the American journalist Jane Kramer and the food writer Pepe Iglesias in a restaurant called La Arcea (another name for the *becada* or woodcock) overlooking the sea in Andrín near Llanes. The fish was sensational. They cooked it in the wonderful Galician Albariño wine, but you can use other fruity dry whites. And you can substitute sea bass for bream.

SERVES 4

Rinse the fish and season inside and out with salt.

Sauté the onion in 1 tablespoon of the oil over a medium heat until soft and golden, then put in a baking dish large enough to hold the fish lined with foil. Boil the potatoes in salted water for 10 minutes, drain and cut them into thick slices. Add them to the onions, drizzle over 3 tablespoons of the oil, add the pinch of saffron and a little salt and mix gently. Then pour in the wine.

Rub the top of the fish with 1 tablespoon of the oil and place it in the baking dish with the potatoes around it. Slash it in two places at the thickest end. Cut 1 thin slice of lemon in half and insert a half in each cut. Put 1 lemon slice inside the fish and the rest on top of the potatoes.

Mix the remaining 1 tablespoon of olive oil with the garlic, breadcrumbs and 1 tablespoon of the parsley, and sprinkle this mixture over the fish. Put the fish in an oven preheated to 250°C/gas 9 to roast for 30 to 35 minutes, or until the fish is cooked (test using the point of a knife in the thickest part – the flesh should be opaque right through to the bone) and the potatoes are tender. Serve sprinkled with the remaining parsley.

※ a large sea bream or sea bass (weighing about 2kg), gutted and scaled

※ salt

※ 1 onion, peeled, halved and sliced

※ 6 tablespoons extra virgin olive oil

※ 8–12 waxy potatoes, peeled

※ a good pinch of saffron threads

※ 250ml Albariño or other fruity dry white wine such as Riesling

※ 1 lemon, thinly sliced

※ 2 garlic cloves, peeled and crushed

※ 2 tablespoons fine breadcrumbs

※ 2 tablespoons chopped flat-leaf parsley

HAKE *in* GREEN SAUCE *with* ASPARAGUS
❊ *merluza en salsa verde con espárragos*

Fishermen in the north of Spain around the Bay of Biscay caught hake when they went whaling in the northern seas and the Basque chefs gave this long slender fish with a delicate flesh a prestigious place in Spanish gastronomy. This is a favourite Basque recipe for cooking hake, but you can use other fish such as monkfish or cod in the same way. Parsley is the Basque herb par excellence. They use it at least four times as much as in any other part of Spain. The sauce in this dish, made with olive oil, garlic and parsley, acquires an unctuous texture from the fish itself. The skin plays a part too, so do not remove it. This version, with asparagus, is also called *a la koskera*. The asparagus cooking water is part of the sauce.

SERVES 2

❊ 1 bunch asparagus (about 200g), hard ends removed ❊ salt
❊ 3 garlic cloves, peeled and finely chopped ❊ 4 tablespoons mild extra virgin olive oil
❊ 1½ teaspoons plain flour ❊ 2 tablespoons very finely chopped flat-leaf parsley
❊ 2 x 200g hake steaks, on the bone

Boil the asparagus for about 4 or 5 minutes in enough salted water to cover them until they are tender. Drain, and keep the cooking water.

In a large frying pan stir the garlic with the oil over a gentle heat for a few seconds only until the aroma rises. Do not let it brown. Add the flour and stir for a minute or so. Add the parsley, then gradually add 250ml of the reserved cooking water from the asparagus, a little at a time, stirring vigorously. Add a pinch of salt and simmer uncovered over a medium heat for about 8 minutes until the sauce thickens a little.

Put in the fish steaks. Now shake the pan in a rotating manner without removing it from the heat, so as to swirl the fish steaks very gently around (or you can cheat by moving the steaks around using a wooden spoon). This allows the white liquid they release to mix with the sauce, giving it a slightly gelatinous texture.

Turn the fish steaks over after 5 minutes, arrange the asparagus around them, and cook over a low heat for 3 to 5 minutes until the fish only just begins to flake away from the bone when you cut into it with a pointed knife.

VARIATIONS

❃ Use peas instead of asparagus.

❃ Make it without asparagus and use 250ml of fish stock instead of the asparagus cooking water. Add 8 to 10 clams (see page 118 for how to prepare them) when you have turned over the fish steaks, and cook with the lid on to steam them open.

HAKE *cooked in* CIDER
�֎ *merluza a la sidra*

Cider in Asturias replaces wine as the local drink and is used in many dishes, including fish dishes.

SERVES 4

✳ 1 large onion, peeled and chopped ✳ 4 tablespoons olive oil ✳ 5 garlic cloves, peeled and finely chopped ✳ 1 large or 2 medium tomatoes (about 200g), peeled and chopped ✳ ½ teaspoon sugar ✳ 350ml strong cider ✳ salt ✳ 4 x 175–200g hake steaks ✳ 4–6 heaped tablespoons plain flour

In a wide frying pan, fry the onion in 2 tablespoons of the oil over a low heat, stirring often, until soft. Add the garlic and stir until the onion and garlic are slightly golden. Add the tomato and the sugar and cook for a few minutes until much of the liquid has evaporated. Add the cider and a little salt and cook over a high heat for 5 to 10 minutes to reduce the sauce.

Season the fish steaks with salt and dredge in flour to cover them well, then shake to remove excess flour. Fry them briefly in the remaining oil in another pan over a high heat for 1 minute on each side to give them a little colour, then transfer them to the sauce. Cook over a low heat for 2 to 5 minutes, or until the fish is cooked through and the flesh begins to flake when you cut into it with the point of a knife.

VARIATIONS

▨ Use monkfish instead of hake. It takes a few minutes longer to cook.

▨ Fry ½–¾ of a red chilli pepper, deseeded and chopped, with the onion and garlic.

▨ Mash the yolk of a hard-boiled egg and stir it into the sauce.

▨ Add the juice of ½ a lemon to the sauce.

▨ Add a handful of clams to the pan on top of the fish. Cook with the lid on until they open and the fish is done.

SALMON *with* PEAS
❋ *salmón con guisantes*

Asturias is famous for the salmon caught in its many fast-flowing rivers. When the fish return from the Atlantic to their spawning grounds in May, the first big catch of the season is called *campanu* because church bells (*campanas*) peal to signal its arrival. A favourite way of cooking salmon in Cangas de Onís in the Picos de Europa is with fresh green peas. Pepe Iglesias explained that the lettuce leaves, which cover the peas and the fish, produce steam that cooks the peas. Without added water the peas have a more intense, sweet flavour.

SERVES 2

Sauté the onion and ham in the oil in a large frying pan over a low heat, stirring occasionally, until the onion is soft. Put in half the butter and all the peas, stir and season with salt. Without adding any water, cover entirely with lettuce leaves and put on a tight-fitting lid so that the peas cook in the steam created by the lettuce. Cook over a very low heat for 15 minutes.

Lift up a few of the lettuce leaves and put in the salmon fillets. Season with salt and lay a piece of the remaining butter on each fillet. Replace the lettuce leaves, put the lid on and cook over a low heat for a further 10 minutes, or until the fish is done to your liking. The peas will be very soft – that is how they are supposed to be. Serve with a squeeze of lemon juice. The lettuce becomes an extra garnish.

- ½ a large onion, peeled and chopped
- 2 slices *jamón serrano* or other raw dry-cured ham, cut into 1.5cm strips
- 1½ tablespoons olive oil
- 25g butter
- 250g fresh green peas (podded weight)
- salt
- 6 or more cos lettuce leaves
- 2 x 150–175g salmon fillets, skin off
- juice of a ¼ lemon

SALMON *in a* BRANDY SAUCE
❊ *salmón al brandy*

The rivers of Asturias that cut gorges into the Cantabrian mountain range are full of beautiful wild salmon. This, too, is a recipe sent to me by Pepe Iglesias (see page 331). It is the way salmon might have been prepared in the homes of wealthy mining families in the first decades of the twentieth century. The sauce would have been put through a *chino*, a conical sieve with a wooden pestle. If you want a smooth, creamy sauce, then use a blender. Otherwise leave it as it is. The brandy gives it a rich taste, the chilli pepper adds a little heat. Serve with boiled new potatoes.

SERVES 4

❊ 1 large onion, peeled and chopped ❊ 3 tablespoons olive oil ❊ 3 garlic cloves, peeled and crushed
❊ 250g tomatoes, peeled and chopped ❊ ½ teaspoon sugar ❊ 250ml fish stock (page144)
❊ 125ml cognac or brandy ❊ 1 red chilli pepper, fresh or dried ❊ salt ❊ 4 x 150–175g salmon fillets

Sauté the onion in the oil in a large covered frying pan or wide casserole over a low heat, stirring occasionally, until soft. Add the garlic and cook briefly, stirring, until the onion and garlic begin to colour.

Add the tomatoes and the sugar. Turn the heat up to fairly high and cook for about 8 minutes until the sauce has a jammy consistency. Pour in the fish stock and the cognac or brandy, add the chilli and salt to taste, and then simmer for 5 minutes.

Put in the salmon fillets and simmer over a low heat for a further 8 to 10 minutes, uncovered, turning them over once, until the fish is done to your liking (I prefer salmon slightly underdone). Taste the sauce occasionally and remove the chilli when the sauce is only just a little peppery.

If you wish, lift out the salmon fillets, blend the sauce to a light cream and return the fillets to the pan to heat through before serving.

CADIZ-*style* SEA BREAM
❋ *urta a la gaditana*

Urta is the sea bream fished off the Cadiz coast, but other firm white fish such as monkfish, cod, halibut or haddock can be used. This is sherry and brandy territory and you find both in all kinds of dishes.

SERVES 4

❋ 1 onion, peeled and chopped ❋ 2 green or red peppers, deseeded and cut into thin strips
❋ 6–7 tablespoons olive oil ❋ 500g tomatoes ❋ 4 tablespoons dry sherry or white wine
❋ salt and pepper ❋ 4 x 150g bream fillets, skin on ❋ plain flour, for dredging ❋ 4 tablespoons brandy

Fry the onion and peppers in 3 tablespoons of the oil in a large frying pan for about 20 minutes, until the onions are golden and the peppers are soft. Cut the tomatoes in quarters and remove the hard bits at the stem end. Blend them, unpeeled, to a cream in the food processor and pour into the pan. Add the sherry or white wine, and season with salt and pepper. Cook for 10 minutes over a fairly high heat to reduce the sauce.

Dredge the fish fillets in flour mixed with a sprinkling of salt and shake off the excess. In a frying pan, briefly shallow-fry the fish in the remaining 3 to 4 tablespoons of the oil, turning the pieces over to brown them lightly on both sides. Pour in the brandy and set it alight.

When the flames have died down, pour the pepper and tomato sauce over the fish and cook for about 3 minutes until the fish is done.

MONKFISH *with* BRANDY
✳ *rape al brandy*

Here is another simple recipe for a tasty fish dish. Catalans call it *rap al conyac*. In the Catalan region of Penedès they make a brandy that is heartier than French cognac and drier than the brandy of Jerez.

SERVES 2

✳ 2 x 175g fillets of monkfish ✳ salt ✳ 2 tablespoons olive oil
✳ 2–3 garlic cloves, peeled and crushed ✳ 1 tablespoon tomato purée
✳ about 50ml water ✳ 4 tablespoons brandy ✳ 2 tablespoons chopped flat-leaf parsley

Season the fish fillets with salt and sauté in the oil in a frying pan over a medium-high heat until lightly coloured. Turn them over once, then lift them out of the pan and on to a plate.

Turn the heat down to low, put in the garlic, and stir for half a minute until the aroma rises and it only just begins to colour, then add the tomato purée and water and stir well.

Heat the brandy in a small pan and ignite it with a long match held over the edge of the pan. When the flames die down, pour it into the pan. Stir well, return the fish to the pan and cook over a low heat, turning the fillets over once, for about 7 minutes or until they are cooked through. Add the parsley and serve.

MONKFISH *with* CARAMELIZED ONIONS FLAMBÉED *in* RUM
❖ *rape con cebolla confitada al ron*

I ate this fish dish at a festival in Sitges on the Costa Brava, a gastronomic event to celebrate the life of the painter Santiago Rusiñol, who had popularized the beautiful resort. A jazz band played and local restaurants offered their best dishes at stands. I was sitting next to Xavier Mestres, who is president of the Fundació Institut Català de la Cuina (the Catalan Culinary Institute – see page 81). He explained that it was the *indianos*, the returnees who came home from Cuba and Venezuela in the nineteenth century, who introduced rum into Catalan cooking. They arrived at a time when the local bourgeoisie had adopted the French style of flambéing. Monkfish is a popular fish in Spain but you can use other firm white fish such as cod, haddock, halibut or turbot.

SERVES 2

❋ 1 large onion, peeled, cut in half and sliced ❋ 2 tablespoons olive oil
❋ 2 x 175g fillets of monkfish ❋ salt ❋ 2 tablespoons rum

In a frying pan, sauté the onion in the oil slowly over a low heat, covered to begin with and stirring often, until soft and golden brown – about 25 minutes.

Season the fish fillets with salt and add them to the pan. Cook gently for 8 to 12 minutes, turning them over once, or until the flesh looks opaque and white when you cut into it with a pointed knife.

Heat the rum in a small pan and ignite it with a long match held over the edge of the pan. When the flames die down, pour over the fish.

FISH *and* SEAFOOD
in a SAFFRON BÉCHAMEL
❊ *bechamel de mariscos*

At that same festival in Sitges (see page 343), I asked Xavier Mestres from the Catalan Culinary Institute about dishes of French origin that had been transformed and Hispanicized. I was given béchamel as an example. Sometimes white wine or sherry is used to flavour it, sometimes tomatoes. Here it is made with fried onions, grated lemon zest and saffron. For the fish fillets you can use cod, haddock or turbot. This is a dish that can be made in advance and refrigerated, then heated through and browned under the grill before serving.

SERVES 6

Sauté the onion in the butter in a medium-sized saucepan over a low heat, covered, until it is soft but not coloured. Add the flour and stir vigorously with a wooden spoon for a minute or so, then gradually add the milk, a little at a time, stirring vigorously off the heat at each addition, until you have a thick, creamy consistency. Whisk the sauce if necessary. Add the grated lemon zest, the saffron and some salt and pepper, and simmer over a low heat for another 10 minutes, stirring occasionally. Then beat in the egg yolks and take off the heat.

Cook the scallops and prawns in the olive oil in a frying pan over a high heat for 30 seconds to 1 minute. Flip the prawns over quickly as they turn pink, and the scallops as they are briefly seared. Then transfer them both to a baking dish. Put the fish in the frying pan and cook very briefly over a medium or high heat, for 5 minutes, sprinkling with salt and turning the fillets over, until the flesh just begins to flake when you cut it. Transfer to the baking dish and flake the fish. Pour the béchamel on top and mix gently. You can prepare ahead to this point and refrigerate the dish.

To make the breadcrumbs, remove the crusts and dry a slice of bread under the grill, then process in the food processor to make slightly coarse breadcrumbs. Sprinkle the breadcrumbs mixed with the melted butter over the dish and put in an oven preheated to 200°C/gas 6 for 10 to 15 minutes, then under the grill to brown the top.

VARIATION

❊ Add 5 tablespoons of sherry to the béchamel.

* 1 onion, peeled and chopped
* 75g butter
* 4 tablespoons plain flour
* 600ml whole milk, heated
* finely grated zest of 1 lemon
* a good pinch of saffron threads or powder
* salt and pepper
* 2 large egg yolks, lightly beaten
* 250g scallops, with roe
* 250g medium or large raw peeled prawns
* 2 tablespoons olive oil
* 250g skinless firm white fish fillet
* 2–3 tablespoons freshly made breadcrumbs, for the topping
* 25g butter, melted, for the topping

FISH *in an* ONION *and* SAFFRON SAUCE
❊ *pescado en amarillo*

This recipe for cooking *cazón* (tope shark) on the Malaga coast is great with other fish such as monkfish. Saffron gives the dish its name, *en amarillo*, which means yellow. The wine and saffron sauce thickened with ground almonds is exquisite.

SERVES 4

❊ 1 large onion, peeled and chopped ❊ 3 tablespoons olive oil ❊ 4 garlic cloves, peeled and chopped ❊ 4 x 175g pieces of monkfish fillet ❊ 350ml dry sherry or white wine ❊ 75ml water ❊ a pinch of saffron threads ❊ salt ❊ 4 tablespoons ground almonds

Fry the onion in the oil in a frying pan or casserole over a low heat, stirring often, until it just begins to colour. Stir in the garlic and, when the aroma rises, put in the fish. Increase the heat slightly and turn the pieces to brown them slightly all over.

Pour in the sherry or wine and water, add the saffron and some salt and bring to the boil. Turn the heat down and cook gently, uncovered, over a low heat for about 5 minutes. Add the ground almonds and cook for 5 minutes more, or until the fish is cooked through and the sauce has thickened.

FISH SOUP *with* MAYONNAISE
❖ *gazpachuelo*

I love this easy-to-make soup, a speciality of Malaga. The garlicky mayonnaise stirred in at the end gives it a creamy texture and adds to the mysterious, slightly winey, delicate flavour. Hake or other firm white fish can be used instead of monkfish. Small clams are usually added (see the variation below) but small or medium-sized scallops are easier to come by in our supermarkets and are perfect in this soup. Serve with toasted or fried bread.

SERVES 4

❋ 250g monkfish fillet ❋ 250ml dry white wine or sherry ❋ 500ml fish stock (page 144) or water ❋ 1 small onion, peeled and finely chopped ❋ 2 bay leaves ❋ salt and pepper ❋ 4 waxy or new potatoes (about 500g), peeled and cut in 7.5mm slices ❋ ½ teaspoon sugar (optional) ❋ 16 medium or large raw peeled prawns ❋ 8 small scallops ❋ 90ml good-quality bought mayonnaise ❋ 3 garlic cloves, peeled and crushed ❋ a sprig of flat-leaf parsley, chopped

Put the monkfish in a large pan or casserole with the wine or sherry and the stock or water. Add the onion and bay leaves, and a little salt and pepper. Bring to the boil and simmer over a low heat for about 5 to 6 minutes until the fish is only just done, then lift the fish out with a slotted spoon and put it aside.

Put in the potatoes and simmer uncovered for 20 to 25 minutes, or until they are tender, but do not let them fall apart. Taste and adjust the seasoning. If the wine is a bit too dry you might like to add a tiny bit of sugar.

Cut the monkfish up into chunks and return them to the casserole. Add the prawns and scallops and cook for 1 to 2 minutes until the prawns turn pink and the scallops lose their translucency.

Put the mayonnaise in a bowl and stir in the garlic. Add a few tablespoonfuls of the fish broth and beat vigorously with a wooden spoon. Then pour the mayonnaise into the soup, stirring very gently so as not to break up the potatoes and the fish, and heat through. Serve sprinkled with the chopped parsley.

VARIATIONS

❁ Use 250g clams instead of scallops. Wash and soak the clams in cold salted water for 1 hour to clean them. Put in a pan with about a finger's depth of water, cover and steam over a medium heat. The shells will open very quickly. Take the clams out of their shells and add them to the soup. Strain the clam cooking water, pour it into the soup and heat through.

❁ Add a drop of vinegar or lemon juice to the broth.

about *bacalao* (salt cod)

When I asked people I met in Spain what their favourite dish was, they often described one with salt cod. In this once fervently Catholic country, before refrigeration, when transport into the interior from the sea was by mule, *bacalao* was the traditional choice for penitential dishes, replacing meat during Lent and days of abstinence, including every Friday and Wednesday. Spaniards have become addicted to its very particular flavour and texture. It is now a much-loved delicacy even in coastal areas. The 'pig of the sea' that replaced the ubiquitous little bits of ham and *chorizo* in so many dishes is the food that evokes memories for everyone.

Cod is not a fish of Spanish waters. Since the tenth century Basque fishermen found a secret source in the high seas off Norway, and they went out as far as Newfoundland off the coast of North America in the North Atlantic to get it. To preserve it for the voyage home they filleted the fish, stacked the fillets between layers of salt to extract their moisture and dried them. It was carried to all parts of the Spanish hinterland by mules and in barges along rivers.

Every region has its own special ways of cooking salt cod. It is difficult to find in Britain at the moment but that might change. It needs to be soaked in plenty of cold water for between 12 hours to 2 days depending on the strength of the cure, and the water must be changed four or five times to remove all the salt. You have to try a bite to see if most of the saltiness has gone, but there should still be a slight taste of salt remaining. In Spain it is often sold soaked and desalted and ready to cook.

To produce something of the flavour and texture of salt cod with fresh cod:
Take thick cod fillets, put them on a plate and sprinkle very generously with coarse sea salt and leave them for at least 1 hour, turning the fillets over every 15 minutes or so and sprinkling with more coarse salt. The crystals will draw out the moisture from the flesh and some will be absorbed (do not use fine sea salt as too much salt would be absorbed). Wipe off the salt and rinse the fillets in cold water under the tap. Then soak in plenty of cold water for 30 to 45 minutes, changing the water three times. Pat dry with kitchen paper.

CREAMED SALT COD *with* MASHED POTATOES *and* GARLIC
❖ *brandada de bacalao*

Serve *brandada* as a starter or *tapa* with fried or toasted bread. Catalans share it with the South of France and the Languedoc. They call salt cod *bacallà*. It can be a creamy emulsion of fish with milk or cream and olive oil beaten in, or a thicker purée with mashed potatoes. I prefer the potato version and make it with plenty of garlic, but you may want to add only a touch. Ask your provider of salt cod how long you need to soak and desalt it, as that varies (see the box opposite). Soak it in cold water and change the water a few times.

SERVES 6

❋ 1–2 floury potatoes (about 200g), peeled and quartered
❋ salt and pepper ❋ 300g desalted salt cod (see page 348), drained
❋ 125ml single cream or whole milk, warmed ❋ 125ml extra virgin olive oil
❋ 2–4 garlic cloves, peeled and crushed

to accompany ❋ 9 or more thin slices white bread / olive oil

Boil the potatoes in salted water until soft, then drain.

Place the desalted and drained salt cod in a saucepan of cold water and bring to simmering point, then remove from the heat and let stand for 15 minutes. Drain, then carefully remove any skin and bones and flake into small pieces with your fingers.

Put the fish in the food processor and blend to a rough paste. Then pour in the warm cream or milk and the oil, a little at a time, alternating them, and blend to a smooth creamy purée that retains a little texture. Add garlic and pepper to taste, and the cooked potatoes, and blend briefly to a fluffy purée. If you have over-soaked the fish and desalted it too much, you may need to add a little salt.

Spoon the *brandada* into a baking dish and warm it in the oven when ready to serve, or serve it at room temperature, accompanied by fried or toasted bread. For this cut away the crusts from the bread and cut the slices into triangles. Then either fry the bread triangles in olive oil or toast them under the grill and brush with extra virgin olive oil.

PEPA'S FISH SOUP
❖ *suquet de peix*

This is an everyday Catalan fish soup that is more like a stew and has several variants. I love the way my friend Pepa Aymami (see page 367) makes it. Like so many Catalan dishes, it starts with a *sofregit* (*sofrito* in Castilian Spanish) of fried garlic and tomato and ends with a *picada* of ground almonds, garlic and parsley stirred in. Pepa uses stock that she makes with prawn shells. I use a good fish or chicken stock that I buy and it is lovely. Use hake, cod, halibut or other firm white fish. If you use monkfish it will need to cook for longer.

SERVES 4

❊ 3 tablespoons olive oil ❊ 4 garlic cloves, peeled and sliced ❊ 1 large or 2 small tomatoes (about 200g), peeled and chopped ❊ 500g waxy potatoes, peeled and cut into 1cm-thick slices ❊ 125ml dry white wine ❊ about 350ml fish or chicken stock (pages 145–5) ❊ salt ❊ a good pinch of saffron threads ❊ ¾ teaspoon sugar ❊ 250g firm white fish fillet (e.g. cod, haddock, hake), cut up into large 2–2.5cm chunks ❊ 250g medium or large raw peeled prawns

For the picada ❊ 10 blanched almonds ❊ 1 large garlic clove, peeled ❊ ½ tablespoon olive oil ❊ 1 tablespoon chopped flat-leaf parsley

Heat the oil in a wide casserole or pan, put in the garlic and tomatoes and cook, stirring often, over a medium heat for about 10 minutes, until the tomatoes are reduced to a jammy consistency.

Put in the potatoes and add the wine and enough stock to cover the potatoes. Add salt, the saffron and sugar, and simmer, covered, over a low heat for about 15 to 20 minutes, until the potatoes are just tender.

In the meantime make the *picada*. Fry the almonds and the whole garlic clove in the oil until both are slightly brown, then drain on kitchen paper. The usual way is to crush and grind them to a paste by hand with a pestle and mortar along with the parsley, but you can use the food processor for this. Then add a ladleful of the stock to dilute it.

Put the fish in the soup and 3 to 4 minutes later put in the prawns and the *picada*. Cook over a low heat until the prawns turn pink.

FISH STEW *with* PEPPERS *and* TOMATOES
❈ *caldereta de pescados y mariscos*

Galicia, Asturias and Cantabria have similar fish stews and soups. Not long ago all the men in the little fishing villages dotting the Atlantic coast went out to fish at night. The name *caldereta* comes from the pot (*caldera*) in which they cooked some of their catch on board their small boats. Nowadays fishermen take pizza along to sustain them while their old traditional stews have developed into prestigious regional dishes. Here is an elegant version. Serve it with toasted slices of country bread brushed with extra virgin olive oil.

SERVES 6

Fry the onion and pepper together in the oil in a large pan, uncovered, over a low heat, stirring often until soft. Stir in the garlic and cook for a minute or so, then add the tomatoes and cook gently for about 10 minutes until reduced. Now add the wine or sherry and water, and season with sugar if necessary (to mitigate the sharpness of the wine), salt and pepper and simmer, uncovered, for about 20 minutes. You can prepare this in advance and reheat it when you are ready to serve.

Ten minutes before serving heat the brandy in a tiny saucepan. When vapours appear, ignite them with a long match and, when the flames die down, pour the brandy into the main pan. Put in the monkfish and cook for 8 minutes (other fish take less time), then put in the prawns and scallops and cook for 1 to 2 minutes, until the prawns turn pink and the scallops become opaque. Serve the soup hot, sprinkled with parsley.

VARIATIONS

❈ For a more substantial version from Galicia, peel and cut 2–3 potatoes into small pieces or slices and add them at the same time as the wine and water.

❈ Put in ½ a deseeded chilli pepper with the wine and water and take it out when the stock is hot enough to your taste.

* 1 large onion, peeled and chopped
* 1 red or green pepper, deseeded and diced
* 3–4 tablespoons olive oil
* 4–5 garlic cloves, peeled and finely chopped
* 3 medium tomatoes, peeled and chopped
* 500ml dry white wine or oloroso sherry
* 500ml water
* 1 teaspoon sugar (optional)
* salt and pepper
* 125ml brandy
* 400g monkfish fillets, or another firm white fish, cut into 3cm chunks
* 280g raw peeled king prawns
* 220g small scallops
* a good bunch of flat-leaf parsley, chopped

ARTICHOKES *with* PRAWNS *and* CLAMS
❖ *alcachofas con gambas y almejas*

This is a delicately flavoured and unusual dish, a speciality of Cordoba. Manuel Andrade (see page 428) cooked it for me in his little restaurant Porta Gayola in Seville. It was exquisite, made with tiny baby artichokes he called *alcahuciles* that he had picked the previous day. I have used frozen artichoke bottoms and you could use frozen artichoke hearts if you manage to find them (they are available in France and hopefully will come here soon). If you are lucky enough to find fresh baby artichokes see how to prepare them on page 120. Manuel says that in Cordoba people cook this dish with the local fino sherry-type Montilla–Moriles wine.

SERVES 4

Throw away any broken clams and those that don't close when you tap them (see page 118). Then wash the clams, put them in a bowl with plenty of cold salted water and leave them for 1 hour to clean themselves of sand.

Heat the oil over a low heat in a wide casserole that you can bring to the table. Put in the onion and cook, stirring, over a low heat until soft. Add the garlic and stir until it begins to colour. Add the flour and stir vigorously, then gradually add the wine or sherry and the stock, stirring all the time.

Season with salt and put in the artichokes. Bring to the boil and cook over a low heat for 10 minutes, or until they are tender. Place the prawns and the drained clams on top and sprinkle with parsley. Cover the casserole with a lid or with foil and cook for 3 to 5 minutes over a medium heat until the prawns turn pink and the clams open (throw away any that do not open).

* 500g clams
* salt
* 3 tablespoons olive oil
* 1 medium onion, peeled and finely chopped
* 2–3 garlic cloves, peeled and finely chopped
* 1 tablespoon plain flour
* 200ml Montilla–Moriles wine, or a dry sherry or white wine
* 200ml fish or chicken stock (see pages 144–5)
* 10–12 frozen artichoke bottoms or hearts, defrosted and quartered
* 200g raw peeled prawns, defrosted if frozen
* 2 tablespoons finely chopped flat-leaf parsley

LOBSTER HOTPOT
❊ *caldereta de langosta*

This sublime Minorcan speciality can be found in restaurants along the coasts of all the Balearic Islands. The spiny lobster, queen of the local seas, was once considered poor food, which only the fishermen who fished it off the rocky coast would eat. This hotpot is in the classic Catalan style – starting with a *sofrito* of fried onion, pepper and tomatoes and ending with a *picada* paste of almonds, garlic and parsley to thicken the sauce. Serve it with toasted slices of good country bread or baguette to dunk in the sauce. Offer lobster picks or skewers for people to extract the meat from the claws and legs, spoons for them to eat the soup with, and finger bowls with water. I added monkfish fillets to the original lobster-only stew and there was just about enough for six. Buy your lobsters live and ask the fishmonger to kill and chop them for you. Discard the black intestinal vein and the green tomalley but keep any roe or coral.

SERVES 6

In a large *cazuela* or casserole, fry the onion and pepper in the oil over a low heat until very soft. Add the tomatoes and sugar and cook until the sauce is reduced and jammy, then blend it to a cream (a hand blender is useful to do this directly in the pan).

Add the fish stock and brandy or cognac, and season with salt and pepper. Add the fennel leaves, if using. Then put in the monkfish and the lobsters, bring to the boil and simmer for 5 minutes.

Meanwhile, for the *picada*, fry the almonds and whole garlic cloves in the oil over a low heat in a small frying pan, for moments only, until they are golden, turning them over once. Pound them to a paste with the parsley using a pestle and mortar, then stir in the brandy or cognac, or blend all the ingredients including the brandy or cognac in the food processor. Stir this mixture into the simmering sauce in the casserole. For a Catalan version, add 2 tablespoons of grated dark chocolate.

Cook for 3 minutes more, or until the lobster shells turn a deep red and the meat is opaque, with a firm texture. Serve the hotpot in bowls and pass around the toasted slices of bread.

* 1 large onion, peeled and chopped
* 1 green or red pepper, deseeded and chopped
* 3 tablespoons olive oil
* 4–5 tomatoes (350g), peeled and chopped
* 1 teaspoon sugar
* 1 litre fish stock (see page 144)
* 125ml brandy or cognac
* salt and pepper
* a few sprigs of fennel leaves, torn into pieces (optional)
* 400g monkfish fillet, cut into cubes
* 2 x 700g lobsters (see note in the introduction for how to cut them up)

For the picada

* 12 blanched almonds
* 3 garlic cloves, peeled
* ½–1 tablespoon olive oil
* a good handful of flat-leaf parsley, coarsely chopped
* 4 tablespoons brandy or cognac
* 2 tablepoons grated dark chocolate (optional)

To serve

* 6 slices of country bread, lightly toasted

SARDINES *in a* PICKLING MARINADE
sardinas en escabeche

Pickling in *escabeche* was originally a way of preserving game such as partridge and rabbit, and fish such as sardines, mackerel and tuna, but it has now become a delicacy in its own right to be served cold. The name originates from the Persian word *sikbaj*, which refers to food cooked in vinegar. Foods '*en escabeche*' are normally dipped in flour and deep-fried before being marinated, but in Andalusia they prefer to simply poach the sardines very briefly in the marinade. This can be a mix of just olive oil and vinegar (which is too sharp for me) or of olive oil, vinegar and dry white wine. I did not have enough leftover dry white wine when I made this dish so I also added some Moscatel wine, which gave the sardines a lovely sweet touch.

Ask the fishmonger to scale and gut the sardines and remove the heads and backbones. The pickled and marinated sardines will keep for a few weeks in the refrigerator. You should make them at least a day before you want to start eating them. Serve 2 to 3 per person as a *tapa* or starter on toasted bread, if you like.

MAKES ABOUT 16

- 1kg sardines, scaled, heads off, gutted and backbone removed
- 150ml dry white wine or a mix with a little Moscatel, or more if needed
- 150ml white wine vinegar, or more if needed
- 150ml olive oil, or more if needed
- salt
- 3 garlic cloves, peeled
- 2 bay leaves
- 10 black peppercorns
- a sprig of thyme or oregano

Arrange the sardines in layers in a wide saucepan. Mix the white wine, vinegar and olive oil together in a bowl and season with a little salt. Stir in the garlic, bay leaves, peppercorns and thyme or oregano, and pour this marinade over the sardines. If the sardines are not covered entirely, add a little more of the liquids in equal quantities. Bring to the boil and simmer for no longer than 3 to 5 minutes. Let cool in the pan before transferring to a glass or ceramic dish. Cover with cling film and keep in the refrigerator. Remove from the refrigerator 1 hour before serving as the oil in the marinade almost solidifies when it is cold.

VARIATION

- You can add a ½ teaspoon of *pimentón dulce* or sweet paprika to the marinade. If you do not have any sweet Moscatel wine, add ½–1 teaspoon of sugar.

POULTRY AND
SMALL GAME

aves y caza

Peasant farmers in Spain kept hens for their eggs and only ate chicken on festive and celebratory occasions. Although there is now intensive farming and chicken is very cheap, the memory of those times is still powerful. That is why Spanish chicken dishes are so special.

Spain is the European country with the greatest tradition of shooting game birds – partridge and woodcock, pheasant and quail, duck and pigeon. For centuries, hunting and shooting were noble sports reserved for the aristocracy – laws once made game the preserve of the landed elites – and noble codes of practice still govern the sport. Peasants were not allowed to shoot or even to take birds that had died accidentally, but of course there were always poachers. Now shooting is a national sport and game cooking has wide appeal. Every region has hunting preserves in national parks and on private wildlife estates. There are hunting and shooting clubs and associations, and organized shooting drives have become an industry. Some farmed birds are raised naturally in their wild environment – they are hatched in nurseries and very quickly allowed into the wilderness.

During their season, game birds are on every restaurant menu. Recipes for cooking game abound in old Spanish cookery books and in recipe collections compiled by monasteries centuries ago. Wild birds have a rich, strong flavour but their meat is tough compared to the farmed game we get at the butcher's and in supermarkets so they have to be well hung and tenderized. Old aristocratic recipes advocate marinating in wine and brandy and pot-roasting or stewing, but innovative restaurants in Spain now serve tender, juicy roasted birds, their meat still slightly pink – sometimes almost raw – accompanied by a sauce. Clandestine peasant game dishes, made with poached game, consisted of hearty soups and stews with beans and vegetables. They included rabbit and hare dishes that are still very popular, such as braised rabbit with herbs and white wine (*conejo al vino*) on page 395 and rabbit cooked like the garlic chicken (*pollo al ajillo*) on page 364.

Now that game is readily available on our supermarket shelves and the price compares favourably with free-range organic chicken, we should be inspired by Spain's ways of cooking it. The season for partridge is from 1 September to 1 February, for pheasant it is 1 October to 1 February, and for woodcock it is 1 October (1 September in Scotland) to 31 January. You can get squab and quail all year round, and all game birds can be bought frozen.

ROAST CHICKEN *with* APPLES *and* GRAPES
✳ *pollo con manzanas y uvas*

Apple trees are mentioned in Asturian monastery documents as early as the eighth century. In the twelfth century, smallholders were contracted to plant and tend a certain number of apple trees for the benefit of their landowners. The clergy, who were major landowners, covered their extensive lands with apple trees. Today apples are used to make cider and are an important part of the local economy. They also appear in both savoury and sweet dishes. When my friend Alicia Ríos and her assistant Simon Cohen sent out emails to their friends on my behalf, asking for their favourite recipes, Ana Isabel Lozano sent me this one, which has become one of my favourites. An apple inside the cavity gives the chicken a fruity aroma and freshly pressed grape juice gives it a caramelized glaze. In Asturias, Reineta apples (see page 465) are used but the Golden Delicious variety is a good substitute.

SERVES 4–6

✳ 5 Golden Delicious apples ✳ juice of ½ a lemon ✳ 1kg white seedless grapes, destalked
✳ 1 x 1.5kg chicken ✳ salt and pepper ✳ 3 tablespoons olive oil ✳ 75g butter

Peel and core the apples. Cut one in half or into quarters, so the pieces will push easily inside the chicken, and the rest of the apples into 8 slices each. Drop the slices into a bowl of water acidulated with the lemon juice to prevent them from discolouring.

Blend half of the grapes in the food processor and collect the juice by pressing the mush through a small-holed sieve with a wooden spoon. Discard the skins left in the sieve. You should get about 250ml of juice.

Stuff the chicken with the halved or quartered apple and put it in a baking dish. Sprinkle with salt and pepper and rub with 1 tablespoon of the oil. Turn the bird breast side down in the baking dish and pour in 125ml of the grape juice. Roast in an oven preheated to 190°C/gas 5 for 45 minutes, then take the chicken out, turn it over, pour the remaining grape juice over it and return to the oven. Cook for another 30 minutes or until the chicken is brown and caramelized and the juices run clear when you cut into the bird between the leg and the body with a pointed knife.

While the chicken is roasting, heat the butter with the remaining 2 tablespoons of oil in a large frying pan. Put in the drained apple slices and the remaining grapes and sauté over a medium heat, turning over the fruits and shaking the pan gently until the grapes are soft and golden and the apples tender and caramelized. It can take 20 minutes. Transfer to a baking dish with their juices and reheat in the oven when you are ready to serve.

VARIATION
✳ Add a handful of raisins or sultanas, or 6–8 moist pitted prunes cut into pieces, instead of the grapes in the frying pan with the apples.

CHICKEN *with* PEPPERS *and* TOMATOES
✼ *pollo al chilindrón*

Chilindrón, also called *fritada*, is a garnish of onions, peppers and tomatoes that is ubiquitous in the parts of north-east Spain where the river Ebro flows. You can choose to use sweet red peppers or green ones that provide a more peppery flavour, or both.

SERVES 6

✼ 1 medium onion, peeled and chopped ✼ 6 tablespoons olive oil ✼ 4 garlic cloves, peeled and chopped ✼ 4 red or green peppers, or a mix of the two, deseeded and cut into wide strips ✼ 750g tomatoes, peeled and chopped ✼ salt and pepper ✼ 1 teaspoon sugar ✼ 1 x 2kg chicken, cut into 6 pieces ✼ 150g *jamón serrano* or other raw dry-cured ham, or streaky bacon, cut into thin strips ✼ 125ml dry white wine

In a wide frying pan or casserole, fry the onion over a medium heat in 3 tablespoons of the oil until golden, stirring often. Add the garlic and peppers and cook for 10 minutes, stirring. Add the tomatoes, season with salt, pepper and sugar and cook over a medium-high heat, uncovered, for 15 to 20 minutes or until the sauce is much reduced.

In another large frying pan brown the chicken pieces lightly in the remaining oil over a medium heat, sprinkling with salt and pepper and turning them over once. Add the ham or bacon and stir for 2 minutes. Then pour in the wine and cook, covered, over a low heat for 20 to 30 minutes. Remove the chicken breasts after about 15 minutes, when they are done, and transfer to a plate. Return them to the pan when the legs are done. Add the tomato and pepper sauce and cook for 5 minutes more or until the chicken is heated through.

GARLIC CHICKEN
❋ *pollo al ajillo*

Cervantes' seventeenth-century romantic 'hero', Don Quixote, kept telling his manservant, Sancho Panza, not to eat garlic as it would betray the vileness in his character. The strong smell of garlic that assailed the knight the first time he saw his beloved Dulcinea del Toboso made him think that an evil magic-man had disguised her as a coarse peasant woman. Scholars of the period have a possible interpretation – that the smell of garlic was a coded message that she was a Conversa (Christian convert), because at the time converted Jews were derided as eaters of excessive amounts of garlic. Today, as the Catalan food writer Xavier Domingo once commented, 'There are many cuisines in Spain but they all have one thing in common – garlic.' However, the lavish use of garlic is a particular characteristic of Castilian cooking. If you are fond of garlic, add the whole peeled cloves of two heads to the dish – they will become soft, sweet and mellow. That is how I like it but it is more common to cook the cloves in their skins and to discard them before serving. Serve the chicken with potatoes or with bread to soak up the sauce.

SERVES 4–6

❋ 4 tablespoons olive oil ❋ 1 x 1½kg chicken, cut into 6 pieces ❋ salt and pepper
❋ cloves of 1–2 garlic heads, peeled ❋ 3 bay leaves, preferably fresh ❋ 250ml dry white wine or dry sherry
❋ 250ml chicken stock (you can use ½ a stock cube)

Heat the oil in a wide, heavy-bottomed casserole or frying pan and put in the chicken pieces. Turn them over a medium heat to brown them lightly all over and season with salt and pepper. Do them in batches if your pan is not wide enough to have them in one layer. Remove the chicken and fry the garlic cloves over a low heat in the same oil, stirring and turning them over, until only just lightly browned.

Return the chicken to the pan, add the bay leaves and pour in the wine or sherry and the chicken stock. Bring to the boil, lower the heat and simmer, covered, for 10 minutes, turning the chicken pieces. Take out the breast meat pieces when they are done. Continue to cook the thighs and legs, uncovered, for another 10 to 15 minutes until they are no longer pink when you cut into them with a knife. Return the breasts to the pan and heat through.

VARIATION
❀ You can substitute a rabbit, skinned and cut into pieces, for the chicken and cook it in the same way.

CHICKEN *cooked in* CIDER
with POTATOES *and* PEAS
❊ *pitu a la sidra con patatinas y guisantes*

Cider, potatoes and peas are major products of Asturias. *Pitu* is the word used there for hens seen running around the villages pecking for grains of maize. They are tasty but tough and need a lot of stewing. Use chicken thighs for this dish because breasts become stringy when they are stewed for a long time.

SERVES 4–6

❊ 1 large onion, peeled and chopped ❊ 3 tablespoons olive oil ❊ 100g *jamón serrano* or other raw dry-cured ham, or streaky bacon, cut into strips ❊ 6 chicken thighs with their skin on ❊ salt and pepper ❊ 3 garlic cloves, peeled and chopped ❊ juice of ½ a lemon ❊ about 500ml extra-strong cider ❊ 500g waxy potatoes, peeled and cut in half or quarters if large ❊ 500g peas or petits pois, fresh shelled or frozen and defrosted

In a wide pan or casserole, sauté the onion in the oil, covered, over a low heat until soft, stirring often. Stir in the ham or bacon, then add the chicken thighs and turn the heat up a little. Turn the chicken pieces to brown them slightly all over and season with salt and pepper. Add the garlic and stir for a moment or two until it just begins to colour.

Add the lemon juice and the cider, and cook, covered, over a low heat for 30 minutes or until the chicken is very tender.

In the meantime, boil the potatoes in salted water for 15 to 20 minutes until tender, then drain and drop them into the pan with the chicken. Add the peas, check the seasoning and simmer, covered, for 5 to 10 minutes more, until the peas are soft.

pepa aymami

Pepa is a glamorous blonde and blue-eyed livewire. I first met her at an international symposium on Mediterranean food in Barcelona in 2004; she was the director and coordinator. Scholars from various Mediterranean countries came together to discuss the histories, peoples, religions, products, cooking techniques and shared food heritage of the area, and chefs were invited to demonstrate their dishes using Mediterranean products. Pepa put together chefs from warring countries (they fell into each other's arms) and initiated the project 'Taste for Peace'. She later persuaded the chefs to help compile a database of all the dishes they had in common for her Fundació Viure el Mediterrani, which aimed to establish the gastronomic heritage of the Mediterranean and to create a Mediterranean Product brand.

She is also the director of the Fundació Institut Català de la Cuina (Catalan Culinary Institute – see page opposite). When I stayed with Pepa in Barcelona I met her colleagues – passionate Catalan gastronomes – over lunch. She sent me a huge book, their *Corpus*, an archive of recipes collected from chefs, farmers, fishermen and housewives, most of them living in mountain and fishing villages. I kept phoning her for advice and information about the recipes in this book. How long can I boil the blood sausage before it explodes? What is *vi ranci*? (It is fortified wine – neither rancid nor simply aged wine.) What is *julivert*? (It is parsley.)

Pepa's office is in a flat above her own and she manages to cook lunch every day for everyone. She has four grown-up children: two daughters and two sons. Her eldest son, Juan, is unusual in that although he comes from a very Catholic family, he became convinced that he was of Jewish origin and wanted to convert to Judaism. When rabbis in Spain would not convert him he went to Israel to study at a yeshiva. His family thought it was a kibbutz. He became Jewish and Israeli, and fought in the first war in Lebanon. He now lives in Barcelona with his Catalan wife and sons and has joined the Jewish community there, which is made up mainly of people from North Africa and Latin America. I am sure that he has had to become lax about kosher laws because it is difficult in Spain to avoid eating ham.

CHICKEN *and* PRAWN STEW
with ALMOND *and* CHOCOLATE SAUCE
❊ *pollo con langostinos*

This is a splendid example of the famous *mar y montaña* ('sea and mountain') Catalan dishes that mix meat and seafood. I asked a Catalan I met at a dinner why they cook the two together so much and I was told, 'The mountain is right by the sea and we use what we have.' My friend Pepa Aymami is famous for this dish. When I asked her for the recipe she sent me the book she and her friends at the Fundació Institut Català de la Cuina (the Catalan Culinary Institute) had just been working on, the *Corpus de la Cuina Catalana* – their archive of Catalan dishes – and marked the page with her recipe. Hers was the grander version that has lobster instead of prawns, and chocolate in the *picada* – the nutty paste that is stirred in at the end of many Catalan dishes to thicken the sauce and add another dimension of flavour. Putting chocolate in savoury dishes was a novelty that came with the Spanish returnees from Mexico in the nineteenth century. Brandy and sherry add other sensational notes.

Catalans grate rather than chop their tomatoes, and that gives a finer texture to their sauce, the famous *sofregit* of fried onion, garlic and tomato. To grate tomatoes cut them in half crossways and grate on the coarse holes of a grater until you get to the skin (see page 121).

SERVES 6

❊ 1 x 2kg chicken, cut into 6–8 pieces ❊ salt and pepper ❊ plain flour, for dredging ❊ 4 tablespoons olive oil ❊ about 20 large raw peeled king prawns, fresh or frozen and defrosted ❊ 2 medium onions, peeled and chopped ❊ 3 tomatoes, halved and grated or peeled and finely chopped ❊ 125ml brandy

For the picada ❊ 70g blanched almonds ❊ ½ tablespoon olive oil ❊ 5–6 garlic cloves, peeled and crushed ❊ a handful of roughly chopped flat-leaf parsley ❊ 25g dark chocolate, grated ❊ 4 tablespoons oloroso or amontillado sherry

»»»

Season the chicken pieces with salt and turn them in the flour to cover them all over, then shake off the excess. Sauté briefly in the oil over a medium heat in a wide casserole, turning to brown them lightly all over, then remove the chicken pieces from the pan.

In the same oil fry the prawns very briefly over a medium heat for 2 minutes until they turn pink, turning them over once, and then remove them.

Now fry the onions in the same oil over a low heat, stirring occasionally, until soft and just beginning to colour. Add the tomatoes and some salt and pepper, and cook for 8 to 10 minutes over a medium-high heat until all the liquid has evaporated and the sauce is reduced to a jammy consistency. Heat the brandy in a small pan and, when vapours appear, ignite them with a long match and pour the flaming brandy into the sauce.

When the flames have died down, put the chicken pieces back in the pan and add just enough water to almost cover them. Simmer over a low heat, covered, for about 20 to 30 minutes (remove the breasts to a plate after 15 minutes and put them back into the pan when the thighs are done).

For the *picada*, fry the almonds briefly over a low heat in the oil in a small frying pan, stirring and turning them over until lightly browned. The traditional method is then to crush all the *picada* ingredients together with a pestle and mortar but it is easier and perfectly fine to blend them in the food processor. Grind the almonds finely first, then add the garlic, parsley and grated chocolate and blend to a paste. Add the sherry and blend again.

Stir the *picada* into the sauce and cook for 5 minutes, then add the prawns and heat everything through.

VARIATION

❊ Make the dish with the cooked meat from 1 lobster instead of the prawns.

CHICKEN *in an* ALMOND *and* EGG SAUCE
❊ *pollo en pepitoria*

In Spain, when this dish is made with an older hen – what our butchers call a boiler chicken – as was common in the past, it is called *gallina en pepitoria* (*gallina* means hen). It is best to use chicken thighs because they can take long stewing. The mix of wine and chicken thickened with almonds, garlic, cinnamon, saffron and egg yolk makes a splendid sauce with a delicate flavour.

SERVES 4

❊ 4 tablespoons olive oil ❊ 6–8 chicken thighs with their skin on ❊ salt and pepper
❊ 1 large onion, peeled and chopped ❊ 250ml dry white wine ❊ 500ml chicken stock
(you may use a stock cube) ❊ 2 bay leaves ❊ ½–¾ teaspoon ground cinnamon ❊ 2 large eggs
❊ 60g blanched almonds ❊ 5 garlic cloves, peeled ❊ a good pinch of saffron threads

You will need a wide casserole or shallow pan with a lid that will hold all the chicken thighs in one layer. Heat 3 tablespoons of the oil in the pan, and put in the chicken thighs. Cook over a medium heat, adding a little salt and pepper and turning them, until lightly browned all over. Take the chicken out, lower the heat and put in the onion. Sauté gently over a low heat until slightly golden, then return the chicken thighs to the pan.

Add the wine and chicken stock, the bay leaves and cinnamon, and simmer gently, covered, over a low heat for 25 minutes or until tender, turning the chicken pieces over a few times and adding a little more salt and pepper to taste.

Boil the eggs for 10 minutes, cool them in cold water and peel them. Cut them in half, take out the yolks, and chop the whites into small dice. Fry the almonds and the whole garlic cloves in a small frying pan in the remaining tablespoon of oil, turning them over, until the almonds brown very slightly – the garlic will turn a darker colour. Do all this while the chicken is simmering.

Blend the almonds and garlic to a paste in the food processor with the hard-boiled egg yolks, plus a few tablespoons of the sauce from the chicken, or mash these ingredients all together with a pestle and mortar.

Stir the paste into the simmering stock, together with the saffron, and cook for 10 minutes or longer, until the chicken is well done and the sauce has thickened.

Serve sprinkled with the chopped egg whites.

VARIATION
❊ In La Rioja, walnuts are used instead of almonds in a similar dish.

ROAST TURKEY *with* STUFFING
✳ *pava relleno*

Turkeys were brought back from what is now Mexico by the conquistadors and were adopted by the nobility as their grand dish for great occasions. In Andalusia and Catalonia, turkey is still the main Christmas fare, served with extraordinary stuffings. My friend Loli Flores, who was a chef in Seville for many years, told me that for Christmas live turkeys are fed brandy and later their meat is injected with brandy to give it a delicious flavour. When Count Ybarra's mother (see page 414) had the nuns debone and prepare a turkey for their family, the nuns too injected the meat with brandy. A common stuffing was made from a mix of sausage meat, chestnuts and brandy. Another was prepared with dried fruit, pine nuts and bread soaked in milk. The family's *pavo trufado* is a complex dish made up of layers of turkey and pork fillet slices, with black truffles and *jamón* in between them. In Catalonia, turkey is stuffed with the same filling as the one given in the capon recipe on page 373. Because turkey meat is very dry it needs special treatment. Here is a good way to keep it juicy and flavoured with brandy.

SERVES 14

✳ 1 x 6.5kg turkey ✳ salt ✳ 1 orange, halved ✳ 150g butter ✳ 175ml brandy
✳ 1½ x the quantity of stuffing prepared as in the capon recipe (page 373)

Lay two large sheets of foil in a roasting pan, one of them widthways and the other lengthways. Lay the turkey on its back in the middle, untie and remove the trussing, sprinkle inside with salt and push the orange halves into the cavity. Blend the butter and the brandy in a bowl with a fork, or in the food processor. Rub the bird with this mixture and push some between the breast and the skin. To do this, starting from the neck lift the skin and gently work your fingers, then your hand, under it. Carefully push the butter and brandy mixture into the gap, pressing to ease it into an even layer over the breast. Tuck the flap of neck skin under the bird to stop the butter leaking out.

Wrap the turkey in the foil so that the parcel is roomy but well sealed. Place in an oven preheated to 220°C/gas 7 for 30 minutes, then lower the heat to 170°C/gas 3 and cook for 2 hours. (Meanwhile prepare the stuffing, put it in a deep baking dish, press it down and cover it with foil. Put it in the oven below the turkey when the turkey has been in for 1 hour and take it out when the turkey is ready.) Open the foil parcel and turn the oven up to 200°C/gas 6. Cook for another 30 minutes, or until the turkey's skin is crisp and brown and the juices run clear when you pierce one of the thighs with a pointed knife. Take the stuffing out of the oven and leave the turkey to rest for 20 minutes before carving. Serve with the juices from inside the foil parcel and the stuffing.

STUFFED ROAST CAPON *or* EXTRA-LARGE CHICKEN
❋ *capón relleno*

Capons, geese, guinea fowl and turkeys are Christmas dishes in Spain. Capons are particularly popular in the north. Every year, on 21 December, there is a capon fair at Vilalba in Galicia where you can buy these birds that are famously raised on a diet of boiled maize meal and potatoes, or chestnuts soaked in milk or white wine. Capons from Vilalba also appear in other Spanish markets. A capon is a cock that has been castrated by hormone injection and is then fattened to reach an enormous weight. The meat is more tender, juicy and full of flavour than that of chicken. 'Caponization' of poultry is banned in Britain on animal welfare grounds, but huge, free-range chickens weighing between 3kg and 5kg that have been fattened and raised for a longer time than usual are sold as 'capons'.

Catalans make glorious stuffings with different combinations of dried fruit, nuts, sausage meat and brandy, which they also use for turkey (see page 371). This recipe is based on one from the Catalan recipe collection, the *Corpus de la Cuina Catalana* (see page 367). I cook the stuffing separately.

SERVES 8

❋ 1 x 3kg 'capon' or extra-large chicken ❋ salt and pepper ❋ 2 tablespoons olive oil ❋ 2 apples, such as Golden Delicious, peeled, cored and halved ❋ 2 onions, peeled and quartered ❋ 1 whole head of garlic, cut in half crossways ❋ 2 ripe tomatoes, peeled and quartered ❋ 250ml sweet white wine such as Moscatel ❋ 2 bay leaves ❋ 1 cinnamon stick ❋ 125ml brandy or cognac

For the stuffing ❋ 250g soft pitted prunes ❋ 250g soft dried peaches or apricots ❋ 175ml brandy or cognac ❋ 1 large onion, peeled and chopped ❋ 2–3 tablespoons olive oil ❋ 250g minced pork ❋ salt and pepper ❋ 250g thin pure pork sausages (about 9), cut into small pieces ❋ 100g pine nuts ❋ 50g ground almonds ❋ 1 teaspoon ground cinnamon

»»»

For the stuffing, chop the prunes and dried peaches or apricots coarsely and put them to soak in a bowl with the brandy or cognac for at least half an hour. In a large frying pan, fry the onion in the oil over a low heat until soft. Add the minced pork and some salt and pepper then cook over a medium heat for about 5 minutes, crushing the meat and turning it over until it changes colour. Make space for the sausages in the pan, put the sausage pieces in and cook, turning them over, for about 5 minutes until they change colour. Add the pine nuts and stir for a minute or two, then stir in the ground almonds and cinnamon. Take off the heat, then mix with the dried fruits and their brandy. Put the stuffing in a deep oven dish, press down and cover with foil.

Remove the neck and giblets, if there are any, from the cavity of the capon or chicken and remove the string and trussing. Rinse it inside and out in cold running water, then pat it dry with kitchen paper. Season generously with salt and rub with the olive oil. Push the apples into the cavity and place the bird breast side down in a roasting pan. Put the onions, garlic and tomatoes around it in the roasting pan and pour in the sweet wine. Add the bay leaves and cinnamon stick, then cover loosely with a foil 'tent'.

Place the capon or chicken in an oven preheated to 190°C/gas 5, placing the pan of stuffing on the shelf below it at the same time. Cook for 1 hour and 10 minutes, then take the roasting pan with the bird out, remove the foil, turn the bird over breast side up and return it to the oven, uncovered. Roast for another 35 to 50 minutes until well cooked and golden brown. It is done when you pierce the thickest part of the thigh with a pointed knife and the juices run clear. (For smaller birds the total cooking time will be about 40 minutes per kg plus an extra 25 minutes.)

Transfer the capon or chicken to a serving dish and take the stuffing out of the oven. Remove some of the excess fat from the bird's juices and place the roasting pan on the hob over a medium heat. Stir in the brandy or cognac and deglaze, scraping up the bits from the bottom of the pan. Season with salt and pepper, and pour into a jug to serve with the capon or chicken. Carve the bird and serve accompanied by the stuffing.

VARIATIONS

- Add 2 peeled and chopped Golden Delicious apples to the stuffing mixture with the soaked dried fruits.
- Add 12 cooked, peeled and coarsely chopped fresh chestnuts to the stuffing mixture. To cook and peel them, make a long cut in the skin on the flat side of each one with a small sharp knife and turn them once under the grill for about 10 minutes until the skin where the cut is curls back. Peel them when they are cool enough to handle. The chestnuts can also be roasted in the oven or boiled.
- Soak a handful of raisins or sultanas in the brandy with the prunes and dried peaches or apricots.
- Use fresh breadcrumbs (see page 120) instead of the ground almonds.
- An aristocratic dish from Majorca is capon stuffed with a mixture of boiled and mashed sweet potatoes, raisins, chopped apples and chopped almonds and hazelnuts.

a rabbit lunch at michael jacobs's house in frailes

Walking with Michael Jacobs and Manolo el Sereno (see page 162) in the village of Frailes in Jaén, Andalusia, is like walking with Don Quixote and Sancho Panza. Michael is a tall, aristocratic-looking Englishman, Manolo a small man of the people. We are stopped by everyone. Michael wrote a book, *The Factory of Light* (John Murray, 2003), about the village and spent a long time interviewing the inhabitants. Now that he lives there, the villagers still want to go on telling him everything. In the local bar carved into the mountain, where men sit playing cards in the dark, one man gives him a rabbit, another offers him an armful of wild asparagus he had just picked. They become part of our lunch in Michael's little house on the hill.

Michael fell for the magic of Spain as a boy and went on to write many learned and witty travel books and guidebooks about the country. He was first drawn to Frailes by the story of the *milagrero*, the healer and miracle man known as *el Santo Custodio*, who had lived as a hermit with his goats at the top of a nearby mountain. A shrine and a little church built on the spot are a place of pilgrimage where people pin photos, light candles and leave gifts. Michael stayed in Frailes because it was a peaceful place for writing, and because he was touched by the friendliness and warmth of the people who adopted him as one of their own. Unlike Gerald Brenan, who wrote about Spain in the 1940s and 1950s but said little about the food, Michael is also a gastronome who writes about Spanish food and takes groups on gastronomic tours.

DUCK *with* PEARS ✸ *pato con peras*

Twenty years ago, when I was working on a BBC television series on Mediterranean cookery, I ate a duck with pears at Remei Martínez's Can Toni restaurant in the port of San Feliu de Guíxols in Catalonia and I have always remembered it. It is one of the crowning dishes of Catalan cuisine. I have since found other versions, all of them rich and complex, but Remei's slightly adapted one is still my favourite. She said that the recipe was originally for goose, but now it is most often made with duck. Other fruits such as peaches, apples, figs and cherries are sometimes used instead of pears. Remei used wild ducks that have little fat, are quite tough and need to be stewed. The ducklings that are now raised in Spain are very tender and, like the ones we buy, very fatty and best roasted.

SERVES 4

Place the duck in a baking dish or roasting pan, breast side down. Rub it with salt and 1 tablespoon of the olive oil and prick the skin in a few places to allow the fat to run out. Place it in an oven preheated to 200°C/gas 6. After 1 hour take the duck out of the dish, pour out the fat and return the duck, breast side up, to the dish, adding about 125ml of water. Cook for 1 hour or until the bird is nicely browned and the juices run clear when you cut between the leg and the body with a pointed knife.

While the duck is cooking, prepare the sauce. Put the almonds on a piece of foil on a baking sheet in the oven and take them out after 5 to 6 minutes when they are lightly browned.

Put the pears in a pan with the wine and simmer uncovered, over a low heat, for 15 to 30 minutes until tender; the time will depend on the type of pears and their degree of ripeness. Watch that they do not fall apart.

In a wide casserole, sauté the onion in the remaining 3 tablespoons of oil over a low heat for about 10 minutes, stirring occasionally, until soft. Add the tomatoes and some salt and the sugar, and cook over a high heat for 8 minutes until the sauce is jammy, stirring every so often. Add the stock, thyme and bay leaf, and pour in the wine from the pears, then simmer for 15 minutes. When the duck is cooked, lift it out of the baking dish and put it aside. Ladle off the fat from the dish and add the remaining juices to the sauce.

Make a *picada* to thicken and add flavour to the sauce: grind the toasted almonds with the garlic cloves into a fine paste with a pestle and mortar or in the food processor, then mix in the brandy. Stir this into the sauce and cook for about 10 minutes. Cut the duck into four pieces and put them in the sauce. Add the pears, heat through and serve.

- ✳ 1 x 2.5kg duck, giblets removed
- ✳ salt
- ✳ 4 tablespoons olive oil
- ✳ 12 blanched almonds
- ✳ 4 small unripe pears, such as Comice or Conference, peeled, halved and cored
- ✳ 500ml dry white wine
- ✳ 1 onion, peeled and finely chopped
- ✳ 2 tomatoes, grated or peeled and chopped
- ✳ 1 teaspoon sugar
- ✳ 300ml chicken stock (you can use 1 stock cube)
- ✳ a sprig of thyme
- ✳ 1 bay leaf
- ✳ 4 garlic cloves, peeled and crushed
- ✳ 3–4 tablespoons brandy or pear brandy

ROAST GUINEA FOWL *with* MARZIPAN *and* DRIED FRUIT STUFFING
❊ *pintada rellena de mazapán y frutos secos*

This medieval dish is still cooked in the houses of the Majorcan nobility. Wild guinea fowl disappeared from the island years ago but they are now farmed. Their flavour is only slightly gamey, less assertive than pheasant or partridge. Guinea fowl have little fat and need barding (covering with pancetta or streaky bacon before roasting) so that the flesh remains juicy. The stuffing given here makes more than will fill the cavities of 4 small guinea fowl or 2 large ones, but because it is so delicious you will want to have extra. Cook the extra stuffing wrapped in foil, or in an oven dish separately (see the variation below).

SERVES 4

❊ 2 x 1–1.25kg large guinea fowl ❊ salt ❊ 2 tablespoons olive oil
❊ 250g pancetta or streaky bacon, in thin slices or rashers ❊ 250ml dry white wine or fino sherry

For the stuffing ❊ 150g soft pitted prunes ❊ 125g soft dried apricots ❊ 100g blanched almonds
❊ 125g caster sugar ❊ 1 teaspoon orange-blossom water (optional) ❊ 1 large egg yolk
❊ 1 tablespoon olive oil or butter, to grease the foil or dish

For the stuffing, boil the prunes and dried apricots in just enough water to cover, over a low heat, for about 20 minutes until they are very soft. Grind the almonds finely with the sugar in the food processor, add the orange-blossom water, if using, and the egg yolk. Blend to a soft paste, adding, if necessary, a few drops of water to bind it. Transfer the paste to a bowl and mix with the drained fruits.

Rub the guinea fowl with salt and oil and fill the body cavity of each one with the stuffing, using a pointed spoon. Wrap the extra stuffing in a greased sheet of foil, or press it in a greased ovenproof dish and cover with foil, and put this in the oven for the last 40 minutes of cooking.

Wrap the pancetta or bacon round the birds and put them, breast side down, in a high-sided oven dish or roasting tin into which they fit snugly. Pour in the wine or sherry, loosely cover with foil and place in an oven preheated to 200°C/gas 6. Cook for 1 hour, then turn the birds over, cover them again with the foil and cook for 15 minutes. (When birds are stuffed, they take much longer to cook than they would normally.) Remove the foil and cook for about 15 minutes more, or until the legs pull away from the body and the juices run clear. Serve with the pan juices, accompanied by the extra stuffing.

VARIATIONS

❊ Put all the stuffing mixture in a small oven dish lightly greased with oil. Press it down firmly and cover with foil. Put it in the oven with the guinea fowl for the last 30 minutes of cooking. As the birds will not be stuffed they may only need about 1 hour of cooking.

❊ Soak the prunes and apricots in brandy instead of boiling them in water.

PHEASANT *with* APPLES
✳ *faisán con manzanas*

When pheasants are hunted wild they are usually no longer young and, while their flavour is richer, they can be quite tough and need slow cooking. Our own pheasants that are available in autumn, or at other times frozen, are farmed. They are young and relatively tender (hen pheasants are the most tender, with more fat) and are good roasted. Asturias is apple country, where they also produce cider and an apple spirit that is like Calvados. Apples cooked with Calvados are sensational but you can use a sweet cider instead.

SERVES 4

✳ 2 young pheasants (approximately 700–750g each) ✳ salt and pepper ✳ 2 tablespoons olive oil ✳ 50g unsalted butter ✳ 5 apples, such as Golden Delicious ✳ 12 slices of pancetta or streaky bacon rashers, rind removed ✳ 125ml Calvados

Pull off any remaining feathers on the pheasants or singe them off over a flame, then rinse the birds inside and out and dry them with kitchen paper. Rub them with salt, pepper and 1 tablespoon of the oil, and put them, breast side up, in a large casserole or oven dish with a lid. Push a small knob of the butter and half a peeled and cored apple in each body cavity and cover the birds entirely with the pancetta slices or bacon.

Peel, core and cut the remaining 4 apples into 8 slices each. Heat the remaining butter and oil in a frying pan, put the apple slices in – in batches if necessary – and cook briefly over a medium to high heat, turning them over once, so that they are lightly browned but not soft. This takes 8 to 10 minutes. Pour in the Calvados and let it bubble for a moment. Arrange the apples around the pheasants in the casserole with their butter and Calvados sauce.

Half-cover the casserole with the lid and put it in an oven preheated to 220°C/gas 7 for 20 minutes. Then take the casserole out, turn the birds over and cook for another 10 minutes or until the birds' legs pull away easily from the bodies and the juices run clear. Cut each pheasant in two down the breastbone and serve accompanied by the apples with the sauce poured over.

VARIATIONS

▩ Use a sweet cider instead of the Calvados.

▩ For *faisán con ciruelas*, instead of apples cooked in Calvados use 500g soft pitted prunes soaked in 250ml brandy for 30 minutes.

▩ In the south of Spain they cook pheasant with grapes. Put 500g white, red or black seedless grapes around the pheasants and pour in 250ml brandy.

PHEASANT *cooked in* PORT
STUFFED *with* DUCK LIVER PÂTÉ
❋ *faisán a la moda de alcántara*

The recipe for this mythical dish appears in the memoirs of Laure Junot, Duchess of Abrantès, which were published in Paris in 1831. According to the duchess, it came from a culinary manuscript her husband, General Jean-Andoche Junot, salvaged when his soldiers sacked the monastery of Alcántara in Extremadura while serving in Napoleon's army during the Peninsular War. The duchess popularized the way of cooking pheasant, woodcock and quail marinated in port wine and stuffed with pâté and truffles, calling it '*à la mode d'Alcántara*'. Auguste Escoffier was to comment later that the manuscript was the only worthwhile French gain from the war. While stuffing game birds with foie gras pâté has long been part of French haute cuisine, especially with quails, Spanish chefs have only recently pulled the style out of their past and developed their own versions. The pheasants are sometimes braised but I prefer this version where they are marinated for 24 hours in port then roasted. I stuffed them with a bought duck liver pâté made with truffles. You can buy cheap port that is good for cooking. In the monastery they would have made the pâté themselves and added truffles to the port during the cooking. It is best to use hen pheasants rather than cocks – they have more fat and are more tender. Serve the dish with mashed potatoes or boiled chestnuts (page 374).

SERVES 4

❋ 2 young pheasants (approximately 750g each) ❋ 350ml port wine ❋ salt ❋ 150g duck liver pâté with truffles ❋ about 10 slices of pancetta or streaky bacon rashers, rind removed

Marinate the pheasants the day before cooking. Pull off any remaining feathers or singe them off over a flame and rinse the birds. Put each one in a separate large plastic bag and pour half the port into each bag. Twist the bags so that they are closed tightly round the birds and leave them in the refrigerator, turning the bags over a few times so as to soak the birds well all over.

Remove the birds from their bags and pour the port into a large baking dish. Season the birds lightly with salt inside and out. Fill the cavity of each with half the liver pâté and truss them – tie the legs together with thread. Cover their bodies entirely with pancetta or streaky bacon (this prevents the flesh from drying out) and place them in the baking dish with the port, breast side up.

Cover the birds loosely with foil and roast in an oven preheated to 200°C/gas 6 for 45 to 60 minutes, or until the legs pull away easily from the body and the juices run clear. Carve the pheasants and serve with the pâté stuffing and the sauce of the port and roasting juices poured over.

PARTRIDGE *in* WHITE WINE
❋ *perdiz a la toledana*

The queen of the Spanish skies is the fast-flying red-legged partridge. She always was the queen. Don Quixote relied on shooting one every week for a meal. When the partridge season opens at the end of summer in Castile, hunters go out in small groups with their entourage – loaders, who look after the guns, and beaters, who thrash the bushes and flush out the birds, shouting, '*Vamos! Vamos!*' In the past, when hunters brought their birds home they were cooked and preserved in a vinegar marinade called *escabeche* so that they could be kept and eaten over several months. These days game butchers are there in the field with their refrigerated vans to buy the birds from the hunt organizers. Partridge is the choice item in restaurants in Toledo during the hunting season. El Bohío in Illescas, on the road between Madrid and Toledo, opened just before the civil war as a modest *mesón* (inn) and became famous for its *perdiz*. The restaurant is still owned by the same family, but now Pepe Rodriguez Rey cooks his sensational modernized versions of the old dishes of La Mancha, while his brother Diego is the maître d'. This way of cooking partridge is one of the classics. Serve it with roast potatoes (page 429) or mashed potatoes.

SERVES 4

Pull off any remaining feathers or singe them off over a flame, then rinse the partridges, dry them with kitchen paper and salt them lightly inside and out. Heat the oil in a wide casserole over a medium heat and turn the birds in it on all sides to brown them all over. Then take them out.

Sauté the onion, carrots and garlic in the same oil over a medium-low heat, uncovered, for about 10 minutes until the onions are soft. Add the wine and water, the bay leaves, thyme, a little salt and the peppercorns. Put the partridges back in and cook, covered, over a low heat for about 40 minutes, turning them over at least once since the sauce does not cover them entirely, until they are very tender and the meat is no longer pink when you pierce the thickest part of the thigh with a pointed knife.

VARIATION

❋ Some people like to blend the sauce to a cream. In the past it would have been pressed with a wooden pestle through a *chino*, a cone-shaped sieve. Now you can use a hand blender straight in the pan, after the birds have been taken out ready for serving.

- ❋ 4 small partridges
- ❋ salt
- ❋ 3 tablespoons olive oil
- ❋ 1 large onion, peeled and chopped
- ❋ 2 large carrots, peeled and thinly sliced
- ❋ 6–7 garlic cloves, peeled and halved
- ❋ 250ml dry white wine
- ❋ 250ml water
- ❋ 3 bay leaves
- ❋ a sprig of thyme
- ❋ 12 black peppercorns

PARTRIDGE *with* GRAPES *and* CHOCOLATE
❖ *perdiz con uvas y chocolate*

When game birds are shot in the wild, they are tough and need braising or stewing. The amount of chocolate in the sauce should be so small that you hardly detect it. It just softens the acidity and lends a mysterious flavour. Do not be tempted to add much more. I overdid the amount once and did not like it at all.

SERVES 4

※ 4 small partridges ※ salt and pepper ※ 4 tablespoons olive oil ※ 1 large onion, peeled, halved and sliced ※ 6 garlic cloves, peeled ※ 1 tablespoon white or red wine vinegar
※ 350ml dry white wine ※ 350ml chicken stock (you may use ½ a stock cube) ※ 2 bay leaves ※ 6 cloves
※ 250g white seedless grapes, destalked ※ 2 teaspoons grated dark chocolate, or to taste
※ 4 slices of dense country-type white bread, crusts removed and fried in olive oil or toasted

Pull off any remaining feathers or singe them off over a flame, then rinse the birds, dry with kitchen paper and season with salt.

In a wide casserole, heat the oil and put in the onion and garlic. Cook over a low heat, stirring often, until they begin to soften. Put in the birds and turn them so that they are lightly browned all over.

Add the vinegar, wine, chicken stock, bay leaves and cloves, and season with salt and pepper. Simmer, covered, over a low heat for 30 minutes, turning the birds over a few times. Add the grapes and the grated chocolate, and cook for 15 to 20 minutes or until the grapes are soft and the birds are done. Remove the lid towards the end to reduce the sauce a little.

Serve the partridges on top of the fried or toasted bread, with the grapes and sauce poured over.

SQUAB *with* RED WINE
✳ *pichón al vino tinto*

Young domesticated pigeons or squabs are an old delicacy of Castile. You see curious old clay-and-straw dovecotes (*palomares*) in wheat fields where the grain was once the readily available feed for thousands of birds. At one time pigeon-rearing was a main agricultural activity and the meat was often pickled or preserved in fat. A squab is a bird killed when it is one month old, before it has flown. There is little meat on a squab – most of it is on the breast – but the dark red meat is very tender and moist because there is young fat under the skin. The flavour is fine and delicate, quite different from the tough, gamey flesh of wild wood pigeons (*palomas torcaces*). It is fashionable nowadays to roast or grill squab and to eat the meat rare or medium-rare, but the traditional way of braising them in a red wine and brandy sauce suits their delicate meat very well. In London, I buy them as *pigeonneaux* from France. Serve the squabs with large slices of fried or toasted bread. Sautéed mushrooms make a good accompaniment.

SERVES 4

✳ 4 squabs, each weighing about 350g ✳ 4 garlic cloves, peeled ✳ 60g butter
✳ 2 tablespoons olive oil ✳ salt and pepper ✳ 1 medium onion, peeled and chopped
✳ 1 leek, trimmed and chopped ✳ 1 carrot, peeled and chopped ✳ 500ml red wine
✳ 100ml brandy ✳ 2 bay leaves ✳ a sprig of thyme ✳ 200ml chicken stock (you may use ½ a stock cube)

Pull off any remaining feathers or singe them off over a flame and rinse the squabs, then put a clove of garlic and a small knob of butter inside each one. In a wide casserole or pan, heat the remaining butter with the oil and brown the birds on all sides, over a medium-low heat, sprinkling them with salt and pepper, then take them out.

Put the onion, leek and carrot in the casserole and sauté gently over a low heat, stirring occasionally, until they are soft and just beginning to colour. Add the wine and brandy, and the herbs, and cook for 15 minutes, then add the stock, season with salt and pepper and put the birds back into the pan. Cook, covered, over a low heat, turning the squabs a few times, for 30 to 40 minutes or until they are well cooked. To test if they are done, pull one of the legs – it should move away easily from the body.

It is usual to take the birds out, and the herbs, and blend the sauce to a cream with a hand blender, but the dish is equally good served as it is.

VARIATIONS

✳ Sauté 100g chopped *jamón serrano* or 1 Golden Delicious apple (peeled, cored and diced) with the chopped vegetables. The apple will add a little sweetness.

✳ A Catalan way to cook squab is to stir 25g grated dark chocolate into the sauce at the end.

✳ Sauté 100g chopped *jamón serrano* with the vegetables.

jesús santos and the *becada*

Jesús Santos was one of the young chefs who pioneered the new Basque haute cuisine. He opened his first restaurant, Goizeko Kabi, in Bilbao in 1982 and now has five Goizeko restaurants across Spain and a catering school. I was taken to his restaurant in the Wellington Hotel in Madrid by Gaspar Rey, editor of the magazine *Cocina Futuro*. It is one of the best and most elegant restaurants in the city, serving exquisite, innovative dishes. During the game season King Juan Carlos and Queen Sophia and the local aristocracy can often be seen there.

When we were there, it was the game season and Jesús had hurt his leg while out shooting, but he was still hobbling round the tables. He stopped to sit with us from time to time to talk about each dish on his tasting menu and the cooking methods (steam, *sous vide*, and so on) now used in modern establishments. We ate crab and all manner of seafood, an exquisite aubergine dish, suckling pig, duck and an absolutely heavenly *becada* (woodcock). The favourite item on the menu is always woodcock, a bird with a strong, gamey taste.

Jesús told us that he was from a peasant family of Palencia, a mountain province of Castile and Leon, and had gone at a young age with his brother to work in the Basque Country where wealthy families employed cooks. As we left, I asked Jesús if he was inspired particularly by the local Castilian gastronomy. 'Yes,' he said, 'Castilian cooking was influenced by Arab and Jewish traditions and I am a Converso.' I told him that when I first heard his name I had guessed he was a Converso because Santos was the name many Jews who fled to Portugal took on when they were forced to convert to Christianity there. Here is the story of the Jews of Palencia that I discovered when I got home. By the fifteenth century, the community was so large that there were two Jewish quarters and Jewish families had spilled out into different parts of the city. After 1492, those who had not converted moved to Portugal where, five years later, they were forced to convert. At the beginning of the seventeenth century many of their descendants found their way back to Spain as Christians.

ROAST WOODCOCK *with* BRANDY
❊ *becada asada al brandy*

The elusive (and expensive) *becada* is considered the most desirable of game birds, succulent, with the most fat and a wonderful gamey flavour. Woodcock is a migratory bird that winters in the mountain woodlands of northern Spain, where it is stalked by hunters who love the challenge of shooting it. When the bird is apprehended, it bursts out of the grass and soars upward almost vertically before racing to safety in a high, swirling flight pattern. It looks haughty with its very long beak and is always cooked with the head and beak left on, except at times when shooting is forbidden and then it appears illicitly in restaurants, unrecognizable, with the beak cut off. It is cooked undrawn, that is with the liver and entrails still inside, like berry-eating songbirds, so that its full flavour can best be appreciated. The bird's trail, or intestines, are choice parts. Buy the birds with the heads left on and the eyes removed.

I asked Basque restaurateur Jesús Santos for several recipes, which his assistant Martine Beaulieu Gracia got for me from the chef. The recipe for his *becada* dish came with step-by-step photographs showing how he prepares it. I tried to cook it but it was incredibly complex with too many ingredients and too many steps. Here, instead, is a simple, traditional way of preparing woodcock that hunters and gourmets alike eulogize about. The birds are roasted and a sauce of caramelized onions is made separately and poured over. Quail is also cooked in this way. For instructions on roasting quail, see the recipe variation at the end. Woodcock are at their best from October to December, but they can also be bought frozen at other times.

》》》

⁎ 1½ large onions, peeled and finely chopped ⁎ 4 tablespoons olive oil, plus
more to oil the baking dish ⁎ 175ml brandy, or to taste ⁎ 4 woodcock
⁎ salt and pepper ⁎ 8 slices of pancetta or streaky bacon rashers, rind removed
⁎ 4 large slices of firm white bread, crusts removed, fried in oil or toasted

Make the sauce first. Sauté the onions in 2 tablespoons of the oil, over a low heat, in a large frying pan or casserole with the lid on, stirring occasionally, for about 30 minutes until very soft. Then cook uncovered over a medium-high heat, stirring often, for another 15 minutes until golden brown and caramelized. Warm the brandy in a small pan, set the vapours alight with a long match and pour it over the onions.

To prepare the woodcock, pull off any remaining feathers or singe them off over a flame, then rinse the birds, dry with kitchen paper and rub each one with salt, pepper and the remaining 2 tablespoons of oil. Cover each bird with 2 slices of pancetta or bacon. Truss the birds by tying their legs together and turn their heads round so that the beaks lie between the legs. Arrange them in an oiled baking dish and place in an oven preheated to 220°C/gas 7 for 10 to 15 minutes, depending on their size, or until tender and done to your taste. Cut into the thickest part of a thigh – the flesh should be pink and juicy. Chefs these days like their *becadas* almost rare. One told me he turns off the oven after 5 minutes and leaves the birds in for another 5 minutes.

When the woodcock are cooked, spoon out the innards, discard the gizzards, chop up the intestines and the livers and add them with the drippings to the onion sauce and heat through. Serve each woodcock on a piece of fried or toasted bread with the sauce poured over.

VARIATIONS

⁑ Place a slice of *mousse de foie* or duck liver pâté on the toast.

⁑ A suggestion from food writer Pepe Iglesias is to accompany the woodcock with chestnuts boiled in milk and sautéed in butter – then mashed or left whole – instead of serving them on toast.

⁑ To prepare quail in the same way, cover each bird with 2 rashers of streaky bacon and roast in an oven preheated to 220°C/gas 7 for 15 to 20 minutes. They must not be rare, only slightly pink. The innards do not go into the sauce.

QUAIL *with* CARAMELIZED ONIONS *and* BRANDY
❋ *codorniz al brandy*

In his book *Homage to Catalonia*, written in 1937, George Orwell described the way peasants spread out nets over the grass at night and lay down making noises like female quails. When male quails came running they got entangled in the nets. Although European Union rules have made it illegal, it is a Mediterranean custom to catch migrating birds that fly over the sea in big nets. In Cyprus, where hunting is a large-scale activity, endless tapes of birdsong are played to lure birds into nets. I wonder if this has caught on in Spain? Anyway, most of the quails you find now in Spain are farmed, as in Britain.

The onions take a long time to caramelize, and are delicious with added brandy. Serve the quails on fried or toasted sliced bread that will soak up the sauce.

You will need to pick up the birds with your fingers when you eat, so provide finger bowls.

SERVES 2 AS A MAIN COURSE, 4 AS A STARTER

* 4 quails
* 5 tablespoons olive oil
* 2 large onions, peeled, halved and sliced
* salt and pepper
* 125ml brandy, or to taste
* 4 large slices of firm white bread, crusts removed, fried in oil or toasted

Pull off any remaining feathers or singe them off over a flame, then rinse the quails and pat them dry with kitchen paper. Heat the oil in a wide, heavy frying pan or casserole and put in the onions. Cover and cook slowly over a very low heat for about 30 minutes until they are very soft and beginning to colour, stirring often.

Push the onions to one side, put the quails into the pan and season with salt and pepper. Turn up the heat to medium. Keep turning the quails to brown them all over – around 7 or 8 minutes – and stir the onions so that they brown evenly. Add the brandy and cook, covered, over a low heat for 25 to 30 minutes until the onions are caramelized and the quails are done. Pull the leg of one of the quails – if it moves easily they are cooked. They should still be a little pink. Serve them on toasted or fried sliced bread.

QUAIL *with* GRAPES
✴ *codorniz a las uvas*

In some Spanish recipes for quail with grapes, the birds are cooked in grape juice rather than wine – the juice is obtained by mashing grapes in the blender and pressing the juice out through a strainer or colander with small holes. In others, the grapes are caramelized in a sugar syrup that is allowed to brown. I particularly like this old Galician recipe, adapted from one sent to me by Pepe Iglesias. It was once cooked with pork fat but now butter is used in this part of Spain (being dairy country), and adding cream gives a luscious sauce. Albariño grapes would be used in Galicia but you can use any flavoursome white seedless grapes. You will need to pick up the birds with your fingers when you eat, so provide finger bowls for your guests as well as paper napkins.

SERVES 2 AS A MAIN COURSE, 4 AS A STARTER

※ 4 quails ※ 60g butter ※ 3 tablespoons olive oil ※ 500g white seedless grapes, destalked
※ 150ml dry white wine ※ 125ml double cream ※ salt and pepper

Pull off any remaining feathers or singe them off over a flame, then rinse the quails and pat them dry with kitchen paper. Heat the butter and oil in a large frying pan. Put in the quails and sauté them briskly over a medium heat for about 8 minutes, turning them in the pan, until lightly browned all over. Put in the grapes, add the wine and the cream and season with salt and pepper.

Bring to the boil and simmer, covered, over a low heat for 15 minutes or until the grapes are soft and the birds are done, turning them so that all parts bathe some of the time in the sauce. To test if the birds are done, cut between the leg and the body of one with a pointed knife – the flesh should still be slightly pink.

VARIATION

✽ For a version from Mediterranean Spain, use Moscatel grapes and a 150ml half-and-half mix of sweet Moscatel wine and chicken stock. Do not add cream.

GRILLED QUAIL
❋ *codorniz a la plancha*

A good way to cook quails is grilled over embers or on a griddle (*a la plancha*). Ask the butcher to spatchcock them, or do it yourself as described below. Serve with garlic mayonnaise or *alioli* (page 149) and remember to provide fingerbowls for your guests.

SERVES 2 AS A MAIN COURSE, 4 AS A STARTER

❋ 4 quails ❋ 1–2 garlic cloves, peeled and crushed ❋ juice of ½ a lemon
❋ 3 tablespoons olive oil, plus more to oil the grill or griddle ❋ salt

Pull off any remaining feathers or singe them off over a flame, then rinse the quails. Lay the birds breast side down and cut them with poultry shears or kitchen scissors along both sides of the backbone, starting from the quail's bottom all the way up to the neck. Now remove the backbone, open each of them out like a book, make a small slit in the skin to release the legs, turn over the birds and press down hard with the palm of your hand along the breastbone until they lie flat. Mix the garlic, lemon juice and olive oil in a large dish, rub the quails with this marinade and leave them in the dish to marinate for 30 minutes to 1 hour in the refrigerator, covered with cling film. Turn them over in the marinade at least once.

Oil the grill or griddle, lay the quails on it skin side up, and cook for 7 minutes over a medium-high heat. Turn over and cook for another 5 minutes, then check they are done by inserting a sharp pointed knife into the bird's thigh. If the juices run clear, the quails are ready. Season with salt and eat with your fingers.

BRAISED RABBIT *with* HERBS *and* WHITE WINE
✳ *conejo al vino*

Mercedes Garcia, who lives in the Andalusian village of Frailes, gave me a wire rabbit trap, one that her father had made for a living. Rabbit was a staple food of the rural population in all of Spain. It was also used as currency to pay the doctor. In the Catalan recipe collection the *Corpus de la Cuina Catalana* (see page 367), I found what seemed like dozens of Catalan ways and variants of cooking rabbit – grilled, roasted, braised; with onions, tomatoes, mushrooms, peppers, snails, prawns, chocolate, whole heads of garlic, olives, prunes, pine nuts; and with vinegar and sugar, red wine or white wine … and the list goes on. I found this Catalan recipe written by hand in Spanish but I cannot remember who it was from.

SERVES 4–6

Ask the butcher to cut the rabbit into six pieces. If you are doing it yourself, trim and discard the flaps of skin and the tips of the forelegs. Using a heavy knife or cleaver, divide the rabbit crossways into three parts: back legs, back and rib cage, and forelegs. Cut between the back legs to separate them and chop the front of the rabbit into two to separate the forelegs. Cut the back crossways also into two, giving six pieces.

Heat the oil in a large casserole, put in the onion and garlic and sauté over a low heat, uncovered, stirring occasionally, until the onion and garlic are soft. Put in the rabbit pieces, season with salt, and continue to cook over a low heat, turning each piece to brown them slightly all over, and until the onions begin to colour.

Add the white wine or sherry, the thyme or oregano and the bay leaves, peppercorns and a little sugar. Bring to the boil and simmer, covered, for about 25 to 35 minutes, turning the rabbit pieces over to cook in the wine on both sides. The rabbit is done when it feels tender when you cut into a thigh with a pointed knife. Uncover the pan for the last 10 minutes of cooking. Do not overcook it or the rabbit will be stringy. The sauce should be reduced and a little syrupy.

✳ 1 x 1–1.25 kg rabbit, cut into 6 pieces

✳ 5 tablespoons olive oil

✳ 1 large onion, peeled and roughly chopped

✳ cloves of 1 garlic head, peeled

✳ salt

✳ 500ml dry white wine or dry sherry

✳ 3 sprigs of thyme or oregano

✳ 2 bay leaves

✳ 8 black peppercorns

✳ 1–2 teaspoons sugar

MEAT DISHES

carnes

The Castilian adage '*Vaca y carnero, olla de caballero*' ('Cow and ram, gentle-man's stew') is a reminder that meat was, for centuries, the food of the nobility. There was a time when most of the population in Spain only ever ate fresh meat at festivals, weddings and funerals, and their everyday meat normally consisted of tiny bits of home-cured ham or *chorizo* added to stews. But today Spain is a country of carnivores.

Lamb is the most common meat eaten in Spain. In the Middle Ages it was the meat of the Muslims and Jews, who could not eat pork, and of the Spanish nobility, who bred sheep for their wool. Pork is ubiquitous in so many dishes in its cured forms, but is still rarely eaten fresh, except in the areas where pig-rearing is an industry, as in parts of Andalusia and Extremadura. In the past, cattle were bred for dairy. The male calves were slaughtered young to be eaten as veal, or were castrated for work in the fields, while fighting bulls were bred for the bullring. Veal was saved for feast days or eaten by the rich. Spanish veal (*ternera*) is not the pale pink veal of milk-fed calves; it is the darker meat of animals that have been slaughtered when they are between nine and twelve months old. Spaniards love their meats very young. The highest points of Spanish gastronomy are roast suckling pig, baby lamb and baby kid cooked in a bread oven.

Beef was hardly ever eaten until a couple of decades ago. The change came about when agriculture was mechanized and the oxen, or *buey* – castrated males who pulled the plough, some as much as twenty years old – were made redundant. Then it was discovered that their muscle, when it was no longer working, turned to fat and that their mature, dark, intricately marbled meat, if well hung, had a magnificent rich taste and silky tenderness. Now that Spain has run out of the old plough oxen and that it is hard to sell milk because of the European Union milk lakes, farmers have turned to rearing indigenous breeds of cattle for beef, which had been neglected in favour of better milk producers in Franco's time. The meat from these mature cows that are fattened for several months before slaughter is of a very high quality.

In the past, offal – tripe, heads, brains, ears, tongues, feet, tails – was not appreciated by the social elites. They ate it only on days of abstinence when eating meat was forbidden by the Church, because offal was not considered 'meat'. The working-class poor got offal cheap from the slaughter houses and specialist butchers. Nowadays offal dishes are much-loved regional specialities.

LAMB STEW *with* HONEY
✳ *cordero a la miel*

This is an old Moorish way of cooking lamb with honey that has been rediscovered by modern chefs in Andalusia. The stew has just a touch of honey in the sauce and a pinch of hot pepper to mitigate the sweetness. The meat should become so tender that it falls apart.

SERVES 5–6

Heat the oil in a wide, heavy-bottomed casserole over a medium heat. Put in the shallots and brown them all over, turning them and shaking the pan frequently. Take them out with a slotted spoon, put in the lamb and turn the pieces to brown them all over. You may have to do that in batches.

Add some salt, the wine and the brandy, the *pimentón*, paprika or cayenne pepper and the honey. Stir well and cook, uncovered, for 10 minutes. Return the shallots to the pan, on top of the meat, and cover with water. Bring to the boil and simmer, covered, for 1½ to 2¼ hours or until the meat is very tender, turning it over a few times and adding water if necessary to keep it covered. Turn the heat up and cook with the lid off to reduce the sauce towards the end.

VARIATION

Some people add a little more honey and a tablespoon of wine vinegar along with the wine, for a sweet-and-sour taste.

- ✳ 3 tablespoons olive or sunflower oil
- ✳ 500g shallots, peeled
- ✳ 1kg lamb shoulder, trimmed of some fat and cut into 5 or 6 large pieces
- ✳ salt
- ✳ 250ml dry white wine
- ✳ 3 tablespoons brandy
- ✳ a pinch of *pimentón picante*, hot paprika or cayenne pepper
- ✳ 1½ tablespoons orange-blossom honey or other runny honey

tiny GRILLED LAMB CUTLETS *with* POTATOES
❋ *chuletitas de cordero a la parilla con patatas*

The nearest thing we have to the tiny, ever-so-tender chops of very young lamb you get in Spain are the small cutlets from a rack of lamb. Serve them on a bed of sautéed potatoes with onions. Prepare the potatoes first as they can be reheated before serving. This dish is wonderful as it is, with no adornments, but look at some of the dressings in the recipe variations below or the *aliolis* (pages 149–50), which you might like to try.

SERVES 2

❋ a rack of lamb (about 6–7 cutlets) ❋ 1 tablespoon olive oil ❋ salt and pepper

For the potatoes ❋ 1 large onion, peeled, halved and sliced ❋ 4 tablespoons olive oil ❋ 500g waxy potatoes, peeled and cut into slices about 7mm thick ❋ salt and pepper ❋ 125ml chicken stock

Cook the potatoes first. Fry the onion in the oil in a large frying pan, covered with a lid, over a low heat and stirring occasionally, until soft. Then add the potatoes and sauté over a low heat, stirring and turning them over with a spatula, until both the potatoes and onion are lightly golden – about 10 minutes. Add some salt and pepper as they cook. Pour in the chicken stock and simmer, covered, for about 15 minutes until it is absorbed and the potatoes are tender.

Cut the rack of lamb into cutlets with a heavy knife or cleaver. Brush them all over with olive oil. Heat an oiled *plancha* (flat griddle) or heavy frying pan and cook the cutlets briefly over a high heat for 2 to 3 minutes on each side until they are brown on the outside but still very pink and juicy inside. Do not overcook them. Cut into one to check whether it is cooked – the cutlets are best eaten medium-rare. Season with salt and pepper and serve hot, beside or on top of the potatoes.

VARIATIONS

❋ To make a garlic and vinegar dressing, stir 2 tablespoons of extra virgin olive oil and 2–3 peeled and crushed garlic cloves in a small pan over a low heat for seconds only until the aroma rises. Do not let the garlic brown. Off the heat add 1 tablespoon of wine vinegar and a ¼ teaspoon of sugar and mix well. When serving, dribble a little of the dressing over each cutlet.

❋ Sprinkle the cutlets with plenty of garlic slices fried in olive oil until golden and crunchy.

LAMB STEW *with* MILK
'SHEPHERDS' *style*'
❊ *cordero a la pastora*

In *Don Quixote*, Cervantes tells of Andrés, a fifteen-year-old boy who looks after the sheep of one Juan Haldudo '*el rico*' (the rich man). His master beats him and withholds wages because, as he explains to Don Quixote, sheep keep going missing and he is certain that the boy either sold or ate them. Don Quixote believes Andrés is innocent and interferes on his behalf, only to make matters worse. Shepherds did eat lamb when they spent months away from home with their flocks. They would have had ewes' milk in which to cook the meat. But would they have had any wine, as in this recipe? Perhaps they exchanged cheese for some. I cooked this dish with lamb neck fillet. It became extra tender, and the wine, milk and herbs gave the potatoes a delicious flavour.

SERVES 4–6

❊ 3 tablespoons olive oil ❊ 750g lamb, such as neck fillet, cut into large pieces (about 6–7cm long) ❊ 4 garlic cloves, peeled and chopped ❊ 250ml dry white wine ❊ 7 cloves ❊ 2 sprigs of thyme ❊ 2 bay leaves ❊ 500g medium new potatoes, peeled and halved ❊ salt and pepper ❊ 1 teaspoon sugar (optional) ❊ 250ml whole milk

Heat the oil in a wide casserole. Put in the lamb pieces and brown lightly on all sides over a high heat. Lower the heat, stir in the garlic and let it just begin to colour.

Add the wine, cloves, thyme and bay leaves. Bring to the boil, then put in the potatoes and season with salt and pepper. Simmer, covered, over a gentle heat for about 1¼ hours until the meat is tender and the liquid has been absorbed. Add a little sugar if the dryness of the wine needs softening.

Stir in the milk, add more salt if necessary, and cook for 5 minutes to heat through.

MARINATED LEG *of* LAMB
❧ *cordero en adobo de guadalajara*

Cookery writer and teacher Rosa Tovar sent me this recipe, which is good for wild goat, venison and wild boar as well as for pork, mutton and lamb. This dish was, she says, made by both hunters and shepherds. It is originally from Alcarria in the province of Guadalajara, but versions of it are eaten in small towns and villages in central Spain all the way down to Andalusia. Alcarria, an area of river valleys and mountains which abounds with flowers on which bees feed, produces a famous honey, *miel de La Alcarria*. The best saffron in the country is also produced in Castile-La Mancha. The extraordinary variety of aromatics gives the meat a delicious flavour. You must start making this dish the day before, because it needs to marinate for 24 hours. Ask the butcher to cut the end of the leg bone so that you can bend it to fit more easily into a large pan or casserole.

SERVES 6

Put all the marinade ingredients in a saucepan, bring them to the boil and simmer for 25 to 30 minutes, then let cool.

Trim any excess fat from the leg of lamb, then put it in a large plastic bag and pour in the marinade. Twist the bag so that it closes tightly around the joint and leave it in the refrigerator for 24 hours, turning the bag a few times so as to soak the meat well all over.

Take out the lamb, dry it with kitchen paper, and season with salt and pepper.

Heat the oil in a large saucepan or casserole. Put in the leg of lamb and turn to brown the meat on all sides over a medium heat. Pour the honey into the bottom of the pan and let it brown a little. Then stir in the vinegar and saffron. Strain the marinade into the pan so that the meat is a little less than half covered with liquid. Bring to the boil and simmer, covered, over a low heat for about 2½ hours or until the meat is very tender, turning it every 20 minutes or so and adding a little water if it becomes too dry. There should be a good amount of sauce left at the end.

- ❋ 1 leg of lamb (about 1.75kg)
- ❋ salt and pepper
- ❋ 2–3 tablespoons olive oil
- ❋ 1 tablespoon runny honey
- ❋ 2 tablespoons white wine vinegar
- ❋ a good pinch of saffron threads

For the marinade

- ❋ 2 tablespoons olive oil
- ❋ 1 onion, peeled and halved
- ❋ cloves of 1 garlic head, peeled
- ❋ 6 black peppercorns
- ❋ 3 cloves
- ❋ 1 cinnamon stick
- ❋ a sprig of fresh thyme
- ❋ 2 bay leaves
- ❋ 2 tablespoons runny honey
- ❋ 100ml white or red wine vinegar
- ❋ 250ml dry white wine

BRAISED LAMB SHANKS *with* POTATOES
✻ *jarrete de cordero con patatas*

These slow-cooked lamb shanks have a marvellous melt-in-the-mouth quality and the wine sauce is enriched by the jelly they produce. They go well with crunchy deep-fried potatoes or the roast potatoes given below, and also with mashed potatoes.

SERVES 4

✻ 4 x 500g small lamb shanks ✻ 3 tablespoons mild olive oil ✻ 1 large onion, peeled and finely chopped
✻ 2 carrots, peeled and sliced ✻ 5 garlic cloves, peeled and finely chopped
✻ 4 tomatoes, peeled and finely chopped ✻ 500ml dry white wine ✻ 4 tablespoons brandy (optional)
✻ 500ml water ✻ salt and pepper ✻ 1 teaspoon sugar

For the potatoes ✻ 750g new potatoes ✻ salt ✻ olive oil

In a large, wide casserole or saucepan, fry the lamb shanks in the oil in batches, over a medium heat, turning to brown them all over. Then remove from the pan. In the same oil cook the onion and carrots over a medium heat until the onion is soft, stirring often. Add the garlic and cook, stirring, until the aroma rises then add the tomatoes.

Cook for about 8 minutes, then put the shanks back into the pan and pour in the wine, brandy, if using, and water. Season with salt, pepper and sugar and cook, covered, over a low heat so that the liquid barely simmers, for 2 hours or until the meat is so tender you can pull it off the bone. Turn the shanks over three or four times and add a little more water to keep them half covered. Let the sauce reduce towards the end. I like to leave the sauce as it is. But if you wish, lift out the lamb shanks, blend the sauce to a cream with a hand blender, as they now do in Spain, and return the shanks to the dish.

For the potatoes, boil them in salted water until barely tender. Drain and cut them in half or into quarters. Place them in a roasting pan or baking dish, sprinkle with salt and pour on a good amount of olive oil to coat them all over. Roast in an oven preheated to 220°C/gas 7 for 30 to 40 minutes, or until crisp and golden.

Serve the lamb with the potatoes.

ROAST SUCKLING PIG
❖ *cochinillo asado*

Cochinillo, or *tostón*, is the most exquisite and aristocratic of foods. A newborn pig, between fifteen and twenty days old and weighing about 4½kg, should be roasted slowly to such melting tenderness that it can be cut with the edge of a plate – which is what happens, dramatically, on festive occasions. Within the triangle delimited by the cities of Segovia, Arévalo and Peñaranda de Bracamonte, reputedly the finest roast suckling pigs are cooked. I ate a fabulous *cochinillo* at the Maracaibo – the best restaurant for miles around – in the hilltop city of Segovia. The Romans built a great aqueduct and the Moors an *alcázar* (fortress) there, and the city is full of Romanesque churches and mansions.

In the past, people brought their little pigs in a clay dish to be roasted in the communal wood-burning baker's oven. At the Maracaibo, as in most grand restaurants today, they are cooked *sous vide* (under vacuum, in an airtight plastic bag placed in not quite boiling water), but I asked for the recipe for the traditional way of cooking suckling pig in a domestic oven. These are the instructions for cooking a 4.5kg suckling pig as sent to me by Oscar Hernando, the owner, head of cooking and sommelier at the Maracaibo.

Ask the butcher to cut the cleaned suckling pig through the belly from top to bottom but to leave the head intact. Salt it on the inside only and lay the pig opened out flat on a rack in a roasting pan, skin side up. Wrap the ears in foil to protect them from burning. Pour 500ml of water into the roasting pan to create steam in the oven and put the pig in an oven preheated to 180°C/gas 4 for 15 minutes. Reduce the heat to 130°C/gas 1 and cook for 2 hours, then increase the heat to 180°C/gas 4 again and cook for a further 15 minutes, or until the skin is crisp and golden. Let it rest for a few minutes and then cut into thick slices.

pigs' ears and feet ❖ *orejas y manos de cerdo*

I have tried a few recipes for pigs' ears and feet. The ears (orejas), cut into little squares and stewed in white wine with a touch of cinnamon, were gelatinous and crunchy. The feet (*manos* – Spaniards call them 'hands'), cooked in fortified wine and a tiny bit of chocolate, were gelatinous and rich in flavour. Both dishes were delicious, but I will not make them again. The offal was difficult to buy, especially ears. Butchers don't sell them. And both ears and feet take too long to prepare before you even begin to cook them. You have to singe off any remaining hairs, then scrub them and blanch them and rinse them in cold water. You then boil them for 3 hours. I cut up the ears and removed the bones from the feet. Most of my guests left much of the tasting portions I offered them on their plates. Pigs' ears and feet are much-loved delicacies in Spain, but these days people eat them when out at a restaurant and hardly ever cook them at home.

ROAST BELLY *of* PORK *with* BAKED APPLES
✤ *panza de cerdo con manzanas*

The crisp crackling and layers of fat in this roast keep the meat meltingly succulent as it cooks. Make sure that the butcher has removed the ribs and that he has scored the skin (or rind) with deep cuts that go right down to the fat. In Asturias, they serve pork with apple purée or whole roasted apples. I was told that Golden Delicious are a good substitute for their local Reineta variety of apple (see page 465). They also serve this dish with mashed potatoes or the chestnut purée in this recipe.

SERVES 6–8

✲ ½ a belly of pork with skin (about 2kg), scored ✲ 2 tablespoons olive oil
✲ salt ✲ 8 Golden Delicious apples ✲ 250ml dry cider

For the optional chestnut purée ✲ 500g chestnuts, fresh peeled, frozen and defrosted or vacuum-packed ✲ about 300ml whole milk, or more (enough to cover the chestnuts) ✲ salt ✲ 35g butter

Put the belly of pork in a roasting pan brushed with 1 tablespoon of the oil or, better still, put it on a rack in the pan. Sprinkle generously with salt, rubbing it into the cuts in the skin. Then wipe the excess salt off the skin with kitchen paper and rub the skin and the flesh side with the remaining tablespoon of the oil. Turn the pork belly skin side up.

Put the pan in an oven preheated to 220°C/gas 7 for 30 minutes until the pork skin has started to puff up, then reduce the heat to 190°C/gas 5 and cook for about 1¾ hours to 2 hours, until the crackling is crisp and brown. Cover with foil and let the meat rest for 15 minutes before cutting it into thick slices.

Meanwhile, put the apples in a baking dish or pan that holds them snugly. Pour in the cider and place the dish in the oven below the roast, after you have lowered the heat. Take the apples out when they are tender when pierced with a knife (the time depends on their size and degree of ripeness). Watch them after about 40 minutes of cooking so that they do not fall apart. Put them back in the oven at the end to heat through.

For the optional chestnut purée, boil the chestnuts over a low heat in enough milk to cover them, in a pan with the lid on, until they are soft. Drain them, reserving the milk, and add salt and butter. Mash the chestnuts with a potato masher or, for a smoother purée, blend them in the food processor, adding as much of the reserved milk as you need to have a soft consistency.

VARIATION
▩ In Andalusia, they rub 1 teaspoon of cumin seeds on the pork skin along with the salt.

PORK LOIN *cooked in* MILK *with* CARAMEL
✳ *lomo de cerdo con leche y caramelo*

I had once eaten pork cooked in milk in Venice but the idea of also adding caramel seemed strange, so the beautiful flavour of this dish was a delightful surprise. For a Spanish version of the dish without caramel, simply omit the caramel step at the end. The milk sauce will curdle but that is how it is meant to be. It is good both hot and cold. You can use 2 or 3 fillets of pork instead of the loin. Serve the dish with mushrooms, sliced and sautéed in a mix of olive oil and butter.

SERVES 6

✳ 3 tablespoons butter ✳ 1 tablespoon olive oil ✳ 1 loin of pork, boned and skinned (about 1kg) ✳ 1.5 litres whole milk, heated ✳ peel of 1 lemon or orange, removed in one or more strips with a small knife ✳ 2 cinnamon sticks ✳ 6 black peppercorns ✳ salt ✳ 6 tablespoons sugar ✳ 4 tablespoons water

Heat the butter and oil in a large casserole or pan and brown the pork on all sides over a medium heat. Pour in the warmed milk to almost cover it. Add the lemon or orange peel, cinnamon sticks, peppercorns and a little salt. Bring to the boil – watch it because the milk can boil over very suddenly – put the lid on slightly ajar, and leave to barely simmer for about 1 to 1½ hours, until the meat is very tender, turning it so that it cooks evenly. The milk will gradually curdle. Remove the meat and discard the peel and the cinnamon sticks.

To make the caramel, heat the sugar in a small pan with the water over a low heat. As the syrup begins to colour, swirl the pan continuously so that the syrup browns evenly, until it bubbles and turns a deep golden brown and the smell of caramel fills the kitchen. Remove from the heat and pour in a ladleful of the hot milk. Be very careful not to burn yourself as it spits. The caramel will harden slightly. Return the pan to the heat and stir until the caramel has melted and dissolved, adding a little more of the milk if necessary. Pour this milky caramel into the casserole, stir well and cook for 10 minutes over a low heat to reduce the sauce. It will be a brown coagulated mass, which is as it should be, but if you like you can blend it to a smooth cream using a hand blender or the food processor. Remove the peppercorns with the meat before blending.

Return the meat to the pan, adjust the seasoning and reheat when you are ready to serve. Cut the pork into slices and pour the sauce on top.

WILD BOAR STEW *with* RED WINE
❈ *estofado de jabalí al vino tinto*

Wild boar is common in many parts of Spain, where it runs free in the countryside. I have found recipes from various regions. Most include onions, carrots, garlic and leeks, some also celery or tomatoes. They are all flavoured with herbs like bay leaves, thyme, rosemary and sage. Sometimes port is added, sometimes a spirit such as Calvados. Some of the most sophisticated recipes with wine and spirits originated in the old monasteries. A lot of game is eaten in Extremadura; every village has its own wild boar recipe.

When I went to buy wild boar at Borough Market in London, the young butcher who served me said, 'Use shoulder because it has some fat – otherwise the meat gets stringy after you cook it for 2½ hours.' He removed the thick outer layer of fat and cut the meat up into large pieces. Serve the stew with slices of good bread to soak up the sauce, or with mashed or boiled potatoes.

SERVES 6

❈ 3–4 tablespoons olive oil ❈ 1kg wild boar from the shoulder (excess fat removed), cut into large pieces about 7–8cm long ❈ 2 large carrots, peeled and diced ❈ 1 large onion, peeled and chopped ❈ cloves of 1 garlic head, peeled ❈ 500ml red wine ❈ 2–3 bay leaves ❈ 2 sprigs of thyme ❈ 1 teaspoon ground cinnamon ❈ salt and pepper

In a large, wide casserole, heat the oil over a medium heat and brown the meat lightly all over, then remove the pieces. Do this in a few batches. Put in the carrots, onion and garlic cloves and sauté, stirring, until they are soft and just beginning to colour. Return the meat to the casserole. Pour in the wine and add just enough water to cover the meat. Add the bay leaves, thyme, cinnamon, salt and pepper. Simmer, covered, for about 2½ hours, until the meat is extremely tender, adding water to keep the meat covered and turning the pieces over.

VARIATIONS

❈ Add 2–3 tablespoons of wine vinegar with the wine.

❈ At the end of cooking, remove the meat and blend the sauce to a cream, then return the meat to the casserole.

❈ For a Catalan version, omit the carrots and add 2 peeled and chopped tomatoes to the onions and garlic. Add about 4 tablespoons of brandy or port and about 3 tablespoons of grated dark chocolate towards the end.

❈ Add 80ml of Calvados 20 to 30 minutes before the end of cooking.

❈ Pepe Iglesias serves this dish with chestnuts boiled in milk and drained and with whole roasted Reineta apples (you can use Golden Delicious), or with a purée of apples or pears.

josé maría conde de ybarra
an andalusian gourmet

I had heard a lot about peasant lives and peasant cooking from people whose parents or they themselves had been subsistence farmers or landless labourers. I also wanted to hear what the Spanish landowning elites had to say about food. I was going to Seville so my friend and mentor Alicia Rios suggested I phone Marina Domecq, a member of the famous sherry family. Marina gave me her cousin José María Count Ybarra's telephone number. She said that he was the ultimate gourmet and gastronome. We met at the Hotel Alfonso XIII in the centre of the city. I recognized the *bon vivant*, a large man with a beautiful smiling face.

Count Ybarra lives in the prestigious residential development of Sotogrande in Cadiz with his wife and young son and has a home in Seville and a converted oil mill on their country estate. The Ybarra family company produces and exports all manner of products, from olives and olive oil to mayonnaise and a number of sauces and preserves, all over the world. Count Ybarra inherited his title as the eldest son but does not run the company. His main interest is food. He is a member of a gastronomic society Tercos y Sordos ('The Stubborn and the Deaf'), where members cook for each other and compete for excellence, which was nominated the best gastronomic society in Europe. He enjoys cooking for friends and neighbours on the coast, many of them British aristocrats and celebrities. He radiates pleasure when he describes what he cooks. I filled pages and pages with notes about dishes and techniques as we went eating from one bar to another over three days in Seville.

I asked if his ancestors had obtained their land by helping to conquer it from the Moors. No, he told me, they were a Basque family who became rich from coal and shipping during the industrial revolution in northern Spain. In the 1840s, the eldest son, José María Ybarra Gutiérrez de Caviedes, came to Andalusia and bought Church land that was being sold off. He planted olive trees and started exporting olives and olive oil to Latin America. He also farmed sturgeon for caviar in the river Guadalquivir. He became mayor of Seville and received a title because of his philanthropy – he built hospitals and paid for public works, including covering many streets with cobblestones. He is remembered for having initiated the most popular festival of Seville, the spring *Feria*, when everyone comes out to dance, eat and drink.

The Andalusian aristocracy doubled during the nineteenth century, when the old aristocracy was joined by newly ennobled industrialists and men grown rich in the Americas. Investors from northern Spain and foreign Catholics from European countries had been invited to settle in Andalusia since the late eighteenth century. Belgians controlled the lead mines, the French the coal mines. At the same time, British wine merchants settled in an area around Cadiz that produced fortified wines, for which there was great demand in England. The production of sherry was in the hands of a few families. Among them were the González family and the Barbadillos; the Domecqs, who came from France; and the Byasses, Garveys and Osbornes, who were all British. These leading dynasties intermarried and formed a wine aristocracy. Around it developed a closed social world of trilingual grandees. Some of the children of these families were brought up by English nannies and sent to Irish convent schools. The aristocracy and landed proprietors combined in a class that owned olive groves and vineyards and bred Arabian horses and fighting bulls.

Jacobo Martínez de Irujo, son of the Duchess of Alba, to whom Count José María is related, once said that 'the Spanish aristocracy no longer exists as a class, neither economically, nor socially, nor culturally'. Perhaps that is so, but their unique Hispano-cosmopolitan cuisine, with English and Gallic touches, has not disappeared in Andalusia. Many of the large wineries have been taken over by multinational companies, but the bread-and-butter puddings, the stuffed turkeys, the sauces with sherry and brandy remain within the families like a secret cuisine. On special occasions, such as horse races on the beach, people can go from one picnicking group to another and taste the foods of other families. José María Count Ybarra knows all the best and finest dishes of Spain but he still remembers nostalgically the simpler family foods his mother taught to their cook Teresa. Several recipes in this book were inspired by him.

BRAISED KNUCKLE *of* VEAL
✳ *jarrete de ternera*

Veal was the meat of choice of the northern bourgeoisie and there are many elegant recipes for it. The slow-cooked knuckle from the hind leg (it is the part that is sawn into rounds to make osso buco), with its rich marrow and gelatinous connective tissue, becomes meltingly tender and produces a sumptuous sauce. Ask the butcher to saw off the end of the bone for you, to expose the marrow.

SERVES 4

Heat the oil in a large ovenproof casserole or roasting pan and brown the veal knuckle on all sides over a medium heat, then remove it from the pan. Add the onion, carrots and butter and cook over a low heat, stirring, for about 7 to 10 minutes until the vegetables are soft. Add the tomatoes and cook for another 5 minutes until they soften. Return the meat to the casserole or pan, along with the garlic and thyme. Season with salt and pepper, pour in the wine and stock and bring to the boil. Cover with a lid or with foil and cook in an oven preheated to 180°C/gas 4 for 2½ to 3 hours, until the meat is very tender. Turn the veal knuckle at least once and add a little more wine and/or stock if the liquid evaporates too quickly.

Take out the casserole or roasting pan and turn the oven up to 220°C/gas 7. Lift out the meat, remove the sprigs of thyme and pour the sauce with the vegetables into a saucepan. Return the meat to the casserole or pan and cook in the oven for a further 20 to 30 minutes, until it is crisp and brown on the outside but still soft and moist inside. Meanwhile, blend the sauce to a cream in the saucepan with a hand blender. Reduce it, if you like, to a thick glaze over a low heat.

Serve the veal cut into four large pieces, with the sauce poured over it.

* 3 tablespoons olive oil
* 1 whole knuckle of veal, weighing about 1½kg
* 1 large onion, peeled and chopped
* 2 medium carrots, peeled and chopped
* 75g butter
* 2 tomatoes, peeled and chopped
* cloves of 1 garlic head, peeled
* 2 sprigs of thyme
* salt and pepper
* 250ml dry, fruity white wine, plus possibly a little more
* 250ml veal or chicken stock (page 145), plus possibly a little more

VARIATIONS

▩ Another way to cook this dish is to let the meat simmer in the casserole on the hob over a very low heat for 2½ to 3 hours. Serve it as it is without blending the sauce.

▩ Instead of the white wine, add 250ml of medium-dry sherry or port.

▩ In Navarre, they add 125ml of brandy to the wine and stock.

BEEF STEWED *in* RED WINE
❖ *estofado de buey*

Young Luis Bertran Bittini Martínez teaches cooking in the biggest catering school in Madrid. It is part of the Fundación Tomillo (*tomillo* means thyme), an independent, not-for-profit organization whose aim is to be of service to society in many different fields. They give training to truanting adolescents, those excluded from school, youths in trouble with the police, the unemployed with severe work difficulties, women alienated from the work market, disabled people and old people who wish to be independent. Luis teaches youths between the ages of sixteen and twenty-one who want to be professional cooks. At the time he invited me and Alicia Rios to lunch at his house, many of his students happened to be Latin Americans from Bolivia, Ecuador and Peru. The year before they had been mostly Moroccans. He told us that when he comes into the class the students jokingly intone: 'Right! Onion, garlic, pepper, tomato!' It is the way so many Spanish dishes start. While we watched him prepare the meal, he explained the courses he teaches. As we ate, his father Rafael Bittini told us what life was like when he was young, and Luis's wife explained that nowadays young people buy ready-cooked pasta dishes to heat up.

Use shin, feather steak, brisket, silverside, flank, chuck, blade or skirt of beef. It should be a bit fatty, otherwise it becomes stringy from long cooking. Luis cooked the meat in a sweet Spanish wine and said that we could use port or red wine. I used a cheap port that made a splendid sauce. If you want to cook the stew in the oven, use a casserole that will go on the hob and also in the oven. Serve the dish with mashed potatoes.

» » »

※ 6–8 tablespoons olive oil ※ 1 onion, peeled and coarsely chopped
※ 1 red or green pepper, deseeded and diced ※ 1 carrot, peeled and diced
※ 1 leek, trimmed and coarsely chopped ※ salt and pepper ※ 1 tomato, peeled and chopped
※ 1kg stewing or braising beef (see 419 for suitable cuts), cut into 3cm cubes
※ 500ml sweet red wine or port ※ 2 bay leaves

Heat about 3 to 4 tablespoons of the oil in a wide casserole. Put in the onion, pepper, carrot and leek, and sauté, uncovered, for about 25 minutes, first over a low heat, then turning up to a medium heat to brown and caramelize the vegetables a little. Turn the vegetables over often and add salt and pepper. Add the tomato and cook for a few minutes more.

Brown the beef on all sides in another 3 to 4 tablespoons of oil in a large frying pan over a high heat. Cook it in batches – if the meat is crowded in the pan it stews rather than browns. Lift the pieces out and add them to the vegetables in the casserole. Pour in the wine or port and enough water to cover. Put in the bay leaves and season again with salt and pepper.

Cook, covered, over a very low heat, so that it is barely simmering, for 2 to 3 hours until the meat is very tender. Stir once in a while to make sure that it does not burn at the bottom. If there is too much liquid, remove the lid at the end to reduce the sauce. Alternatively, put the casserole, with the lid on, in an oven preheated to 160°C/gas 3 for about 2½ to 3 hours.

When he made this dish, Luis lifted out the meat and bay leaves and blended the sauce to a cream with a hand blender, but he said you do not need to do that. I like to leave the sauce as it is without blending. Serve the stew with mashed potatoes.

VARIATIONS

※ For a version from the Pyrenees, instead of the sweet wine or port use 250ml of red wine and 125ml of brandy. Pour the wine into the casserole. Heat the brandy in a small pan, touch the rising vapours with a lighted match and pour it into the casserole once the flames have died down. Then add 2 cinnamon sticks and 5 cloves.

※ For an *estofado de toro con chocolate* from Navarre, add 1 or 2 tablespoons of grated dark chocolate plus 4 tablespoons of wine vinegar and 2 cinnamon sticks along with the wine or port. Put in 500g of peeled, boiled and halved or quartered new potatoes to heat through towards the end.

BARBECUED STEAK
❊ *chuletón a la brasa*

The first *asador* (roaster) to serve ox steaks over embers was Julián Rivas in the Basque town of Tolosa in 1961. The fashion for grilled ox steak swept through the cider houses of the Basque Country and eventually through cattle-raising northern Spain and across the rest of the country. *Churrasquerías* – steakhouses where meats are cooked over embers – have become immensely popular in northern Spain. In Tolosa, they have *chuletón fiestas* (steak festivals). Nowadays the meat comes from well-hung indigenous cows that have been specially fattened. In the more distant past, *maestros asadores* (master roasters) were hired to roast meats at village feasts. Today many chefs and *churrasquería* owners are Argentinian emigrants. At home many men expect to be in charge of the barbecue when they are cooking for family and friends. Buy large T-bone steaks that include the fillet and sirloin. And serve them with garlic mayonnaise or *alioli* (page 149).

SERVES 6–8

❊ 2 large T-bone steaks, about 5–6cm thick ❊ olive oil ❊ salt and pepper

Start the fire, and wait until it has reduced to glowing coals.

Take the steaks out of the refrigerator and bring them to room temperature. Trim off some of the fat and any sinews, and brush them lightly with olive oil. Oil the grill well. Put the steaks on the grill and sear for 1 to 2 minutes over the hottest part of the barbecue. Then move the steaks to a cooler part of the barbecue, or raise the grill, and continue to cook, turning them a few times, until the meat is cooked to your taste. Allow 10 to 15 minutes for rare steak and a little longer for medium. You can judge the cooking time by the feel of the meat – if it feels soft when pressed it is rare, if it feels springy it is medium. If it feels firm and stiff it will be overdone.

Move the steaks to a carving board, season with salt and pepper, cover them with foil and allow to rest for 10 minutes. To serve, cut the meat across the grain into thick slices.

VARIATION

❊ You can cook the steaks on a heavy iron griddle or in a large frying pan on the hob. Heat it until it is very hot. Lightly oil the pan before you put the meat in, to stop it sticking. Press the meat well down with a heatproof spatula and cook for 10 to 15 minutes, turning the steaks over a few times.

MEATBALLS *in an* ALMOND SAUCE
✷ *albóndigas en salsa con picada de almendras*

In Spain, meatballs and minced meat stuffings are usually made with a mix of different meats, most commonly a half-and-half mix of veal and pork. When I asked people why this was so, the answer I got was that veal used to be the prestigious, expensive meat and pork the plebeian partner that made the mixture cheaper and provided some fat. But you can use one or the other of the meats alone. The use of bread soaked in milk or water and a raw egg makes the mix go further and gives the meatballs a soft, moist texture. They are poached in a variety of sauces. Here the sauce has white wine and is thickened and given a characteristic Catalan flavour with a *picada* – a paste of fried almonds, bread and garlic. The meatballs are traditionally rolled in flour before frying but some people now omit this step. Although meatballs are supposed to be a poor man's food, this recipe is anything but. The flavours make an extraordinary combination.

SERVES 4–6 (MAKES 18–20 MEATBALLS)

Soak the bread in water for 5 minutes. Lightly beat the egg in a large bowl. Add the minced meat, the bread (squeezed dry and mashed in your hand), the onion, garlic and parsley, and some salt and pepper. Work the mixture with your hands into a soft, well-mixed paste. Shape into balls the size of large walnuts and roll in plenty of flour.

Fry the meatballs briefly, for 2 to 3 minutes, in a wide frying pan, in hot oil to a depth of about 1.5cm, turning them once, until lightly browned all over, then lift them out with a slotted spoon and drain on kitchen paper. They will not be cooked through. Do this in batches.

For the sauce, pour the stock and wine into a wide saucepan and bring to the boil. Add the saffron and lemon zest, then the salt, pepper and sugar.

Make a paste called a *picada* to thicken the sauce. Fry the bread, the almonds and the whole garlic cloves very briefly in the oil in a small frying pan over a medium heat until lightly browned. Lift them out, let them cool a little, then grind to a paste with a pestle and mortar, or blend them in the food processor. Stir this mixture into the sauce, add the meatballs and simmer, covered, over a very low heat for about 20 minutes.

- 1 hunk of white bread (about 100g), crusts removed and cut in slices
- 1 large egg
- 500g minced pork or veal, or a half-and-half mix of both
- ½ a small onion, peeled and very finely chopped
- 2 garlic cloves, peeled and crushed
- 2 tablespoons finely chopped flat-leaf parsley
- salt and pepper
- flour, to roll the meatballs in
- olive or sunflower oil, for frying

For the almond sauce

- 300ml chicken stock (you may use ½ a stock cube)
- 200ml fruity dry white wine
- a good pinch of saffron threads
- grated zest of 1 lemon
- salt and pepper
- 2 teaspoons sugar
- 1 small, thin slice of white bread (about 20g), crusts removed
- 40g blanched almonds
- 3–4 garlic cloves, peeled
- 3 tablespoons olive oil

MEATBALLS *cooked in* TOMATO SAUCE
✳ *albóndigas con salsa de tomate*

Meatballs cooked in this sauce are common all over Spain. You find them in tapas bars.

SERVES 4–6

✳ 1 x quantity of meatballs from the previous recipe (page 422)

For the tomato sauce ✳ 1 medium onion, peeled and chopped ✳ 2 tablespoons olive oil
✳ 750g tomatoes, peeled and chopped ✳ salt and pepper ✳ 1 bay leaf ✳ 1 teaspoon sugar

Make the meatballs as explained in the previous recipe (page 422) and briefly fry them until browned but not cooked through.

For the sauce, fry the onion in the oil in a wide saucepan over a low heat, stirring occasionally, until soft. Add the tomatoes, some salt and pepper, the bay leaf and sugar. Cook over a low heat for 5 minutes, then add the meatballs and continue to cook, covered, for about 20 minutes, turning the meatballs over once.

NOTE: It is possible to brown the meatballs by turning them under the grill instead of frying them. In that case do not roll them in flour.

✺ BASQUE COUNTRY

ROAST VENISON *with* CHESTNUT PURÉE
and PEAR COMPOTE
✳ *corzo con puré de castañas y confitura de pera*

In 1180, King Sancho VI of Navarre declared in a code of regulations on hunting that big game and animals of the woodland might only be hunted 'by the king, grandees, nobles and knights'. Today, in Spain, hunting big game is a macho trophy sport. Venison and wild boar are much less of a gastronomic tradition than game birds. Only a few Spanish restaurants and hunting clubs are known for their venison and wild boar specialities. Deer are hunted in the high mountains of northern Spain – in the Cantabrian range and the Pyrenees. The hunted meat is mostly sold to Germany and France, or turned into preserves such as pâtés and sausages.

The meat of young, farm-raised animals can be roasted briefly but needs to marinate for 24 hours.

» » »

✳ about 500ml red wine ✳ 5 tablespoons olive oil ✳ 1 onion, peeled and chopped ✳ 10 black peppercorns
✳ 2 bay leaves ✳ 1 fillet of young, farmed venison (about 750g) ✳ salt

For the chestnut purée ✳ 500g chestnuts, fresh peeled, frozen and defrosted or vacuum-packed
✳ about 300ml whole milk, or more (enough to cover the chestnuts) ✳ ½ teaspoon ground cinnamon
✳ salt ✳ 30g butter

For the pear compote ✳ 250ml dry red wine ✳ 4 tablespoons sugar ✳ 4 pears, peeled, quartered and cored

For the marinade, put the wine, 2 tablespoons of the olive oil, the onion, peppercorns and bay leaves in a glass or ceramic bowl and mix well. Then add the venison fillet, curled over to fit in the bowl, and cover with cling film. Refrigerate for 24 hours, turning the meat over once.

For the chestnut purée, put the chestnuts in a saucepan with enough milk to cover and bring to the boil. Add the cinnamon and cook, covered, over a low heat for about 15 minutes until they are soft, then pour out the milk. Add some salt and the butter, and mash with a potato masher or blend in the food processor.

For the pear compote, pour the wine into a wide pan with the sugar, then put in the pears and cook over a low heat, covered, for 8 to 10 minutes, or until they are tender, turning them over once.

Lift the venison out of the marinade, pat it dry with kitchen paper, and sprinkle with salt. Bring the marinade to the boil in a small saucepan and reduce to about half the volume.

Heat the remaining 3 tablespoons of oil in a large frying pan over a high heat, put the meat in and turn it around to sear it all over. Then put it in a baking dish with about 125ml of the marinade and roast in an oven preheated to 200°C/gas 6 for about 20 to 30 minutes, until it is done to your liking. It is best eaten rare or medium-rare, while still juicy inside (the meat is dry if well done). It should still be pink inside.

Let the venison rest for 5 minutes. Then serve the meat carved into slices, accompanied by the reheated chestnut purée and pear compote.

CALVES' LIVER *with* ONIONS *and* BRANDY
✣ *higado de ternera encebollado al brandy*

Offal was always the food of the poor and levels of consumption went down as Spain grew rich. But since immigrants from Latin America have arrived in large numbers, over a decade or so the offal stands that had almost disappeared from city markets are doing a booming trade once again. Calves' liver, though, has always been considered a delicacy. It is important not to overcook it.

SERVES 4

✳ 2 large onions, peeled, cut in half and sliced ✳ 3–4 tablespoons olive oil
✳ 500g calves' liver, thinly sliced and cut into 2cm strips ✳ salt and pepper ✳ 4 tablespoons brandy

Sauté the onions in the oil over a low heat, covered, in a large frying pan until they are soft, stirring occasionally. It can take up to 25 minutes because of the large amount of onions. Then cook, uncovered, over a medium heat, stirring often, until golden.

Put the liver in with the onions. Sauté briefly for 1 minute, adding salt and pepper and turning the strips over quickly to brown them lightly on both sides. Pour the brandy all over them and then cook over a high heat for 1 minute to reduce the sauce – the time depends on the thickness of the liver. Cut into a piece; it should still be pink inside.

VARIATION

✣ For an Andalusian version, use chicken livers instead of calves' liver, and sauté very briefly, stirring and turning them constantly to brown them all over. Add oloroso sherry instead of the brandy.

OXTAIL STEW
❊ *rabo de toro*

This recipe for *rabo de toro* (bull's tail) was given to me by Manuel Andrade, who was for many years head chef at El Burladero in the Hotel Colón in Seville, where bullfighters have lodged during the season since the Exposición Ibero-Americana world's fair held in the city in 1929. Manuel now has his own restaurant, the Porta Gayola in Calle Barcelona, where he cooks some of the best foods I have eaten in Seville in a tiny upstairs kitchen.

Manuel's is the classic recipe for this famous dish, the way it was made with the trophy tails that were given to the *picadores*, the horsemen who pierce the bull's back with a lance early in the bullfight. There are many estates in Andalusia where fighting bulls are raised for the *corrida*. The dish is served in all the *tapas* bars in Seville and also in Cordoba, where the tails of ordinary cows are used. What we call oxtails in Britain are not the tails of oxen – castrated bulls that were once used for the plough as work animals – but of ordinary beef cattle. Butchers sell them cut up into pieces consisting of vertebrae surrounded by meat fat and connective tissue. After long, slow cooking the meat becomes silky tender and the sauce rich and gelatinous. With the heady flavours imparted by wine and brandy this is a real luxury dish. Serve the stew with mashed potatoes or the roast potatoes given below. In grand restaurants in Spain they remove the meat from the bones and serve it up with the sauce, atop a little ball of mashed potatoes.

SERVES 6

❊ 1 oxtail (about 2.5kg) ❊ 6 tablespoons olive oil ❊ 2 medium onions, peeled and chopped
❊ 3 carrots (about 350g), peeled and diced ❊ 1 large leek, trimmed and cut into small pieces
❊ 4 garlic cloves, peeled and chopped ❊ 3 bay leaves ❊ a sprig of thyme ❊ 6 tomatoes (about 500g),
peeled and chopped ❊ 250ml dry white wine ❊ 250ml brandy ❊ 500ml red wine ❊ salt and pepper

Cut away much of the excess fat from the oxtail – the larger pieces have the most fat – but leave the skin on as it disappears during the cooking. Then place the oxtail pieces on a sheet of foil on an oven tray and roast in an oven preheated to 240°C/gas 9 for 30 minutes, until they have browned and released more fat. This fat is to be discarded.

Meanwhile, in a very large saucepan, heat the oil and add the onions, carrots, leek, garlic, bay leaves and thyme, and cook, stirring often over a medium heat, for about 10 minutes. Add the tomatoes and cook for another 10 minutes.

» » »

Put the pieces of oxtail into the pan, pour in the white wine, brandy and red wine, and season with salt and pepper. Simmer, uncovered, for 10 minutes then add enough water to cover the oxtail and cook, covered, for 3 to 4½ hours. The meat should be meltingly tender and fall away from the bone easily. Let the stew rest for about 20 minutes and then skim off the fat from the surface with a ladle and absorbent kitchen paper. Reheat before serving with the roast potatoes below.

It is usual in Spain to lift out the oxtail, the bay leaves and sprig of thyme and to blend the sauce to a cream in the pan with a hand blender, before returning the oxtail and reheating. Personally I like the sauce with the vegetable bits and prefer not to blend it

ROAST POTATOES
❖ *patatas al horno*

SERVES 6

❋ 1.5kg floury potatoes ❋ salt ❋ 125ml olive or sunflower oil

Peel the potatoes and cut them in half, or into quarters depending on their size. Put them in a large saucepan with enough cold water to cover and add salt. Bring to the boil and simmer for about 10 minutes, until the surface of the potatoes is slightly fluffy. Drain off the water and shake the pan to roughen the surface of the potatoes so that they will absorb more oil and become crispier. Another way is to scratch them with a fork.

Arrange the potatoes in a large baking dish or roasting pan and sprinkle with a little salt. Pour the oil over them and turn to coat them all over. Place in an oven preheated to 220°C/gas 7 for 50 to 60 minutes, turning the potatoes over once, until crisp and golden.

POTATOES *with* CHORIZO
✤ *patatas a la riojana*

This is an earthy, strongly flavoured dish that is served as a starter or main course. By tradition the potatoes are cut only to halfway through with a wide knife, then snapped open by twisting the blade. This is meant to release more starch, which makes the sauce thicker and allows the potatoes to absorb more flavour. Small pork ribs, shallow-fried or roasted in the oven, are sometimes added to make it a meatier dish.

SERVES 2 AS A MAIN COURSE

Sauté the onion in the oil over a low heat in a wide frying pan, stirring often, until it is really brown – almost caramelized – about 20 minutes. Add the chorizo slices and garlic and cook, stirring, for about 2 minutes. Put in the potatoes and cook for 5 minutes, turning them over.

It is usual to add *pimentón* or paprika, but I did not add any as there was enough flavour to my taste from the *chorizos*. Add salt and pour in enough water to cover. Simmer over a low heat, uncovered, for about 25 to 35 minutes until the potatoes are soft and the liquid is very much reduced, turning the potatoes over if necessary, so that they are well cooked right through. You should be left with a sizzling sauce that coats the potatoes and *chorizo* slices. If there is too much liquid, increase the heat towards the end to reduce it.

VARIATIONS

- Chop ½ a green pepper and ½ a red pepper, and put them in the pan when the onion is soft and continue to cook until lightly browned.

- Add 1 peeled and chopped tomato to the fried onions when they are brown.

- Put in a whole dried or fresh chilli pepper.

- 1 large onion, peeled and chopped
- 3–4 tablespoons olive oil
- 200g spicy *chorizos*, fully cured or semi-cured (the cooking type), cut into 1cm slices
- 2 garlic cloves, peeled and chopped
- 500g new potatoes, peeled and cut into 3cm pieces
- ½–1 teaspoon *pimentón dulce* or sweet paprika (optional)
- salt

FRESH PORK SAUSAGES ❖ *botifarres*

Catalan *botifarres* are fresh, pure pork sausages with only salt and pepper as flavouring. Catalans have wonderful ways of cooking these sausages, stewed in red or white wine, in sparkling cava or in cider. They accompany them with mashed potatoes and apple purée, caramelized onions or caramelized pears, and also with white beans. They make a wonderful cheap meal, but you must buy good medium-coarse pork sausages, such as Cumberland sausages.

PORK SAUSAGES *cooked in* WINE *or* CIDER ❖ *botifarra amb vi o sidra*

Prick the sausages in one or two places with a pointed knife. Heat 1 tablespoon of olive oil in a frying pan over a low heat, add the sausages and turn them to brown them lightly all over. Then pour out the excess fat and pour in enough red or white wine, sparkling cava or cider to at least half cover the sausages and cook over a medium to high heat, covered, turning them over once, until they are cooked right through and the wine or cider has almost disappeared – about 20 to 25 minutes.

PORK SAUSAGES *with* APPLE PURÉE ❖ *botifarra amb poma*

Prick the sausages and fry them in a little oil in a frying pan over a low heat, turning them over until they are done and well browned – about 20 to 25 minutes – or cook them in wine or cider as above. Peel, core and quarter 1 apple per person. Put the apples in a pan with about a finger's depth of water and cook with the lid on over a very low heat until they are soft. This will take about 20 minutes. Watch the pan, as the water can evaporate too quickly and the apples can burn. Remove the lid and carry on cooking to evaporate any remaining water, then mash to a rough purée. Serve with the sausages.

PORK SAUSAGES *with* CARAMELIZED PEARS ❖ *botifarra amb peres*

Prick the sausages and fry them in a little oil in a frying pan over a low heat, turning them over until they are cooked right through and well browned – about 20 to 25 minutes – or cook them as above in wine. Use 1 slightly unripe pear per person. Peel, core and cut each pear into 6 slices, then sauté in a little oil in another pan over a medium heat, turning them over, until the pears are soft and lightly browned all over. This will take about 6 to 10 minutes. Serve them with the sausages.

PORK SAUSAGES *with* CARAMELIZED ONIONS ❖ *botifarra amb cebes*

Prick the sausages and fry them in oil in a frying pan over a low heat for 20 to 25 minutes, turning them over until they are cooked right through and well browned, or cook them in wine as above. To make enough for 3 people, peel, cut in half and slice 2 large onions. Put them in another large frying pan with 3 tablespoons of olive oil, cover and cook over a low heat, stirring occasionally, for about 30 minutes until they are very soft (they stew in their own juices). Remove the lid and cook, stirring often, over a medium heat for up to 15 minutes more or until they are brown and caramelized. Serve the onions with the sausages.

DESSERTS AND PASTRIES

postres

he usual way to end a meal in Spain is with fruit, sometimes followed by bought ice creams or pastries. 'Sweet dishes do exist in Spain, but more as vestiges of history . . . the traditional man considers this kind of food to be a feminine weakness, while for women it is a disaster for the waistline,' is how Alicia Rios introduces the chapter on desserts in *The Heritage of Spanish Cooking* (Ebury Press, Random House, 1992), the book she co-wrote with Lourdes March. However, Spaniards do eat fritters called *churros* with hot chocolate for breakfast and for their *merienda* (teatime snack), and they buy *magdalenas* (madeleine cakes) by the bagful from the supermarket.

A huge range of pastries, including deep-fried doughnuts, raisin and nut breads and cakes based on almonds, hazelnuts or walnuts are the 'historic' festive foods that celebrate the landmarks of the Christian year – Christmas, Epiphany, Candlemas, Easter, Ascension Day, the Feast of St John the Baptist, St Michael's Day, St Martin's Day, and so on, plus the many feasts celebrating the Virgin Mary. Every village honours its own patron saint with parades and fireworks, re-enactments of legends and always with a special pastry. During the festival of San Isidro, which goes on for three weeks in Madrid in May with processions, music, dancing and bullfights, bakeries and pastry shops go into a baking frenzy. The traditional pastries attached to a special day are now eaten all the year round. Many are made by cloistered nuns and are known as convent sweets.

I have a sweet tooth so I went looking for those sweet dishes that are a 'feminine weakness'. Every region has its specialities. In the north, which is dairy country, they make milk puddings, custards, rice puddings and cheesecakes. The ubiquitous *flan* we know as crème caramel is served everywhere in Spain. Some of the loveliest sweets are made with fruit. There are compotes, flans, tarts, cakes, fritters and sweet omelettes. At an international pudding competition you would be able to tell which were the Spanish entries because almost all of them would be flavoured with lemon peel and cinnamon.

ORANGE FLAN
✳ *flan de naranja*

I love this refreshing, slightly tangy, creamy custard. It is just what you need to end a rich meal. You must use freshly squeezed orange or clementine juice and it is best if you squeeze the juice yourself.

SERVES 8

✳ 600ml fresh orange or clementine juice ✳ 125g sugar ✳ 10 large egg yolks ✳ 2 large eggs

Heat the citrus juice with the sugar in a saucepan over a low heat and stir to dissolve the sugar.

Beat the egg yolks and the whole eggs lightly with a fork in a large bowl. Then gradually beat in the citrus juice. Ladle the mixture into 8 x 175ml ramekins. Place them in a large shallow pan, pour in boiling water to come halfway up the sides of the ramekins (this water bath is called a bain-marie) and bake in an oven preheated to 150°C/gas 2 for 30 minutes or until the custard sets. It needs to be cooked at a low temperature to get a perfectly smooth texture without bubbles.

Take the ramekins out of the pan and let cool, then chill in the refrigerator, covered with cling film.

BREAD PUDDING
✳ pudín de pan

British and Irish wine merchants began setting up fortified wine businesses around Jerez de la Frontera in the province of Cadiz in the late eighteenth century. Their names are still on the sherry labels even though the companies may now be under Spanish or multinational ownership. A Spanish version of English bread pudding is still part of the traditional cooking repertoire of an Andalusian upper class that was brought up speaking English and taking tea every day with toast and biscuits. The pudding can be served hot or cold, with or without a crisp caramel topping. For the caramel you will need a mini blowtorch. These are now quite easy to find.

Do also try the Ibizan pudding in the recipe variation below. It is extremely quick and easy to make, and is a delightful comfort food.

SERVES 6

Use a baking dish that will fit the slices of bread in two layers – cut them to fit if necessary – and grease the dish with butter. Put the bread in the dish, sprinkling the almonds and sultanas between the two layers.

In a bowl, beat the eggs lightly with the sugar, add the lemon zest, then beat in the milk and cream and, if using, the sherry or sweet wine. Pour the mixture over the bread in the baking dish. Bake in an oven preheated to 180°C/gas 4 for 40 minutes until golden, risen and lightly set, and serve hot.

Alternatively, let it cool and then chill in the refrigerator. Just before serving, sprinkle the top evenly with the optional 2 to 3 tablespoons of sugar and caramelize with a mini blowtorch.

VARIATION

❋ GREIXONERA DE IBIZA, a pudding made with leftover ensaimada pastries – croissants are a perfect substitute – is served in all the restaurants on the island of Ibiza. Greixonera is the name of the clay dish in which it is baked. Tear 4 croissants (mine weighed 175g) into pieces and spread them out in a buttered baking dish, about 25cm in diameter. Bring to the boil 500ml of whole milk with 150g of sugar in a saucepan and stir to dissolve the sugar. Lightly beat 4 large eggs in a bowl, add the grated zest of ½ a lemon, then beat in the milk. Pour this over the croissants and bake in an oven preheated to 200°C/gas 6 for 30 minutes. It is good hot or at room temperature, dusted with a ¼ teaspoon of ground cinnamon.

* 6–8 slices of white bread or brioche (about 200g), crusts removed

* butter, to grease the baking dish

* 100g blanched almonds, coarsely chopped

* 60g sultanas

* 4 large eggs

* 60g caster sugar, plus a further 2–3 tablespoons for the optional caramel topping

* grated zest of 1 lemon

* 300ml whole milk

* 300ml double or single cream

* 4 tablespoons Pedro Ximénez sherry or sweet Malaga liqueur wine (optional)

CRÈME CARAMEL
✣ *flan*

Originally from France, *flan* spread from the north of Spain and has become popular all over the country.

SERVES 6

Make the caramel first. Put the sugar and water in a stainless-steel saucepan over a medium heat. When the syrup starts to bubble and colour, swirl the pan to spread the caramel evenly, and cook until it turns to a deep amber, continuing to swirl the pan. Watch it as it can turn too dark very quickly, which results in a bitter taste. Pour the caramel immediately into a mould (which can be metal, porcelain or Pyrex, but not non-stick, that will hold at least 1 litre), turning and tilting the mould to coat the bottom and sides. You have to do this very fast because the caramel hardens quickly.

To make the custard, put the milk in a pan with the sugar and vanilla extract and bring slowly to simmering point, stirring to dissolve the sugar. Let it cool slightly for 10 minutes. Meanwhile, beat the eggs lightly by hand with a fork or whisk in a large bowl, then gradually beat in the milk, starting with a ladleful, until well blended. Pour the mixture into the caramel-lined mould.

Place the mould in a large shallow pan and pour in boiling water to come halfway up the side of the mould (this water bath is called a bain-marie). Bake in an oven preheated to 160°C/gas 3 for 1 hour or until the custard has set. Take the mould out of the pan of water, let it cool, then chill in the refrigerator, covered with cling film, for 3 hours or overnight.

Turn out the *flan* just before you are ready to serve. Run a pointed knife all round the edge of the mould, place a serving dish on top of the mould and quickly turn upside down, then lift off the mould. There will be a lot of caramel sauce, so the dish should be deep enough to collect it.

For the caramel
* 100g sugar
* 4 tablespoons water

For the custard
* 600ml whole milk
* 100g sugar
* 1 teaspoon pure vanilla extract
* 4 large egg

CHEESE PUDDING
✻ greixonera de brossat

This very simple and light cheese pudding from the island of Menorca is baked in a *greixonera* – the local name for an earthenware *cazuela* (see page 116). *Brossat* is the fresh cream cheese made from cow's milk (the English brought dairy cows when they occupied the island) – ricotta is a good substitute.

Miguel Montez Martínez, who for many years cooked in the Balearic Islands during the tourist season, gave me this recipe and also the one for the *greixonera de Ibiza* (see page 438). Now living in his home village of Frailes in Andalusia he is called upon to cook giant stews and *paellas* for hundreds of people during festivals.

SERVES 6–8

Blend the ricotta, sugar, lemon zest and eggs to a cream in the food processor. Pour into a greased baking dish about 26cm in diameter and bake in an oven preheated to 180°C/gas 4 for about 30 to 45 minutes, or until it feels firm.

Serve at room temperature in the dish in which it was baked.

* 500g fresh ricotta cheese
* 125g caster sugar
* grated zest of 1 lemon
* 5 large eggs
* butter, to grease the baking dish

VARIATIONS

* Serve it with a fragrant honey. The honey produced in neighbouring Majorca is an orange-blossom honey.

* Dust the top with icing sugar and ground cinnamon. For *flaó*, a speciality of Ibiza, a similar cheese mix is used to fill a thin pastry base.

* It is flavoured with 3–4 mint leaves and 2–3 tablespoons of an anise-flavoured spirit (you can use pastis, ouzo or arak).

* Serve it covered with icing sugar or a drizzle of honey.

BURNT CREAM
✻ crema catalana

This creamy custard with a crisp caramel topping is found everywhere in Spain as *crema catalana* but in Catalonia it is known as *crema cremada,* which means 'burnt cream', and *crema de Sant Josep,* because it is served to celebrate Saint Joseph's Day on 19 March. This recipe comes from the Fundació Institut Català de la Cuina (see page 81).

SERVES 6–8

✻ 4 tablespoons cornflour ✻ 1 litre whole milk ✻ peel of 1 lemon, cut into 1 or 2 long strips
✻ 1 cinnamon stick ✻ 8 large egg yolks ✻ 150g caster sugar, plus about 4–8 tablespoons for the caramel

In a cup dissolve the cornflour in 4 tablespoons of the cold milk (the cornflour will prevent the egg yolks from curdling). Heat the rest of the milk in a large saucepan with the lemon peel and cinnamon stick until it just begins to boil.

Beat the egg yolks and 150g sugar to a pale cream in a bowl, then beat in the cornflour mixture. Now beat in a ladleful of the hot milk.

Remove the lemon peel and cinnamon stick from the hot milk and add the egg and sugar mixture to the pan, stirring vigorously as you pour. Bring to the boil slowly over a low heat and continue to cook over a low heat, stirring continuously, until the mixture thickens, then pour into 6 or 8 small clay *cassoles* or large ramekins. Let cool, then chill.

Just before serving, sprinkle the top of each custard with 2 to 3 teaspoons of sugar and gently shake the ramekin to spread it evenly. Caramelize the sugar with a mini blowtorch, or use a red-hot salamander as they do in Spain (see page 117), until the sugar turns a dark amber colour.

CRÈME BRÛLÉE *with a* SPANISH FLAVOUR

Some Spanish chefs now make *crema catalana* like crème brûlée, but flavoured with lemon or orange peel and sometimes cinnamon. I have to include it as I just adore the contrast of the light silky cream with a slight orange flavour and the crisp layer of caramel on the top. Do try it. To make a good caramel topping you will need a mini blowtorch. Putting the cream under the grill to caramelize does not work as well.

SERVES 6

⁂ 6 large egg yolks ⁂ 90g caster sugar, plus about 6 tablespoons for the caramel topping
⁂ 500ml double cream ⁂ grated zest of 1 orange or 1 lemon

Whisk the egg yolks with the sugar in a large bowl until pale and creamy.

Heat the cream in a saucepan with the orange or lemon zest (I love it with orange zest) over a low heat until almost boiling and then very gradually pour it into the egg and sugar mixture, starting with half a ladleful so that the eggs do not curdle, whisking constantly.

Ladle into 6 small ramekins so that they are not quite full to the brim. Place them in an oven dish or pan and pour in boiling water to come about halfway up the sides of the ramekins (this water bath is called a bain-marie). Bake in an oven preheated to 150°C/gas 2 for about 25 minutes, or until the custards are set but still slightly wobbly in the middle. Remove the ramekins from the water and let them cool, then chill in the refrigerator for 4 hours or overnight, covered with cling film.

When you are ready to serve, cover the top of each chilled cream with about 1½ teaspoons of sugar and very gently shake each ramekin to spread the sugar evenly. Caramelize with a mini blowtorch until a thin layer of amber caramel is formed. Then sprinkle another 1½ teaspoons of sugar over the caramel, gently shaking the ramekins to spread it evenly, and caramelize again to form a thick, crunchy, dark amber caramel. Do not let it get too dark or the caramel will taste bitter.

ALMOND SOUP ❖ *sopa de almendra*

In Spain this soup is eaten as the first course of the meal on Christmas Eve. Although it is unusual to have a soup as a dessert, that is how I like it best. Bought almond paste is normally dissolved in the milk but it is also very good and just as easy to make using ground almonds. You can serve it sprinkled with toasted pine nuts and a dusting of cinnamon.

SERVES 4

※ 500ml whole milk ※ 100g sugar, or to taste ※ grated zest of 1 lemon ※ 100g ground almonds ※ 2 slices of brioche, cut into 2.5cm pieces, lightly toasted

Bring the milk to the boil in a pan with the sugar and grated lemon zest and stir very well so that the sugar is entirely dissolved. Add the almonds and stir again. Simmer for a minute or two then turn off the heat. Let it rest until it cools and the ground almonds absorb the milk, and the consistency of the soup thickens. Serve at room temperature in little bowls over a few pieces of toasted brioche.

VARIATION
※ Boil the milk with a pinch of saffron threads along with the lemon zest.

NAVARRE

RICE CAKE ❖ *pastel de arroz*

A rice cake or pudding is always homely, but this one is elegant enough to serve at a dinner party. Navarre is famous for its crystallized fruit. Try to get a variety.

SERVES 8 OR MORE

※ 125g short-grain ('round' or pudding) rice or risotto rice ※ 1.5 litres whole milk ※ 125g sugar ※ 50g unsalted butter, plus a little more to grease the baking dish ※ 3 large eggs, separated ※ 50g raisins ※ 75g crystallized fruits, cut into small pieces

In a large saucepan, cook the rice in the milk over a very low heat for 45 minutes or longer, until the rice is very bloated but there is still quite a bit of liquid left.

Add the sugar, butter and lightly beaten egg yolks to the pan, then stir in the raisins and crystallized fruits. Beat the egg whites until stiff and fold them in.

Pour the mixture into a buttered baking dish and bake in an oven preheated to 180°C/gas 4 for 1 hour. Cover with foil for the first 30 minutes so that the top does not become too brown.

Serve warm or cold, cut like a cake.

RICE PUDDING
✳ *arroz con leche*

Rice pudding is popular all over Spain, but especially in the north, which is dairy country. It is always flavoured with a cinnamon stick and a strip of lemon peel. Most versions are made quite thick; some are baked in the oven, others are cooked on the hob. In Asturias they may add butter and caramelize the top. My favourite is this very creamy version, which has a good amount of liquid left at the end, thickened with egg yolk. You will be surprised how lovely it is. Be prepared for a long cooking time. You can serve it cold, at room temperature, or warm.

SERVES 4–6

Bring the milk to the boil in a large pan with the cinnamon stick and lemon peel. Add the rice and continue to cook gently over a very low heat for 45 minutes to an hour until the rice is very soft and much, but not all, of the liquid has been absorbed. Stir occasionally with a wooden spoon so that the rice does not catch on the bottom of the pan – especially at the start when it tends to stick.

Stir in the sugar and cook over a very low heat, stirring occasionally, for another 10 to 15 minutes. Remove the lemon peel and cinnamon stick. There should still be a good amount of liquid left.

In a small bowl, beat the egg yolks with a few tablespoonfuls of the milk and rice taken from the pan, then pour them into the pan, stirring vigorously over a low heat for seconds only, until the liquid becomes creamy. Do not let it boil or the yolks will curdle. Take off the heat and pour into a serving dish or little bowls. Serve chilled, at room temperature or warm.

VARIATIONS

※ Serve with a light dusting of ground cinnamon.

※ Just before serving, sprinkle the top with 3 tablespoons of sugar and caramelize with a mini blowtorch.

※ 1.5 litres whole milk

※ 1 cinnamon stick

※ peel of ½ a lemon, cut into 1 or 2 strips

※ 100g medium-grain Spanish rice or risotto rice

※ 100g sugar, or more to taste

※ 4 large egg yolks, lightly beaten

EGG *and* SYRUP FLAN
❖ *tocino de cielo*

This pudding made with egg yolks originated in monasteries in the wine-producing areas of Jerez de la Frontera and Montilla–Moriles where, in the late nineteenth century, the *bodegas* (wineries) used egg whites to clarify their wines and gave the leftover yolks to the local convents. The name means 'heavenly bacon'. It has a crème caramel aspect and feel. The texture varies depending on the proportion of egg yolks to sugar, and whether whole eggs are also used. This version uses some whole eggs, which give it a firmer texture. Even though it is not as sweet as those you will find in pastry shops in Andalusia it is still very sweet, so should be served in small portions.

SERVES 8–10

Make the caramel first. Put the sugar and water in a stainless-steel saucepan over a medium heat. As soon as it starts to bubble and caramelize in parts, swirl the pan to spread the colour evenly, and cook until it turns to a deep amber, continuing to swirl the pan and watching that it does not turn too dark, which would result in a bitter taste. Pour the caramel immediately into a mould (it can be metal, porcelain or Pyrex, but not non-stick, that will hold at least 1 litre), turning and tilting the mould to coat the bottom and sides. You have to do this quickly because the caramel hardens very fast. Let it cool.

For the flan, make a sugar syrup: put the water and sugar in a saucepan and simmer for a minute or two until the sugar has dissolved. Let it cool until still just warm. Beat the yolks and whole eggs lightly by hand with a fork or whisk, then gradually beat in the warm sugar syrup until well blended. Pour into the caramel-coated mould.

Place the mould in a large shallow pan and pour in boiling water to come halfway up the side of the mould (this water bath is called a bain-marie). Bake in an oven preheated to 160°C/gas 3 for 1¼ to 1½ hours or until the custard has set. Take the mould out of the pan, let it cool, then chill in the refrigerator, covered with cling film, for 3 hours or overnight.

Just before you are ready to serve, turn out the *tocino de cielo* – run a pointed knife all round the edge of the mould, place a serving dish on top and quickly turn upside down then lift off the mould. There will be a lot of caramel sauce so the dish should be deep enough to collect it.

❋ 500ml water

❋ 500g sugar

❋ 10 large egg yolks

❋ 4 large eggs

For the caramel

❋ 6 tablespoons sugar

❋ 3 tablespoons water

NOUGAT ICE CREAM
✳ *helado de turrón*

Turrón, a kind of nougat confection made of almonds and honey, is produced in Alicante and the neighbouring little hill town of Jijona. It was once sold by Morisco (see page 24) street vendors. For this ice cream you must use the softer type of *turrón* from Jijona. At a men's gastronomic society lunch in the Basque Country, I was offered an instant version – vanilla ice cream topped with crumbled *turrón* and a dash of rum. It was delicious. This recipe is also extremely easy to make.

SERVES 6

✳ 600ml double cream ✳ 50g caster sugar ✳ 300g soft *turrón* from Jijona

Beat the cream with an electric mixer in a large bowl until it is quite thick and forms stiff peaks (be careful that it does not turn to butter), adding the sugar when it begins to stiffen. Crumble the *turrón* with a fork then beat it into the cream until you have a homogeneous cream.

To give the ice cream a dome shape, line a bowl with cling film, pour the cream mixture in and cover with more cling film, then put in the freezer. Freeze for at least 6 hours or overnight. To serve, remove the top piece of cling film and turn it out on to a serving plate, then peel off the other piece of cling film.

ALMOND ICE CREAM
✳ *helado de almendra*

People visit the island of Majorca in January and February for the joy of seeing the almond trees in blossom – a magnificent pink-and-white spectacle that fills the air with a bitter-sweet perfume. The trees provide Spain with many of the almonds that are used in the country's famously long repertoire of almond pastries and confectionery. This ice cream is a speciality of the island, often served with their famous *ensaimada* pastry. It is a water ice but the almond milk gives it a creamy texture. Instead of using ready-ground almonds, buy whole blanched almonds and grind them yourself for a much better flavour and texture. Adding a few drops of almond extract will give a more pronounced flavour, but be careful not to add too much, though, as the taste will be really unpleasant if you do.

SERVES 8

✳ 250g whole blanched almonds ✳ 300g sugar ✳ 1 litre water ✳ 3 drops of almond extract (optional)

Grind the almonds as finely as possible in the food processor. Bring the sugar and water to the boil in a saucepan and stir to dissolve the sugar, then stir in the ground almonds and the almond extract, if using, and bring to the boil again. Remove from the heat and let cool before pouring the mixture into ice cube trays. Cover the trays with cling film and leave to freeze hard overnight in the freezer.

The next day, turn out the iced almond cubes and drop them into the food processor in two or three batches. As they are rock hard you will have to wait a few minutes for them to soften. Process to a very fine creamy slush. You can serve the slush right away, but crushing the ice cubes makes such a noise that you may not want to do it while people are there, so pour the slush into a serving bowl or little individual bowls and return to the freezer, covered with cling film. Take the ice cream out of the freezer 10 minutes before serving.

NOTE: To shape the ice cream into a dome that is easy to turn out, line a bowl with cling film, pour the processed mixture in and cover with another piece of cling film. Freeze overnight. To serve, remove the cling film from the top, then turn out the ice cream dome and remove the other piece of cling film.

RAISIN *and* SWEET WINE ICE CREAM
❋ *helado de pasas y vino dulce*

This ice cream is fabulous. Because it is a custard it does not need an ice cream machine or regular beating by hand to prevent crystallization. The base is a rich vanilla ice cream. The raisins and a sweet, dark Pedro Ximénez sherry or a sweet Malaga Moscatel wine are mixed in when it is almost firm.

SERVES 10 OR MORE

❋ 100g raisins ❋ 100ml sweet Pedro Ximénez sherry or Malaga Moscatel wine, plus more to pass around
❋ 700ml double cream ❋ 300ml whole milk ❋ 1 small cinnamon stick
❋ 1 teaspoon pure vanilla extract ❋ 8 large egg yolks ❋ 100g caster sugar

Put the raisins in a small bowl and pour over the sweet sherry or fortified wine. Leave them to soak for 1 hour or longer. Heat the cream and milk in a large saucepan with the cinnamon stick and vanilla extract until almost boiling. Remove from the heat and leave for half an hour to infuse before removing the cinnamon stick and reheating.

In a large bowl, beat the egg yolks with the sugar to a pale thick cream with an electric mixer. Add a ladleful of the hot milk and beat well, then pour this egg and sugar cream into the saucepan, off the heat, beating vigorously to mix well. Now return the pan to a low heat and stir constantly with a wooden spoon or heatproof spatula until the mixture thickens. Do not let it boil or it will curdle (if the mixture does curdle you can still save it by beating thoroughly with the electric mixer until it is smooth).

Pour the custard into a serving bowl and let it cool, then cover with cling film and put it into the freezer. After about 3 to 3½ hours, when it has firmed enough but is not yet hard, take it out of the freezer and thoroughly mix in the raisins together with their sherry or wine. You must do this before the ice cream becomes too hard to mix but when it is firm enough so that the raisins remain suspended evenly and do not sink to the bottom. If you do not mix thoroughly there will be little white lumps in the ice cream, but that too is lovely. Return to the freezer and freeze for at least 6 hours or overnight.

Take the ice cream out of the freezer 10 to 15 minutes before serving, then cut it into slices. If it proves difficult to dislodge the pieces from the bottom, dip the serving bowl in a bowl of hot water for a few seconds.

Pass the bottle of Pedro Ximénez or sweet wine around for everyone to drizzle a little over their ice cream.

NOTE: To shape the ice cream into a dome that is easy to turn out, line a second bowl with cling film, pour the finished mixture in, cover with another piece of cling film and freeze. To serve, remove the cling film from the top, then turn out the ice cream and remove the other piece of cling film.

QUINCE PASTE
✳ *dulce de membrillo*

I adore everything made with quinces. This soft, creamy, fragrant paste is another thing entirely from the industrial *dulce de membrillo* – the firm, dark wine-red, usually overly sweet block – that is traditionally served with cheese. It makes a marvellous dessert accompanied by a bland fresh cheese such as ricotta. It keeps for weeks in the refrigerator.

SERVES 8 OR MORE

✳ 4 quinces, weighing about 1.25 kg ✳ 150g sugar

Wash the quinces and scrub them if they still have the down on their skins. Place them on a sheet of foil on a large baking tray and bake in an oven preheated to 150°C/gas 2 for about 2 hours until they are soft. If the quinces are larger they will take longer.

When cool enough to handle, peel them, cut them in half and cut out the cores with a sharp pointed knife, then cut the flesh into pieces. Put the quince flesh in the food processor with the sugar and blend to a soft, creamy paste.

Pour the paste into a wide non-stick pan and cook gently over a low heat for about 30 minutes, stirring often, until it thickens and turns a deep pink colour. Stir with a wooden spoon and keep scraping up and stirring in the paste that caramelizes on the bottom of the pan – it will give the mixture a stronger colour and enhance the flavour.

Scrape the paste into a shallow dish, let it cool, then chill in the refrigerator. Serve it with a soft, mild fresh cheese such as ricotta.

---

cheese and honey ✳ *queso y miel*

In the old days, when shepherds travelled far with their sheep, when they got together during Lent the shepherds toasted bread dipped in olive oil on the embers of a fire and topped it with slices of aged hard cheese fried in a little pork fat or olive oil until it softened. Sometimes they poured honey over it. They called this *quesomiel,* which means 'honey-cheese'. Try it after dinner. Cheese and honey are still sold together by vendors in mountain villages.

Mel y mató is a popular dessert in north-east Spain, a combination of the fresh bland, creamy goat's cheese of the Pyrenees, called *mató,* served with the local honey (*mel* in Catalan). It is part of the Catalan, high Aragonese and Basque shepherds' culture. You can use ricotta – eat it with a fragrant runny honey. In the Pyrenees the honey might be chestnut honey.

PEACHES MACERATED *in* WINE
❖ *melocotones al vino*

The people of Aragon have been growing a special type of sweet yellow-fleshed peach, the *melocotón de Calanda*, since medieval times. The peaches we get in our supermarkets may not be as good, but macerating them in sweet wine, as they do in Aragon, will give you a delightful dessert.

SERVES 4

5 large, ripe but firm orange-fleshed peaches
about 250ml sweet white wine, such as Moscatel, or sweet red wine

To skin the peaches, put them in a bowl and pour boiling water over them. Leave them in the water for a few minutes. Drain and skin them, then cut each into quarters straight into a serving bowl or into individual wine glasses. Pour the wine over them (there should be enough to cover the fruit), cover the bowl or glasses with cling film and leave to macerate for 2 to 3 hours in the refrigerator.

VARIATIONS

You can also make this with a dry wine mixed with 2–3 tablespoons of sugar.

Serve the peaches in a bowl and put the peel of 1 lemon, cut into strips, and 1 cinnamon stick in with the wine.

ORANGES *in* SWEET MALAGA WINE
✳ *naranjas al vino de málaga*

This is a Malaga recipe using the region's own sweet fortified wine and marmalade made with the bitter oranges of Seville. One of the most extraordinary sights in Seville in January and February is the orange trees that line the streets, bursting with fruit.

SERVES 6

Peel the oranges, removing the white pith entirely. Cut them into medium-thick slices, then into pieces and arrange them in a wide serving dish.

Heat the marmalade in a pan with the wine over a low heat, stirring to mix well, until the jelly melts. Let the mixture cool, then pour over the oranges and leave for at least an hour before serving at room temperature.

- 8 sweet oranges
- 250g coarse-cut Seville orange marmalade
- 250ml Malaga Moscatel or Pedro Ximénez wine

VARIATIONS

- Instead of marmalade, Murcians dissolve a little honey in the wine and stir in ½ a teaspoon of ground cinnamon.
- For a Valencian version, put a mix of orange and grapefruit slices on a platter with sweet wine or Grand Marnier poured over, a little drizzle of honey and a sprinkling of chopped crystallized lemon or orange peel. Just before serving, sprinkle over toasted flaked almonds.

DRIED FRUIT COMPOTE *with* CUSTARD
❋ *zurracapote con crema pastelera vasca*

Zurracapote, also called *mermelada de frutos secos* is a New Year's Eve special in the Basque Country and in Navarre. It is great served with the Basque custard that can be flavoured with rum or cognac. I love it with rum. This recipe is from Carlos Posadas Gomez, a young Basque chef at the Santo Mauro restaurant in Madrid. *Zurracapote* did not feature on his sensational tasting menu – it came out of his childhood memories when I asked him about traditional Basque dishes. He said you can add nuts – pine nuts, blanched almonds, walnuts – when serving.

SERVES 6

Soak the dried fruits in the wine and water for 2 hours, then put the fruits and their soaking liquid in a pan with the sugar. Simmer, covered, over a low heat for 20 to 30 minutes until they are very soft. Uncover towards the end to reduce the liquid if necessary. Let them cool, then chill in the refrigerator.

For the custard, bring the milk to the boil in a heavy-bottomed saucepan, watching that it does not boil over, and remove from the heat. In a bowl, beat the egg yolks with the sugar to a light pale cream with an electric mixer, then beat in the flour.

Gradually pour in the hot milk, a little at a time, beating vigorously until well blended. Then pour the mixture back into the pan. Stir constantly with a wooden spoon or heatproof spatula over a very low heat for about 10 minutes until the custard thickens. If any lumps form at the start they will disappear as you work the custard vigorously. Add the rum and mix well. Pour the custard into a serving bowl. Let it cool, cover with cling film and chill.

Serve in little bowls, the custard at the bottom and the cooked fruits on top with their wine sauce. There will be a lot of custard; pass around what is left for people to help themselves to more. You may also like to pass around a bowl of toasted almonds, pine nuts or walnuts, or a mix of all three, for people to sprinkle on top.

❋ 250g prunes

❋ 250g dried peaches or apricots

❋ 250ml red wine

❋ 750ml water, or more to cover

❋ 100g sugar

For the custard

❋ 500ml whole milk

❋ 6 large egg yolks

❋ 175g caster sugar

❋ 3 tablespoons plain flour

❋ 3–4 tablespoons rum

To serve with

❋ toasted almonds, pine nuts and walnuts (optional)

FRESH FRUITS STEWED *in* WINE
❊ *compota de frutas*

Navarre is known for the quality of its fruits. This compote goes well served with the rice pudding on page 447. The fruits turn a beautiful purplish red and their flavour is rich and delicious.

SERVES 6

Put the wine and sugar in a large pan with the lemon peel and cinnamon stick. Peel the pears and apples, cut them into quarters and cut the cores out, then cut them into eighths and drop them into the pan. Bring to the boil and simmer, uncovered, for 25 to 30 minutes until they are only just tender. The cooking time depends on the degree of ripeness of the fruit and takes longer in the syrup than it would in water.

To peel the peaches, poach them in boiling water for less than a minute and drain. The skin will come off easily. Cut them into quarters, remove the stones and add them to the pan when the apples and pears are almost tender. Simmer a few minutes more until all the fruits are soft.

Serve the compote cold or at room temperature, sprinkled with lightly toasted almonds or pine nuts if you like.

- 1 x 750ml bottle of Rioja or other dry red wine
- 125g sugar
- peel of 1 lemon, cut into 2 or 3 strips
- 1 cinnamon stick
- 3 unripe pears
- 3 apples
- 3 peaches
- 75g blanched almonds or pine nuts, lightly toasted (optional)

PUMPKIN DESSERT
✳ *arnadí de calabaza*

This is an Easter pudding from the Costa del Azahar (the 'orange blossom' coast), made with a large type of sweet orange-fleshed pumpkin. The finished dish looks like a pyramid spiked with almonds and has a soft, moist texture and an unusual flavour. If you like pumpkin you will love *arnadí*. But much depends on the taste of the pumpkin. The pumpkin you need is usually sold by the slice, weighing between 500g and 1kg, with the seeds and stringy fibres removed. You can also use butternut squash – it is now often sold already peeled and cubed. Andresito (see page 268) had lots of huge pumpkins growing in his garden in Alicante. This is his recipe. He sometimes mixes boiled and mashed sweet potatoes (*boniato*) in with the pumpkin, which makes the pudding sweeter and firmer.

SERVES 8–10

To prepare the pumpkin or butternut squash, if necessary, scrape away any seeds or stringy bits from the slice – halve it first if it is a whole fruit. The rind is thin but very hard so it is more easily removed if you first cut the pumpkin or squash into large chunks. Lay down the chunks on a chopping board and cut the skin away by pressing down with force with a large heavy knife.

Cut the pumpkin or squash flesh into pieces of about 3 to 4cm. Put them in a wide saucepan with 250ml water and cook, tightly covered so that they steam, over a low heat for about 15 to 20 minutes or until soft. Have a look to see that all the water has not evaporated too quickly and add a little more if necessary. Drain and mash the flesh with a potato masher. Continue to cook, uncovered and stirring, over a medium heat for about 5 minutes until most of the liquid has evaporated.

Stir in the sugar – the amount will depend on the sweetness of the pumpkin or squash – and continue to cook until nearly all the moisture has evaporated, stirring often and making sure that the purée does not burn. This can take about 15 to 25 minutes.

Remove the pan from the heat, add the ground almonds, eggs, lemon zest and cinnamon, and mix very well.

Scrape the pumpkin and almond paste into a round shallow baking dish and shape it into a pyramid. Push the blanched almonds half in on their pointed ends, to form lines down the sides of the pyramid. Then dust the whole thing with icing sugar.

Bake in an oven preheated to 190°C/gas 5 for 50 minutes. Let it cool and serve at room temperature.

- 750g cleaned pumpkin or butternut squash flesh
- about 250g sugar, to taste
- 125g ground almonds
- 2 large eggs, lightly beaten
- grated zest of 1 lemon
- 1 teaspoon ground cinnamon
- 50–75g whole blanched almonds
- 2–3 tablespoons icing sugar

APPLE OMELETTE
✤ *tortilla de manzana*

There are seventeen varieties of indigenous apples in Asturias ranging from sweet and semi-sweet to tart and slightly bitter, many of them used for making cider. The local Reineta apples are used for baking and cooking. According to the British National Fruit Collection, there are at least fifteen different types of this apple, most of them grown in France, but none in Britain. When I asked people in Asturias and elsewhere in northern Spain what apples we could substitute, they all said Golden Delicous.

You can cook the apples in advance but the omelette must be made at the last minute.

SERVES 4

Melt the butter with the olive oil in a large frying pan and then take off the heat while you cut up the apples. Cut each of the apple quarters into two slices and sauté them all in the pan over a medium-low heat for 15 to 20 minutes, turning them over once, until soft and lightly browned on both sides. Sprinkle evenly with 1 tablespoon of the sugar as soon as they go in, then sprinkle again with the remaining sugar when you have turned them over.

Beat the eggs lightly in a bowl. Lift out the apples from the pan, leaving the butter mixture in the pan, and gently fold the apples into the eggs.

Preheat the grill. A few minutes before serving, heat the pan and, when the butter mixture sizzles, pour in the egg and apple mixture and cook for 2 to 3 minutes over a medium-low heat until the eggs set at the bottom. Put the pan under the grill to set the top of the omelette. It should still be a little creamy inside. Serve it hot.

* 50g unsalted butter
* 1 tablespoon olive oil
* 3 Golden Delicious or other sweet dessert apples, peeled, quartered and cored
* 3 tablespoons caster sugar
* 4 large eggs

VARIATIONS

* You can add 2–3 tablespoons of Calvados or Asturian apple brandy to the apples towards the end of the sautéing.
* Sprinkle ½ a teaspoon of ground cinnamon on the apples when you begin to cook them.

APPLE CREAM
�֍ *crema de manzana*

This is a simple dessert that Asturians make with the local Reineta variety of apples (see opposite). The region is awash with them. Golden Delicious apples are a good substitute. It is another sweet dish that Spaniards like to caramelize.

SERVES 4–6

Peel, quarter and core the apples, dropping them into a bowl of water acidulated with the lemon juice as you go, to stop them discolouring. Then drain and put them in a pan with about 100ml of water. Put the lid on and cook over a low heat – they will steam – for about 15 minutes until they are very soft.

Mash the apples, stir in 150g of the sugar, and cook uncovered, stirring, over a medium-high heat for about 5 to 10 minutes to allow most of the liquid to evaporate.

Beat the egg yolks with the cream in a bowl. Add this to the apple purée and cook, stirring vigorously, over a low heat for 1 to 2 minutes until the mixture thickens slightly. Do not let it boil.

Pour the apple cream into a serving bowl. Let it cool, cover with cling film and chill in the refrigerator.

Just before serving, sprinkle the top with the remaining sugar and caramelize with a mini blowtorch. When it cools it will form a thin crisp sheet of caramel, with brown patches.

- ✺ 1kg Golden Delicious or other dessert apples
- ✺ juice of ½ a lemon
- ✺ 225–250g sugar
- ✺ 5 large egg yolks
- ✺ 150ml single or double cream

SWEET OMELETTE *with* RUM
✢ *tortilla al ron*

This flambéed omelette is delicious and so simple to make. If you have a mini blowtorch you can caramelize the top, but it is just as good without that. Rum was produced in the Caribbean from molasses from the sugar cane introduced there by Spanish colonizers. A Catalan who emigrated to Cuba, Don Facundo Bacardí Massó, developed a way of refining the rough local product and set up a distillery in 1862. In the late nineteenth century, rum was popularized in northern Spain and especially Catalonia by the returning emigrants grown rich in the Cuban tobacco trade. They, like the newly rich industrial bourgeoisie of the north, adopted French haute cuisine and flambéeing was in fashion.

SERVES 2–4

Soak the bread in the milk for about 10 minutes. Beat the eggs lightly with the sugar. Mash the bread with your hands and add it to the egg mixture, leaving behind any excess milk. Beat well with a fork, or use an electric mixer if you want a very smooth texture.

Preheat the grill. Heat the butter in a 26cm frying pan and, when it begins to sizzle, pour in the egg mixture. Cook for 2 to 3 minutes over a low heat until the bottom sets, then place the pan under the grill for 1 to 3 minutes until the top has set. Slip the omelette on to a serving plate.

If you like, sprinkle the omelette with the 2 tablespoons of icing or caster sugar and caramelize the sugar using a mini blowtorch.

Heat the rum in a ladle or in a small metal cup. Hold a lighted match over the edge and, when you see blue flames, pour the flaming rum all over the omelette. Serve hot.

* 3–4 slices of firm white bread, crusts removed (about 100g without the crusts)
* 175ml whole milk
* 5 large eggs
* 60g caster sugar
* 30g unsalted butter
* 2 tablespoons icing or superfine caster sugar (optional)
* 2 tablespoons rum

PANCAKES FILLED *with* APPLE PURÉE
✳ *frisuelos de manzana*

Thin pancakes like French crêpes are a speciality of Asturias and also of Galicia, where they are called *filloas*. They are often simply served folded and dusted with icing sugar and cinnamon, or with a trickle of honey, or a liqueur or whipped cream. This version, stuffed with apple purée, is absolutely delicious and elegant to serve. The version stuffed with custard on the following page is also delicous. The pancakes can be made in advance, even days before, and kept in the refrigerator, covered with cling film, to be filled later.

MAKES ABOUT 25 X 19CM PANCAKES

For the pancakes, put the flour in a bowl. Add the milk and water gradually, beating vigorously with an electric mixer. Add the eggs, salt, oil and brandy and beat until the batter is smooth and free of lumps. Cover with cling film and leave to rest for 1 to 2 hours.

For the filling, peel, quarter and core the apples, dropping them in a bowl of water acidulated with the lemon juice as you go, to prevent them from discolouring. Drain and put the apples in a pan with a tight-fitting lid. Add 4 to 5 tablespoons of water. Cook, covered tightly, over a very low heat for about 15 to 20 minutes until the apples fall apart (they will steam in their own juice), then mash and continue to cook, uncovered and stirring often, until much of the liquid has evaporated. Add the sugar and Calvados and stir until the sugar has dissolved.

Now make the pancakes. Heat a non-stick frying pan with a base diameter of about 19cm over a medium heat and grease it with oil, using a folded piece of kitchen paper. Stir the batter well and pour about 2 tablespoonfuls into the frying pan. Tilt the pan around very quickly until its entire bottom surface is covered with the batter. The pancake should be thin. When it becomes detached from the pan and the bottom is lightly browned, flip it over with a large heatproof spatula (or pick up the edge with your fingers) and cook for a few moments only on the other side until it just becomes detached. Continue this process until all the batter is used up, rubbing the pan with oil each time, and stacking the pancakes in a pile on a plate.

To fill the pancakes, put a heaped tablespoon of apple purée in a line on one end of the pancake and roll it up. Place the stuffed pancakes, seam side down, in two baking dishes greased with butter. Finish by pouring over a little Calvados or apple brandy and sprinkling with sugar. Heat through in an oven preheated to 200°C/gas 6 for 10 to 20 minutes. Serve hot.

For the pancakes
- ✳ 300g plain flour
- ✳ 600ml whole milk
- ✳ 300ml water
- ✳ 2 large eggs, lightly beaten
- ✳ 1 teaspoon salt
- ✳ 1 tablespoon olive or sunflower oil, plus more to grease the frying pan
- ✳ 1 tablespoon brandy

For the apple filling
- ✳ 1kg Golden Delicious apples
- ✳ juice of ½ a lemon
- ✳ 6 tablespoons sugar
- ✳ 4 tablespoons Calvados or other apple brandy, or to taste

To finish
- ✳ butter, to grease the oven dish
- ✳ 4 tablespoons Calvados or other apple brandy
- ✳ 4 tablespoons caster sugar

PANCAKES FILLED *with* CUSTARD
❊ *frisuelos con crema pastelera*

Make the pancakes as in the previous recipe and fill them with this custard instead of the apple purée. This quantity fills 16 of the 19cm pancakes. My favourite flavour for the custard is rum but see the variations for the other common flavours. Keep the leftover unfilled pancakes for another day.

❋ 1 x quantity of pancakes from the previous recipe (page 467)

For the custard filling ❋ 175g caster sugar ❋ 5 large egg yolks ❋ 3 tablespoons plain flour
❋ 500ml whole milk ❋ 3 tablespoons rum

Follow the instructions on page 467 to make the pancakes.

For the filling, beat the sugar in a large bowl with the egg yolks, using an electric mixer, until you have a smooth pale cream. Then beat in the flour.

Bring the milk to the boil in a heavy-bottomed pan – be careful not to let it boil over. Pour the milk into the egg mixture, a little at a time, beating until well blended. Pour this back into the pan and stir constantly over a low heat with a wooden spoon or heatproof spatula until the custard thickens and almost reaches boiling point. Beat in the rum towards the end. If lumps form they will disappear as you work the custard vigorously.

Let the custard cool before filling the pancakes following the instructions in the previous recipe.

VARIATIONS
▩ Omit the rum and add 1 teaspoon of pure vanilla extract to the milk as you bring it to the boil.
▩ Omit the rum and add the grated zest of ½ an orange to the milk as you bring it to the boil.

APPLE *and* SPONGE PUDDING
❀ *dulce de manzana con bizcocho*

There is a big tradition of making sponge cake in Spain and it is often eaten dipped or soaked in sweet wine. Here, layers of sponge fingers (also called boudoir biscuits) dampened in sweet wine alternate with layers of apple purée. Make this dish with sweet dessert apples such as Coxes or Golden Delicious.

SERVES 6–8

Peel, quarter and core the apples and drop them, as you go, into a large bowl of water acidulated with the lemon juice to prevent them discolouring.

Drain the apples and put them in a pan with about 100ml of the wine. Cook with the lid on over a low heat for 15 to 20 minutes, until the apples are soft. Mash them with a potato masher and then continue to cook, uncovered and stirring, over a medium to high heat for a further 15 to 20 minutes until all the liquid has evaporated (the bottom of the pan should look dry) and you have a smooth purée. Let it cool.

Line a 24cm round mould or cake tin with enough cling film so that it overhangs generously all the way around the edges. Spread half the apple purée at the bottom.

Pour the remaining wine into a wide soup plate. Moisten the sponge fingers in the wine, a few at a time, and leave them in for seconds only (if they absorb too much wine they will be soggy and fall apart). Arrange half the sponge fingers in a layer on top of the apple purée, trimming some as necessary to make them fit in the round surface. Cover with the remaining apple purée and then a second layer of sponge fingers dampened in sweet wine.

Cover with the overhanging cling film and another piece on top. Chill in the refrigerator for 3 hours or overnight. To serve, remove the cling film from the top, turn upside down on to a platter, lift off the mould or tin and remove the second piece of cling film.

VARIATION

❀ Use a sweet cider instead of the two wines.

- ❀ 1kg apples
- ❀ juice of ½ a lemon
- ❀ about 500ml sweet white wine such as a Moscatel (the amount depends on the type of sponge fingers)
- ❀ 1 x packet of ladyfingers (about 175g)

ALMOND CREAM
✤ *bienmesabe*

Bien me sabe means 'tastes good to me'. This is a thick, dense almond cream – more like a paste – that accompanies pastries and ice cream and is spread on toast. It is very rich so serve small amounts. It keeps for several days in the refrigerator. Use blanched almonds and grind them finely, or buy them already ground. Serve it with sponge fingers dipped, if you like, in sweet wine – it can be the Canary Island's Malvasia wine or a sweet Malaga wine, or dip them in rum.

SERVES 8

Bring the sugar and water to the boil in a pan with the cinnamon stick and stir with a wooden spoon until the sugar has dissolved. Then remove the cinnamon stick and put in the ground almonds.

Cook, stirring constantly, over a low heat for about 7 minutes until the mixture thickens to a paste. Stir in the almond extract, if using, and the grated lemon zest, and take off the heat. Be very careful not to add too much almond extract as that could give it a nasty taste. Let it cool a little.

Beat the egg yolks vigorously, then stir them into the almond paste. Put the pan back over a low heat and stir constantly until you see one or two bubbles come up to the surface, then take off the heat. Serve the cream at room temperature – spoon small amounts on to individual plates. Pour a little sweet wine in people's glasses and pass around sponge fingers to dip in at the same time.

* 250g sugar
* 250ml water
* 1 cinnamon stick
* 250g ground almonds
* 2 drops almond extract (optional)
* grated zest of ½ a lemon
* 9 large egg yolks
* sponge fingers, to serve
* Malvasia or sweet Malaga wine, for dipping

ALMOND CAKE
✳ *tarta de santiago*

This is a splendid cake which is normally made in a wide cake or tart tin and comes out low, but it is equally good as a thicker cake. I have eaten almond cakes in other parts of Spain but this one is special. Pilgrims and tourists who visit the great Cathedral of Santiago de Compostela in Galicia, where the relics of the apostle Saint James are believed to be buried, see the cake in all the windows of every pastry shop and restaurant, decorated with the shape of the cross of the Order of Santiago. I have watched the cake being made in many sizes, big and small, over a pastry tart base at a bakery called Capri in Pontevedra. This deliciously moist and fragrant homely version is without a base. When I suggested to a man associated with the Galicia tourist office that the *tarta* was a Jewish Passover cake, he dragged me to a television studio to explain all. The presenters liked the idea. The Galician city of Corunna is on the Jewish tourist route. There is a synagogue and an old Jewish quarter there. Jews from Andalusia fleeing the Berber Almohads' attempts to convert them came to Galicia in the twelfth and thirteenth centuries.

SERVES 10

Grind the almonds finely in the food processor. Beat the egg yolks with the sugar to a pale cream with an electric mixer, then beat in the orange and lemon zests and almond extract. Add the ground almonds and mix very well.

With the cleaned mixer, whisk the egg whites until stiff and fold them into the egg and almond mixture – the mixture is so thick that you need to turn it over quite a bit into the egg whites. Grease a spring-form cake tin around 28cm in diameter (preferably non-stick) with butter and dust it with flour, then pour in the cake mixture.

Put the cake into an oven preheated to 180°C/gas 4 for 40 minutes or until it feels firm. Let it cool before turning out. Dust the top with icing sugar. If you like, cut the shape of a Santiago cross out of paper and place it in the middle of the cake before dusting with icing sugar. Then remove the paper shape.

VARIATIONS

※ Add 1 teaspoon of ground cinnamon to the almond and egg mixture.

※ In Majorca, they make a similar almond cake called *gató d'ametla*, which is flavoured with the grated zest of 1 lemon, 1 teaspoon of ground cinnamon and sometimes a few drops of vanilla extract.

※ In Navarre, they cover the cake with apricot jam.

- ※ 250g blanched almonds
- ※ 6 eggs, separated
- ※ 250g caster sugar
- ※ grated zest of 1 orange
- ※ grated zest of 1 lemon
- ※ 4 drops almond extract
- ※ butter, to grease the cake tin
- ※ flour, to dust the cake tin
- ※ icing sugar, for dusting the cake

PUFF PASTRY FILLED *with an* ALMONDY CUSTARD
❖ *costrada con crema franchipán*

This is a Spanish take on the French *gâteau basque*, a flaky-crust pie filled with custard. It is easier to make and more delicious than the French version, with its combination of crisp, light puff pastry and luscious *crema franchipán* – a custard made with almonds. The flavouring for the filling can be vanilla or grated orange zest, but my favourite is rum. I use a ready-rolled bought puff-pastry sheet weighing 375g and measuring about 35cm by 22cm, but use the type of pastry that is most easily available to you and roll it out if necessary. The pastries are best eaten warm and can be reheated. You must try them. Another name for them is *milhojas calientes* (hot millefeuilles).

MAKES 8 PASTRIES

To make the custard, beat the sugar with the 5 egg yolks in a large bowl with an electric mixer to a smooth, very pale cream. Then beat in the flour thoroughly.

Bring the milk to the boil in a heavy-bottomed pan then very gradually pour this into the egg mixture, beating vigorously until well blended. Pour the mixture back into the pan and gradually bring almost to the boil over a low heat, stirring constantly with a wooden spoon or spatula until the custard thickens. If lumps form at the start they will disappear as you work the custard vigorously. You can also take it off the heat and whisk it with the electric mixer. Stir in the almonds and the rum.

Unroll the pastry on to a lightly oiled sheet of foil on a baking sheet and cut it into 8 rectangles. Brush the tops with the remaining 1 egg yolk mixed with a drop of water, and bake in an oven preheated to 200°C/gas 6 for about 20 to 25 minutes or until the pastries have puffed up and are golden brown. When the pastries have cooled a little, cut them horizontally through the middle with a pointed serrated knife and fill each one with about 5 tablespoons of the thick custard – warmed up a little or left as it is.

If you make the pastries in advance, you can heat them through briefly before serving. Dust, if you like, with icing sugar.

VARIATIONS
- Omit the rum and add 1 teaspoon of pure vanilla extract to the milk.
- Omit the rum and put the grated zest of 1 orange in the custard.

- 175g caster sugar
- 5 large egg yolks, plus 1 more for the glaze
- 4 tablespoons plain flour
- 500ml whole milk
- 100g blanched almonds, coarsely ground in the food processor
- 3 tablespoons rum
- 1 x 375g chilled, ready-rolled puff-pastry sheet
- oil, to grease the baking sheet
- icing sugar, to dust the tops of the pastries (optional)

PASTRY ROLLS FILLED *with* WALNUTS
❊ *casadielles*

In Asturias, I stayed with the *New Yorker* journalist Jane Kramer (she was writing a piece about me) in Jaime Rodriguez and his wife Marichu's farmhouse in Llenín near Cangas de Onís. We had met Jaime in the street and he had invited us to stay. It is a little mountain paradise with a sweeping view of the Picos de Europa mountains. Now the farmhouse has been transformed into a beautiful and welcoming *casa rural*, a family guest house called Heredad de la Cueste. Marichu's mother cooks traditional food with local produce for the guests. We had *casadielles*, fried pastry rolls filled with walnuts, for breakfast. At home I tried several different pastry doughs. This one with olive oil worked best. It can be rolled out easily to make a thin, crisp crust for the soft, moist, aromatic walnut filling. In Asturias it is usual to fry the pastries but I find they are better baked.

MAKES 12 *CASADIELLES*

❊ 125ml olive oil, plus a little more to grease the baking sheet ❊ 125ml warm water
❊ ½ teaspoon caster sugar ❊ about 350g plain flour ❊ 1 egg yolk, beaten with 1 teaspoon water
❊ icing sugar, to dust the pastries

For the filling ❊ 200g walnuts ❊ 100g caster sugar ❊ 30g unsalted butter
❊ 3–4 tablespoons anise-flavoured spirit, such as pastis, ouzo or arak

For the dough, mix the oil, water and sugar in a bowl, beating vigorously with a fork. Then gradually work in enough flour to have a soft, smooth, malleable dough that does not stick. Begin by stirring the flour in with the fork, then work it in with your hands and knead briefly. You may use the dough right away, or keep it, wrapped in cling film at room temperature, not chilled in the refrigerator, until you are ready to use it.

To make the filling, grind the walnuts fairly coarsely in the food processor with the sugar and butter, then add the anise-flavoured spirit and blend very briefly.

Divide the dough into two pieces to make rolling easier. Roll each piece out thinly to about 2 or 3mm thick. Do not flour the surface or the rolling pin – the dough is oily and does not stick. Cut each sheet of dough into 6 rectangles about 13cm by 9cm.

Take a lump of filling the size of a walnut, shape it into a loose sausage and lay it along the edge of a long side of a dough rectangle. Using your little finger or a cotton bud, paint a thin line of egg yolk mixed with water along the three remaining edges (this is to make the dough stick better). Then roll up like a cigar and pinch the two ends firmly. Do the same with the remaining dough rectangles and filling. Arrange the *casadielles* on a lightly oiled baking sheet and brush the tops with the remaining egg yolk and water mixture.

Bake the *casadielles* in an oven preheated to 150°C/gas 2 for about 30 minutes, or until slightly golden. Let them cool before moving them to a serving plate and dusting them with icing sugar.

FRIED CREAM
✳ *leche frita*

Leche frita, literally meaning 'fried milk', can be bought in pastry shops, where the creamy pastries are most often made with cornflour. I prefer the texture of this homely version that uses wheat flour as the thickener. They can be eaten hot or cold and can be reheated. Straight out of the oil, they are crunchy outside and very creamy inside.

MAKES 16 PASTRIES

✳ 150g plain flour ✳ 750ml whole milk ✳ 100g caster sugar ✳ grated zest of 1 lemon or 1 orange ✳ 2 large egg yolks ✳ about 100g fine breadcrumbs or matzo meal ✳ 1 large egg, lightly beaten ✳ sunflower oil, for deep-frying and for oiling the dish ✳ 4 tablespoons icing sugar, to dust ✳ 1 teaspoon ground cinnamon, to dust

In a bowl dissolve the flour in 250ml of the cold milk, adding the milk gradually and beating vigorously with an electric mixer to get rid of any lumps.

Bring the rest of the milk to the boil in a saucepan with the sugar and lemon or orange zest. Add the flour and milk mixture, stirring vigorously, and cook, stirring constantly, over a low heat until you get a thick cream. If lumps form you can get rid of them by beating with an electric mixer straight in the pan. Continue to cook very gently over a low heat, stirring often, for about another 10 minutes. Add the egg yolks, and stir vigorously for a few seconds more. Do not let the cream boil or the yolks will curdle.

Lightly oil a square or rectangular dish and pour in the cream so that you have a layer about 2cm thick. Let the cream cool, then chill, covered with cling film, in the refrigerator for about 2 hours until set very firm.

Cover a plate with the fine breadcrumbs or matzo meal. Beat the whole egg lightly in a soup plate. Turn the cream out on to a large flat oiled platter or surface and cut it into 16 squares or rectangles. Lift each piece very carefully, turn it gently in the egg then in the breadcrumbs or matzo meal so that it is well covered. Heat plenty of oil (about 2cm depth) in a frying pan until a piece of bread sizzles when it is dropped in but does not brown too quickly. Deep-fry the coated cream squares in batches until golden brown, turning them over once. Lift them out and drain on kitchen paper.

Serve hot or cold, dusted with icing sugar and cinnamon.

WALNUT CAKE *with* BRANDY
✤ *tarta de nuez con brandy*

The lower slopes of the Asturian mountains are covered with walnut and chestnut trees. Walnut cakes are common there. This version with a syrup poured over is sensational. It has a marvellous texture and a pure walnut taste with a touch of brandy. Make sure the walnuts you use are good and fresh without a rancid taste by trying one.

SERVES 8–10

Coarsely grind the walnuts in the food processor. Beat the eggs and sugar with an electric mixer until you have a thick, pale cream. Add the slightly cooled melted butter and the brandy or cognac and beat well. Then fold in the walnuts and pour into a greased and floured spring-form cake tin about 28cm in diameter. Bake in an oven preheated to 180°C/gas 4 for 45 minutes or until it feels firm.

For the syrup, heat the sugar and water in a pan so that the sugar melts and then simmer for about 5 minutes and add the brandy or cognac. Pour it hot all over the surface of the cake as it comes out of the oven. Let the syrup seep into the cake while in the tin for at least 1 hour before serving.

※ 500g walnuts

※ 4 large eggs

※ 200g caster sugar

※ 75g unsalted butter, melted

※ 3 tablespoons brandy or cognac

※ butter, to grease the cake tin

※ flour, to dust the cake tin

For the syrup

※ 100g sugar

※ 250ml water

※ 1 tablespoon brandy or cognac

WALNUT CAKE
❋ *pastel de nuez*

I have tried an Asturian walnut cake made with only egg whites beaten stiff but I prefer this one with the yolks as well because it is moist, the way I like nutty cakes. These measures give a small, thin cake. I bake it in a 22cm cake tin and it comes out 2cm thick. It is quick and easy to make.

SERVES 4–6

Beat the eggs and egg yolks with the sugar to a pale thick cream with an electric mixer, then add the grated orange zest. Coarsely grind the walnuts in the food processor and add them to the egg mixture. Mix well and pour into a greased and floured spring-form cake or tart tin. Bake in an oven preheated to 200°C/gas 6 for 40 minutes. Let it cool before removing from the tin. Dust with icing sugar.

- 2 whole eggs
- 2 egg yolks
- 125g caster sugar
- grated zest of 1 orange
- 125g walnuts
- butter, to grease the cake tin
- flour, to dust the cake tin
- icing sugar, to dust the top of the cake

about chocolate cakes and desserts

According to legend, chocolate was first encountered by the Spaniards as a drink in Mexico in 1519, when the conquistador Hernando Cortés met the Aztec ruler Moctezuma, and it was Cortés who introduced the chocolate drink to the Spanish court. Chocolate remained known only as a drink in Spain until the nineteenth century and was always something that only the rich could afford. It was also associated with the Church because monks in the Americas sent cocoa beans to their monasteries back home. The clergy encouraged the use of chocolate during Lent, believing it to have restorative and medicinal properties. In the mid seventeenth century, Pope Alexander VII declared that liquids, including chocolate, did not break the fast.

The first Spanish cocoa factory was in Astorga in Leon (there is now a chocolate museum there) and the Maragato muleteers (see page 71) transported the powder all over Spain. A Basque trading company, the Real Compañía Guipuzcoana de Caracas, held the monopoly on the Venezuelan cocoa trade in the eighteenth century. Cocoa beans arrived in the Basque ports and were re-exported to cities all over Europe. One of these was the French Basque city of Bayonne, just over the border, where Spanish and Portuguese Converso families started a chocolate industry, the first in France. That is where the Basques and Catalans first got the hard block chocolate that they used to make cakes.

Chocolate cakes and desserts are part of the bourgeois cuisines of Spain that developed in the late nineteenth and early twentieth centuries in the industrialized north of the country. It was the time when Spain gradually lost its colonies and many Spaniards who had made their fortunes overseas came back to settle in large numbers in Asturias, the Basque Country and Catalonia, and in port cities like Cadiz and Santander. They built fabulous houses painted pink, orange, mauve, blue and green, inspired by the colonial houses in Mexico, and invested in the emerging industries. The newly rich local bourgeoisie and these *indianos* (returnees from the Americas) employed cooks and demanded from them a refined, mostly French, sophisticated style of cooking and baking.

CHOCOLATE *and* WALNUT CAKE
✳ *tarta de chocolate con nueces*

Chocolate was only known as a beverage and there were no chocolate cakes in Spain until they appeared in Catalonia and the Basque Country in the late nineteenth century. This chocolate cake is extremely rich, so do not serve large portions. It has two layers – one is firm and nutty and the topping is light and creamy.

SERVES 12

Beat the egg yolks with the cognac and sugar in a large bowl using a fork. Melt the chocolate in a double boiler, or in a Pyrex bowl or small pan sitting on top of a pan containing water over a low heat so that the top pan or bowl does not touch the boiling water (this is to avoid overheating and spoiling the chocolate), and mix it into the egg mixture.

Coarsely chop the walnuts in the food processor – some will be finely ground in the process – and fold them in. Beat the egg whites with an electric mixer until stiff and forming peaks and fold them into the cake mixture.

Grease a spring-form cake tin about 25cm in diameter (preferably non-stick) with butter and dust it with flour. Pour the cake mixture in and bake in an oven preheated to 180°C/gas 4 for about 45 minutes or until firm. Leave in the tin until cool before turning out.

For the topping, melt the chocolate as above, over boiling water. Stir in the rum, and let it cool slightly. Beat the whipping cream until it forms stiff peaks and fold into the melted chocolate.

Remove the cake from its tin when it has cooled and spread the topping over the top and sides.

* 6 large eggs, separated
* 4 tablespoons cognac
* 150g caster sugar
* 100g dark bitter chocolate, broken into pieces
* 200g walnuts
* butter, to grease the cake tin
* flour, to dust the cake tin

For the topping

* 150g dark bitter chocolate, broken into pieces
* 2 tablespoons rum
* 300ml whipping cream

CHESTNUT *and* CHOCOLATE TRUFFLE CAKE
❋ *trufas de castañas y chocolate*

This cake has a smooth truffle-like texture. It is very rich, so expect to serve it in small portions. Chestnuts appear during winter festivals. All Saints' Day in Catalonia is celebrated with a *castanyada*, when roasted chestnuts, sweet potatoes and *panellets*, marzipan balls covered in pine nuts (page 492) are eaten.

SERVES MORE THAN 12

Boil the chestnuts in the milk for about 10 minutes over a low heat until they are soft, then stir in the vanilla extract. Melt the butter and chocolate in a Pyrex bowl or small pan sitting on top of a pan containing water over a low heat so that the top pan or bowl does not touch the boiling water (this is a double boiler).

Blend the chestnuts and milk to a purée in the food processor. Add the sugar, the melted chocolate and butter, the egg yolks and the cognac or brandy and blend until smooth and homogeneous.

Beat the egg whites with an electric mixer until they form stiff peaks, then fold them into the chocolate and chestnut mixture.

Line a 23cm spring-form cake tin with foil and grease the foil with butter, then pour in the cake mixture. Bake in an oven preheated to 160°C/gas 3 for 30 to 35 minutes until just set but still slightly wobbly. It will firm as it cools.

VARIATION
❋ For a rougher texture, mash the chestnuts with a potato masher and mix them thoroughly by hand with the other ingredients.

- 250g chestnuts, fresh peeled, vacuum-packed or frozen and defrosted
- 250ml whole milk
- 1 teaspoon pure vanilla extract
- 250g unsalted butter, cut into pieces
- 250g dark chocolate, broken into pieces
- 125g caster sugar
- 4 eggs, separated
- 3 tablespoons cognac or brandy
- butter, to grease the cake tin

CHOCOLATE *and* ALMOND CAKE
❋ *pastel de chocolate y almendras*

This is a moist cake that is good to serve as a dessert with cream. The recipe comes from a little book that Carolina Zendrera, my Spanish publisher, gave me, entitled *Recetas tradicionales: La ermitaña de la cocina, cocina burguesa del siglo XX* ('Traditional Recipes: The hermit in the kitchen – bourgeois cooking in the twentieth century'), published by Zendrera Zariquiey in 1999. The recipes are those of Águeda Bienzobas, who cooked for Carolina Zendrera's grandparents and family in Catalonia for fifty years. Águeda was born in a village in Navarre in 1907 and went to work in the Martí-Codolars' kitchen in Barcelona as a young girl. The Martí-Codolars, Zendrera's grandparents, were an illustrious family involved in shipping. On their farm they kept rare animals, including an elephant that was later donated to Barcelona Zoo. What Águeda learnt from the family cook, and what became her repertoire gathered over the years, which her husband wrote down, is a distinctive mix of Spanish and French haute cuisine. A family friend of the Martí-Codolars called her 'the hermit' because she spent her time alone in the kitchen.

SERVES 10

Heat the chocolate with the water in a Pyrex bowl or small pan that is sitting on top of a pan containing water over a low heat so that the top pan or bowl does not touch the boiling water (this is a double boiler), until almost melted. Add the butter and let them both melt.

In a bowl mix the egg yolks, sugar, ground almonds, baking powder and rum very well. Add the melted chocolate and butter and mix vigorously. Beat the egg whites until stiff with an electric mixer and fold them into the mixture.

Grease a spring-form cake tin about 23cm in diameter (preferably non-stick) with butter and dust it with flour. Pour in the cake mixture and bake in an oven preheated to 160°C/gas 3 for about 35 minutes until firm. Turn out when it is cool.

For the optional topping, melt the chocolate with the water in the small bowl or pan over boiling water, as above. Add the sugar and the butter, let them melt and mix well. Spread over the cake.

- 150g dark bitter chocolate or baking chocolate such as the Menier Chocolat Patissier, broken into pieces
- 3 tablespoons water
- 150g unsalted butter, cut into pieces
- 4 large eggs, separated
- 100g caster sugar
- 100g ground almonds
- 1 teaspoon baking powder
- 4 tablespoons rum
- butter, to grease the cake tin
- flour, to dust the cake tin

For the optional topping

- 50g dark bitter chocolate, broken into pieces
- 2 tablespoons water
- 50g caster sugar
- 25g unsalted butter

CHESTNUT *and* CHOCOLATE FLAN
❊ *flan de castañas y chocolate*

Chestnut trees and forests are found all over Spain. Chestnuts were a staple food of the peasantry before the arrival of potatoes and maize from the Americas. In the time of the first Bourbons, cooks in the homes of the aristocracy made marrons glacés and chestnut puddings, and the Andalusian bourgeoisie and those of northern Spain adopted their ways.

SERVES 10

Make the caramel first. Put the sugar and water in a stainless steel saucepan over a medium heat. When the syrup begins to bubble and colour in patches, swirl the pan to spread the caramel evenly. Cook until it turns to a deep amber, swirling the pan (watch it as it can turn too dark very quickly, which results in a bitter taste). Pour the caramel immediately into a heatproof mould (it can be metal, porcelain or Pyrex, but not non-stick) about 23cm to 26cm in diameter and at least 6.5cm high, moving and tilting the mould to coat the bottom and sides well. You have to do this very fast because the caramel hardens quickly.

Put the chestnuts and 500ml of the milk in a saucepan and simmer over a low heat for 10 minutes until the chestnuts are soft, then drain and discard the milk.

Add the vanilla and sugar to the remaining 500ml of milk in a pan and slowly bring to simmering point, stirring to dissolve the sugar, and then remove from the heat.

Grind the chocolate as fine as possible in the food processor. Add the drained chestnuts and blend to a soft paste. Gradually add the warm milk and then the cognac or brandy.

Beat the eggs with a fork in a large bowl, then gradually beat in the chestnut mixture and pour into the caramel-coated mould. Place the mould in a large shallow pan and pour in enough boiling water to come about halfway up the side of the mould (this water bath is called a bain-marie).

Bake in an oven preheated to 160°C/gas 3 for 1 to 1¼ hours, or until the flan feels firm. Let it cool, then chill in the refrigerator for 2 to 3 hours, covered with cling film. Before serving, run a pointed knife round the edge of the flan, place a serving dish on top of the mould (there will be some caramel sauce, so the dish should be deep enough to collect it), turn the flan upside down and lift off the mould.

❊ 200g chestnuts, fresh peeled, vacuum-packed or frozen and defrosted

❊ 1 litre whole milk

❊ 1 teaspoon pure vanilla extract

❊ 200g sugar

❊ 150g dark bitter chocolate, broken into pieces

❊ 6 tablespoons cognac or other brandy

❊ 7 large eggs

For the caramel

❊ 100g sugar

❊ 3 tablespoons water

DULCES DE CONVENTO
pastries and confectionery from
the hidden world of cloistered nuns

I rented a room at El Monasterio de Santa María del Socorro, the convent of a Conceptionist Franciscan order of nuns on the Calle de Bustos Tavera in the old quarter of Seville. From the outside it looks like an ordinary house on a narrow street. Inside, the decor is Mudejar. Blue-and-white tiles line the walls and there is an interior patio and a small church. A picture of the Virgin Mary looked down on my bed. I thought of the room I shared with my Slovene–Italian nanny Maria in Egypt. She had been a novice Catholic nun but was convinced by her family that it was better for her to find work in Egypt, as many Slovene women did at the time, and to send money home. A crucifix, images of the Virgin and icons of saints hung on our walls. There was a branch from the 'Virgin's Tree' in Matariya under which Joseph and Mary are believed to have rested.

I had hoped to see the nuns making pastries and did not realize that it would not be possible because they are cloistered. I only saw Sor Inmaculada Romero, who is in charge of the rented rooms, and an older, very cheerful nun who passed the pastries round on a wooden *torno* (lazy Susan). The monastery was founded in 1522 in an existing house by Doña Juana Ayala for women of the nobility who wished to live a life of prayer and contemplation. The nuns today spend their time in prayer and silent contemplation and make pastries to support themselves and maintain the convent. Seville has more monasteries and churches than any city in Spain and is famous for its convent pastries made by cloistered nuns. Santa María del Socorro has the widest range – a list of sixty pastries is pinned near the hatch where the orders are given and the pastries appear. Sister Inmaculada says their secret ingredient is *alegría* – joy. They have brought out their own cookery book.

The only time the closed world of Seville's cloistered nuns interacts with the world of the street is when they come out to sell Christmas specialities in the great patio of the baroque Palacio Arzobispal on 8 December, the annual feast of the Immaculate Conception – *la Purísima, la Inmaculada*. In the old days nuns came to Seville from all over Spain. Now they are more likely to be from Latin America, Africa and India. New nuns learn to make the old traditional pastries whose secrets have been handed down for centuries.

Some convents have their own specialities. At the Monasterio de Santa Paula, an Indian nun sold me jasmine and orange-blossom jams, tomato marmalade, chestnut cream, chillies in syrup and quince paste. San Leandro is famous for its *yemas* – egg yolks cooked in sugar syrup (page 493). I adore them but they are so rich I could only eat one. The nun who served me remained unseen behind the door but answered my questions. She said that by ancient tradition convents had always made pastries to thank their noble protectors and sponsors. They then started selling them after the Spanish Civil War to support themselves. A nun in a convent in Toledo once told me that convent pastries were 'Moorish' because long ago, when mosques and synagogues were first converted into churches and monasteries, aristocratic nuns came to the convents with their Morisco maids.

Around the corner from Santa María del Socorro, the Convento de Santa Inés also sells pastries. It contains the remains of its founder, Doña María Coronel, a Sevillian noblewoman who disfigured herself by throwing boiling oil on her face to escape the persistent amorous advances of Pedro I the Cruel, who had her husband executed. I knew a Jewish family called Coronel in Egypt so I looked up Doña María Coronel, and yes, she was from an illustrious Converso family. My friend Cuqui Gonzales de Caldas, who is from Seville, says that the city has so many churches and monasteries because there had been many wealthy Conversos living there and it is they who donated the funds for the buildings.

Here are some of the traditional pastries that figure in the menu lists of convents: *mazapanes*, *piñonates*, *mantecados*, *mostachones*, *pestiños*, *rosquillas*, *bizcochos*, *cocos*, *milhojas*, *bollos maimones*, *glorias*, *turrones*, *marquesitas*, *torrijas*. And here are those with colourful names: *huesos de santo* ('saints' bones'), *orejas de fraile* ('friars' ears'), *tetas de novicias* ('novice nuns' breasts'), *suspiros de monja* ('nuns' sighs'), *borrachuelos* ('drunkards'), *tocinos de cielo* ('heavenly bacon') and *polvorones* ('dust cakes'). Some convents, inspired by the creativity of modern innovative chefs – they can see them on the internet – now add pastries of their own creation to the old traditional ones.

TOLEDO MARZIPAN ✳ *mazapán de toledo*

Toledo, the old capital of Visigothic Spain and the capital of La Mancha, is also the world capital of marzipan. It is known as the 'city of three cultures' because Christians, Muslims and Jews coexisted there for centuries. I visited Toledo with María Rosa Menocal, the medieval scholar who wrote *The Ornament of the World: How Muslims, Jews and Christians Created a Culture of Tolerance in Medieval Spain* (Little Brown US, 2002). She made me aware of the Mudejar architecture and design in the churches, palaces and synagogues. The inlaying of gold, copper and silver thread into metal, called *damasquino* (Damascene), is a speciality of Toledo that refers to the city of Damascus in Syria.

Cookery teacher and writer Rosa Tovar (see page 250), who sent me this recipe, says there are two ways of making marzipan in Spain. This one, which is used in the two Castiles and in Andalusia, is her favourite. In the other method, common in Catalonia, sugar syrup is boiled down, then ground almonds are added with a little orange-blossom water and the paste is cooked and stirred until it comes away from the sides of the pan. My relatives, who came from Aleppo in Syria, made marzipan in the manner of Toledo and those who came from Istanbul made it in the Catalan way.

Marzipan lasts for weeks. You can get your children to roll it into balls or shapes. In Toledo they form the marzipan into a variety of *figuritas*, shapes such as fish, snails, shells, *huesos de santo* ('saint's bones'). They glaze them and brown them under the grill.

Rosa advised using the Spanish Marcona almonds if you can, which are round and creamy, but those I bought in London were stale. I have made marzipan for years with ordinary blanched almonds or bought ground almonds.

MAKES ABOUT 26 BALLS

✳ 200g ground almonds ✳ 200g icing sugar ✳ 3 drops almond extract ✳ 2–3 tablespoons water

For the glaze ✳ 1 egg white ✳ 1 tablespoon icing sugar

Blend the ground almonds and sugar in the food processor. Add the almond extract, being careful not to add more than a few drops as the taste can become overpowering. Add the water, a tablespoonful at a time, and blend to a thick paste. You need very little water (I used 2 tablespoons only) as the oil from the almonds will hold it together. Knead to a smooth, soft paste. You will see how greasy it is as the almonds release their oils. Shape into firm balls of about 3cm diameter by rolling lumps between the palms of your hands until they are firm and compact. Lay them on a baking tray in a cool, dry place, covered if you like with a tea towel, and leave for 12 to 24 hours.

Make a glaze by beating 1 egg white until firm with an electric mixer, then beating in 1 tablespoon of icing sugar until thick and shiny. Brush the balls with this (you will only need very little) and put them under the grill for 1 minute or until the tops are lightly browned. Alternatively, bake them in an oven preheated to 200°C/gas 6 for about 2 minutes.

PINE NUT *and* MARZIPAN SWEETS
❋ *panellets de piñones*

Panellets are the traditional sweets of All Saints' Day (1 November) in Catalonia, when they are eaten with roasted chestnuts and sweet wine. Mashed potatoes or sweet potatoes are commonly mixed with the marzipan almond paste when they are made industrially, but the sweets do taste best using ground almonds alone. The tricky part is pressing the pine nuts into the marzipan balls and making them stick. These are the kind of sweets that you would make as a special Christmas gift. It is best to make the marzipan paste ahead, even the day before.

MAKES ABOUT 20 *PANELLETS*

❋ 200g ground almonds ❋ 150g caster sugar ❋ grated zest of 1 lemon ❋ 2½ tablespoons water
❋ 1 egg white, lightly beaten ❋ 200g pine nuts

Put the ground almonds, sugar and lemon zest in the food processor with the water and blend to a paste. You will not need any more water to produce the right consistency, but you will have to blend for a long time until the oil from the almonds is released and binds the ingredients into a firm, soft paste. Wrap the paste in cling film and refrigerate for at least 1 hour.

Take small lumps of the marzipan paste and roll them into small balls, about 2½cm in diameter, between the palms of your hand. When you have made them all, take one ball at a time and roll it in the egg white, then take a handful of pine nuts and press them into the ball in your hand. It is not easy to make the pine nuts stick – you will have to push them in with your finger. Roll the pine nut-encrusted ball in the palm of your hand again so as to cover it with a further film of egg white.

Repeat this with all the balls and place them on greaseproof or baking paper on a baking sheet. Bake them in an oven preheated to 200°C/gas 6 for about 10 minutes until they are slightly golden. Do not try to take the *panellets* off the baking sheet while they are hot – they will be too soft. Wait until they are cold and have firmed up.

EGG-YOLK SWEETS
✳ *yemas de santa teresa*

These famous sweets are named after the mystic Carmelite nun of Ávila who was canonized in 1622. They are made in monasteries and convents all over Spain. According to legend, in the early seventeenth century King Philip III obliged wineries, which used egg whites to clarify their wines, to give their yolks to the nuns, and that remained the custom. Now the nuns give away their leftover egg whites.

This recipe is from the book *Los dulces del convento – Recetas del Monasterio de Santa María del Soccoro* ('Convent Sweets: Recipes from the Santa María del Soccoro Monastery'), written by the nuns at the convent where I stayed in Seville. The nuns say that *yemas* are their favourite sweets and warn you that they do not always come out right when you first attempt to make them. They encourage you to try again since 'hens are not about to die out and there are plenty of eggs'. Sor Jesús María, the *maestra repostera* (head pastry chef), said the recipe was not meant for the public domain, but nevertheless gave it with her special tips. The secret is to arrive at a thick enough syrup so that the sweets are firm. Making them is a fiddly matter of rolling the very soft, slightly sticky mass into small balls on a bed of fine sugar.

MAKES ABOUT 10

✳ 100g sugar ✳ 4 tablespoons water ✳ 6 large egg yolks ✳ caster or icing sugar, to coat

In a small non-stick pan (if the corners are rounded or sloping at the base it will make it easier to work the paste without leaving some behind) bring the sugar and water to the boil, then simmer over a low heat for about 10 minutes, until the syrup is thick enough to coat a spoon. If it is not thick enough the sweets will not firm up. Let the syrup cool a little.

Beat the egg yolks vigorously by hand with a whisk or fork, then gradually pour them into the syrup, beating with a wooden spoon or heatproof spatula. Put the pan back over a low heat and keep stirring vigorously until the mass thickens to a paste that comes away from the sides of the pan. It will take about 10 minutes. Leave to cool, then chill in the refrigerator. It is best to leave the mixture to chill overnight.

Cover a large plate with caster or icing sugar. Using a teaspoon, drop small lumps of the chilled paste, each the size of a large quail's egg, one at a time in the sugar and roll them into balls about 2.5cm in diameter, covering them lightly all over with the sugar. Dampen your hands slightly so that the paste does not stick. Put the balls into little paper cases. The *yemas* keep well for many days in the refrigerator.

ALMOND CUPCAKES

❊ *marquesas*

This too is Rosa Tovar's recipe. (marchionesses) or are little cupcakes that are most typical of Sonseca in the province of Toledo, where they are made at Christmas time. They are soft, moist and lemony.

MAKES 24–30, DEPENDING ON THE SIZE OF THE CAKE CASES

❊ 3 large eggs, separated ❊ ¼ teaspoon freshly squeezed lemon juice
❊ 200g caster sugar ❊ 2 large egg yolks ❊ grated zest of 1 lemon
❊ 50g cornflour ❊ 300g ground almonds ❊ icing sugar, for dusting

With an electric mixer, beat 2 of the egg whites with the lemon juice and 4 tablespoons of the sugar until stiff.

In another bowl, beat the 5 egg yolks and the remaining egg white with the remaining sugar to a pale cream. Then beat in the grated lemon zest and the cornflour and mix in the ground almonds thoroughly. It should make a thick paste. If it is too dry, add 1 or 2 tablespoons of water (I did not need any).

Gently fold in the egg whites and spoon the batter into small paper cases so that the cases are three-quarters full. Bake for 10 to 13 minutes in an oven preheated to 180°C/gas 4. The cakes will be very soft when you press the top lightly with your finger. They will harden a little when they cool but will still be very soft and moist.

Dust with icing sugar as they come out of the oven.

DRINKS

bebidas

There are various types of traditional drinking places in Spain. *Tabernas* and *tascas* sell wine and other alcoholic drinks, *cervecerías* are beer houses and *sidrerías* are cider houses. Cider is produced in apple-growing northern Spain, mainly in Asturias, which is famous for it, and in the Basque Country. Every region except Asturias makes wine. You can read about the emergence of Spanish wines on pages 114–15 and you will find names of wines in each region in the chapters on regional cuisines. Brandies distilled from fermented grape juice are produced mainly by the sherry houses of Andalusia and in Catalonia, and strongly alcoholic spirits called *aguardientes*, made from fermented and distilled fruit and grain musts, are produced in various parts of Spain. Many refreshing, fruity, alcoholic and non-alcoholic drinks are a part of Spanish gastronomic traditions and these drinks are worth adopting.

RED WINE
❉ *sangría*

The barman in a small bar in Seville served me *sangría* from a large bowl with chopped apples and peaches floating on top. He told me it was made from wine, brandy, rum and fizzy lemonade. *Sangría* is a drink that people make very much to their own taste and different fruits can be added. It is a wonderfully refreshing festive drink to serve on a hot day. It tastes better if you use soda water and lemon juice rather than fizzy lemonade.

SERVES 8 OR MORE

Put the diced fruit in a large glass jug or bowl with the sugar, orange and lemon juices, lemon peel, brandy or cognac and rum. Stir and leave to macerate in the refrigerator for an hour or so. Just before serving, pour in the chilled red wine and chilled soda water and stir well.

Let everyone help themselves to ice for their glasses.

- ❋ 2 apples or 2 peaches, or 1 of each, peeled, cored and diced
- ❋ 3–4 tablespoons sugar
- ❋ juice of 4 oranges
- ❋ juice of 1 lemon and a strip of the peel
- ❋ 100ml brandy or cognac
- ❋ 100ml dark rum
- ❋ 1 x 750ml bottle chilled red wine
- ❋ 500ml chilled soda water
- ❋ ice cubes, to serve

WHITE WINE *or* SHERRY
with FIZZY LEMONADE
❋ *rebujito*

Served long, over ice, this is the thirst-quenching summer drink of Seville. While tourists ask for *sangría*, this is what the locals want. You can see everybody drinking *rebujito* from jugs filled with ice in their *casetas* (tented stalls) during the fantastic spring festival there in April – the *Feria de Abril*. It is light and refreshing, a mix of fino sherry or wine and fizzy lemonade. Cities such as El Puerto de Santa María, Jerez, Cordoba and Sanlúcar de Barrameda have their own versions made with their own dry sherries and their favoured proportions of wine and lemonade. Bottled Casera, a Spanish fizzy lemonade which is like Spritzer or 7 UP, is used but plain soda or sparkling water with freshly squeezed lemon juice and sugar tastes so much better. Experiment with the proportions – have more wine or more soda – and with the amounts of lemon and sugar.

SERVES 4

❋ 250ml fino or manzanilla sherry, or white wine, chilled ❋ 250ml soda or sparkling water, chilled
❋ 4 tablespoons freshly squeezed lemon juice, or to taste ❋ 4 tablespoons sugar, or more to taste
❋ ice cubes ❋ a small bunch of fresh mint leaves

Pour the sherry or wine and soda or sparkling water into a large glass jug. Add the lemon juice and sugar and mix very well to dissolve the sugar, then put in some ice cubes. Serve in long glasses, with ice cubes and 2 or 3 mint leaves in each.

VARIATION

❋ To make *tinto de verano* ('summer red wine'), another refreshing drink that is very popular in Andalusia, use a medium-bodied red wine instead of the white. You can also add 2–3 tablespoons of rum.

VALENCIA 'WATER'
�֎ *agua de valencia*

Agua de Valencia started as a cocktail in Valencia. The late Constante Gil (Tino to his friends), an artist and bar owner who painted the people who came to his Café Madrid in Valencia, created it in 1959, and it caught on as a favourite drink. Gil made it with cava (Spanish sparkling wine), orange juice and vodka. Nowadays, bars use vodka, gin or rum, or an orange liqueur such as Cointreau or Grand Marnier, for the spirit. I prefer it as a simple mix of cava and orange juice, but you might like to experiment with added spirits. It is like our Buck's Fizz. I drank a little too much when I experimented and had to lie down and sleep.

SERVES 4

֎ 250ml chilled cava ֎ 125–250ml freshly squeezed orange juice ֎ sugar, to taste (optional) ֎ ice cubes

Mix the chilled cava and freshly squeezed orange juice in a large glass jug. Add some sugar, if you like, stir well to dissolve it, then put in a good handful of ice cubes. Serve in wide cocktail or wine glasses.

THICK HOT CHOCOLATE DRINK
❊ *chocolate a la taza*

Thick, creamy, rich dark hot chocolate served with *churros* – long, ribbed, crisp dough fritters – is a popular breakfast in Spain. *Chocolaterías* specialize in the drink, which is made with dark bitter chocolate and a little cornflour to thicken the milk. The amount of sugar needed depends on the sweetness of the chocolate.

SERVES 2

❊ 2 teaspoons cornflour ❊ 500ml whole milk ❊ 100g dark bitter chocolate, grated or finely chopped in the food processor ❊ 2–3 teaspoons sugar, or to taste

Dissolve the cornflour in 2 tablespoons of the cold milk. Bring the rest of the milk to the boil in a saucepan and pour in the cornflour mixture, stirring with a wooden spoon. Cook over a low heat for 2 to 3 minutes, stirring until the milk thickens slightly and becomes creamy.

Add the chocolate and keep stirring until it has melted entirely. Then stir in the sugar to taste.

TIGER NUT MILK
❋ *horchata de chufa*

A drink that I adore is made with *chufas* (tiger nuts). It is a speciality of Valencia, where the nuts grow. The village of Alboraya is famous for its tiger nut *horchata* and is full of *horchaterías* where you can get the real drink (the industrial bottled one is nothing like it). It was adopted from the Muslims who originally made it in the area. The recipe follows the same method that we used to make almond milk in Egypt. I find tiger nuts in health food shops.

SERVES 4

❋ 250g tiger nuts ❋ about 1 litre water ❋ about 4 tablespoons sugar, or more to taste

Wash the tiger nuts, then soak them in fresh water for 12 hours. Throw away any that float on the surface – they are likely to be bad. Drain and rinse them again, then put them in the food processor with a glassful of the measured water and blend to a soft paste. Add another glass of the water, blend again, and pour into a jug. Add the remaining measured water, mix well, and leave in the refrigerator for 2 to 3 hours.

Strain the chilled 'milk' containing the finely ground nuts. Place a fine cloth in a colander and pour the mixture in, letting the liquid drain into a bowl. Extract as much liquid as possible from the nuts by squeezing them with your hands in the cloth. Pour into a serving jug and add sugar to taste, and more water if you want to dilute it further, and serve the drink chilled.

VARIATION

❋ I like pure *horchata de chufa* as it is, but some people put a strip of lemon peel in the milk before the mixture goes into the refrigerator, and sprinkle on a little ground cinnamon in the glasses when they serve it.

FLAMBÉED RUM *and* COFFEE ❖ *ron cremat*

Ron cremat is a festive drink that was brought back from Cuba by returning sailors in the nineteenth century. In Catalonia, it is served during concerts of *habaneras*, which are songs that have roots in Cuba. The songs are romantic and nostalgic about lost loves, faraway lands and sailing ships with cargoes of rum. Once they were sung by fishermen in taverns, but now the concerts take place on the beaches of the Costa Brava. At such events, the *cremat* has a higher proportion of rum than coffee, includes coffee beans and is served flaming (*cremat* means 'burnt' in Catalan) out of earthenware *cazuelas*. For us at home, *cremat* made with a greater proportion of coffee makes for a sumptuous and spectacular after-dinner drink. You can burn off all of the alcohol content by letting the flames die down on their own, or burn off as little as you like by dousing the flaming rum sooner with hot coffee, or by covering the pot with a lid. If you are going to bring the dish to the table from the hob you have to be careful not to spill the hot liquid and start a fire. You can make this with brandy instead of rum.

SERVES 6

❋ 500ml rum ❋ 2–3 tablespoons sugar ❋ 2 cinnamon sticks ❋ peel of 1 lemon, cut into 4 strips ❋ 1 litre freshly made strong hot black coffee

Put the rum, sugar, cinnamon sticks and lemon peel in a shallow *cazuela*, casserole or large and deep frying pan (the best thing I have found to make it in is a fondue dish) and stir over a low heat. When the rum is hot but not boiling, ignite the vapours that are given off with a long match, being careful because tall blue flames will flare up. Let the flames almost die down for a minute or so, then pour in the coffee – it will put them out. Stir, then pour into cups using a ladle.

LACED COFFEE ❖ *carajillo*

Drinking coffee laced with rum began in Cuba. *Carajillo* is now made in northern Spain with brandy or *orujo* – a fiery alcohol made from grape residue – as well as with rum.

SERVES 1

For each person, fill a small cup three-quarters full with strong black coffee. Sweeten it, if you like, with sugar, add a tablespoon or more of rum, brandy or *orujo* and stir.

INDEX

SELECTED BIBLIOGRAPHY

I have consulted a large number of old and new regional Spanish cookery books. Among the cookery books in English that I have found useful are those of the writers Colman Andrews, Teresa Barrenechea, Penelope Casas, Sam and Sam Clark, Don Harris, Clarissa Hyman, Elisabeth Luard, Janet Mendel, Marimar Torres and Steve Winston. I have learnt much about Spanish culinary history from *El libro de la cocina española: gastronomía e historia* by Néstor Luján and Juan Perucho (Ediciones Danae, 1970); from *El buen gusto de España* edited by Ana de Letamendía, Lourdes Plana and Gonzalo Sol for the Ministerio de Agricultura, Pesca y Alimentación (the Ministry of Agriculture, Fishing and Food) (1991); from *Sabores de España* by Ismael Díaz Yubero (Ediciones Pirámide, 1998); from Xavier Medina's *Food Culture in Spain* (Greenwood, 2005) and from *Spain Gourmetour*, the food, wine and travel quarterly magazine published by ICEX (the Spanish Institute of Foreign Trade) in Madrid.

Of the books on the history of Spain not mentioned in the text, the following have been especially helpful:

- Braudel, Fernand, *The Mediterranean and the Mediterranean World in the Time of Philip II* (Penguin US, 1993)
- Bolens, Lucie, *La Cuisine Andalouse, un art de vivre XI–XIII siècle*, (Albin Michel, 1990)
- Carr, Raymond (ed.), *Spain: A History* (Oxford University Press, 2001)
- Casey, James, *Early Modern Spain: A Social History* (Routledge, 1999)
- Kamen, Henry, *Spain in the Later Seventeenth Century: 1665–1700* (Longman, 1980)
- Kamen, Henry, *Empire: How Spain Became a World Power: 1492–1763* (HarperCollins US, 2003)
- Kedourie, Elie, *Spain and the Jews: The Sephardi Experience, 1492 and after* (Thames and Hudson, 1992)
- Marin, Manuela (ed.), *The Formation of Al-Andalus, Part 1: History and Society* (Ashgate, 1998)
- Menocal, María Rosa, *The Ornament of the World: How Muslims, Jews, and Christians Created a Culture of Tolerance in Medieval Spain* (Back Bay Books, 2003)
- Meyerson, Mark D. and Meyerson, Edward D. (eds.), *Christians, Muslims and Jews in Medieval and Early Modern Spain: Interaction and Cultural Change* (University of Notre Dame Press, 2000)
- Morris, Jan, *The Presence of Spain* (Faber and Faber, 1964)
- Perry, Charles, *A Baghdad Cookery Book* (Prospect Books, 2005)
- Perry, Charles, *Medieval Arab Cookery* (Prospect Books, 2006)
- Read, Jan, *The Catalans* (Faber and Faber, 1978)
- Ruiz, Teofilo, *Spanish Society: 1400–1600* (Longman, 2001)
- Thomas, Hugh, *Rivers of Gold: The Rise of the Spanish Empire from Columbus to Magellan* (Random House, reprint 2003)

ACKNOWLEDGEMENTS

Much of what is in this book fills me with nostalgia about people: I asked everybody I met in Spain during the five years I took to research this book to tell me about their favourite dishes. Some gave me recipes; some spent hours, even days, talking to me about food and life, about the history of their country and about the produce. Friends cooked for me and took me to restaurants and on *tapas* crawls; many were always available to answer questions by telephone or email; colleagues gave me their books and sent me recipes; and mentors made contacts for me in different regions.

So many people helped me that I cannot thank them all, but I do remember them all – every recipe reminds me of somebody. I am immensely grateful to the following: Alicia Ríos, Pepa Aymami, Rosa Tovar, the late Gaspar Rey, Angelita García de Paredes Barreda, Pepe Iglesias, José María Conde de Ybarra, Lourdes March, Cuqui Gonzáles, Loli Flores, José Luis Alexanco, Andrés Bertomeu, Manolo Ruiz Lopez, Michael Jacobs, Ana Lorente, Luis Bertran Bittini Martínez, Jaime Rodriguez, Sister Inmaculada Romero and Carolina Zendrera. I have written about them all in the book. I am much indebted to Simon Cohen and Vicky Hayward, to Abraham Parrish, who designed the map, to food historians Xavier Medina and Antoní Riera Melis, to Edith Grossman, Aliza Ginio and María Rosa Menocal, to Josep Lladonosa i Giró and to the architect Miquel Espinet – who is president of the Catalan Academy of Gastronomy – and to Jose Alba Mendoza of the Instituto de la Grasa de Sevilla (the 'Institute of Fats of Seville'). I also owe special thanks to Maria Jose Sevilla, Antoni Campins, Rosa María Esteva Grewe, Martine Beaulieu Gracia, Hilary Pomeroy, Elena Santonja, Encarna Vicente and Sonia Ortega.

I thank my editor Lindsey Evans for her enthusiastic support and valuable advice and for seeing the book through every stage; my agent Lizzy Kremer for her unceasing encouragement; Lizzie Dipple for her intelligent and painstaking copy-editing; Jason Lowe for the splendid photographs; and John Hamilton and Sarah Fraser for the design of this very beautiful book.